"The notion of religious pluralism has just received a major philosophical and theological defense in this finely crafted series of essays on the theme of religious diversity. Bookended between contributions by Griffin and Cobb is an exemplary set of essays that articulate the value, purpose, and range of reflections on religious pluralism, including major statements from Jewish, Islamic, Christian, Buddhist, Hindu, and Confucian and Daoist perspectives. These are critical essays for anyone fascinated by the current debate on the philosophical and theological relevance of religious pluralism in the twenty-first century and for those who defend a philosophical and theological notion of robust pluralism as a worthy goal."
—John Berthrong, Boston University School of Theology;
author of *The Divine Deli* and *All under Heaven:*
Changing Paradigms in Confucian-Christian Dialogue

"A ripe and rigorous contribution to religious pluralism: this is a groundbreaking text, invaluable for advancing the conversation beyond fusion or fragmentation."
—Catherine Keller, Professor of Constructive Theology,
Drew University; author of *Face of the Deep*

"I found this book to be as unsettling as it was exciting. In its opening chapters, Griffin rehearses and strengthens current criticisms leveled against pluralist theologians; then he comes to their rescue by offering a new foundation that will assure a more authentic, or deeper, pluralistic understanding of religious differences. The remaining multifaith contributions build on this foundation. Both in its intent and its content, this is a book that will certainly challenge—maybe change—the current conversation about religious pluralism."
—Paul F. Knitter, Professor Emeritus, Xavier University; author of
One Earth Many Religions: Multifaith Dialogue and Global Responsibility

"In a world torn by religious antagonism, strife, and crusades, David Ray Griffin's collection *Deep Religious Pluralism* offers a path of hope. Building on the foundations of a serious engagement with the most enlightened elements within each religious tradition, assessing them from the standpoint of Whitehead's process philosophy, the articles in this book offer serious engagement with these traditions and challenge each of them to go further in integrating into their theological foundations a recognition that there is more than one path to religious truth."
—Rabbi Michael Lerner, editor, Tikkun Magazine; author of
Jewish Renewal: A Path to Healing and Transformation

"What can process thought contribute to inter-religious dialogue? This state-of-the-art collection demonstrates how a Whitehead-based approach encourages more genuinely pluralistic forms of religious pluralism. Scholars from many traditions reflect deeply on the interaction between a process approach and their own religions."
—David R. Loy, Besl Professor, Xavier University;
author of *A Buddhist History of the West* and
The Great Awakening: A Buddhist Social History

"As an evangelical, I welcome forms of religious pluralism that do not, as this book does not, undermine the distinctive truths of Christianity and whose pluralism thus does not end up in debilitating relativism."

—Clark H. Pinnock, Professor of Theology Emeritus at
McMaster Divinity College; author of *Most Moved Mover:
A Theology of God's Openness*

"Alfred North Whitehead is rightly viewed as one of the great modern philosophers. This collection of essays, on the many complex issues associated with religious pluralism, engages widely and impressively with the philosophico-theological tradition deriving from this great thinker."

—Kenneth Surin, Duke University; author of
Theology and the Problem of Evil

"This volume of essays is a very important clarification of the current discussion of religious plurality and a strong proposal for the next step in a theory of religious pluralism. The editor, David Ray Griffin, has done a superb job of presenting and organizing these essays, which represent all the major religious traditions and which are focused on the possibility of a 'deep religious pluralism' based on Whitehead's philosophy as interpreted by John Cobb."

—Owen Thomas, Professor of Theology Emeritus,
Episcopal Divinity School; author/editor
of *Attitudes Toward Other Religions*

"No Christian theologian has attended to the issue of religious pluralism—from his earliest work to the present—more than John Cobb. This book shows how deeply we are all in his debt."

—David Tracy, Professor of Philosophy of Religion and Theology,
University of Chicago; author of *Dialogue with the Other:
The Inter-Religious Dialogue*

DEEP RELIGIOUS PLURALISM

Edited by

David Ray Griffin

WESTMINSTER JOHN KNOX PRESS
LOUISVILLE · KENTUCKY

© 2005 Westminster John Knox Press

All rights reserved. No part of this book may be reproduced or transmitted in any form or by any means, electronic or mechanical, including photocopying, recording, or by any information storage or retrieval system, without permission in writing from the publisher. For information, address Westminster John Knox Press, 100 Witherspoon Street, Louisville, Kentucky 40202-1396.

Book design by Sharon Adams
Cover design by Lisa Buckley

First edition
Published by Westminster John Knox Press
Louisville, Kentucky

This book is printed on acid-free paper that meets the American National Standards Institute Z39.48 standard. ∞

PRINTED IN THE UNITED STATES OF AMERICA

05 06 07 08 09 10 11 12 13 14 — 10 9 8 7 6 5 4 3 2 1

Library of Congress Cataloging-in-Publication Data

Deep religious pluralism / edited by David Ray Griffin.—1st ed.
    p. cm.
    Includes bibliographical references.
    ISBN 0-664-22914-X (alk. paper)
    1. Religious pluralism—Congresses.   I. Griffin, David Ray, 1939–

BL85.D375 2005
201'.5—dc22   2004056958

"The overarching task [of a more adequate approach to religious diversity] is to find a fruitful way of combining recognition of truth or validity and *difference across the religions. . . . A perspective is needed which can recognize the effective truth of what is truly other."*

—S. Mark Heim

"I continue to push [my Whiteheadian proposal] forward against great resistance because I believe it helps those who accept it to acknowledge the deep differences among religious traditions without denying that each has its truth."

—John B. Cobb Jr.

Contents

Contributors

David Ray Griffin is emeritus professor of philosophy of religion and theology at Claremont School of Theology and Claremont Graduate University and codirector of the Center for Process Studies. He is the author of many books, including *Two Great Truths: A New Synthesis of Scientific Naturalism and Christian Faith* and *God, Power, and Evil: A Process Theodicy*, and coauthor (with John B. Cobb Jr.) of *Process Theology: An Introductory Exposition* (all are available from Westminster John Knox Press).

Steve Odin is professor of philosophy at the University of Hawaii at Manoa and the author of many books, including *Process Metaphysics and Hua-Yen Buddhism* and *The Social Self in Zen and American Pragmatism*.

John Shunji Yokota is professor of inter-religious studies at Kyoto Women's University and the author of numerous essays on Buddhism and process thought, including "Continuity and Novelty: A Contribution to the Dialogue between Buddhism and Process Thought," in Santiago Sia, ed., *Charles Hartshorne's Concept of God*, and "A Call to Compassion: Process Thought and the Conceptualization of Amida Buddha," *Process Studies* 23/2.

Sandra B. Lubarsky is professor of religious studies at North Arizona University. She is the author of *Tolerance and Transformation: Jewish Approaches to Religious Pluralism* and coeditor (with David Ray Griffin) of *Jewish Theology and Process Thought*.

Jeffery D. Long is assistant professor of religious studies at Elizabethtown College. His University of Chicago dissertation was titled "Plurality and Relativity: Whitehead, Jainism, and the Reconstruction of Religious Pluralism." His first book, tentatively titled *Universal Hinduism: Truth, Diversity, and the Incomplete Project of Hindu Modernity*, should appear in 2006.

Mustafa Ruzgar, a Muslim theologian from Turkey, is a PhD candidate at Claremont Graduate University. He is writing a dissertation on Mohammed Iqbal and Islamic religious pluralism.

Christopher Ives is professor of religious studies at Stonehill College. He is the editor of *Divine Emptiness and Historical Fullness: A Buddhist-Jewish-Christian Conversation with Masao Abe* and the coeditor (with John B. Cobb Jr.) of *The Emptying God: A Buddhist-Jewish-Christian Conversation.*

Michael Lodahl is professor of theology at Point Loma Nazarene University and the author of *Shekhinah/Spirit: Divine Presence in Jewish and Christian Religion* as well as *God of Nature and of Grace: Reading the World in a Wesleyan Way* and coeditor of *Embodied Holiness: Toward a Corporate Theology of Spiritual Growth.*

Chung-ying Cheng is professor of philosophy at the University of Hawaii at Manoa. He is widely known for his books and essays in Chinese philosophy, including *New Dimensions in Confucian and Neo-Confucian Philosophy* and "Categories of Creativity in Whitehead and Neo-Confucianism," *Journal of Chinese Philosophy* (1979).

Wang Shik Jang is professor of philosophy of religion and theology at Methodist Theological Seminary in Seoul, Korea, and the author of numerous essays on religious dialogue and Whitehead's philosophy, including "A Philosophical Evaluation of Western and Eastern Civilization from a Whiteheadian Perspective," *Process Studies* 33/1.

John B. Cobb Jr. is Ingraham Professor of Theology Emeritus at the Claremont School of Theology. He is the founding director of the Center for Process Studies and the cofounder of Progressive Christians Uniting. His many books include *A Christian Natural Theology; Christ in a Pluralistic Age; Beyond Dialogue: Toward a Mutual Transformation of Christianity and Buddhism;* and (with David Ray Griffin) *Process Theology: An Introductory Exposition.*

For Marjorie Hewitt Suchocki

Preface

Whereas "religious diversity" refers to the simple sociological fact that there are many religious traditions, often within a single country, "religious pluralism" refers to beliefs and attitudes. Religious pluralists do not believe that their own religion is the only legitimate one. They believe that other religions can provide positive values and truths, even salvation—however defined—to their adherents.

The articulation of religious beliefs, including beliefs about religious diversity, inevitably involves the use of philosophical ideas. Some philosophical positions discourage religious pluralism. Other positions encourage pluralism, but only superficial versions thereof. The present book is based on the conviction that the philosophy articulated by Alfred North Whitehead encourages not only religious pluralism in the generic sense, but *deep* religious pluralism. This deep religious pluralism is offered as an alternative to the version of religious pluralism that has dominated the recent discussion, especially among Christian thinkers in the West—a version that has evoked a growing call to reject pluralism as such.

This volume arose from a conference organized by the Center for Process Studies, held in March of 2003 in Claremont, California. Long associated with religious pluralism, Claremont was the location of the 1986 conference that led to *The Myth of Christian Uniqueness: Toward a Pluralistic Theology of Religions*, edited by John Hick and Paul F. Knitter. That book is, indeed, probably the one that has provoked the strongest criticisms of religious pluralism among Christian philosophers and theologians. In addition to the criticism that the book's dominant position, as articulated especially by its editors, is not very pluralistic, the other major criticism has been that although this position purports to offer a Christian theology of religions, it is not adequate to Christian faith.

The intention of the present Claremont-based book is to show that if religious diversity is approached from perspectives informed by Whiteheadian philosophy—as distinct from, say, the Kantian philosophy informing Hick's approach—more satisfactory results can be achieved. This book shows, in the first place, how a Whitehead-based approach can help us articulate forms of religious pluralism that are deeply pluralistic. It shows, in the second place, that this approach can help Christian theologians articulate a form of Christian pluralism that does not undermine the distinctive truths and values of Christian faith. And it shows, in the third place, that this approach can help philosophers and theologians from various other traditions articulate forms of religious pluralism that do not undermine the distinctive truths and values of those traditions.

The conference behind this book was organized in honor of Marjorie Suchocki, one of the directors of the Center for Process Studies, on the occasion of her retirement from the Claremont School of Theology, where she had taught theology and served as dean of the faculty for many years. Special thanks go to President Philip Amerson for his enthusiastic willingness to have the School of Theology cosponsor the conference to thank Marjorie for her many years of faithful and inspiring leadership. Those who find the present book helpful should also be grateful to John Buchanan, without whose support neither this conference nor much of the Center's other work would be possible.

In addition to earlier versions of the chapters in this book, the conference included some presentations from other participants of material from forthcoming books. One of these participants was Marjorie Suchocki herself, who gave us an oral preview of her *Divinity and Diversity: A Christian Affirmation of Religious Pluralism* (Abingdon, 2003). Also, Jay McDaniel presented an early draft of *Gandhi's Hope: Learning from Others as a Way to Peace* (Orbis, 2005).

References to Works of
Alfred North Whitehead

References to the works of Alfred North Whitehead will be placed parenthetically in the text, using the following symbols:

AI   *Adventures of Ideas* (1933). New York: Free Press, 1967.

FR   *The Function of Reason* (1929). Boston: Beacon Press, 1958.

IS   *The Interpretation of Science: Selected Essays.* Ed. A. H. Johnson. New York: Bobbs-Merrill, 1961.

MT   *Modes of Thought* (1938). New York: Free Press, 1968.

PR   *Process and Reality* (1929). Corrected edition. Ed. David Ray Griffin and Donald W. Sherburne. New York: Free Press, 1978.

RM   *Religion in the Making* (1926). New York: Fordham University Press, 1996 [reprint].

S   *Symbolism: Its Meaning and Effect.* New York: Macmillan, 1927.

SMW   *Science and the Modern World* (1925). New York: Free Press, 1967.

PART ONE
WHITEHEAD, COBB, AND DEEP RELIGIOUS PLURALISM

Chapter 1

Religious Pluralism
Generic, Identist, and Deep
David Ray Griffin

For members of a particular religious tradition to accept religious pluralism is to accept two affirmations—one negative, the other positive. The negative affirmation is the rejection of religious absolutism, which means rejecting the a priori assumption that their own religion is the only one that provides saving truths and values to its adherents, that it alone is divinely inspired, that it has been divinely established as the only legitimate religion, intended to replace all others. The positive affirmation, which goes beyond the negative one, is the acceptance of the idea that there are indeed religions other than one's own that provide saving truths and values to their adherents. This twofold statement provides a summary account of what can be called "religious pluralism in the generic sense." To accept generic religious pluralism is not necessarily to deny that one's own religious tradition has distinctive truths and values of universal importance, the acceptance and implications of which members of that tradition should seek to spread. But it means that, if the adherents of that tradition do believe they have such truths and values, they assume that other religions do as well.

The present book is based on five convictions. The first of these is that the effort to promote the acceptance of religious pluralism in our world today is vitally important. If civilization is to have much hope of surviving even the present

3

century, we must find solutions to our global problems, especially the problems of war, imperialism, weapons of mass destruction, global apartheid, massive human rights violations, genocide, and the ecological crisis. The religions of the world, with their ability to motivate people, could provide a powerful force for the kind of civilizational transformation we need if they would cooperate toward that end in the name of their common values. But thus far the religions have been as much sources of discord as sources of solidarity. The growth of religious pluralism in the various traditions could encourage a mutual respect and appreciation that would facilitate cooperation.

A second conviction is that this growth of religious pluralism is now especially important among Christians. This is because the tendency to religious absolutism has been very strong among Christians and also because Christians have in recent centuries had far more power—militarily, economically, and culturally—than adherents of other religions, making the Christian tendency to absolutism the most destructive. This tendency is, furthermore, far from a thing of the past. Indeed, the possibility of "civilizational wars," with the "(Christian) West against the rest," is probably more discussed now than at any time in the past.

The third conviction upon which this book is based is that most of the discussion of this issue in the Christian West in recent decades has been based on a wrong turn. The very idea of "pluralistic Christian theology" is being brought into disrepute because it has become largely associated with a very problematic image of what such a theology would be. This image has evoked a fourfold critique of pluralistic Christian theology: that it falsely claims a neutral universality, that it is not really Christian, that it is not even truly pluralistic, and that it entails a debilitating relativism.

The fourth conviction behind this book is that Whiteheadian philosophy provides a basis for articulating a version of pluralistic Christian theology that does not pretend to an impossible neutrality, that is clearly Christian, that is truly pluralistic, and that avoids a debilitating relativism. It is hoped that the essays in this book written by Christian theologians will help show fellow Christians that the emergence of pluralistic Christian theology is a development to be celebrated and promoted, not bemoaned and rejected—that the "pluralistic turn" in theology is not itself a wrong turn.

The fifth conviction is that Whitehead's philosophy also provides a basis in terms of which thinkers from other religious traditions can articulate versions of religious pluralism that can be found helpful by members of their traditions. A Whitehead-based approach can, in other words, undergird versions of religious pluralism that are truly Buddhist, versions that are truly Confucian, versions that are truly Hindu, versions that are truly Jewish, versions that are truly Islamic, and so on.

In spite of the wider purposes expressed in the first and fifth points, my two introductory essays focus on religious pluralism as it has emerged and been debated within Christian circles. There are three reasons for this focus. First, as already stated, the Christian form of religious absolutism is the one with the most destructive potential. Second, most of the discussion of religious pluralism in the West has occurred among Christian thinkers. And third, the wrong turn taken by pluralism, mentioned above, is a turn taken primarily by Christian thinkers.

This introduction proceeds in the following way. The first section discusses the notion of "generic religious pluralism" as that which all versions of religious pluralism have in common. The second section further clarifies the meaning of generic pluralism by discussing four bases for the emergence of pluralism in Christian theology. The third section discusses the wrong turn taken by the recent Christian discussion, illustrating, by means of Mark Heim's critique of Christian pluralistic theology, how the equation of religious pluralism with one problematic type of it can lead to the conclusion that pluralistic theology as such is to be rejected. The conclusion brings out the point implicit in this discussion—that a better version of religious pluralism is needed.

The title of this volume reflects the difference between its version of religious pluralism and the hitherto dominant version. Although that dominant version has widely been criticized as not really pluralistic, the more accurate critique is that its pluralism is superficial. Whitehead's philosophy provides the basis for a deep pluralism.

1. GENERIC RELIGIOUS PLURALISM

For Christians to accept religious pluralism involves the rejection of Christian absolutism, the idea that Christianity is the absolute religion, the sole vehicle of divine salvation.[1] This Christian absolutism has taken two major forms: "exclusivism," according to which only Christians can be saved, and "inclusivism," according to which people in other religious traditions can be saved—perhaps if they have followed the light available to them in those traditions—by virtue of the salvation effected by Jesus Christ.[2] Alan Race, whose 1983 book is usually credited with first articulating the exclusivist-inclusivist-pluralist typology, mentioned Paul Tillich, John Hick, Wilfred Cantwell Smith, and John Cobb as four examples of Christian pluralists in the then-contemporary discussion.[3] In the more recent discussion of prominent advocates of pluralism, Tillich has largely

---

1. As I indicated in the opening paragraph, this rejection of absolutism constitutes only the negative half of pluralism. Full-fledged pluralism involves not only the rejection of any a priori denial that other religions *could be* authentic means of salvation but also the affirmation that other religions *are* in fact such means. One of the merits of Schubert Ogden's writings about pluralism (see later notes and section 4 of chapter 2) has been to draw attention to the distinction between these two dimensions of pluralism (only the former of which he affirms).

2. As Ogden has emphasized, the crucial issue here is christological. Absolutists, whether of the exclusivist or the inclusivist type, have a *constitutive* Christology, according to which God's saving act in Jesus Christ is constitutive of all salvation whatsoever. See Ogden, "Problems in the Case for a Pluralistic Theology of Religions," 505, 507; *Is There Only One True Religion or Are There Many?* 31, 84, 92–96.

3. Race, *Christians and Religious Pluralism*, 71, 88, 98.

been replaced by Paul Knitter. I will, accordingly, use Cobb, Hick, Knitter, and Smith as my four primary examples of recent pluralists.

My main purpose here is simply to show that these pluralistic theologians do clearly affirm what I am calling generic pluralism. This point is important because in much of the criticism of pluralism, as will be seen in section 3, this generic meaning of pluralism tends to drop from view as critics focus on more particular theses of this or that pluralist. What needs to be more clearly seen is that religious pluralism as such should be equated simply with generic pluralism. Because Hick is the pluralist in relation to whom this distinction is most often ignored, I will document his affirmation of generic pluralism first.

John Hick

In an essay titled "The Non-Absoluteness of Christianity," Hick rejects the "absolutist position," which affirms "a Christian monopoly of salvific truth and life," and thereby the conviction that the Christian religion should seek "to dispossess the non-Christian religions."[4] The pluralistic position, he says, holds instead that "Christianity is not the one and only way of salvation, but one among several."[5] In a chapter titled "The Pluralistic Hypothesis," Hick says that pluralism rejects the view that "there can be at most one true religion, in the sense of a religion teaching saving truth." The traditional belief that "God must intend [Christianity] to supersede all other religions and to embrace the entire human race," Hick adds, is "incompatible with a pluralist understanding of Christianity as one salvific response among others." In a chapter with the title "A Christianity That Sees Itself as One True Religion among Others," Hick attributes an "implicitly pluralistic theology" to Christians who assume that their "Jewish or Muslim or Hindu or Sikh or Buddhist friends and acquaintances are as fully entitled in the sight of God to live by their own religious traditions as we are to live by ours," because they have "their own authentic form of faith."[6] All these statements, while underlying Hick's particular hypothesis about the Real and the universal movement from self-centeredness to Reality-centeredness (to be discussed later), could be affirmed by many theologians who reject that particular hypothesis. Hick's particular hypothesis has led to the charge that his position is not really pluralistic or is at best superficially so. But those charges, even insofar as they are true, should not prevent us from seeing that Hick clearly affirms, and is motivated by, pluralism in the generic sense.

---

4. Hick, "The Non-Absoluteness of Christianity," 16–17.

5. Ibid., 33. As the statements quoted in this discussion suggest, Hick does not clearly distinguish between the negative dimension of pluralism (the rejection of Christian absolutism, according to which there in principle *cannot be* other valid religions) and the positive dimension (the affirmation that there *are* other valid religions). But that he affirms both dimensions is clear. The same twofold fact will be seen in the other pluralists.

6. Hick, *A Christian Theology of Religions*, 24, 87, 125.

Paul Knitter

This generic pluralism is also clearly affirmed by Paul Knitter, who speaks of "the simple but profound insight that *there is no one and only way*" and of the "possibility that other religions may be ways of salvation just as much as is Christianity."[7] Describing the "paradigm shift" from either exclusivism or inclusivism to pluralism as the move from an insistence on the absoluteness of Christianity "toward a recognition of the independent validity of other ways,"[8] Knitter holds with other pluralists that there are "many equally valid religions" and that "no one religion can claim to be absolutely . . . superior over all others."[9] Whereas absolutists insist that Christianity has a total or virtual monopoly on religious truth, Knitter affirms "the plurality of religious truth."[10] Endorsing "historical consciousness," which realizes that "insofar as every existing reality is historical, it is limited," Knitter explicitly draws the conclusion that Christianity, like every other religion, is limited. This conclusion leads to the "dialogical imperative," because it is through dialogue with members of other religious traditions that "we can expand or correct the truth that we have," thereby overcoming the "limitations of our own viewpoint."[11]

Wilfred Cantwell Smith

Wilfred Cantwell Smith's endorsement of generic pluralism is illustrated by his dismissal of the "fallacy" held by traditional Christians that "they alone were in God's grace, were saved."[12] He instead affirms "pluralism," according to which "the figure of Christ" is only "one form among others [through] which God has entered history," so that we can hold that "God has played in human history a role in and through the Qur'an, in the Muslim case, comparable to the role in the Christian case in and through Christ." Given the notion that the meaning of *idolatry* is "to treat, mistakenly, something mundane as if it were divine," Smith considers idolatrous the tendency of Christians "to hold that their own forms [doctrines and practices] are given by God, others' forms are not."[13]

John Cobb

This generic pluralism is also clearly affirmed by John Cobb. In *Christ in a Pluralistic Age*, he indicates that the pluralism he accepts involves the rejection of the

---

7. Knitter, *No Other Name?* 5, 17.

8. Knitter, Preface, *The Myth of Christian Uniqueness*, viii.

9. Knitter, in Cobb, *Transforming Christianity and the World*, 3, 61. (Knitter, who edited this collection of Cobb's essays, wrote an introduction to the volume [1–11] and also an introduction to each of the essays.)

10. Knitter, *Jesus and the Other Names*, 28.

11. Knitter, *No Other Name?* 36; *Jesus and the Other Names*, 29, 31.

12. Smith, "Theology and the World's Religious History," 61.

13. Smith, "Idolatry in Comparative Perspective," 63, 64–65.

traditional view "that Christianity is the one right or true way."[14] In his book on interreligious dialogue, he says, after having indicated that he endorses pluralism, that he "join[s] with Paul Knitter, John Hick, and Wilfred Cantwell Smith in their rejection of the deep-seated tendency of Christians to absolutize their tradition in some way."[15] Cobb's endorsement of generic pluralism is also illustrated by his acceptance of the normative judgment "that in a plurality of religious movements each deserves respect in its own terms and that Christians should not make claims for their doctrines of a sort that they do not accept as equally legitimate for others to make about theirs"—a judgment that implies that the various movements are "on the same level." Besides recognizing the *descriptive* fact that we live in a pluralistic age, meaning one in which "almost everyone is forced to come to terms with religious differences," Cobb endorses the *normative* interpretation that "the diversity is acceptable and that people should learn to live with it in mutual appreciation."[16] As well as supporting the need for Christians to engage in dialogue with members of other religious traditions, Cobb explicitly endorses the implication of this engagement, which is that the Christian thereby "sets aside all claims of an exclusiveness that entails a monopoly of wisdom" and respects the other traditions "as comparable in worth."[17] While regarding the Christian experience of salvation as distinctive, he accepts "the Hindu account of *moksha* or the Zen Buddhist account of *satori* [as] just as authentic."[18]

2. FOUR BASES FOR THE EMERGENCE OF CHRISTIAN PLURALISM

Each of these pluralists has his own specific proposal for the best way to develop a pluralistic theology suitable for Christians in our time. These specific proposals differ from each other, and some of the proposals, especially Hick's, have provoked an enormous amount of debate. Most of this debate has tended to blur the distinction between pluralism as such, which I am calling generic pluralism, and one or more specific proposals as to how to develop a pluralistic Christian theology. The nature of generic pluralism can be brought into clearer focus by seeing the various bases for affirming it.

Because it is important to have a conception of generic pluralism that applies to all theologians who would normally be considered pluralists, I will now expand

14. Cobb, *Christ in a Pluralistic Age*, 18.

15. Cobb, *Beyond Dialogue: Toward a Mutual Transformation of Christianity and Buddhism*, 14, 41. Alan Race's inclusion of Paul Tillich among the pluralists is supported by Cobb, who says in a discussion of Tillich and several other major theologians—Hendrik Kraemer, Karl Barth, Hans Küng, Jürgen Moltmann, and Wolfhart Pannenberg—that "only Tillich seems to be completely exempt" from the tendency to absolutize his own tradition (41).

16. Cobb, *Transforming Christianity and the World*, 35, 50.

17. Leonard Swidler, John B. Cobb Jr., Paul F. Knitter, and Monika Hellwig, *Death or Dialogue? From the Age of Monologue to the Age of Dialogue*, 10.

18. Cobb, *Transforming Christianity and the World*, 86.

my examples of recent pluralists to include Langdon Gilkey, Huston Smith, Gordon Kaufman, Alan Race, Marjorie Suchocki, and Paul Tillich. For a list of religious pluralists to be representative, furthermore, it must take account of the fact that pluralism did not arise suddenly in recent decades but has a much longer history. Alan Race points out, for example, that forms of pluralism were articulated in the early part of the twentieth century by William Ernest Hocking, Arnold Toynbee, and most notably Ernst Troeltsch, whose work, says Race, "represents the real beginning of the argument for pluralism in the Christian theology of religions." Although Troeltsch was certainly a pivotal figure, it is probably more correct to call him, as does Cobb, "the first great Christian relativist."[19] Religious pluralism as such must be traced back to some of the eighteenth-century deists, such as Matthew Tindal and G. E. Lessing.[20] In this discussion of various bases for the emergence of pluralist forms of Christian theology, nevertheless, I will limit the examples to pluralists from the time of Troeltsch. Of the various bases for this emergence, four seem especially important: sociological, theological, ethical, and ontological.

Sociological

One of the reasons for the recent growth of religious pluralism among Christians in the West has been a twofold sociological change. One side of this change involves the fact that there is now much more knowledge of other religions, based not only on books and other forms of mass media but also on increasingly having neighbors who belong to these other religions. This greater knowledge has broken down old stereotypes and brought awareness of the spiritual riches in the other traditions and the beautiful lives they can produce. In Hick's words, "it has become a fairly common discovery that our Muslim or Jewish or Hindu or Sikh or Buddhist fellow citizens are in general no less kindly, honest, thoughtful for others, no less truthful, honourable, loving and compassionate, than are in general our Christian fellow citizens."[21] Occurring concurrently with this rising appreciation of the wisdom and beauty in other traditions has been a more critical appraisal of Christianity. In the process of decolonization after World War II, Langdon Gilkey observes, the Christian faith came to be widely seen as more morally culpable, more imperialistic, and less spiritual than other religions.[22] This twofold sociological change has made increasingly implausible the idea that

---

19. Race, *Christians and Religious Pluralism*, 82; Cobb, *Beyond Dialogue*, 13.

20. Tindal, *Christianity as Old as Creation* (1730); Lessing, *Nathan the Wise* (1779). The distinction between identist and differential pluralists, to be introduced below, extends back to them, with Tindal being an identist pluralist, arguing that the essence of Christianity is the same as the essence of all religions, and Lessing being a more differential pluralist.

21. Hick, *A Christian Theology of Religions*, 13. See also Hick, "The Non-Absoluteness of Christianity," 17–20, and "Religious Pluralism and Salvation," 57–65; Knitter, *No Other Name?* 2–4; and Philip Quinn, "Towards Thinner Theologies: Hick and Alston on Religious Diversity," 226–27.

22. Gilkey, "Plurality and Its Theological Implications," 40.

Christianity is somehow different in kind from the other religions in terms of the ability to mediate saving truth.

Theological

Another basis for the shift to pluralism is a theological judgment about the primacy of the doctrine of divine love.[23] Many modern Christian thinkers came to see Christian absolutism as in conflict with this doctrine. Arnold Toynbee argued, for example, that the Jewish-Christian "vision of God as being a jealous god, the god of *my* tribe as against the gentiles *outside* my tribe or my church," should be rejected in favor of "the Jewish and Christian vision of God as being love," which makes it seem "unlikely that He would not have made other revelations to other people as well."[24] Langdon Gilkey, more recently, has said that the emphasis put on "the width of the divine love" by modern Christian theologians has given rise to a rhetorical question: "Could the divine agape choose us because of the external 'religion' in which we live, and not reach out to others because of the external religions in which they grew up and which they now affirm?"[25] Huston Smith, affirming the form of religious pluralism embodied in the "perennial philosophy" articulated by Frithjof Schuon, says that "it follows" from the divine benevolence that God's "revelations must be impartial, which is to say equal: the deity cannot play favorites."[26]

This primacy of the divine love plays a central role in Knitter's account, in his first book, of the modern theological move toward pluralism. Saying that traditional Christian faith involved a tension "between two fundamental beliefs: God's universal love and desire to save, and the necessity of the church for salvation," he gives priority to the former, saying that "Troeltsch's foundational conviction that God's revelation is offered to all peoples and to all religions" is demanded by "Christian belief in a God who loves all human beings."[27] Endorsing Karl Rahner's point of departure in the doctrine of God's universal salvific will, Knitter says that this doctrine should be seen to imply that the revelation given to oth-

---

23. As Ogden points out, insofar as a pluralistic theology presents itself as a *Christian* theology, it cannot justify its rejection of Christian absolutism solely in terms of contemporary needs and criteria. It must also provide a *theological* justification, showing that "a serious attempt to understand the Christian witness in terms of its own real intention leads to the elimination of all absolutism" ("Problems in the Case," 495). At the core of Ogden's theological justification for this move is the doctrine that God's love is "the sole and sufficient source of human salvation"—a doctrine that would be contradicted by Christian absolutism's constitutive Christology because the latter makes God's act in Jesus an additional necessity for salvation (505). Ogden has argued this point in *Is There Only One?* (92) and earlier in *Christ without Myth, The Reality of God* (esp. chaps. 6 and 7), and *The Point of Christology*. For a precise summary of Ogden's position on this point, see Philip E. Devenish and George L. Goodwin, "Christian Faith and the First Commandment: The Theology of Schubert Ogden," especially the first section, "Christocentrism as Radical Monotheism" (2–12).

24. Toynbee, "What Should Be the Christian Approach to the Contemporary Non-Christian Faiths?" 161.

25. Gilkey, "Plurality and Its Theological Implications," 39.

26. Griffin and Smith, *Primordial Truth and Postmodern Theology*, 41.

27. Knitter, *No Other Name?* 121, 33.

ers must be a potentially *saving* revelation, so that "Christians not only can but must look on other religions as possible *ways of salvation*."[28]

This motivation has also been central to Hick's adoption of a pluralistic outlook. In one of his earlier books on the subject, for example, Hick said that "in wrestling with the problem of evil I had concluded that any viable Christian theodicy must affirm the ultimate salvation of all God's creatures. How then to reconcile the notion of there being one, and only one, true religion with a belief in God's universal saving activity?"[29] In another book published about the same time, Hick spoke of an "acute tension" between the Christian teaching that "God is the Creator and Lord of all mankind and seeks mankind's final good and salvation," on the one hand, and the idea that "only by responding in faith to God in Christ can we be saved," on the other; this latter idea would mean that "infinite love has ordained that human beings can be saved only in a way that in fact excludes the large majority of them."[30] To be sure, the particular way in which Hick has developed his pluralistic hypothesis means, as we will see, that he can no longer attribute love or benevolence to Ultimate Reality as it is in itself, except in a mythological sense, so it would now be incoherent for Hick to appeal to this theological justification for generic pluralism. The fact that Hick's later thought has undermined this original justification, however, does not negate the fact that his turn to pluralism *was* originally motivated, at least in part, by the implications of the doctrine of the universal divine love.

Ethical

In the recent discussion, even more emphasis has been given to the ethical basis for the shift to pluralism. This ethical basis is very evident in Hick, who devotes several pages to the "destructive effects of the assumption of Christian superiority."[31] Speaking of these effects in relation to Jews, Hick says that "there is a clear connection between fifteen or so centuries of the 'absoluteness' of Christianity, with its corollary of the radical inferiority and perverseness of the Judaism it 'superseded,' and the consequent endemic anti-Semitism of Christian civilization, which has continued with undiminished virulence into and through [the] twentieth century."[32] With regard to the evils of the European colonization of most of the planet, Hick says that "the moral validation of the imperial enterprise rested upon the conviction that it was a great civilizing and uplifting mission, one of whose tasks was to draw the unfortunate heathen up into the higher, indeed highest, religion of Christianity."[33] The moral passion behind Hick's pluralist

28. Ibid., 125, 116–17, 140.
29. Hick, *God Has Many Names*, 17. For perhaps the best treatment of the way in which Christian exclusivism aggravates the already difficult problem of evil, see Ogden, *Is There Only One?* 33–41.
30. Hick, *Philosophy of Religion*, 117–18.
31. Hick, "The Non-Absoluteness of Christianity," 18.
32. Ibid., 18.
33. Ibid., 19.

project is especially evident in his discussion of the ways in which political con-flicts can be intensified by religious differences, with the biggest obstacle to peace-ful solutions coming from those people on both sides "with the most absolute religious beliefs." Saying that "the absolutist aspect of each faith motivates young men to be willing to kill and be killed for a sacred cause," Hick adds that "if this absoluteness were dismantled by the realization that one's own religion is one among several valid human responses to the Divine, religion could become a heal-ing instead of a divisive force in the world."[34]

This ethical motivation for rejecting Christian absolutism is sometimes expressed in terms of the implications of the centrality of the commandment to love our neighbors. "In light of the primary, foundational role that love of neigh-bor plays in Christian life," says Knitter, there is "something wrong with . . . the way traditional Christian theology has instructed me to look upon [my neigh-bors in other faiths] and treat them." Knitter's point is that we cannot really love these neighbors if we, instead of listening to their religious witness, are trying to convert them to *our* religion.[35]

Marjorie Suchocki makes this point in terms of the idea of the "reign of God." Pointing out that Jesus' message of the reign of God invoked the prophetic demand to extend kindness and well-being to the stranger within the gates, which involves a reversal of the typical human proclivity to show kindness only to our own kind, Suchocki suggests that today the challenge to live the reign of God "meets its ultimate test in relation to those whose religious ways are not our own—those strangers who are now indeed 'within our gates' in this increasingly small world." Contrasting this demand with Christian kindness to others based on the missionary aim of conversion, Suchocki adds that we are called "to extend well-being to those whom we neither require nor expect to become like our-selves." We are today called, she concludes, "to live a reign of God that reaches not toward an imperialism of one religion—our own!—sweeping the planet, but that reaches toward a new form of community: a community made up of diverse religious communities, existing together in friendship."[36]

This ethical passion motivating the theological pluralists has been emphasized by critic Mark Heim, who considers this passion to constitute their *primary* moti-vation: "The pluralist's Copernican revolution begins with revulsion at the crimes of religious pride. . . . Before it is any kind of theory, pluralism is a commitment to exorcise the religious sources of human oppression."[37]

Ontological

Although these sociological, theological, and ethical bases are all crucial, there is yet another basis for the modern shift from Christian absolutism to pluralism,

---

34. Hick, *A Christian Theology of Religions*, 123.
35. Knitter, *Jesus and the Other Names*, 39–40.
36. Suchocki, *Divinity and Diversity*, 80, 81, 86.
37. Heim, *Salvations: Truth and Difference in Religion*, 72.

which in the current discussion is usually more presupposed than explicitly acknowledged. Indeed, it is arguably obvious that there *must* be another basis for the shift, because the sociological fact of religious diversity is not *wholly* new and the theological and ethical motivations, rooted in the doctrine of divine love and the commandment to love our fellow human beings, have been present in Christianity all along. To explain why pluralism has arisen among Christian theologians only in modern times, we require some distinctively modern basis for it. This basis is surely the rejection of supernaturalism, in the sense of the belief in a divine being that occasionally interrupts the world's normal causal processes. Although supernaturalism in this sense was still affirmed by some of the founders of distinctively modern science, including Newton, it quickly lost support. As early as the eighteenth century (in France and Germany) and certainly by the middle of the nineteenth century (in Great Britain), it was widely assumed that the "scientific worldview" rules out any divine interruptions of the world's normal causal processes.[38]

Given this definition of supernaturalism, its rejection could be called the affirmation of *naturalism*. Simply to say that pluralistic theologians have affirmed naturalism, however, could be misleading, because the term "naturalism" has come to be used for a doctrine far more particular than simply the denial of supernatural interruptionism. It is now widely used, as by Hick,[39] to designate an atheistic worldview. It is also often equated with a materialistic worldview, which, among other things, identifies the mind with the brain and thereby denies the possibility of life after death (given the denial of supernaturalism and thereby the possibility of any "resurrection of the body"). This materialistic naturalism is also usually regarded as involving the sensationist theory of perception, according to which all perception is *sensory* perception, because of the presumed impossibility of any nonphysical and hence nonsensory perception. This sensationism thereby implies, among other things, the impossibility of theistic religious experience understood as a nonsensory perception of a Holy Reality. Using "s" to stand for sensationism, "a" for atheism, and "m" for materialism, I refer to naturalism in this sense as "naturalism$_{sam}$."[40] One need not affirm naturalism$_{sam}$, however, to reject supernaturalism in the sense of a divine being that sometimes interrupts the world's normal causal processes. Using "ns" to mean "nonsupernaturalist," I have called naturalism in this more limited sense naturalism$_{ns}$.[41]

---

38. At the beginning of the nineteenth century, Friedrich Schleiermacher seemed to rule out such interruptions, saying: "It can never be necessary in the interest of religion so to interpret a fact that its dependence on God absolutely excludes its being conditioned by the system of Nature" (*The Christian Faith*, 178). He made an exception, however, for the origin of the life of Jesus (389–415), for which he was criticized by David Friedrich Strauss (*The Life of Jesus Critically Examined*, 771).

39. Hick, *An Interpretation of Religion*, 1, 111.

40. Griffin, *Reenchantment without Supernaturalism* and *Religion and Scientific Naturalism*.

41. I usually define "supernaturalism" to mean belief in a divine being that (ontologically) *could* occasionally interrupt the world's most fundamental causal processes (*Religion and Scientific Naturalism*, 33, 60), not simply, as here, belief in a being that actually does so. I usually, therefore, define naturalism$_{ns}$ to mean the denial of the existence of a being that (ontologically) *could* interrupt the

Naturalism$_{ns}$ is embodied, of course, in naturalism$_{sam}$ and other forms of atheism (including doctrines that, while using the term "God" positively, think of God as an imaginary projection or in some other way that denies any causal efficacy to the referent of the term "God"). But it can also be embodied in many other worldviews. It is embodied in the deism affirmed by Matthew Tindal and the early John Hick. It is also embodied in Spinozistic pantheism, Kantian idealism, Hegelian idealism,[42] and Whiteheadian-Hartshornean panentheism. As some of these examples illustrate, it is not self-contradictory, given the definition of naturalism as simply the rejection of supernatural interruptionism, to speak of "naturalistic theism." Naturalism$_{ns}$ does not, therefore, necessarily imply the denial of theism, in the sense of belief in a Holy Actuality distinct from the world. It does not even imply the denial that this Divine Actuality exercises variable causal influence in the world.[43] But it does mean that interruptions of the world's normal causal relations are never to be affirmed.

Naturalism$_{ns}$ is a (negative) ontological doctrine, asserting that events of a certain type never occur.[44] It most clearly rules out the occurrence of miracles as traditionally defined—that is, as events that are brought about by divine causation in a way that is different in kind from the way in which most events are brought about. In the scheme of primary and secondary causation, which was long the standard framework for understanding the nature of miracles, God as the primary cause of all events was said to bring about most events by means of secondary (natural, finite) causes, whereas miracles were regarded as events in which God brought about the events directly, without the use of secondary causes.[45] The acceptance of some version of naturalism$_{ns}$ involves the affirmation that there are *no* events devoid of natural, in the sense of finite, causes. But, whether or not the language of primary and secondary causation be employed, the more general point of naturalism$_{ns}$ is that if there is divine causation in the world, it is integral to the world's normal causal processes, never an interruption of them.

This ontological doctrine has epistemic implications. Human beings are fallible, their belief-forming processes being shaped by cultural conditioning, sin,

---

world's causal processes. I have here loosened the definition, however, to include the de facto naturalism$_{ns}$ affirmed by a consistent deism, according to which God, having created the world out of nothing, has the power to interrupt the world's basic causal processes but never does so.

42. While holding a Hegelian worldview, David Friedrich Strauss said that the presuppositions of the modern world include the conviction that "all things are linked together by a chain of causes and effects, which suffers no interruption" (*The Life of Jesus*, 78). This presupposition lay behind Strauss's criticism of Schleiermacher, referred to in note 38, above.

43. See my *Religion and Scientific Naturalism*, 39–40, 80, 94–95.

44. Actually, given the modification I have made in my usual definition of naturalism$_{ns}$, as indicated in note 41, it would more properly be called an ontic, rather than an ontological, doctrine, as it merely states what (de facto or ontically) *does* not happen, not what (ontologically) *could* not happen. I will here, however, ignore this fine point, continuing to speak of naturalism$_{ns}$ as an *ontological* doctrine, because for the purposes of this discussion the distinction makes little if any difference. (It does become important, however, when the discussion is expanded to include the problem of evil or the relation between theology and science.)

45. See my *Religion and Scientific Naturalism*, 27, 38–40.

and ignorance. Ontological supernaturalism, however, allows for divine causation to override the normal belief-forming processes of particular human beings, canceling out the causes of fallibility and error, so that human beings could be vehicles of *infallible* revelation and *inerrant* inspiration. Ontological supernaturalism can thereby support *epistemic* supernaturalism, according to which certain doctrines can be affirmed as true simply on the basis of their alleged mode of origination. Questions of truth can be settled, in other words, by appeal to authority. The rejection of ontological supernaturalism in favor of naturalism$_{ns}$ implies the rejection of epistemic supernaturalism, with its authoritarianism. The question of the truth of a given worldview must be settled by appeal to the normal rational-empirical criteria of self-consistency and adequacy to the facts, not by the "way of authority."[46]

This rejection of ontological and epistemic supernaturalism can be seen to be common to the various pluralistic theologians. Troeltsch explicitly rejected "the theory that the truth of Christianity is guaranteed by miracles," whether "the so-called 'nature-miracles,' involving an infringement of natural law" or the so-called inward miracles of interior conversion, in which "an entirely different type of causation comes into operation from that which is operative anywhere else in the world." Regarding the latter type, Troeltsch rejected the idea that we could be justified "in tracing the Platonic *Eros* to a natural cause, while we attribute a supernatural origin to the Christian *Agape*."[47] Alan Race, in dating the beginning of pluralism with Troeltsch, points to the connection between Troeltsch's rejection of Christian claims to truth based on a supernatural account of Christian origins and his emphasis on the consequences of a historical consciousness. Race himself, in fact, evidently endorsed this connection. "Some form of pluralism in the Christian theology of religions is inevitable," said Race, "if historical studies are treated seriously."[48] This rejection of supernaturalism could also be documented in the other early pluralists named by Race. Divine interruption of the world's normal causal processes is clearly ruled out, for example, by Tillich's doctrine that God is being itself, not *a* being.

The rejection of the idea that God acted supernaturally in Christian origins can also be seen in the writings of *contemporary* pluralists. Hick, for example, says that insofar as Christianity has "believed in miracles which arbitrarily disrupt the order of nature," it is "incompatible with the scientific project." At the center of Hick's revision of traditional Christian doctrines to make them compatible with pluralism is his rejection of a substance Christology based on a social trinity, which says that Jesus "was God—more precisely, God the Son, the second person of the Holy Trinity—incarnate."[49] This doctrine would imply "that Christianity, alone among the religions, was founded by God in person," making it

---

46. On the "way of authority," see Farley and Hodgson, "Scripture and Tradition."
47. Troeltsch, "The Place of Christianity among the World Religions," 76–78.
48. Race, *Christians and Religious Pluralism*, 82, 97.
49. Hick, *A Christian Theology of Religions*, 53, 15.

"God's own religion in a sense in which no other can be"—a point that Hick makes repeatedly.[50] Given this supernaturalistic Christology, the superiority of Christianity to all other religions is guaranteed a priori.[51] Arguing that "this kind of arbitrary superiority-by-definition no longer seems defensible," Hick says that if the question of superiority is raised, it must be treated as an empirical issue, to be settled by an examination of the facts.[52]

This empirical approach involves the rejection of another dimension of the supernaturalism of traditional Christianity, its *soteriological* supernaturalism, according to which salvation involves a divine decision, based on arbitrary standards, that saves one from eternal damnation. Recognizing that Christian exclusivism and inclusivism both depend on this kind of understanding of salvation, such as "being forgiven and accepted by God because of the atoning death of Jesus," Hick suggests that "we define salvation . . . as an actual change in human beings, a change which can be identified . . . by its moral fruits."[53] This actual change, which he usually calls the shift from self-centeredness to Reality-centeredness, is "a long process," not a sudden, supernaturally effected transformation. Hick decides that, even on this empirical or a posteriori approach, there is no basis for affirming the superiority of Christianity, because this salvific process seems to take place within all the great traditions "to a more or less equal extent," leading Hick to attribute "rough parity" to all of them with regard to their salvific effectiveness. The more fundamental point, however, is Hick's denial of "any a priori overall superiority" based on a supernaturalistic understanding of Christian origins.[54]

The importance of the rejection of supernaturalism is also clear in Langdon Gilkey's discussion of the reasons why the plurality of religions came to be understood as "rough parity." Besides connecting this notion of the "rough parity of religions" with "removing the absolute starting point of each," he also defines the shift to parity as the move "from Christianity as the definitive revelation . . . to some sort of plurality of revelations." Perhaps most significantly, Gilkey, with reference to "the liberal theology that grew out of the Enlightenment," refers to the

---

50. Ibid., 15, 23, 87, 126; *Problems of Religious Pluralism*, 34.

51. Hick, *Problems of Religious Pluralism*, 36.

52. Hick, "The Non-Absoluteness of Christianity," 23. Ogden is at one with Hick on this point. Holding, as he always has, that theology should acknowledge that its claims "can be validated as credible only in terms of our common human experience and critical reflection," Ogden agrees that "all judgments about the truth or validity of religions must be a posteriori, not a priori" ("Problems in the Case," 498, 502). Ogden finds, however, that some Christian pluralists, having rejected the *negative* a priori judgment that other religions *could not possibly* provide true revelation and salvation, make the *positive* a priori judgment that they *do* (501, 504). With regard to Hick in particular, Ogden believes that he seems to assume that the rejection of absolutism, with its a priori assertion that "there *cannot be* several ways of salvation," logically implies pluralism, according to which "there actually *are* several ways of salvation of which Christianity is only one." However that may be, the logical implication of the rejection of absolutism, Ogden is right to say, is only "that there *can be* these several ways" (504; see also *Is There Only One?* 54–55).

53. Hick, *A Christian Theology of Religions*, 16, 17.

54. Ibid., 18, 68, 23.

cultural forces through which "the doctrines of faith—creeds, confessions and even the words of scripture itself—began to be seen as human, as therefore historical and hence relative expressions."[55]

The rejection of supernaturalism can also be discerned in W. C. Smith's form of pluralism. Smith says that our theology needs to be true to "our modern perception of the world."[56] He rejects the idea "that God has constructed Christianity" in favor of the idea that God "has inspired us to construct it, as He/She/It has inspired Muslims to construct what the world knows as Islam, or . . . Ramanuja to write his theological commentaries." He rejects the idea "that God has given [Christianity a privileged status]." And he says that the assumption by Christians that "they have been accorded quite special treatment by God, available to no one else in like measure," is "theologically awry."[57] Smith's rejection of the idea of God as an omnipotent being who, whether always or only sometimes, simply determines the events of our world is suggested by his statement that part of the truth about God is that "God is confronted with the recalcitrance . . . of us human beings." It is also expressed in his rejection of the idea that "the flow of time is interrupted by the intrusion of the divine into the historical," as if "God's presence [were] an interruption."[58]

The rejection of supernaturalism involved in Knitter's affirmation of pluralism is suggested by his favorable description of Troeltsch as "dissatisfied with concepts of revelation that had God swooping down from heaven and intervening into history at particular spots"; in his rejection of "supernaturalism," according to which deity would "have to 'step down' and enter history here and there," in favor of "a *nondualism* between God and the world"; and in his endorsement of those who see "God's incarnation in Jesus as an expression of the *nondualistic* unity between divinity and humanity," so that "[i]ncarnation is not a one-time event."[59] Knitter's rejection of supernaturalism also lies behind his seeming rejection of the "uniqueness" of Jesus and Christianity.[60]

Knitter's point here has been widely misunderstood. Although in the preface to *The Myth of Christian Uniqueness* he said that by calling "Christian uniqueness" a myth he did not mean to say that it is simply false, but only that it must be carefully interpreted,[61] critics have taken him, along with other pluralists, to be denying Christian uniqueness altogether. What needs revision, said Knitter,

55. Gilkey, "Plurality and Its Theological Implications," 44, 39, 38.

56. Smith, *Towards a World Theology*, 125.

57. Smith, "Idolatry in Comparative Perspective," 59, 66, 68 n.12.

58. Smith, "Theology and the World's Religious History," 72, 68.

59. Knitter, *No Other Name?* 26, 68, 191.

60. The importance this issue has taken on is evident in the title of the 1990 book edited by Gavin D'Costa, *Christian Uniqueness Reconsidered.* Knitter has later conceded that his and Hick's decision to title their edited volume *The Myth of Christian Uniqueness* "was perhaps a mistake" (Swidler et al., *Death or Dialogue?* 127). This issue is confusing because Hick and Smith, with whom Knitter has been closely associated, deny Christian uniqueness not only in the supernaturalist sense but also in the more general sense, against which Heim, Cobb, and some other critics have reacted.

61. Knitter, Preface, vii.

are "*traditional* understandings of 'the uniqueness of Christ and Christianity' (together with similar understandings of the Qur'an)."[62] But even the usually careful John Cobb responded by saying that "I affirm and celebrate the uniqueness of Christ, of Christianity, of the Qur'an,"[63] thereby implying that Knitter rejected such uniqueness altogether. If Knitter had said that he rejected the idea that Christianity is unique in the sense of being the only religion to be supernaturally founded, his point would have been clearer (and seconded by Cobb, who also rejects the "metaphysical uniqueness of Jesus"[64]). That this is Knitter's meaning seems clear from his statement that what he is rejecting is "the *absolute superiority*" of Christianity, his affirmation that "Jesus is unique . . . without being exclusively unique," and his assertion that Christians cannot "really play the game of dialogue [if they believe that] they have been given all the trump cards by God."[65] Knitter's rejection of a supernatural account of Christian origins is also reflected in his criticism of theologians who believe that present experience can be ignored in favor of biblical authority.[66]

The rejection of supernaturalism behind Gordon Kaufman's affirmation of pluralism is shown by his denial that the assertions of Christian theology are "directly and uniquely authorized or warranted by divine revelation," his affirmation that Christian theology should "understand itself in essentially the same terms that it understands other religious activity and reflection," his rejection of "[b]eliefs about divine inspiration and revelation [that have] enabled theologians in the past to [claim] that this or that affirmation or position is grounded directly in the very truth of God,"[67] and his rejection of the view that the Christian gospel is "grounded in God's own special revelation in and through Jesus Christ" in a way "taken to set Christian faith apart from all other religious orientations."[68]

John Cobb has thought in terms of Whitehead's nonsupernaturalistic understanding of divine power for so long that he for the most part simply assumes, rather than explicitly stating, an understanding of Christianity that is not supernaturalist. But some more or less explicit statements can be found. In an early essay on Christology, for example, Cobb says that God was present in Jesus as prehended or experienced (*not* as experiencing), that this divine presence involved no "displacement" of any feature of Jesus' humanity, that "the actual occasions constituting Jesus as a living person were not in any instance the . . . actual occasions constituting the divine life," and that "[s]trict identity of Jesus with God is simply nonsensical."[69] In his book on Christology he explicitly rejects the traditional "supernaturalist and

---

62. Cobb in Swidler et al., *Death or Dialogue?* 32; emphasis added.
63. Ibid., 83.
64. Ibid., 14.
65. Knitter in Swidler et al., *Death or Dialogue?* 127, 94, 12. An examination of Knitter's denial of the "exclusive uniqueness" of Jesus in his first book will show that what he was rejecting was the idea that Jesus is "the one and only Savior" so that "all salvation is *constituted* by the Christ event" (*No Other Name?* 116–17).
66. Knitter, *No Other Name?* 90–91.
67. Kaufman, "Religious Diversity, Historical Consciousness, and Christian Theology," 12.
68. Ibid., 15 n. 3.
69. Cobb, "A Whiteheadian Christology," 384–85, 390.

exclusivist" interpretations of the incarnation of the divine Logos in Jesus, according to which Jesus was "a supernatural being," namely, "the transcendent, omnipotent, omniscient ruler of the world . . . walking about on earth in human form."
Furthermore, after saying that Christianity is "one historical movement alongside
others," Cobb adds: "Nothing historical is absolute; so any tendency to absolutize
any feature of Christianity is idolatry." Cobb has also endorsed a naturalistic soteriology in dealing with "salvation as something we participate in here and now
rather than, or in addition to, life beyond."[70] Finally, he has encouraged Christians
not to resist "appropriation of the universal truth offered by modern science,"
which could well be taken to include the truth of naturalism$_{ns}$.[71]

Whereas the examples of the rejection of supernaturalism summarized thus
far have emphasized the negative point that this rejection undermines the basis
for assuming that God's participation in the origin of Christianity was ontologically unique, Marjorie Suchocki shows how this rejection can lead to a positive
argument for pluralism. Over against the traditional view of *creatio ex nihilo*,
Suchocki suggests that we should think of "creation through call and response."
In place of the idea of a passive creation, she suggests that "the world has the
capacity for novelty, or freedom, within itself."[72] Although at the outset of our
universe, the chaos is sufficiently unresisting that "God can set down the para-
meters of all future becomings," each stage of the creative process, in bringing
forth creatures with greater complexity, provides the conditions for increasing
diversity of response, with each divergence laying the ground for even greater
diversity in the future. Although God's call in each context is for the greatest possible well-being, given the past history of the creatures in question, the divine
calls to different creatures become increasingly diverse. Her conclusion: "If creaturely response is so integral to the creator's call, then there is simply no way there
could even be a world without great diversity."[73]

Because freedom is greatest at the human level, furthermore, diversity within
the human race will be the greatest. The divine calls to the various cultures will
therefore be very diverse. Although God is always calling each culture to the most
inclusive form of well-being possible for it, "the type of response God gives within
any culture depends upon the type of response those within the culture have
given to God's call."[74] Given the Christian belief in the faithfulness of God, we

70. Cobb, *Christ in a Pluralistic Age*, 27, 163; *Transforming Christianity and the World*, 44; and in
Swidler et al., *Death or Dialogue?* 13. Some theologians think that to reject a supernaturalistic understanding of salvation means to reject life after death. As both Cobb and Hick see, however, the real
issue is whether any salvific state to be experienced in a life beyond this one is in continuity with the
soul's growth in the present life, as opposed to being a state unilaterally effected by God as an extrinsic reward. A nonsupernaturalistic understanding of salvation is suggested by Mark Heim's statement
that "[r]eligious ends are not extrinsic awards granted for unrelated performances, like trips to Hawaii
won in lotteries. . . . The way and the end are one" (*Salvations*, 162).
71. Cobb, *Beyond Dialogue*, x. I have argued for this conclusion in *Religion and Scientific Naturalism*.
72. Suchocki, *Divinity and Diversity*, 28, 29.
73. Ibid., 29–30, 30.
74. Ibid., 33.

should assume that, even though aboriginal culture is very different from ours, "God is as surely creatively involved in the evolution of aboriginal culture as in Jewish and Christian culture." Arguing that "diverse communities of peoples develop as a result of the creative interaction between God and the world," she concludes: "We can affirm other religions because God has been at work in calling them as well as ourselves into being."[75] In this way, Suchocki shows how the ontological rejection of supernaturalism leads to a view of the God-world relation that not only makes religious diversity theologically expected, rather than a theological aberration, but also shows how God can be understood as equally involved in radically diverse religious traditions.

The ontological basis for religious pluralism, I am suggesting, is crucial for explaining the rise of generic pluralism and for understanding its nature. This positive relation between the modern rejection of supernaturalism and the affirmation of pluralism is not, to be sure, a necessary relation. One could become a pluralist while continuing to affirm supernaturalism. And one could reject supernaturalism without become a pluralist. But there is, nevertheless, a strong correlation between the two. The rejection of the belief that the origin of our own religion involved a supernatural interruption of the normal causal principles of the universe tends to lead us to religious pluralism, and most pluralists have, in fact, rejected supernaturalism.

However, whereas pluralists see this relationship as a good thing, it can provide a reason for critics to claim that Christian pluralistic theologies, by accepting an alien ontology from modernity, are not really Christian. For critics who oppose pluralistic theology because of its generic pluralism, rather than simply because of defects in one or more of its species, Christian faith as such involves the claim to be the only true religion, or at least the claim that all salvation comes through Jesus Christ, with this claim being based on the conviction that God *did* act supernaturally in Christianity's originating events. These critics would, in effect, be rejecting the compatibility of naturalism$_{ns}$ with authentic Christian faith. The Christian belief in God, they would say, involves belief that God has the power to interrupt the world's basic causal processes—which, they would say (perhaps with a reference to the doctrine of *creatio ex nihilo*), were freely established by God, so they can be freely interrupted—and that God used that power in founding Christianity. Insofar as these critics see the fundamental error of pluralists to be their acceptance of naturalism$_{ns}$, their critiques may involve negative comments about (uncritical) acceptance of "modern" or "Enlightenment" rationality.

The observation that modern assumptions are central to the pluralist project is not, however, necessarily connected to criticism of the rejection of supernaturalism. This centrality has been noted by pluralists, such as Gilkey (in statements cited above), and by critics whose criticism is not necessarily dependent on supernaturalist assumptions. One such critic is Mark Heim, who speaks of "an under-

---

75. Ibid., 75.

lying similarity in Hick, Smith, and Knitter which has very much to do with liberal Christianity's appropriation of modernity." Heim says, in particular, that pluralists assume the universality of "Western academic principles."[76] He is not
necessarily critical of this assumption. His point is rather that pluralists need to
provide an *argument* for the universal validity of the principles they are assuming.[77] He believes, in fact, that the task of "mak[ing] explicit their case for the
global normativity of the Western critical principles" they are employing is "[t]he
primary challenge to pluralist theories."[78] Whether or not this should be considered the *primary* challenge to pluralists, Heim is certainly right about both the
centrality of modern assumptions and the need to argue for their universal validity. This is one of the issues that should be addressed by Whiteheadian pluralists.
I give my own view, which I believe also to be Cobb's view, in the first section of
the following chapter. For now, however, I turn to the recent criticism of Christian pluralism that is based not on its rejection of supernaturalism but on the fact
that pluralism as such has become widely identified with one version of it.

3. HEIM'S CRITIQUE OF PLURALISTIC THEOLOGY

The hitherto dominant proposals for how to develop a pluralistic theology have
evoked an enormous amount of criticism.[79] In his 1995 book, *Salvations*, Mark
Heim provides an acute and extensive critique that is to a large extent a systematic synthesis of much of the prior criticism.[80] I will use it to illustrate the way in
which the widespread tendency to equate theological pluralism with one type of
it—a type that is not very pluralistic—has been creating a negative impression of
pluralistic theology as such.

Heim's Examples of Pluralistic Theology

Part I of Heim's book, entitled "Pluralisms," contains critiques of three pluralist
theologians: John Hick, Wilfred Cantwell Smith, and Paul Knitter. Heim's stated
reason for focusing on them is that they provide "the most extensive and consistent
cases for 'pluralistic' interpretations of religious diversity." The implication of this

76. Heim, *Salvations*, 9, 60. Heim also points to Lesslie Newbigin and Kenneth Surin as two critics who had previously made this point (9 nn. 6, 7).
77. Ibid., 92–93, 123–24, 214.
78. Ibid., 123.
79. A list of books and articles printed in an appendix to Hick's *A Christian Theology of Religion*
(1995), which contains responses only to his own proposal, fills almost five pages.
80. Heim drew most heavily on the critiques contained in D'Costa, ed., *Christian Uniqueness
Reconsidered: The Myth of a Pluralistic Theology of Religions*. Other sources that seem to have been
especially influential include DiNoia, "Varieties of Religious Aims: Beyond Exclusivism, Inclusivism,
and Pluralism," and *The Diversity of Religions: A Christian Perspective*; Griffiths, *An Apology for Apologetics*; Milbank, *Theology and Social Theory*; Ogden, *Is There Only One True Religion or Are There
Many?*; and Ward, "Truth and the Diversity of Religions."

statement is that if *their* versions of theological pluralism turn out on examination to be inconsistent and otherwise problematic, pluralism as such will have been shown to be unsatisfactory. Indeed, Heim suggests at the outset that this will be his conclusion. While saying that the pluralists have raised real questions, he adds: "If their accounts of religious diversity are seriously wanting, then . . . we may learn from them and search further."[81] By the end of the book, he is consistently speaking negatively of "pluralism" and "the pluralists"—alternatively "the pluralist hypotheses," "pluralistic theologies," "pluralistic theology," "pluralistic theories," "pluralistic doctrine"—and calling for "a 'post-pluralistic' conversation."[82]

However, although this is the central thread in the book, it is not the only one. A paradoxical feature of Heim's critique is that although he consistently refers to Hick, Smith, and Knitter as "the pluralists" and of their positions as "the pluralistic hypotheses," he contends that their positions are not really pluralistic—a point that has been made by several other writers.[83] Referring with scare quotes to "'pluralistic' theologies," Heim says: "Despite their appropriation of the title, these theologies are not religiously pluralistic at all." Compounding the paradox, Heim indicates that he considers pluralism a good thing by offering a "true religious pluralism," a "more pluralistic hypothesis," "a truly pluralistic hypothesis."[84]

This paradox raises the question as to why Heim continues to call Hick, Smith, and Knitter pluralists. If he believes they are not really pluralists, why not call them *alleged* pluralists, *self-styled* pluralists, or *pseudo*pluralists? This change in language would remove the paradox, as there would be nothing inconsistent in offering a hypothesis that is more pluralistic than a pseudopluralistic hypothesis. This change would also mean that the rhetoric of the book would not be directed against pluralism. If all the negative comments were about pseudopluralists and pseudopluralist hypotheses, the book would not seem to suggest that pluralism as such should be left behind. The call for a "postpseudopluralistic conversation" might be a mouthful, but it would make clear that what we now need is a *genuinely* pluralistic conversation. As it is, however, the dominant message of Heim's book is that the pluralistic turn as such has been a mistake.[85]

To understand this conclusion, along with the paradox in Heim's position, we need to look more closely at his decision to let "pluralism" in theology be represented by Hick, Smith, and Knitter. It is always dangerous to judge a genus in

---

81. Heim, *Salvations*, 8, 2.

82. Ibid., 87, 88, 89, 90, 101, 103, 109, 125, 130, 226.

83. For example, Gavin D'Costa, in the introduction to *Christian Uniqueness Reconsidered*, says that "'pluralistic theology' ironically often seems to hinder rather than aid a proper recognition of religious plurality" (xi). Another contributor to this volume, Christoph Schwöbel, says that Hick's version of pluralistic theology "seems in danger of undermining what it sets out to preserve, that is, the plurality of religions" ("Particularity, Universality, and the Religions," 32). Joseph DiNoia, who also has an essay in the D'Costa volume, elsewhere says that his essay's thesis is that pluralist accounts "turn out upon examination to be markedly nonpluralistic" (*The Diversity of Religions*, 194).

84. Heim, *Salvations*, 129, 7, 8, 130.

85. That this is indeed the message received by readers is suggested by the fact that Paul Griffiths's (rave) review of the book is titled "Beyond Pluralism."

terms of a limited number of species, to judge a type on the basis of a few tokens. Due to limitations of time and space, however, this practice is often necessary. The danger must nevertheless be kept in sight, the danger that one will make generalizations about the genus (type) that in reality apply to only some of the species (tokens). This danger is especially acute in polemical writing. With regard to a type of thought of which one is critical, one way to guard against this danger is to include among one's samples the positions that are arguably the best or strongest versions of that type. Heim suggests that he did this, saying that his three writers provide "the most extensive and consistent cases for 'pluralistic' interpretations." Of Hick's pluralistic hypothesis in particular, Heim says that "[n]o other version of pluralistic theology has reached the same level of breadth, clarity and consistency."[86] The dozens of critiques of Hick's position that have been published, however, are replete with charges of inconsistency.[87] Heim's statement comes, in fact, at the close of a chapter in which he demonstrates that Hick's position is full of inconsistencies. That demonstration, in conjunction with other problems Heim finds in his trio of pluralists, supports, of course, the conclusion toward which his book is headed—that pluralistic theology is to be left behind. That conclusion would follow, however, only if the problems that Heim identifies as belonging to pluralistic theology apply to every version of it. But they do not apply, for example, to the version put forth by John Cobb.

The fact (to be shown below) that Cobb is an exception to Heim's generalizations about pluralistic theologies raises the question of why he was not included among the representative pluralists. The criteria Heim mentions in justifying his decision to use Hick, Smith, and Knitter as the "three primary versions of pluralistic theology" are five: the *extensiveness, clarity,* and *consistency* of the case they have made for pluralism and their *prominence* and *influence.*[88] In terms of these five criteria, Cobb clearly should have been included.[89] The reason for Cobb's exclusion, however, is not Heim's doubts about his prominence or the clarity and consistency of his writing. Although there are only a few references to Cobb's writings in Heim's book, they are all positive.[90] The reason is that

---

86. Heim, *Salvations,* 8, 42.

87. See, for example, the critiques published in D'Costa, ed., *Christian Uniqueness Reconsidered,* and the essays reprinted in Quinn and Meeker, eds., *The Philosophical Challenge of Religious Diversity,* especially those by Philip L. Quinn, Paul R. Eddy, George I. Mavrodes, Ninian Smart, and Keith Ward. For example, Ward says that Hick's hypothesis is "riddled with difficulties" ("Truth and the Diversity of Religions," 110).

88. Heim, *Salvations,* 102, 8, 42.

89. At the time Heim's book was published (1995), Cobb's writings on the topic included *The Structure of Christian Existence* (1967), *Christ in a Pluralistic Age* (1975), *Beyond Dialogue* (1982), and (with Swidler, Knitter, and Hellwig) *Death or Dialogue?* (1990), along with twenty-some articles. Cobb, furthermore, was already mentioned as an important pluralist in Alan Race's 1983 landmark book, *Christians and Religious Pluralism,* 88, 98.

90. It is puzzling, however, that Heim mentions none of Cobb's books and only one of his articles. Given this virtual ignoring of Cobb's position, Heim can say of his own "hypothesis of multiple religious ends, salvations," that it is "a perspective little canvassed in the contemporary discussion of religious diversity" (*Salvations,* 157).

Heim considers Cobb a critic, not an advocate, of pluralistic theology.[91] To see the reason for this surprising view, we need to look more closely at how Heim's equation of a particular species of pluralistic theology with the genus leads him to characterize pluralistic Christian theologies as not really pluralistic and not really Christian.

Pluralistic Christian Theologies as Not Pluralistic

Although there are many varieties of pluralism in the generic sense, they can be divided into two broad types, which can be called "identist pluralism" and "differential pluralism." In these expressions, the noun (*pluralism*) refers to *generic* pluralism while the adjectives refer to ontological and soteriological theses about the relations of the various religions to each other. According to *identist* pluralism, all religions are oriented toward the same religious object (whether it be called "God," "Brahman," "Nirvana," "Sunyata," "Ultimate Reality," "the Transcendent," or "the Real") and promote essentially the same end (the same type of "salvation").[92] Identist pluralism is, in other words, identist both ontologically and soteriologically. *Differential* pluralism, by contrast, says that religions promote different ends—different salvations—perhaps by virtue of being oriented toward different religious objects, perhaps thought of as different ultimates. Differential pluralism is, in other words, pluralistic soteriologically and perhaps also ontologically.[93] There can, of course, be various versions of both identist and differential pluralism.

In light of these distinctions, there are two basic problems with Heim's use of Hick, Smith, and Knitter to characterize pluralistic theology. First, they are all *identist* pluralists, so Heim's sample includes no differential pluralists. The second problem is that Heim fails to distinguish between these thinkers' religious pluralism as such, which I have called their generic pluralism, and their identist versions of it. This second problem, more precisely, is that Heim ignores their generic pluralism in favor of their particular hypotheses. Because these particular hypotheses are all identist, Heim comes to think of this identism as, paradoxically, that which all pluralists have in common. In Heim's mind, in other words, the pluralism that is generic to the pluralistic theologians is a *denial* of pluralism. He says, for example, that the "principles of 'pluralistic theology' have the odd similarity of denying precisely any pluralism of authentic religious con-

91. Ibid., 88.

92. An identist version of pluralism that has much in common with Hick's is articulated by Fritjof Schuon in *The Transcendent Unity of Religions*. Schuon's view has been endorsed by Huston Smith in his introduction to Schuon's book, in his own *Forgotten Truth*, and in his portion of Griffin and Smith, *Postmodern Theology and Primordial Truth*.

93. Some Christian theologians remain identist ontologically, while affirming soteriological pluralism, by means of the doctrine of the Trinity, suggesting that different types of salvation involve orientation to different dimensions (or "persons") of one and the same divine reality. Heim's section on "Plenitude and Trinity" (*Salvations*, 163–71) suggests a version of this position. He later developed this suggestion in *The Depth of the Riches: A Trinitarian Theology of Religious Ends*.

sequence."[94] It is no wonder that he concludes that pluralistic theology is not really pluralistic.

Although Heim does see all three members of his trio as exemplifying what he calls the principles of pluralistic theology, it is plain that his characterization has been derived primarily from Hick, whose "pluralistic hypothesis" Heim considers "the most extensive and detailed case yet made for a pluralistic account of the religions," adding: "No other version of pluralistic theology has reached the same level of breadth, clarity and consistency."[95] Because Heim thinks of Hick as the paradigmatic pluralist, he especially equates Hick's version of pluralism with pluralism as such. This tendency is evident even in the title of the chapter devoted to Hick's position. Although one might have expected a title such as "John Hick's Pluralistic Hypothesis," which would indicate that Hick's is one pluralistic hypothesis among others, the chapter is titled simply "John Hick and the Pluralistic Hypothesis." In the first section, headed "The Pluralistic Hypothesis," Heim says that Hick "summarizes the 'pluralistic hypothesis' this way. An 'infinite Real, in itself beyond the scope of other than purely formal concepts, is differently conceived, experienced and responded to from within the different cultural ways of being human' (Hick 1989, 14)."[96] Part and parcel of this hypothesis, Heim adds, is that in each tradition a "transformation of human existence from self-centeredness to Reality-centeredness is taking place." In later summarizing "the pluralistic hypothesis," Heim says that it rests on two dubious assumptions: "a metaphysical dogma that there can be but one religious object, and a soteriological dogma that there can be but one religious end."[97]

What Heim is here discussing, however, is not a hypothesis that is held in common by all pluralistic theologians, but only Hick's particular hypothesis. Hick himself, in fact, has made this point by referring to "religious pluralism as a family of theories about the relationship between the religions." Contrasting these pluralistic theories with exclusivist and inclusivist theories, he says that they all "acknowledge the other great world religions as independently authentic spheres of salvation/liberation/enlightenment." Pointing out that this "broadly pluralistic view" is expressed in a "range of pluralistic points of view," he distinguishes between "[his] own particular version of religious pluralism" and "other forms of religious pluralism."[98]

To be fair to Heim, however, I must immediately add that this statement, in which Hick distinguishes clearly between generic pluralism and his own version of it, was published only after Heim had written his book. Hick's statement is in

94. Heim, *Salvations*, 7.
95. Ibid., 8, 42.
96. Ibid., 15.
97. Ibid., 15, 23.
98. Hick, *A Christian Theology of Religions*, 149. Although Hick thereby properly distinguishes between a "broadly pluralistic view" and his own version of it, Paul Griffiths, in his review of Heim's book ("Beyond Pluralism," 50), summarizes what he calls a "broadly pluralistic" view in terms that apply to Hick's position (and to some extent Smith's and Knitter's) but not to that of many other pluralists, such as Cobb.

A Christian Theology of Religions, which was published in 1995, the same year that Heim's book appeared. Prior to that statement, Hick himself had tended to write as if pluralism as such could be equated with his version of it. Indeed, in Hick's 1989 book, *The Interpretation of Religion*, which was Heim's primary source for understanding his position, Hick referred to his own view as "The Pluralistic Hypothesis" (the title of chapter 14), which Hick in turn seemed simply to equate with "Religious Pluralism" (the title of part 4). According to this hypothesis, Hick explained, there is only one religious ultimate, to which all the world religions are oriented, and salvation in each of them is essentially the same, being "the transformation of human existence from self-centredness to Reality-centredness."[99] Even in his 1995 book, furthermore, Hick's distinction between religious pluralism as such and his particular version of it is not prominent.[100]

Other commentators have also been misled by Hick into equating religious pluralism as such with his particular version of it. For example, Keith Ward, having said that Hick's 1989 book "is a statement of the position which has come to be known as religious pluralism," adds, "The pluralistic hypothesis is that religions provide different valid but culturally conditioned responses to a transcendent reality, and offer ways of transcending self and achieving a limitlessly better state centred on that reality."[101] Probably the clearest example of this equation is provided by Kevin Meeker and Philip Quinn. After rightly distinguishing *religious diversity* (which refers simply to "the undisputed fact that different religions espouse doctrines that are at least apparently in conflict and offer alternative paths of salvation") from *religious pluralism*, they "reserve [the latter] term to refer to the position John Hick adopts in response to the fact of religious diversity."[102] By this definition, Hick and those who adopt his position would seem to be the only religious pluralists in the world! In any case, Heim is far from alone in equating religious pluralism as such with Hick's version of it.[103]

---

99. Hick, *An Interpretation of Religion*, 234, 248, 347, 300.

100. The statement quoted above from page 149 of *A Christian Theology of Religions* is contained in an appendix. In the main body of the book, aside from an allusion to the distinction between pluralism as such and his version of it on page 18, Hick makes the same identification he had in prior writings. For example, he begins the book with a chapter titled "The Pluralistic Hypothesis," in which his own solution to the problem raised by a diversity of religions is labeled simply "the pluralist answer" (11, 27). Although there are several statements expressing what I call the generic meaning of pluralism (ix, 15, 18, 24, 30, 33, 87, 125, 126, 135), Hick does not call attention to the distinction between this generic meaning and his specific version of pluralism. In most of the book, Hick gives the impression that religious pluralism can simply be equated with his own position, according to which "there is one ineffable reality to which [all the religions are] pointing" and, although the aims of the various religions are "*specifically* different, [they] are *generically* the same" (69, 41).

101. Ward, "Truth and the Diversity of Religions," 109–10. The continuation of Ward's statement, however, summarizes what I would call the generic dimension of Hick's pluralism, and Ward later speaks of "his [Hick's] version of pluralistic religious realism" (122), thereby showing his awareness that there can be other versions.

102. Quinn and Meeker, eds., "Introduction: The Philosophical Challenge of Religious Diversity," in *The Philosophical Challenge of Religious Diversity*, 3.

103. One critic who clearly sees the distinction is Schubert Ogden. Arguing in an essay titled "Problems in the Case for a Pluralistic Theology of Religions" that there are problems in Hick's case for religious pluralism, Ogden points out that there may be "other logically independent lines

This said, however, this equation *is* a confusion, and one with unfortunate consequences. The principal consequence is that Heim, who sees Hick as making "the philosophical case for a pluralistic outlook," regards Hick's position, which "grounds the cognitive and experiential cores of the great religious traditions in one common object and one common salvific process,"[104] to be representative of "pluralistic theologies" as such. Heim says, for example, that the "assumption that there is and can be only one religious end is a crucial constitutive element of 'pluralistic' theologies." He also says that pluralistic theologies are *opposed* to the view that "different religions may offer alternative religious objects."[105]

Although this characterization seems to be derived primarily from Hick, Heim sees all three members of his trio of pluralists as making similar points. Having said that in spite of their significantly different approaches, they have "real similarities," Heim continues:

> One of the most dramatic is the way that each appears to deconstruct the pluralism it seeks to affirm. They insist that despite any apparent indications to the contrary, there is no diversity in the religious object (Hick), in the human religious attitude (Smith), or the primary religious function (Knitter).[106] Thus they agree that the faiths cannot be regarded as serious religious alternatives.[107]

Having thereby equated pluralism with the identist type of it, Heim offers, as "A More Pluralistic Hypothesis" (the title of his fifth chapter), the idea that there are "various realities . . . which are religiously significant and which ground diverse religious fulfillments (for instance, both some form of personal deity and a condition similar to that described as nirvana)." In contrast with Hick's view "that 'Sunyata' and 'God' are mythological cultural forms which represent 'the Real,'" [Heim's] hypothesis presumes that they are real religious ineffables available to their seekers."[108] Another point Heim makes against the position of Hick

---

of argument by which the case for pluralism might be made" (493). In Ogden's *book* on the subject, however, his conclusion about pluralism—"that there are a number of difficulties with the case that pluralists make for it and that these difficulties are sufficiently serious to make one question its validity" (*Is There Only One?* 79)—is based, except for a very brief discussion of Alan Race, on the positions of Hick and Knitter. There is no discussion, for example, of John Cobb.

104. Heim, *Salvations*, 15, 16.

105. Ibid., 129, 103.

106. The reference to Smith summarizes Heim's critique of him as equating human religiosity with "faith" understood as an attitude or disposition that is identical in people in all religious traditions, regardless of how they conceive the object to which it is directed (ibid., 55–57, 61). The reference to Knitter summarizes Heim's critique of him as insisting that all religion should be—so that all "authentic" religion *is*—oriented toward liberation from injustice (76, 91–97).

107. Ibid., 102.

108. Ibid., 146, 154. In Heim's use, I should point out, to say that something is ineffable does not mean that it is, like Hick's (Kantian noumenal) "Reality," *wholly* beyond description. It merely means that "short of actually experiencing [something, such as a pain], no description gives anything like a full understanding of it" (145 n. 6). This understanding of ineffability had previously been offered, in criticism of Hick's use of the term, by Keith Ward ("Truth and the Diversity of Religions," 113–18).

and the other (identist) pluralists is that, by regarding all the religions as essentially the same, they provide no motivation for dialogue among them, because their view implies that "the specific and special aspects of another faith tell us [nothing] that is of significant importance," whereas Heim's more pluralistic hypothesis "offers real hope for mutual transformation."[109]

However, as anyone knows who has read John Cobb's *Beyond Dialogue* or some of his essays on religious pluralism—some of which have been helpfully collected by Knitter in *Transforming Christianity and the World*—these points are central to Cobb's version of religious pluralism. Cobb criticizes, for example, the assumption that "what is approached as 'ultimate reality' must be one and the same." He rejects, in particular, the idea that the terms "God" and "Sunyata" (or "Emptiness") refer to the same reality.[110] In a criticism of Hick's position, Cobb says that in light of the fact "that Emptiness is not an object of worship for Buddhists . . . , it is not illuminating to insist that Emptiness and God are two names for the same noumenal reality."[111] Cobb has long insisted, furthermore, that the "nirvana" or "satori" experienced or sought by the Buddhist is radically different from the salvation experienced or sought by the Christian.[112] In response to the statement by fellow Christian theologian Monika Hellwig that "we have a common starting point and a common end in the transcendent ultimate" and that "what is truly ultimate is unified so that all quests for communion with the ultimate are in process of converging," Cobb argues that "there are many Buddhists who do not understand themselves as seeking communion with the ultimate," so their Buddhism offers "a different path to a different goal, a different name of a different aspect of reality, a different language through which something quite different from communion is sought."[113]

On these bases, Cobb has not only pointed out that members of different religious traditions can learn from each other but has also advocated that the various traditions can undergo "mutual transformation." In fact, although Heim employs this phrase with no reference to Cobb's use of it, the prevalence of this phrase in discussions of interreligious dialogue is surely due primarily to the influence of Cobb, who employed it in, among other places, the subtitle of his *Beyond Dialogue*. What Heim is proposing as an *alternative* to pluralistic theologies is, in sum, what Cobb's version of pluralistic theology has been proposing for some time. Rather than leaving pluralistic theology behind, therefore, we

---

109. Heim, *Salvations*, 125, 123.

110. Cobb, *Transforming Christianity and the World*, 87; *Beyond Dialogue*, 87–90, 110; *Death or Dialogue?* 116.

111. Cobb, *Beyond Dialogue*, 43.

112. Cobb, *The Structure of Christian Existence*, chaps. 6, 10–12; *Beyond Dialogue*, chaps. 4–6.

113. Cobb in Swidler et al., *Death or Dialogue?* 81–82. Having been questioned by Hellwig about his suggestion that the biblical God and Buddhist Emptiness refer to different "aspects" of reality, Cobb says that he should not have used that term, which suggests that Buddhists and Christians simply apprehend an identical reality in different ways, but should have more clearly said that they focus on a different "principle, element, reality, or ultimate" (100, 115–16).

perhaps need merely to cease equating pluralistic theology solely with identist versions of it.[114]

This equation creates yet another problem for Heim. As we have seen, he often says that the positions of the (identist) pluralists are not really pluralistic. But at one point, Heim says that their "pluralism is real but superficial."[115] This is a more accurate statement. However, given Heim's characterization of their positions—according to which, for example, Hick's pluralism is equated with his "pluralistic hypothesis" about a common salvific process oriented toward a common Reality—Heim has no way to explain in what sense Hick's pluralism can be called real. This explanation requires our explicit recognition of the generic pluralism underlying Hick's particular hypothesis. Then, once we have seen that Hick's professed pluralism is real, our distinction between identist and differential pluralism allows us to explain why the pluralistic position developed in Hick's particular hypothesis is superficial. I earlier made the tongue-in-cheek proposal that Heim should have referred to his trio of pluralists as "pseudopluralists." A more serious proposal, suggested by Heim's own statement, would be "superficial pluralists."[116] A differential pluralism, by contrast, would be a deep pluralism.

Heim's critique can, accordingly, be seen as a call for a deep pluralism—one that recognizes that religious diversity involves real differences in the diagnosis of the basic human problem, the type of "salvation" needed, and the nature of the ultimate reality to which attention is directed. A deep pluralism would, furthermore, see truth in other religions in relation to aspects in which they are different from one's own tradition, as well as in relation to aspects in which they are similar. This book is intended as a response to that call—with part of this response being the demonstration that John Cobb has already gone far in the direction of articulating a deeply pluralistic Christian position.

114. Heim is not the first one to suggest that problems in one of its types provide grounds for rejecting pluralist theology as such. For example, Gavin D'Costa, after referring to dissatisfaction with "the pluralist project so defined in *The Myth of Christian Uniqueness*," goes on to "raise questions as to whether 'pluralist theology' is an appropriate or even adequate interpretation of religious plurality" (*Christian Uniqueness Reconsidered*, x–xi). Whereas the first statement suggests the inadequacy of pluralistic theology of a particular type, the second statement suggests that pluralistic theology as such is problematic.

115. Heim, *Salvations*, 7.

116. The pluralism suggested by much of Knitter's writing is also open to the charge of being, like Hick's and Smith's, superficial. For example, although Knitter raises critical questions about the doctrine, affirmed in various ways by Arnold Toynbee, W. C. Smith, and Fritjof Schuon, that all the religions have a common essence (*No Other Name?* 37–54), he does hold that all religions focus on the same object—that "what is being experienced in the religions [is] basically the same" (ibid., 51). The fact that Knitter has remained committed to the view that all the religions are oriented toward the same ultimate, even after editing a book of Cobb's essays, is shown by his comment that "Cobb is *tempted* to speak of differing but related Ultimates" (*Transforming Christianity and the World*, 114; emphasis added). The other feature of Knitter's position making his pluralism less than deep is his insistence, mentioned in note 106, on making liberative justice the criterion for any religion to be judged authentic. One can agree with Knitter that religions today should cooperate to promote liberative justice without regarding this as the criterion of authentic religion as such.

Pluralistic Theologies as Falsely Claiming a Neutral Universality

Another point in Heim's critique of pluralistic theologies is that they pretend to have transcended particularity—to have a neutral, universal perspective from which to decide what is valid and invalid in historic Christian faith and other particular religious traditions. They assign normative cognitive status, in other words, to an allegedly neutral metatheory of religion, which is thought to stand equidistantly above Christian faith and all other particularistic religious commitments.[117] Rejecting the "imperialism" involved when Christians judge other religions by their own norms, these pluralists "claim not to impose a particular norm as universal." But, says Heim,

> [T]his is largely an optical illusion. There is no 'God's eye view' from which to discern [the general facts of the religions or human existence]. A metatheory claims to offer a view which is not a Christian one or a liberal Western one alongside an orthodox Jewish one or a liberal Muslim one, but rather a view on a different level and in some qualitative way beyond such particularity. It is a claim that cannot be validated. To demonstrate that one, for instance, no longer grants authority to Christian or Muslim norms is no evidence that one does not hew to others just as particular.[118]

This twofold criticism—that pluralistic theologians unrealistically and even incoherently insist that it is wrong to use the norms of one's particular religious tradition to evaluate others, and that they then turn around and use their own norms, which are in fact just as particularistic, to judge all the religious traditions—is one that Heim reverts to time and time again.[119] It is, along with his related point that pluralistic theologies are not really pluralistic, his fundamental criticism.

It is, however, a criticism that does not apply to Cobb's version of pluralistic theology. The denial of a neutral standpoint has, in fact, been central to Cobb's perspective from the outset. Two of Cobb's earliest books argue that, on the one hand, Christian theology proper requires a natural theology in the sense of a *philosophical* account of God, humanity, and the world, and that, on the other hand, there is no such thing as a *natural* theology in the sense of a purely *neutral* account, unaffected by some particular historical tradition with a particular vision of reality.[120] What the Christian theologian needs, therefore, is a *Christian* natural (philosophical) theology,[121] because the normative employment of a philosophy embodying some other vision of reality will inevitably lead to a distortion of the Christian message.

117. Heim, *Salvations*, 4, 10, 30, 34.
118. Ibid., 105.
119. Ibid., 4, 10, 30, 34, 66, 91, 120, 124, 138, 141–42, 190, 210.
120. Cobb, *Living Options in Protestant Theology* (1962); *A Christian Natural Theology* (1965).
121. Here Cobb's position is parallel to that of Heim, who rejects not the need for a metatheory of religion but only the assumption that such a theory can be neutral rather than confessional (*Salvations*, 10, 124, 141).

This standpoint is reflected in an essay written for a volume edited by Leonard Swidler titled *Toward a Universal Theology of Religion*. Cobb begins with a critique of that title, saying that he fears that the phrase "universal theology" suggests "that theology can begin with a perspective shaped neutrally by all the ways rather than by any of them in particular," which would mean that "a universal theology will replace specifically Christian theology." In a paragraph that could have been written by Heim, Cobb continues:

> If that is the meaning, then I protest in the name both of realism and of Christian faith. In the name of realism I protest that the pretense to stand beyond all traditions and build neutrally out of all of them is a delusion. In the name of Christian faith I protest against the implicit relativization and even negation of basic Christian commitments.[122]

It would seem, therefore, that pluralistic theologians need not be unaware of the impossibility of shedding their historical spectacles in favor of a God's-eye point of view.

Pluralistic Christian Theologies as Not Christian

Besides characterizing pluralistic Christian theologies as not really pluralistic and as falsely claiming to have transcended particularity, Heim also portrays them as not really Christian, by virtue of the fact that they call for "an unequivocal denial of Christian uniqueness," thereby rejecting the idea that the Christian tradition has any "unique religious value."[123] This complaint is closely related to the idea of a neutral metatheory of religion. Any allegedly neutral metatheory adopted by a Christian theologian will be either implicitly Christian, which is Heim's critique of Knitter's attempt to employ "justice" as a neutral norm,[124] or else hostile to Christian faith, as is Hick's metatheology. In the latter case, employing it normatively will lead to emptying Christian faith of its substance.

In Hick's case, the metatheory in question is the hypothesis that the various ideas of ultimate reality—whether they be ideas of ultimate reality as personal or as impersonal—are all phenomenal appearances of "the Real," understood as a noumenal reality, in the Kantian sense, with this taken to mean that no categories applying to worldly beings can apply to it, even analogically. One implication of this metatheory, brought out by Hick himself, is that none of the substantive predicates that Christians apply to God—such as "being good," "being powerful," and "having knowledge"—can be thought to apply to the Real in itself.[125] The result is that, as Heim says, "Any language within a religious tradition which

---

122. Cobb, "Toward a Christocentric Catholic Theology," 79.

123. Heim, *Salvations*, 2.

124. Ibid., 91–98, 127. This is another point at which Heim notes that Cobb's position is the same as his own (76).

125. Hick, *An Interpretation of Religion*, 239.

intends to be about the Real in itself . . . can only be mythological"—with myths being true if, as Hick says, they "evoke in us attitudes and modes of behaviour which are appropriate to our situation *vis-à-vis* the Real."[126] Although Hick means to validate the cognitive content of religion, the cognitive content of the theistic religions that is validated is identical, Heim points out, with the cognitive content of the nontheistic religions. Accordingly, although Hick says that religions evoke dispositions "appropriate to the Real," this phrase, Heim rightly says, "tells us literally nothing," because we are said to have no idea what the Real is like.[127] This position supports Hick's view that nothing about the salvific process as understood in Christianity (or any other tradition) has any essential importance, nothing beyond the abstract description of the move from self-centeredness to Reality-centeredness. In the name of this metatheory of religion, Heim complains,

> Hick is willing to limit sharply the extent of the truth value he could otherwise grant to particular traditions. For instance, since he is committed to the conclusion that the religions are all talking about "the Real" and about the same identical ultimate human destiny, he is committed to the assumption that everything the faith traditions say or do which points to another conclusion is fundamentally mistaken.[128]

Hick's use of his metatheory leads to the denial, Heim adds, that the Christian (or any other) tradition has unique religious value:

> It seems to be a paradoxical axiom in [Hick's] hypothesis that anything about which it is possible to differ religiously cannot be *religiously* significant to the extent of leading toward a different religious fulfillment than others. By means of your religious tradition you achieve religious fulfillment. But absolutely nothing which is distinctive in your tradition, in the life of faith that you lead, can be integral to that fulfillment itself.[129]

Seeing a similar denial of Christian uniqueness in Smith, with his reduction of Christian faith to a disposition or attitude that is identical with the "faith" of all religious people, and in Knitter, who wrote the preface to *The Myth of Christian Uniqueness*,[130] Heim concludes that a position that would "include grounds for crediting as valid and appropriate the various traditions' testimony regarding their own uniqueness" would require going "beyond the existing pluralistic theories."[131]

---

126. Ibid., 351; Heim, *Salvations*, 20.

127. Hick, *An Interpretation of Religion*, 353; Heim, *Salvations*, 21, 30.

128. Heim, *Salvations*, 34.

129. Ibid., 2, 26.

130. It would be a mistake, I believe, to put Knitter entirely in the same camp with Smith and Hick on this issue. Knitter's apparent denials of the uniqueness of Jesus and Christianity are correctly understood, I have suggested (see notes 60 and 65, above), as denials of their uniquely *supernatural* character. The problem with Knitter's position is not that he empties Christian faith of its distinctive content but that he, as Heim points out (see note 106, above), covertly uses the distinctively biblical concern with social-economic justice as the norm for authentic religion as such, thereby failing to acknowledge the uniqueness of either the biblical faiths or the other religious traditions.

131. Heim, *Salvations*, 125.

That conclusion follows, however, only because Heim has drawn his picture of pluralistic theories from identist pluralists alone. Heim's generalizations are again disproved by Cobb's differential pluralism. Cobb explicitly affirms that Christianity is unique in the sense that it "achieves something fundamentally different from other religions." "It is quite likely," he adds, "that the precise salvific experience brought about through faith in Jesus Christ occurs in no other way."[132] Similarly to Heim, who wants a position that will allow each tradition to affirm its own uniqueness, Cobb declares, in response to the question whether he is affirming Christian uniqueness: "Certainly and emphatically so! But I am affirming the uniqueness also of Confucianism, Buddhism, Hinduism, Islam, and Judaism. . . . Further, the uniqueness of each includes a unique superiority, namely, the ability to achieve what by its own historic norms is most important."[133]

That reference to each tradition's "own historic norms" might sound too relativistic for Heim, given his insistence that we cannot help but use our own norms to judge the beliefs and practices of other religions. Cobb, however, explicitly says that "[a]s a Christian I can, and do, evaluate other communities and traditions by [my] norm," meaning "what I would like everyone and every community to be about," namely, "[c]ontributing to the indivisible salvation of the whole world." This statement is not antithetical to Cobb's pluralism, however, because he recognizes the equal right of people in other traditions to evaluate Christianity by their own norms.[134]

We can see, therefore, that Heim's reasons for considering pluralistic Christian theology not really Christian do not apply to Cobb's position. This is not a judgment with which Heim would disagree. Heim, in fact, cites Cobb favorably for holding that, in Heim's words, "there is no reason for religious traditions not to bring convictions of uniqueness and the universal validity of their special beliefs into [interreligious] dialogue." What *is* at issue, as I indicated above, is whether Cobb should be considered a pluralist. Heim assumes not. On the page just cited, Heim contrasts Cobb's position with "contemporary pluralistic views." Heim elsewhere mentions Cobb as one of the theologians who contributed to a "collection of essays critical of pluralistic theology."[135] Heim's reference is to *Christian Uniqueness Reconsidered: The Myth of a Pluralistic Theology of Religions,* edited by Gavin D'Costa (which was written in opposition to *The Myth of Christian Uniqueness: Toward a Pluralistic Theology of Religions,* edited by Hick and Knitter).[136]

---

132. Cobb, *Transforming Christianity and the World,* 62, 86.
133. Ibid., 72; Heim, *Salvations,* 125.
134. Cobb, *Transforming Christianity and the World,* 182.
135. Heim, *Salvations,* 144, 88.
136. Heim is not the only one who, having accepted the equation of identist pluralism with pluralism as such, has trouble accepting Cobb as a pluralist. In his preface to *The Myth of Christian Uniqueness,* Knitter refers to Cobb as one of the *critics* of "the pluralist move" (viii). In the introduction to his collection of Cobb's essays, Knitter says that Cobb, while not being either an exclusivist or an inclusivist, also cannot be ranked with the pluralists (*Transforming Christianity and the World,* 3). Although Knitter there defines pluralism as the view that there are "many equally valid religions"

To sort out this issue, we need to look at Cobb's contribution to the D'Costa volume, which he titled "Beyond 'Pluralism.'"[137] The possibility that Cobb did not mean to be rejecting pluralism as such, but only a position that has misleadingly usurped the name, is suggested by the scare quotes around the word "pluralism."[138] That this is indeed the case is confirmed in the essay's first paragraph, in which Cobb says:

> How odd I find it to be writing for a collection of essays in criticism of theologies espousing religious pluralism! Yet I have agreed to do so because of the very narrow way—indeed an erroneous way, I think—in which *pluralism* has come to be defined. By *that* definition of pluralism, I am against pluralism. But I am against pluralism for the sake of a fuller and more genuine pluralism.[139]

In the following paragraph, Cobb explains that he had declined to write a paper for the conference on which *The Myth of Christian Uniqueness* was based, because he rejected "the consensus that conference was supposed to express and promote," which was that "the several major religions are, for practical purposes, equally valid ways of embodying what religion is all about. The uniqueness that is rejected is any claim that Christianity achieves something fundamentally different from other religions."[140] The crucial point for our purposes is that Cobb rejects the idea

---

(which Cobb does *not* deny), he later in the book makes clear that the claim of "the pluralists" that Cobb denies is the claim that "all religions have the *same* basic (or essential) task which each carries out with rough parity" (ibid., 61). Knitter sees that Cobb is "really accusing the pluralists of not being pluralistic enough." Knitter even speaks of "his [Cobb's] own more authentic pluralism," which says that "all of the religions have *different* tasks" (61). When he wrote the introduction to the volume, nevertheless, he said that Cobb could not be called a pluralist. Knitter, like Heim, evidently believes that one can be considered a pluralist only if one is not very pluralistic. The reactions of Knitter and Heim to Cobb, in any case, suggest that the attempt to break the equation of religious pluralism with the identist version of it will not be easy. The extent of the failure to recognize Cobb as a pluralist is illustrated by the fact that even Marjorie Suchocki, one of his former students, has characterized him as an inclusivist rather than a genuine pluralist—see note 94 of the following chapter.

137. Cobb, "Beyond 'Pluralism,'" originally in D'Costa, ed., *Christian Uniqueness Reconsidered* (1990); reprinted in Cobb, *Transforming Christianity and the World*, 61–75 (the latter pagination is followed).

138. It is perhaps significant that in the citation of Cobb's essay in the bibliography of Heim's book (*Salvations*, 231), the scare quotes are omitted, so that the title seems to indicate that Cobb wants to go beyond pluralism as such.

139. *Transforming Christianity and the World*, 62. As this statement shows, Cobb cannot be held responsible for the fact that some interpreters have taken his essay "Beyond 'Pluralism'" to mean that he rejects religious pluralism as such. But Cobb has not always been consistent on this point. For example, in "Being a Transformationist in a Pluralistic World," Cobb, having described the three usual options as exclusivism, inclusivism, and pluralism, proceeds to equate pluralism with an identist version of it (as seeing "the ends to which all the great traditions tend as identical" [749]). On this basis, he identifies himself with a fourth position, "transformationism." In the context of Cobb's other writings, we can see that he is here affirming a transformationist, in contrast with an identist, pluralism. Taken by itself, however, this essay would give the impression that Cobb rejected pluralism. But the widespread failure to regard Cobb as a pluralist does not seem to be significantly due to this essay, which I have not seen cited in this regard.

140. Cobb, *Transforming Christianity and the World*, 62.

that religion has a "normative essence"—an essence ("what religion is all about") that can be used *normatively* to evaluate the various religions—so that one could say, as Hick and Knitter wish to say, that all the religions have "rough parity" in the sense that "they all accomplish the same goal equally well."[141]

Cobb's criticism, based on his conviction that different religions have different goals, which he calls "radical pluralism," is the same as Heim's criticism of Hick's belief that, because "one identical salvific process is taking place in them all," we can comparatively evaluate the religions by asking "how well is each doing at what all are about." The only difference between Cobb and Heim here is that Cobb makes this criticism in the name of a "fuller and more genuine pluralism,"[142] whereas Heim, having accepted the definition of pluralism that Cobb regards as narrow and erroneous, makes this criticism in the name of a *rejection* of pluralism. The fact that Heim has accepted this definition, however, leads to several problems.

Resulting Problems in Heim's Position

One problem resulting from Heim's acceptance of the term "pluralism" for a position he rejects is that although he, like Cobb, wants a more truly pluralistic position, he must come up with some other term for it. He chooses the term "inclusivism." But this is confusing. Inclusivism as usually understood, as Heim knows, is a *soteriological* doctrine affirming a twofold inclusiveness of Christianity. It asserts that Christianity is the only religion in full possession of saving truth, so that whatever religious truths are found in other religions are already included in Christianity. And it asserts that although all salvation comes through Jesus Christ, people in other religions can be included in this salvation.[143] Heim rejects inclusivism in this classical sense, arguing instead that other religions provide alternative fulfillments, different "salvations," involving different religious truths. Heim calls this position "pluralistic inclusivism," suggesting that it simply involves moving "a step beyond" classical inclusivism.[144]

---

141. Ibid., 64–66. There are also passages in which Cobb rejects not only this notion of a *normative* essence of religion but even the idea that there is anything that all religions have in common so that we can give a definition of religion (62–63, 78, 131). This denial seems extreme, unnecessary, and unsupported. I have, for example, offered a formal account of the nature of religion that, as far as I can see, could not be used normatively in the way Cobb (rightly) opposes (*Reenchantment without Supernaturalism*, 10–14, 249–55).

142. Heim, *Salvations*, 26; Cobb, *Transforming Christianity and the World*, 72. In another statement showing that he rejects not pluralism as such but only the hitherto dominant versions of it, Cobb says: "As a Christian theologian I commend all efforts to break Christianity out of its parochial limits and especially out of its implicitly or explicitly negative relationship to the other great ways of humankind. But I am troubled by the dominant proposals for carrying out this task. . . . Hence I am calling for a different approach" (90).

143. Heim, *Salvations*, 131, 159, 224. In Alan Race's words, although Christian inclusivism recognizes the spiritual power in other religions, "it rejects them as not being sufficient for salvation apart from Christ, for Christ alone is saviour" (*Christians and Religious Pluralism*, 38). Given the fact that Race is widely acknowledged as the creator of the inclusivist-exclusivist-pluralist typology, it would be confusing to begin using any of these terms in a way that differs from his usage.

144. Heim, *Salvations*, 152.

In Heim's usage, however, "inclusivism" no longer has a soteriological meaning. The soteriological dimension of Heim's position—the fact that salvation (of
one type or another) can be realized by members of various religious traditions—
is carried by the adjective "pluralistic." The term "inclusivism" has for Heim only
an *epistemic* meaning, referring to the aforementioned fact that we necessarily
regard the grounds of our own judgments as the best, which Heim takes to mean
that one inescapably believes that "one follows the most inclusive true religion."[145] Because this epistemic point and the point about a plurality of salvations are notions that his "pluralists" deny, Heim means his position to be an
advance—to a "post-pluralistic" position. However, given what the term "inclusivism" has usually been taken to mean, at least in contrast with exclusivism and
pluralism, Heim creates confusion by using it for a purely epistemic doctrine.[146]
And in light of the fact that inclusivism as usually understood rules out pluralism, the label "pluralistic inclusivism" is oxymoronic.[147] But, because Heim had
accepted the equation of "pluralism" with a theological position that he found
untenable, he needed *some* other term, and "inclusivism" evidently seemed the
best candidate, given the fact that identist pluralists tend to deny that Christians
should use their own norms to evaluate other religious-ethical positions. Seeing
a reason for this choice of terms does not, however, remove the confusion.

A second problem is that Heim's characterization of theological pluralism simply does not apply to most of the theologians who call themselves pluralists
and/or would normally be considered pluralists. Besides Cobb, there are many
such theologians that Heim himself recognizes as pluralists. For example, on a
page in which he is justifying his selection of Hick, Smith, and Knitter to represent pluralism, Heim includes a footnote in which he explains that he did not
include Raimundo Panikkar, even though Panikkar's work is sufficiently broad
and extensive, because "he literally breaks the mold which pluralistic theology
has set for itself."[148] One problem here is Heim's reifying language, as if "pluralistic theology" were itself a thing, even an agent, that could set a mold for itself.
Would it not be more accurate to say that certain *theologians* have articulated a
type of pluralism that they hoped would become the mold for pluralistic theology, and that Heim (among others) has accepted this mold?

145. Ibid., 138, 222, 227.
146. Ibid., 26. This shift of meaning is evident in Heim's initial definition of Christian inclusivism as the doctrine "that salvation is available through other traditions because the God most deci-
sively acting and most fully revealed in Christ is also redemptively available within or through those
traditions" (4). Although this definition does refer to salvation, it does not assert, as Christian inclusivism has standardly been understood to assert, that everyone's salvation is dependent upon God's
saving act in Jesus Christ. The focus is, instead, on the epistemic point that Christians believe that
everyone's salvation is dependent upon the activity of the God *most fully known* in the Christian tradition, a point that Heim makes repeatedly (29–30, 102, 118, 225).
147. That said, and given the use of "inclusivism" to make a purely epistemic point, the label is
at least more appropriate for Heim's position than it is for that of Schubert Ogden, who had earlier
suggested it as a possible label for his own position (*Is There Only One?* x). Ogden's position, as I will
suggest in chapter 2, is better called "semipluralistic."
148. Heim, *Salvations*, 14n.

The more important problem, however, is that Heim has admitted that there is at least one *bona fide* pluralist who does not fit his characterization. Moreover, Heim also mentions Aloysius Pieris and Stanley Samartha as theologians who, along with Panikkar, are "on somewhat different wave-lengths than my three primary subjects, despite their own willingness to be identified in some way as 'pluralists.'" Heim also mentions still more pluralists—David Krieger, Marjorie Suchocki, Grace Jantzen, and George Bosworth Burch—to whom his characterization would not apply. One could, furthermore, come up with a list of many other pluralistic theologians who would not fit the mold. Contained in such a list would be theologians from previous generations, including Ernst Troeltsch, whom Heim himself called the "Protestant pioneer in the field of religious pluralism."[149]

These problems in Heim's position—that his characterization of theological pluralism leads him to regard Cobb as not a pluralist; that it does not fit all or even most other theological pluralists; that it leads him to the paradoxical position of rejecting pluralism while offering "a more pluralistic hypothesis"; and that it leads him to resort to a confusing label for his own position—suggest the need for something that Heim does not provide: a characterization of generic religious pluralism—of what religious pluralism in the most general sense is—on the basis of which different species of religious pluralism can then be identified. That is, of course, what I provided in the previous sections.

CONCLUSION

In a defense of his pluralistic hypothesis, which is intended to explain the fact that religious experience results in conflicting truth claims, John Hick says that "critics who don't like it should occupy themselves in trying to produce a better one."[150] He is absolutely right. There is little point in continuing to churn out criticisms of Hick's version of pluralism. Although some of this criticism has been repeated here as a basis for pointing out the need for a more adequate hypothesis, the main target of this critique has not been Hick's version of pluralism, or even identist pluralism more generally, but the widespread tendency to equate pluralism as such with this version of it. This point having been made, the task now is to make available a better hypothesis.

At the same time, it is important to emphasize that the cultural move from absolutism to pluralism is the most important issue. Ernst Troeltsch, John Hick, Wilfred Cantwell Smith, Paul Knitter, and the others who have pioneered and popularized this move in the Christian West are to be commended and honored for their service. The question of the adequacy of their particular ways of developing a pluralistic position is a secondary matter, criticisms of which do not

149. Ibid., 8, 173.
150. Hick, *A Christian Theology of Religions*, 50.

detract from the importance of their achievement in calling attention to the need to make the pluralistic turn.

Nevertheless, this issue of adequacy *is* important, especially since now the charge of inadequacy of the hitherto dominant formulations is being used as a basis to call the pluralistic turn as such into question. One of the purposes of the present book is to show how Whitehead's philosophy provides a basis for pluralistic Christian theology that is not subject to the criticisms that have been rightly directed at religious pluralism understood in terms of its identist form—that it is not really pluralistic or at best only superficially so, that it is based on a false claim to neutral universality, that it leads to a debilitating relativism, and that it is not really Christian.[151] In the following chapter, I show how John Cobb has employed Whitehead's philosophy to provide such a position.

---

151. A finally convincing answer to this last issue would, of course, involve showing that a theology can be adequate to Christian faith without presupposing supernatural intervention. The importance of this challenge can be illustrated with reference to a comment by Hick that the "present divide between fundamentalist/evangelical and liberal Christianity" could lead to a complete split, so that there would be "visibly two Christianities" (*A Christian Theology of Religions*, 133). Hick rightly says that "this would be a highly regrettable development" (134). I would add, however, that if liberal Christianity were by and large to accept Hick's version of religious pluralism, the likelihood of such a split would be greatly increased. In any case, the task of responding to this challenge is a huge one that is far beyond the scope of the present volume.

Chapter 2

John Cobb's Whiteheadian Complementary Pluralism

David Ray Griffin

If the task before us is to make available an alternative to the identist form of religious pluralism that is free from its inherent problems, the first part of this task is simply to draw attention to the fact that such an alternative is, to a significant extent, already available, primarily thanks to John Cobb, who over the past three decades has been developing a Whiteheadian Christian version of pluralist theology.[1]

The alternative to identist pluralism, I suggested in the previous chapter, can be called "deep" or "differential" pluralism. But just as there is more than one type of identist pluralism, there can also be more than one type of deep or differential pluralism. One type, which says that different religions emphasize the different salvific implications of different aspects or dimensions of the total truth, sees a central task of theological dialogue to be the discovery of how these various doctrines are complementary rather than contradictory. Complementary pluralism can in turn be rooted in various perspectives, one of which is Whitehead's philosophy.[2] And there can, in turn, be more than one version of Whiteheadian

1. See note 89 of the previous chapter.
2. The idea that different religions can be understood as emphasizing complementary truths and values, based on insights into different dimensions or aspects of reality, has been suggested by some

39

complementary pluralism.[3] I explicate it here primarily in terms of the version that has thus far been most fully developed, that of John Cobb. Although Cobb's version of pluralistic Christian theology was referred to frequently in the introductory essay, those references were primarily aimed at showing that Cobb's position provided an alternative to the kind of pluralism criticized by Heim and his sources. Here Cobb's position is laid out more systematically and in terms of its rootage in Whitehead's philosophy.

In the first section, I discuss the relation between science and theology, suggesting that the Whiteheadian attempt to see them as providing complementary truths leads to naturalistic theism. The second section brings out the connection between naturalistic theism and the distinction between God and creativity, which provides the basis for Cobb's view of theistic and nontheistic religions as complementary. The third section discusses Cobb's complementary pluralistic hypothesis. The fourth section brings out the distinctiveness of Cobb's position by contrasting his position with that of Schubert Ogden. The final section points out how Cobb's view of complementarity is fundamental for his articulation of pluralism without relativism.

1. SCIENCE, THEOLOGY, AND NATURALISTIC THEISM

In a section of *Religion in the Making* headed "The Three Traditions," Whitehead begins by speaking of two of them, Buddhism and Christianity. Having earlier described them—in terms of the combination of "clarity of ideas, generality of thought, moral respectability, survival power, and width of extension over the world"—as "the two Catholic religions of civilization,"[4] he has also described them both as in decay, as having "lost their ancient hold upon the world" (RM 44). Whitehead now suggests that this decay "is partly due to the fact that each religion has unduly sheltered itself from the other. . . . Instead of looking to each other for deeper meanings, they have remained self-satisfied and unfertilized" (RM 146). Whitehead, who published this statement in 1926, would surely be

---

previous writers. For example, E. L. Allen, in *Christianity among the Religions* (1960), suggested that the various religions may be asking different questions (135). In a book cited favorably by Heim (*Salvations*, 130), George Bosworth Burch suggests that there are, in the words of the title, *Alternative Goals in Religion* (1972). (It is perhaps noteworthy, incidentally, that Burch had attended lectures by Whitehead in 1926–27, his notes for which have been published in *Process Studies* 4/3.) The idea that the various religions present complementary truths has also been suggested by William Ernest Hocking in *Living Religions and a World Faith* (1940) and *The Coming World Civilization* (1956), Paul Tillich in *Christianity and the Encounter of the World Religions* (1963), and Robley Edward Whitson in *The Coming Convergence of the World Religions* (1971). But Hocking, Tillich, and Whitson all had conceptions of ultimate reality that prevented any real complementarity to be conceived (as I pointed out in "Can Christians Learn from Other Religions?" [1976]).

3. There might also be forms of Whitehead-based pluralism that would not be versions of complementary pluralism.

4. Their chief challenger, Whitehead added, has been Islam.

pleased to see, three-quarters of a century later, not only that Buddhist-Christian dialogue is a going enterprise, but also that Whitehead-inspired thinkers have been playing a major role in it.

This dialogue by itself would not suffice to arrest the decay of Buddhism and Christianity, Whitehead notes, because that decay has been due in part to "the rise of the third tradition, which is science" (RM 146). Whitehead can put science in the same category as Buddhism and Christianity because, he says, it

> appeared as a third organized system of thought which in many respects played the part of a theology, by reason of the answers which it gave to current theological questions. Science suggested a cosmology; and whatever suggests a cosmology, suggests a religion. (RM 141)

The reason why the first two universal traditions lost their hold on the world, partly because of this third one with its new cosmology, was that "neither of them had retained the requisite flexibility of adaptation" (RM 146). Theology and science, Whitehead insists, cannot be sheltered from each other. Each must allow its doctrines to be modified in the light of the truths discovered by the other (RM 79–80). The key to this mutual modification is the recognition that thinkers tend to formulate the truths they have seen in an "over-assertive" way that implies "an exclusion of complementary truths" (RM 145, 149). A clash between the doctrines of science and religion, Whitehead says elsewhere (SMW 185), provides the opportunity for a reconciliation resulting in "a deeper religion and a more subtle science." The reconciliation will involve a modification of either the scientific doctrine, or the religious one, or (often) both, so that neither excludes the truth expressed in the other.[5]

Whitehead meant his own philosophy to provide a basis for such a reconciliation, and Whitehead-inspired thinkers have continued this effort. Such a reconciliation would involve, as Whitehead indicates, mutual modifications, with received ideas from the scientific tradition as well as received ideas from the religious tradition being modified, so that neither will exclude complementary truths from the other. Our concern here, however, is with what the Christian tradition needs to incorporate from modern science. This concern is expressed in Cobb's statement, cited in the previous chapter, about the church's need to appropriate "the universal truth offered by modern science."[6] The liberal tradition in theology has, of course, been modifying itself in the light of the presumed truths of science for a long time, and much of this self-modification has been ill-advised, as liberal theologians have all too often evacuated theology of its traditional substance on

5. Cobb, having described his goal of modifying contradictory statements from diverse religious traditions so as "to render them non-contradictory—and, ideally, coherent," points out that he holds "the same hope for the relation of religious and scientific statements." When contradictions appear, he sees this "as an occasion to re-examine statements made on both sides with the goal of avoiding contradiction and even attaining coherence" (Cobb in Swidler et al., *Death or Dialogue?* 121).

6. Cobb, *Beyond Dialogue*, x.

the basis of doctrines that, while claiming science's imprimatur, did not deserve it. Theologians need to ask, more critically than have many in the past, exactly which part of the so-called scientific worldview now reigning really deserves to be considered "the universal truth offered by modern science."

Whitehead believed that many of the ideas now associated with science are not true. One of these is the mechanistic theory of matter, according to which the ultimate units of nature are devoid of experience and spontaneity—an idea that, besides making the mind-body problem insoluble, has made the idea of divine influence in the world seem impossible. Another of these ideas is the notion that all perception is through our sensory organs—a notion that rules out not only the extrasensory perception documented by parapsychology but also the possibility of genuine moral and religious experience. Still another widely held idea that Whitehead rejected is the Darwinian doctrine of evolution, according to which evolutionary developments have occurred without any divine influence in the process. I have argued elsewhere that the empirical facts support White-head's rejection of these ideas.[7]

Whereas, I hold with Whitehead, these and many other ideas thought to be scientifically established are at best half-truths, there are many other ideas produced by modern science that really are true. Many of these true ideas are of a purely factual nature, such as the idea that our universe is billions of years old and that the present state of the universe came about through a long evolutionary process. But at least one of these true ideas is of a philosophical nature, being the doctrine that I have called naturalism$_{ns}$, according to which there are never any supernatural interruptions of the world's normal cause-effect principles.[8] I have argued that, although Whitehead does not explicitly say so, part of his own attempt to reconcile science and religion, by producing a worldview that is adequate for both, is his naturalistic theism.[9] Although Whitehead affirms divine influence in the world, even *variable* divine influence,[10] this influence is always a dimension of, never an interruption of, the normal causal processes. This denial of divine interruptions of the causal principles exemplified in other actualities is implicit in Whitehead's dictum that "God is not to be

---

7. On the mechanistic view of the ultimate units of nature, see my *Unsnarling the World-Knot* (1998); on the sensationist view of perception in relation to paranormal and religious experience, respectively, see chap. 2 of my *Parapsychology, Philosophy, and Spirituality* and chap. 2 of *Reenchantment without Supernaturalism*; on the (neo)Darwinian view of evolution, see chap. 9 of my *Religion and Scientific Naturalism*.

8. As stated in the previous chapter, my preferred definition of naturalism$_{ns}$ is that there (ontologically) *cannot* be any such violations. For the purposes of this volume, however, I am allowing the weaker definition, according to which there (factually) *are* no such violations, in order to be inclusive of thinkers such as the early John Hick, whose religious pluralism is based on this less ontological rejection of supernatural interventionism.

9. See my *Religion and Scientific Naturalism*, esp. chaps. 1 and 4, or my *Reenchantment without Supernaturalism*, esp. chaps. 1 and 4. One thing I show in chap. 4 of the former book is that although Whitehead did not himself thematize the notion of "naturalism," his worldview is presented as a (theistic) form of naturalism in James Bissett Pratt's *Naturalism* (1939).

10. See my *Religion and Scientific Naturalism*, 39–40, 80, 94–95.

treated as an exception to all metaphysical principles" but as "their chief exemplification" (PR 343).

Implicitly, therefore, Whitehead has accepted the naturalism of the modern scientific worldview as a "universal truth offered by modern science." He does *not*, however, simply accept what has passed, since the time of Darwin, for the "scientific worldview." He is mainly critical of this worldview, which, because of its sensationism, atheism, and materialism, I call naturalism$_{sam}$. He argues the need, for the sake of science as well as for the sake of religion, to replace naturalism$_{sam}$ with what I call naturalism$_{ppp}$, with the first "p" standing for Whitehead's *prehensive* doctrine of perception (according to which sensory perception is derivative from a more fundamental nonsensory prehension), the second "p" for *panentheism*, and the third for *panexperientialism*.[11] With regard to the issue of panentheism, Whitehead's view is that traditional theism rightly saw the need to posit a divine being, but exaggerated the truth it saw, whereas atheistic naturalism has rightly seen that there is no omnipotent being with the power completely to determine events in the world, but has exaggerated this truth by denying the reality of divine influence altogether. Whitehead's panentheism, which is his version of naturalistic theism, is his reconciliation of the truth in these two views.

This distinction between the two kinds of naturalism is relevant to the question, raised in chapter 1, of the extent to which religious pluralism is based on modern liberal ideas. Whereas some pluralists have said or at least implied that their position is based on some universal perspective, neutral with regard to all particular traditions, Tom Driver, in his contribution to *The Myth of Christian Uniqueness*, says, "It will be the better part of wisdom to acknowledge, even to stress, that the whole discussion about 'religious pluralism,' as it is represented in this book, belongs to Western liberal religious thought at the present time."[12] I agree. But I would also emphasize, at least with regard to "religious pluralism" more broadly construed, that it is not necessarily in agreement with much that is widely thought to be included in "Western liberal religious thought" (or "modernity," or "Enlightenment thinking"). Pluralism is connected by Heim, for example, with what Raimundo Panikkar calls the "modern Western myth."[13] But Whiteheadian pluralists certainly would not accept many of the beliefs said by

---

11. Having naturalism$_{ns}$ embodied in naturalism$_{ppp}$ rather than naturalism$_{sam}$ makes an enormous difference with regard to a vast range of issues. For example, Heim points to the way in which the Victorians' employment of a "naturalistic view of the universe" led them to construct a historical Gautama and a historical Jesus "purged of mythical elements." The naturalistic worldview in question involved naturalism$_{sam}$, which excludes any genuine religious experience as well as all events of the type traditionally classified as "miracles," including those involving life after bodily death. Although Whitehead's philosophy, being naturalistic, excludes a supernaturalistic *interpretation* of such events, it does allow for the *occurrence* of such events as perfectly natural, if extraordinary, happenings, as I have shown elsewhere (*Parapsychology, Philosophy, and Spirituality* and "Parapsychology and Philosophy").

12. Driver, "The Case for Pluralism," in *The Myth of Christian Uniqueness*, 206.

13. Heim, *Salvations*, 108; Panikkar, "The Ongoing Dialogue," xiii.

Panikkar to belong to this myth, such as individualism, social Darwinism, and the neutrality of technocracy.

The modern ideas that *do* belong to religious pluralism as such, I have suggested, are two: the acceptance of naturalism$_{ns}$ (ns = nonsupernaturalist) and (thereby) the rejection of the authoritarian method for determining truth, including religious truth.[14] In fact, combining Cobb's reference to "the universal truth offered by modern science" with Heim's (evidently ironic) reference to "the revelatory conditions of pluralism,"[15] I would argue that pluralism (in the generic sense) is based on a distinctively modern revelation of a universal truth, revealed primarily through modern science and reflection thereon—the truth of naturalism$_{ns}$ (which the divine spirit, as the spirit of truth, has led us to see).[16] It belongs to complementary pluralism to assume that every great tradition is based on some deep insight into, some revelation about—whichever language one prefers—the nature of things. It would be strange to assume, as some postmodern thinkers seem to, that "modernity," or "the Enlightenment tradition," is the one tradition that is an exception. Generic religious pluralism, in any case, is based, at least implicitly, on the belief that the universal truth offered by modernity, especially as represented by modern science, is the truth of ontological naturalism and thereby the appropriateness of epistemic naturalism. The Whiteheadian version of pluralism embeds this naturalism$_{ns}$ in a naturalistic theism.

2. THE DISTINCTION BETWEEN GOD AND CREATIVITY

Part and parcel of this naturalistic theism is Whitehead's distinction between God and creativity. Creativity, which takes the place of Aristotle's prime matter and of the "being" or "being itself" of other philosophers, is, to use Paul Tillich's synonym, the "power of being." It is, more precisely, the twofold power to exert efficient and final (or self-) causation. This twofold power is necessarily embodied in both God and a world of finite actualities. Traditional theism, of course, also said that power is embodied both in God and in finite beings, but it said that all power *essentially* belongs to God alone, so that any power embodied in finite beings is there only contingently, due to a voluntary divine grant. This contin-

---

14. Franklin Gamwell argues that at the heart of modernity is the commitment to defend all claims in terms of experience and reason, rather than in terms of an appeal to authority (*The Divine Good*, 4).

15. Heim, *Salvations*, 104.

16. I would argue, further, that this negative truth, which is not unique to modernity—it has been held, for example, by atheists of all times—is only the first half of a fuller truth that is gradually being revealed, the truth of naturalistic theism, which *is* a distinctively modern, or postmodern, truth (see my "Panentheism: A Postmodern Revelation")—although Whitehead suggests, in effect, that theists could have learned this lesson long before the rise of modernity. I refer here to his statement that Plato's final conviction, "that the divine element in the world is to be conceived as a persuasive agency and not as a coercive agency," is "one of the greatest intellectual discoveries in the history of religion" (AI 166).

gency of the world's power, even its existence, was expressed in the doctrine of *creatio ex nihilo*, with the "nothing" meaning *absolutely* nothing. Whitehead denies this doctrine, holding instead that the creation of our particular universe (our "cosmic epoch") was "not the beginning of [finite] matter of fact, but the incoming of a certain type of order" (PR 96).[17]

Because creativity is embodied in the world as naturally and necessarily as it is embodied in God, there can be no divine interruptions of the principles normally involved in the causal processes between finite beings. Those causal principles, being simply the principles inherent in creativity as such, are metaphysical principles, inherent in the very nature of things, including the nature of God. Supernaturalistic theism's doctrine of *creatio ex nihilo* implied that God *could* suspend the causal principles of our world now and then, because what has been freely created can be freely interrupted. Whitehead's naturalistic theism exists, therefore, in a relation of mutual implication with his distinction between God and creativity. This distinction between God and creativity is at the heart of Cobb's version of complementary pluralism, to which I now turn.

3. COBB'S COMPLEMENTARY PLURALISTIC HYPOTHESIS

John Hick's particular pluralistic hypothesis arises out of a combination of three factors: (1) his recognition that religious experience gives rise to two fundamentally different conceptions of ultimate reality—as personal and as nonpersonal; (2) his belief that there is only one ultimate reality, which leads him to say that "when the different traditions speak of the God of Abraham, Isaac and Jacob, or of . . . Brahman, or the Dharmakaya/Nirvana/Sunyata," they are affirming the same "putative transcendent reality";[18] and (3) his desire to take religious experience as cognitive without showing favoritism to one kind of religious experience over another. Hick's way of reconciling these three factors is to hold that ultimate reality as it is in itself is neither personal nor impersonal, so that neither type of religious experience is more correct than the other. What this amounts to, however, is saying not that each type of religion is correct, but that each is equally mistaken. This drastic conclusion follows from Hick's apparently unshakable commitment to the idea that there is only one ultimate reality.[19] As Heim points out, "were Hick

---

17. Recent scholarship, which I have summarized elsewhere ("Creation out of Nothing, Creation out of Chaos, and the Problem of Evil"), shows that, unbeknownst to Whitehead himself, it is his view that is in harmony with the Bible and even with the early Christian tradition up to the end of the second century—as well as with the cosmogonies of most other religious traditions.

18. Hick, *An Interpretation of Religion*, 10.

19. Given the importance of this belief in determining Hick's whole hypothesis, his arguments for it in *The Interpretation of Religion* (248), I have pointed out elsewhere (*Reenchantment without Supernaturalism*, 277), are remarkably weak. (He has two arguments. His first one—that since the ultimates of the various traditions are different, they "cannot all be truly ultimate"—simply begs the question. Hick's second argument—that the idea that there is only one ultimate is "the simplest hypothesis"—assumes, wrongly, that simplicity is more important than adequacy.) There is no advance in his

not so intent that the traditions should express the same truth, they would have more room to be simultaneously accurate. . . . If God and the Dharma are each real, for instance, then the Muslim and Buddhist traditions are both much more concretely correct than Hick would allow."[20] The alternative hypothesis to which Heim points is the one that Cobb has long been developing.[21]

Hick presents his view as the best hypothesis to take account of the fact of different experienced-based concepts of ultimate reality in a way that validates theistic and nontheistic religious experiences as equally valid. But Cobb finds it unilluminating to say that God, who is *worshipped*, and Emptiness, which is *realized*, are "two names for the same noumenal reality."[22] Cobb's opinion that this hypothesis is not illuminating is supported, if unintentionally, by Caroline Franks Davis's discussion of religious experience. Reflecting on the fact that both kinds of religious experience are reported to be experiences of *ultimate* reality, Davis asks: "How can 'ultimate reality' be both a personal being and an impersonal principle, identical to our inmost self and forever 'other,' loving and utterly indifferent, good and amoral, knowable and unknowable, a plenitude and 'emptiness'?"[23] Although seemingly contradictory reports of some types can be reconciled by distinguishing between the experience and its interpretation, she points out, this type of solution would not seem possible in this case. In support, she quotes Stephen Katz, who says: "There is no intelligible way that anyone can legitimately argue that a 'no-self' experience of 'empty' calm is the same experience as the experience of intense, loving, intimate relationship between two substantial selves."[24] Although Hick does not claim that the experiences as such are

---

discussion in *A Christian Theology of Religions*, in which he insists that there is only one ultimate or Real, even while holding—because the Real is beyond all substantive predicates, including numbers—that it is impossible "to say that the Real is one in distinction from two or three" (71).

20. Heim, *Salvations*, 34. Cobb makes a similar point in saying that Hick has shown more willingness to revise theology than to revise his metaphysics (*Transforming Christianity and the World*, 88–89).

21. Given the tendency to consider Hick the paradigmatic pluralist, part of the reason for the failure to recognize Cobb as presenting an alternative version of pluralism may be Hick's refusal to respond in his books to Cobb's version (in spite of the fact that Hick and Cobb were colleagues in Claremont for many years). In Hick's *Interpretation of Religion* (1989), for example, there is no reference to Cobb's *Beyond Dialogue* (1982) or to any of his essays on the subject of religious pluralism and Christian-Buddhist dialogue. In *A Christian Theology of Religions* (1995), Hick, in response to the question of whether there may be a plurality of ultimates, says that "[s]ome have suggested a single finite generic God together with just one of the nonpersonal absolutes," for which he has a footnote saying, "This seems to be the position of John Cobb" (after which he mentions *Beyond Dialogue* and a few of Cobb's essays). Leaving aside the accuracy of Hick's characterization of Cobb's God as "finite," it is noteworthy that he dismisses this alternative suggestion in a single sentence, saying that it "would be a selective, and indeed arbitrarily selective, theory which it would be very hard to justify" (70). It is interesting, incidentally, to compare Hick's treatment of Cobb's position here with his excellent suggestions, in the introduction to the book (4–6), about how to improve the quality of criticism in the academy.

22. Cobb, *Beyond Dialogue*, 43.

23. Davis, *The Evidential Force of Religious Experience*, 172–73.

24. Katz, "Language, Epistemology, and Mysticism," 39–40.

identical, Cobb also finds it unilluminating to claim even that two such radically different kinds of experience are experiences of the same ultimate reality.

"[T]he evidence," suggests Cobb, "counts in favor of a different hypothesis."[25] One element of this hypothesis is that "the totality of what is, is very complex, far exceeding all that we can ever hope to know or think." A second element is that "in different parts of the world at different times, remarkable individuals have penetrated into this reality and discovered features of it that are really there to be found," so that "alongside all the errors and distortions that can be found in all our traditions there are insights arising from profound thought and experience that are diverse modes of apprehending diverse aspects of the totality of reality." A third element in this hypothesis is that "in the full complexity of reality . . . , 'Emptying' identifies one truly important aspect, and 'God' another."[26]

The connection with Whitehead's distinction between God and creativity is the idea that the term "creativity" points to the same reality to which some Buddhists point with the term "emptying" or "emptiness." More generally, Cobb's hypothesis, which involves "a pluralistic metaphysics,"[27] is that there are at least two ultimates. One of these, corresponding with what Whitehead calls "creativity," has been called "Emptiness" ("*Sunyata*") or "Dharmakaya" by Buddhists, "Nirguna Brahman" by Advaita Vedantists, "the Godhead" by Meister Eckhart, and "Being Itself" by Heidegger and Tillich (among others). It is the *formless* ultimate reality. The other ultimate, corresponding with what Whitehead calls "God," is not Being Itself but the *Supreme* Being. It is in-formed and the source of forms (such as truth, beauty, and justice). It has been called "Amida Buddha," "Sambhogakaya," "Saguna Brahman," "Ishvara," "Yahweh," "Christ," and "Allah."[28]

This recognition of two ultimates leads to a simple solution to the problem of the two kinds of religious experience discussed by Davis and Katz. That is, the two types of experience can be taken to be equally veridical if we think of them as experiences of different ultimates.[29]

This recognition of two ultimates also leads to two kinds of interreligious dialogue for the sake of discovering truth. Dialogue with those from other traditions that are attending to the same ultimate, as when Christians talk with Jews, Muslims, and theistic Hindus, can be a dialogue of *purification*. Dialogue with those who focus on the other ultimate can be a dialogue of *enrichment*, in which one's comprehensive vision is enlarged.[30] In this latter type of dialogue the notion of complementarity plays an especially central role. Against those who "insist on a

---

25. Cobb in Swidler et al., *Death or Dialogue?* 43.

26. Cobb, *Transforming Christianity and the World*, 135, 74; Swidler et al., *Death or Dialogue?* 6. On Cobb's use of "aspect," see note 113 of chap. 1, above.

27. Cobb, *Transforming Christianity and the World*, 88.

28. Ibid., 184–85; *Beyond Dialogue*, 124–28; Swidler et al., *Death or Dialogue?* 116.

29. I have discussed this issue in chap. 7 of *Reenchantment without Supernaturalism*.

30. Cobb in Swidler et al., *Death or Dialogue?* 5–7. Cobb's discussion does not, I should say, correlate these two terms, "purification" and "enrichment," as closely with the two kinds of dialogue as my discussion suggests. But I find this way of naming the distinction helpful.

pre-established common ground as a basis for dialogue," Cobb urges "complementarity as an alternative mode." On the assumption that both types of religion reflect genuine insights into the nature of things, the challenge of dialogue is "to transform contradictory statements into different but not contradictory ones," thereby moving "toward a more comprehensive vision in which the deepest insights of both sides are reconciled."[31]

One basis for such reconciliation is to recognize that claims that may at first glance seem contradictory are really answers to different questions. "[T]here is no contradiction in the claim of one that problem A is solved by X and the claim of the other that problem B is solved by Y. . . . The claims are complementary rather than contradictory."[32] On this basis, Cobb argues, the different religions can each be seen as proclaiming universally valid insights, which can be synthesized.

> Consider the Buddhist claim that Gautama is the Buddha. That is a very different statement from the assertion that God was incarnate in Jesus. The Buddha is the one who is enlightened. To be enlightened is to realize the fundamental nature of reality, its insubstantiality, its relativity, its emptiness. . . . That Jesus was the incarnation of God does not deny that Gautama was the Enlightened One. In that vast complexity that is all that is, it may well be that God works creatively in all things and that at the same time, in the Buddhist sense, all things are empty. . . . To affirm both that Jesus is the Christ and that Gautama is the Buddha is to move our understanding closer to the truth.[33]

Cobb suggests that this approach can reconcile the seeming contradiction between Christian theism and Buddhist atheism.

> When a Buddhist says that no God exists, the main point is that there is nothing in reality to which one should be attached. When a Christian says that God exists, the meaning may be that there is that in reality that is worthy of trust and worship. *If* those translations are correct . . . , then it is not impossible that both be correct. . . . [T]he Buddhist could in principle acknowledge the reality of something worthy of trust and worship without abandoning the central insight that attachment blocks the way to enlightenment. And the Christian could come to see that real trust is not attachment in the Buddhist sense.[34]

Although this notion of complementary truths plays its largest role in reconciling affirmations of theistic and nontheistic religions, it also can play a role in dialogue between religions of the same basic type, as Cobb illustrates with the tension between the Christian assertion "that Jesus is the Christ" and the Jewish insistence "that the Messiah has not come." Jews and Christians, he suggests,

---

31. Ibid., 80, 120; *Transforming Christianity and the World,* 74.
32. Cobb in Swidler et al., *Death or Dialogue?* 14.
33. Cobb, *Transforming Christianity and the World,* 140.
34. Ibid., 74.

should "work together repeatedly to clarify the difference between what Jews mean by 'Messiah' and what Christians legitimately mean by 'Christ.'" Having made this distinction, Cobb adds, Christians should then "join the Jews in their longing for the coming of the Messiah and the messianic age."[35]

Before concluding this section, I need to point out that Cobb's complementary pluralism has another dimension. The idea of God and creativity as two ultimates has played by far the central role, partly because of its helpfulness in understanding how theistic Christianity and nontheistic Buddhism could both be oriented toward something ultimate in the nature of things. However, as I hinted earlier in saying that Cobb's hypothesis is that there are "at least two ultimates," he affirms *three*, with the third being the cosmos, the universe, "the totality of [finite] things." Cobb relates these three ultimates to the three types of religion described by Jack Hutchison: theistic, acosmic, and cosmic.[36] The distinction between God and creativity helps us understand only the theistic and acosmic types of religion. But there is also a type of religion, illustrated by forms of Taoism and many primal religions, including Native American religions, that regards the cosmos as sacred. By recognizing the cosmos as a third ultimate, we are able to see that these cosmic religions are also oriented toward something truly ultimate in the nature of things.[37]

Although traditional Christian theology, with its doctrine of *creatio ex nihilo*, could not regard the cosmos as in any sense ultimate, Whitehead's philosophy does. Although our particular cosmos—our "cosmic epoch"—is contingent, being rooted in a divine volition, the fact that there is *a* world—some world or other consisting of a multiplicity of finite actual entities—is not contingent. What exists necessarily is not simply God, as in traditional Christian theism, and not simply the world understood as the totality of finite things, as in atheistic naturalism, but God-and-a-world, with both God and worldly actualities being embodiments of creativity. Although these three ultimates within the totality are distinct, they are, Cobb emphasizes, "not in fact separable from one another," adding: "I would propose that without a cosmic reality there can be no acosmic one, and that without God there can be neither. Similarly, without both the cosmic and acosmic features of reality there can be no God."[38]

Those who have been conditioned, especially through the doctrine of *creatio ex nihilo*, to believe that there can be only one ultimate tend to hear any talk of multiple ultimates as polytheism. But this characterization would not, Cobb points out, be appropriate for his Whiteheadian worldview, because the three ultimates do not exist on the same level. They differ as the one Supreme Being, the many finite beings,

---

35. Ibid., 86–87.
36. Ibid., 185 (see Hutchison, *Paths of Faith*).
37. Ibid., 120–23, 136–37, 140, 185.
38. Ibid., 121. Cobb is here reflecting the position of Whitehead himself, who said "there is no meaning to 'creativity' apart from its 'creatures,' and no meaning to 'God' apart from the 'creativity' and the 'temporal creatures,' and no meaning to the 'temporal creatures' apart from 'creativity' and 'God'" (PR 225).

and Being Itself, which is embodied by both God and finite beings. Creativity, as Being Itself, is in no way a second god alongside the Supreme Being, because it is not a being and has no reality apart from its embodiments in the divine and finite actualities. It makes no sense to say, as some have, that Whitehead's God is subordinate to creativity, because, as Cobb argues, "between reality as such and actual things there can be no ranking of superior and inferior. Such ranking makes sense only among actualities. Among actualities [God] is ultimate."[39] This statement also makes clear that Whitehead's position does not make the world of finite being equal with God. Although Tillich said that a Supreme Being would be merely "one being alongside other beings," this pejorative description would not fit the Whiteheadian idea of God. As the "worldsoul," understood as "a unity of experience that contains all the multiplicity of events," God is "the being that includes all beings."[40]

This pluralistic ontology allows us to understand the possibility that a wide variety of religious experiences could be authentic. Although these three ultimates are inseparable, individuals and religious traditions can concentrate on one or two features alone. Insofar as there is concentration solely on God, on the universe in distinction from God, or on creativity, there would be the pure case of theistic, cosmic, or acosmic religious experience.[41] However, Cobb adds, "much religious language blurs the distinctions and relates to more than one of the three ultimates." For example, the fact that "[t]he universe reverenced as ultimate is the embodiment of Being Itself or [nirguna] Brahman and is pervaded by God . . . is often attested unintentionally in the rhetoric of those who find meaning in appreciating their part in this whole." Likewise, "[l]anguage about God often draws on what is strictly true only of Being Itself."[42] This mixing occurs especially in Western theism, Cobb points out, because "it has incorporated acosmic elements from its Neo-Platonic sources" with the result that "the religious experience of Western mystics seems to be at once of theistic and acosmic reality—one might say that it is of the theistic as embodying the acosmic reality, or of the acosmic as qualified by the theistic reality." As a final example, the truth that "Being Itself does not exist at all except in God and the creatures" is reflected in a twofold fact. On the one hand, "Being Itself, being the being of all things, is also closely associated with the thought of the whole." On the other hand, "Very little is said of Being Itself or [nirguna] Brahman that does not hint at characteristics that actually belong to God."[43]

39. Cobb, "Being Itself and the Existence of God," 19.

40. Cobb, *Transforming Christianity and the World*, 122.

41. Ibid., 121. As Cobb mentions here, Aurobindo reports having had all three types of experience. Aurobindo's experiences and his attempt to understand them are discussed in a dissertation by Ernest Lee Simmons Jr., "Process Pluralism and Integral Nondualism: A Comparative Study of the Nature of the Divine in the Thought of Alfred North Whitehead and Sri Aurobindo Ghose" (1981), which was written under Cobb's guidance. See also Simmons's essay "Mystical Consciousness in a Process Perspective," in which some of the material from the dissertation is summarized.

42. Cobb, *Transforming Christianity and the World*, 186, 185.

43. Ibid., 124, 186. Cobb illustrates this latter point by the fact that although many Buddhists would say that Emptiness or *Dharmakaya* can be realized "as such apart from all forms," it is always expected that those who fully realize ultimate reality thus understood will be characterized by wisdom and compassion (*Beyond Dialogue*, 127).

Cobb's view that the totality of reality contains three ultimates, along with the recognition that a particular tradition could concentrate on one, two, or even all three of them, gives us a basis for understanding a wide variety of religious experiences as genuine responses to something that is really there to be experienced. "When we understand global religious experience and thought in this way," Cobb emphasizes, "it is easier to view the contributions of diverse traditions as complementary."[44]

Heim, who subtitled his book "Truth and Difference in Religion," says that the overarching task of a more adequate approach to religious diversity is "to find a fruitful way of combining recognition of truth or validity *and* difference across the religions." His twofold contrast is with (identist) pluralists, who "are committed to limiting their attribution of truth to what is convergent," and inclusivists, who "are almost equally inclined to stress the truth of what is similar . . . and to deny validity to what is different." What is needed, he says, is a perspective that "can recognize the effective truth of what is truly other."[45] Cobb, as we have seen, has been developing a version of pluralism that can do just that. The subtitle of Heim's book, in fact, could have been employed by Cobb. "I continue to push [my proposal] forward against great resistance," Cobb says, "because I believe it helps those who accept it to acknowledge the deep differences among religious traditions without denying that each has its truth."[46]

4. COBB'S PLURALISM CONTRASTED WITH OGDEN'S SEMIPLURALISM

The distinctiveness of Cobb's pluralism can be made clearer by contrasting it with the position of Schubert Ogden, who has also been heavily influenced by Whitehead, especially as mediated through the philosophy of Charles Hartshorne. Although Ogden has widely been considered a process theologian because of his employment of Hartshorne's doctrine of God and his metaphysical position more generally, equally formative for Ogden's position is a demythologized—which for

---

44. Cobb, *Transforming Christianity and the World*, 186. As I reported in a chapter titled "The Two Ultimates and the Religions" in *Reenchantment without Supernaturalism*, Gene Reeves has also suggested that one should say that worldly actual occasions constitute a third ultimate in Whitehead's philosophy. "As both a Unitarian Universalist and a Lotus Sutra Buddhist," I explained, "Reeves makes this point in support of the ultimate importance of the world, fearing that a religion oriented around only God and/or Creativity as such might encourage a religiosity in which this world is trivialized" (281n.). As this statement suggests, Reeves favors a religion in which all three ultimates are emphasized. Although for various reasons I there resisted Reeves's suggestion, I now wish that I had incorporated it. Marjorie Suchocki, I have belatedly realized, had made a similar suggestion. Whereas Whitehead had included three notions—"creativity," "many," "one"—within the Category of the Ultimate (PR 21), Suchocki suggested that we could think of these as "three different ultimates," each of which can be seen as the central focus of different religions (*God-Christ-Church*, 172). In making this suggestion, of course, she is thinking of "the one" as God.

45. Heim, *Salvations*, 124.

46. Cobb, *Transforming Christianity and the World*, 186.

Ogden means a *dehistoricized*—version of Rudolf Bultmann's kerygmatic theology.[47] Given the fact that Ogden's resulting position leads him to endorse the negative half of pluralism—the rejection of any a priori denial that there could be any other equally authentic religions—but not the positive half—the affirmation that there are in fact some such religions—Ogden can be called a semi-pluralist. Ogden affirms, in his language, "the possibility of pluralism" but not "the actuality of pluralism."[48] Although he holds that the "completely universal reality of God's love" is savingly "at work in all religions," which not only grounds the possibility of pluralism but also provides an a priori reason to expect it to be actual,[49] he has been unable to say that it *is* actual. The purpose of this section is to clarify why Cobb and Ogden differ on this issue.

Ultimate Reality

We can begin this comparison by looking at Ogden's notion that we have a "basic faith (or confidence) in the meaning of life," which is "the faith that there is . . . an authentic self-understanding—that the ultimate reality of one's own existence together with others in the whole is such that some way of understanding oneself is uniquely appropriate, or authorized."[50] Every human being in every historical tradition, Ogden argues, is confronted with the challenge to live in terms of this authentic self-understanding. Cobb has argued, by contrast, that the various axial religions promote various structures of existence, each one of which can be actualized in either authentic or inauthentic modes. Ogden could reply that, even granting that supposition, Cobb's acceptance of the realist view that "reality is as it is" means that he must accept Ogden's view that "ultimate reality in itself has one structure rather than another."[51] Cobb, accordingly, must agree that there is some way of being human that is more appropriate to the nature of reality than the rest. Although Cobb would in fact agree, he would add that he sees no reason to suppose that any of the modes of existence recommended by any of the world's religions or philosophies in their past or present forms coincides with this uniquely authorized mode of existence. Part of the reason for Cobb's view here is his pluralistic metaphysics, with its affirmation that reality is indefinitely complex, with part of this complexity being that there is more than one ultimate relevant to human existence. So, although "ultimate reality in itself" must indeed have "one structure rather than another," the full apprehension of this structure by human beings is still a work in progress, to which we can expect interreligious dialogue to contribute.

47. See especially Ogden, *Christ without Myth: A Study Based on the Theology of Rudolf Bultmann* (1961) and "Bultmann's Demythologizing and Hartshorne's Dipolar Theism."
48. Ogden, "Problems in the Case for a Pluralistic Theology of Religions," 505.
49. Ogden, *Is There Only One True Religion or Are There Many?* 103.
50. Ibid., 7.
51. Cobb in Swidler et al., *Death or Dialogue?* 120; Ogden, *Is There Only One?* 18.

By contrast, Ogden speaks—with Hartshorne—in terms of only one ultimate, which he identifies with God, as illustrated by his reference to "the strictly ultimate reality called 'God'" and his assertion that "the structure of [ultimate] reality in itself, in its strictly ultimate aspect, must be as individual as it is universal." Ogden sometimes refers to the ultimate reality as the *love of* God, as in his statement that the Christian witness is that the "love of God . . . is the strictly ultimate reality with which every human being has to do." He holds, accordingly, that "the kind of trust in God's love and loyalty to its cause that are Christian faith are, in fact, authorized by ultimate reality." At least partly because he affirms only one ultimate, Ogden's position is not merely that this mode of human existence is authorized by ultimate reality, but that *only* this mode is authorized. There is, in other words, only one salvation: "If persons are saved, it can only be because or insofar as they so entrust themselves to God's love as thereby to be freed to live in loyalty to it."[52] Given Ogden's view of ultimate reality and salvation, therefore, the only kind of pluralism he would be able to endorse would be an *identist* pluralism.[53]

True Religion

This point can be brought out more clearly by turning to the central concept in the title of Ogden's book, "true religion." It belongs to very nature of religion, Ogden says, to claim authority with regard to the understanding of human existence, so that "every religion at least implicitly claims to be the true religion."[54] This statement implies that a Christian by definition believes Christianity to be the true religion. How, then, can the question in the title of Ogden's book make sense? If Christianity is taken to be *the* true religion, how could there be any other true religions?

52. Ogden, *Is There Only One?* 47, 100, 47, 101. Although Heim agrees with Ogden on epistemic issues, especially his argument for (epistemic) "inclusivism," he disagrees, he says, with Ogden's "unitary notion of salvation" (*Salvations*, 225).

53. This fact is illustrated in Ogden's critique of Rosemary Radford Ruether's argument for pluralism. Her argument for the pluralistic conclusion that the various religions are equal in integrity and adequacy, Ogden points out, is based on the assumption of a truly universal Divine Being that, as she puts it, "generates, upholds, and renews the world" and is "the father and mother of all peoples without discrimination" ("Feminism and Jewish-Christian Dialogue: Particularism and Universalism in the Search for Religious Truth," 141–42). Given this "broadly theistic assumption," Ogden argues, "then, clearly, any religion or ideology that denied or failed to affirm theism in the same broad sense could not possibly be equal in integrity or adequacy with any religion or ideology that affirmed it" ("Problems in the Case," 501). Cobb, by contrast, can regard theistic and nontheistic religions as equally adequate in a cognitive sense insofar as they seem to be equally adequate to different truths. He would consider a religion cognitively even more adequate, of course, insofar as it involved a synthesis of these complementary truths.

54. Ogden, *Is There Only One?* 4, 12. The point about religion is based on Ogden's description of it as the *primary* form of culture in which the existential question of the meaning of ultimate reality for us is explicitly asked and answered (5–6), so that "a religion claims to be the authorized representation of the answer to this question" (11).

To understand Ogden's question, we need to see precisely what he means by "true religion." He understands this concept, he tells us, by analogy with the concept of a "true church" in classical Protestant ecclesiology.[55] According to that concept, a church is "substantially true provided that its doctrine and practice agree with those of the apostles, whose church alone may be said to be formally true." By analogy, Ogden says, a religion

> may be said to be *formally* true provided that its representation of the meaning of human existence is that with which all others must agree in order themselves to be true religions. On the other hand, it may be said to be *substantially* true provided that it exhibits just such agreement with whatever religion is correctly said to be the formally true religion.[56]

In claiming to be *the* true religion, then, any specific religion is claiming to be *formally* true, which leaves open the possibility that other religions may be, from its perspective, (merely) *substantially* true. "[I]t belongs to a religion to claim to be *the* true religion, and hence the formal norm by which all other true religion, if any, has to be determined."[57]

From the Christian's perspective, therefore, the question whether there is more than one true religion is the question whether there are any other religions that "give expression to substantially the same religious truth." This condition means, more precisely, that these other religions "must express substantially the same self-understanding, the same way of understanding ourselves in relation to others and the whole. And this means . . . that they must also have substantially the same necessary implications, both metaphysical and ethical." Ogden sees, however, that Christianity and Buddhism—at least the type of Buddhism with which he has been in dialogue—have radically different metaphysical and ethical implications.[58] Given this view of what it would take to affirm the actuality of religious pluralism, Cobb, who has emphasized the great differences in the religious worldviews and the "salvations" they produce, would find the affirmation at least as difficult as does Ogden.

One of the differences between the two theologians is that Cobb's understanding of the God-world relation provides no basis for him to accept Ogden's notion of "true religion." As Ogden points out, his idea that a religion can be "the formally true religion" is understood by analogy with the traditional Protestant concept of the apostolic church as the standard by which all other churches are to

---

55. Ibid., x.

56. Ibid., 12–13.

57. Ibid., 13. It is essential to Ogden's position—which he calls a fourth option beyond exclusivism, inclusivism, and pluralism—to endorse the possibility that adherents of another religion could just as validly consider *it* to be the formally true religion (100). From their perspective, Christianity, if it agreed with their religion's understanding of existence, would be considered substantially true. If this substantial agreement obtained between Christianity and some form of Buddhism, then the Christians would rightly consider the Buddhists "anonymous Christians," while the Buddhists would rightly consider the Christians "anonymous Buddhists" (101–2).

58. Ibid., 103, 60–66.

be measured. Cobb would emphasize, however, that this traditional concept pre-supposed traditional theism, according to which God could provide *complete* and *infallible* revelation recorded in *inerrant* scripture. Traditional Protestants could reasonably assume, accordingly, that the witness of the apostolic church contained not only truth but the *whole* truth and *nothing but* the truth. It was fully self-consistent, therefore, for them to take it as *the* norm for measuring the truth of all subsequent churches. However, given Cobb's Whiteheadian rejection of tradi-tional theism's doctrine of omnipotence, which entailed that God could unilater-ally determine human thought, speech, and writing, the necessary presupposition for the traditional idea of complete and infallible revelation is removed. This pre-suppositional change is, in fact, reflected in Ogden's own criteria for theology, according to which appeal to the apostolic witness can answer only the question whether a theology is Christian, not also, as it did for traditional theology, whether it is true; that question must now be settled in terms of common experience and reason.[59] Ogden's acceptance of a notion of true religion based on analogy with the traditional doctrine of the formally true church is rooted in the part of Ogden's theology that Cobb does not share. From Cobb's more strictly Whiteheadian the-ology, there is no basis for the assumption that Christianity's understanding of real-ity expresses the *whole* truth about the essential structure of reality.[60]

It is precisely this notion of true religion, furthermore, that separates Ogden's position so radically from Cobb's. Some of Ogden's formulations could, to be sure, be endorsed by Cobb. Ogden says, for example, that "it is the very nature of a religion to make or imply the claim to formal religious truth."[61] If this state-ment were taken to mean only that a religion claims to represent *a* universally valid truth and thereby to be *a* norm for measuring all other religions, Cobb would enthusiastically endorse it. This interpretation, besides avoiding rela-tivism, would allow for another religion to be seen as expressing a different but complementary universally valid truth, so that this religion would be normative with respect to that part of the full truth that *it* has seen. There would be two "true religions" that are *not* substantially the same.[62] Ogden, however, rules out this way of interpreting his statement. In saying that a religion makes "a claim to formal religious truth," he means that it claims "to be *the* true religion, and hence

---

59. Ibid., 36–37.
60. This same difference of perspective is reflected in Ogden's assumption, cited earlier, that the fact that God's love is savingly active in all human existence and therefore in all religions should lead us to expect pluralism, understood in an identist sense, to be true (ibid., 103; "Problems in the Case," 505). As I pointed out in the previous chapter, Marjorie Suchocki, working from a more Cobbian perspective, has argued in her *Divinity and Diversity* that a Whiteheadian understanding of God's mode of action would lead us *not* to expect diverse cultures to come up with identical understand-ings of ourselves and the universe.
61. Ogden, *Is There Only One?* 13.
62. This Cobbian view is in agreement with Heim's rejection of Ogden's "simple dichotomy of true and false religions" in favor of the view that "[r]eligions may be seen as both true and alter-native . . . , and thus two 'true' religions need not be assumed to represent the same thing" (*Salva-tions*, 225).

the formal norm by which *all* other true religion, if any, has to be determined."[63] He rules out, accordingly, the kind of complementarity that Cobb advocates. From Ogden's perspective, a Christian can consider other religions to be true only "insofar as they give expression to substantially the same religious truth."[64] It is mainly because of this difference that Cobb is a radical pluralist whereas Ogden, assuming that pluralism would have to be *identist* pluralism, is a semipluralist,[65] endorsing only the possibility that there could be other true religions.

Philosophy as a Norm

Ogden does add a qualification that could open the way to an acceptance of Cobb's position and thereby full-fledged pluralism. Although he often writes as if we must take our own *religion* as the norm for judging the truth-value of other religions, Ogden's position is really that we must have *some* norm, which might well be a philosophy. This allowance is reflected in his observation that we can make a reasoned judgment about the truth of the religions "only by employing, openly or tacitly, some one of them, or some philosophy, as the norm required to make

63. Ogden, *Is There Only One?* 13; latter two emphases added.
64. Ibid., 103.
65. The label "semipluralist" is mine. Ogden himself, after saying that he had not found an entirely satisfactory term for his "fourth option" (beyond exclusivism, inclusivism, and pluralism), suggests that "if we could agree to qualify what is here as well as elsewhere distinguished simply as 'inclusivism' by speaking instead of '*monistic* inclusivism,' we could appropriately speak of the fourth option as '*pluralistic* inclusivism'" (ibid., x). But this term is doubly problematic. On the one hand, the term "inclusivism" has traditionally had a primarily *soteriological* meaning, as illustrated by Ogden's own description of inclusivism as the doctrine that "the possibility of salvation uniquely constituted by the event of Jesus Christ is somehow made available to each and every human being" so that "salvation itself is thus universally possible, and in this sense is all-inclusive" (31). Ogden does, to be sure, also bring out the epistemic implication of (monistic) inclusivism, which is that "Christianity alone can be the formally true religion, since it alone is the religion established by God in the unique saving event of Jesus Christ" (31). Ogden's agreement with this epistemic dimension of inclusivism, properly modified, is reflected in his statement that "pluralists who want to avoid relativism cannot finally escape what they often seem to regard as a difficulty peculiar to inclusivism—the difficulty, namely, of taking some one specific religion to be formally true, and hence the norm for determining all other religious truth" (71). It is because Ogden accepts this alleged difficulty as a necessity that he calls his position a version of inclusivism. It is confusing, however, for Ogden to adopt this label by virtue of endorsing only this secondary feature of inclusivism in abstraction from its primary, soteriological meaning, which Ogden emphatically rejects (by endorsing a representational rather than a constitutive Christology). Equally misleading, on the other hand, is Ogden's use of the term "pluralistic" to signal his rejection of the monism of (traditional) inclusivism. The reason that Ogden can think of his position as in *any* sense pluralistic is evidently rooted in an ambiguity in his use of "monism." In his book's first instances of the term, it means that "there is only one true religion" (22; see also 23, 26). In the later instances, however, monism means that "there not only is but can be only one true religion" (32; see also 28, 54–55, 56, 80, 82). On the basis of this second meaning, Ogden says that "to make a clean break with Christian monism" one need not assert "that there actually *are* many true religions, but only that there *can be*" (83; see also 55). However, given the *first* meaning of "monism"—which is the meaning reflected in the book's title, which asks whether there *are* many true religions, not merely whether there *can be*—Ogden's "fourth option" does *not* constitute "a clean break with monism." Indeed, if Ogden's position is that, insofar as he can presently see, there seems to be only one true religion, then his position would represent only a transition from an a priori monism to an a posteriori monism. For both of these reasons, therefore, "pluralistic inclusivism" is a less accurate label for his position than "semipluralism."

it."[66] Cobb's pluralism, at least arguably, employs Whiteheadian philosophy as such a norm. From Cobb's perspective, this employment is not in conflict with taking Jesus Christ as normative, because he sees Whitehead's philosophy as "a *Christian* natural theology."[67] This philosophy, nevertheless, provides a basis for recognizing truths that have not been present in historic Christian thought, at least explicitly, because this philosophy has also been informed by insights from other traditions. Whitehead himself famously observed that his philosophy approximates "some strains of Indian, or Chinese thought" (PR 7).

With regard to the question of how we can recognize truths other than those embodied in our own particular tradition, Whitehead's tuning-fork analogy suggests an answer: Saying that an expressive sign "elicits the intuition which interprets it," Whitehead adds, "It cannot elicit what is not there. A note on a tuning fork can elicit a response from a piano. But the piano has already in it the string tuned to the same note. In the same way the expressive sign elicits the existent intuition *which would not otherwise emerge into individual distinctiveness*" (RM 133; emphasis added). In other words, insofar as a doctrine of another religion is an explication of a universal intuition that had not arisen to consciousness in my experience because it had not been thematized by my own religious tradition, I can, upon being exposed to it, recognize its truth.[68] This seems to be Ogden's position with regard to people in nontheistic traditions being exposed to the idea of God as creator and redeemer. From Cobb's viewpoint, there may be other doctrines, such as the doctrine of *sunyata*, with the same formal status. The Christian could, accordingly, see nontheistic Buddhism as representing a universally valid salvific truth, even though it is not the truth historically represented by Christianity. Ogden, however, has not developed this possible implication of Whitehead's philosophy. For example, one of his statements—that "the truth in any philosophy not only has to confirm that in any religion, but also has to be confirmed by it"[69]—seems to foreclose the possibility that a philosophy, while containing much truth, might not contain a truth expressed by a particular religion, or that a religion, while expressing a universally valid salvific truth, might not contain every universally valid truth expressed by a particular philosophy.

Religion in a Pluralistic Situation

Another feature of Ogden's position that separates his position from Cobb's is his contention that a religion necessarily claims to be *the* formal norm of all true religion whatsoever. Consistently with this contention, Ogden says that "to be a

66. Ibid., 73.
67. See Cobb, *A Christian Natural Theology*.
68. This notion is developed in the chapter on "Doctrinal Beliefs and Christian Existence" in Cobb and Griffin, *Process Theology* (1976). I received an approving note from Ogden regarding this chapter, indicating that it expressed a less relativistic position than he had previously understood Cobb to have advocated.
69. Ogden, *Is There Only One?* 72.

Christian and to take Christianity to be the formally true religion are one and the same thing." Cobb would withhold assent from this view in terms of Ogden's own third test for a theological position, namely, that besides being appropriate to Jesus Christ and credible in light of common human experience and reason, it also be "fitting to its situation." Part of the present situation is precisely its religious plurality combined with the fact that many Christian theologians, partly because of new forms of theism (of which the process theism shared by Cobb and Ogden is one instance), believe that pluralism is theologically appropriate. Ogden himself, in fact, says that more and more Christian theologians "are religious pluralists precisely as Christians and theologians" and that "this is why the challenge they pose to Christian witness and theology is new, and importantly new at that."[70]

One of the implications of this importantly new situation, Cobb would suggest, is that it can lead adherents of the various religions to make a somewhat more modest claim. Granted that religions traditionally have claimed to be *the* formally true religion, could not believers in this new situation be content to see their own religion as *a* formally true religion? Could they not come to see, furthermore, that this new understanding of Christianity's place among the religions of the world is more appropriate to their founding events than the claim to be *the* formally true religion? It is this slight but crucial change that Cobb's complementary pluralism makes. With regard to Christian faith in particular, Cobb would fully endorse Ogden's statement if it were slightly modified to say that "to be a Christian and to take Christianity to be [a] formally true religion are one and the same thing." One could argue, in fact, that this is a reformulation of the meaning of Christian faith that many Christians in our time have, largely implicitly, already made, so that Cobb's complementary pluralism is simply providing a way to explicate this new self-understanding. This is not a move, however, that Ogden has made.[71]

Ogden's rejection of pluralism is based, at least in part, on his realization that pluralism, at least in many of its best-known versions, is either incoherent or implicitly, if not explicitly, relativistic. In the present section, I have alluded to the way in which Cobb's position allows him to affirm pluralism without relativism.[72] In the next section, I address this issue directly.

5. PLURALISM WITHOUT RELATIVISM

The idea of religious pluralism has from the outset raised the specter of relativism. Troeltsch, as we have seen, has been called both the pioneer of religious plural-

70. Ibid., 100, 35, 4.

71. Or, to be more precise, this is at least not a move Ogden had made at the time that he wrote the things employed for this exposition of his position.

72. In *Tolerance and Transformation: Jewish Approaches to Religious Pluralism* (1990), Sandra Lubarsky uses the term "veridical pluralism" for Cobb's type of pluralism to emphasize its rejection of relativism as well as absolutism (2, 6, 129 n. 4).

ism and the first great Christian relativist. Having defined "debilitating relativism" as the view that all religions are equally true, therefore equally false, Alan
Race says: "The pertinent question mark which hovers over all theories of pluralism is how far they succeed in overcoming the sense of 'debilitating relativism'
which is their apparent danger." Langdon Gilkey, in his contribution to *The Myth
of Christian Uniqueness*, opines that a theoretical solution is probably impossible.
Seeing "no consistent theological way to relativize and yet to assert our own symbols," he says that plurality as "rough parity," which means giving up our absolute
starting point, seems to lead to an "unavoidable relativism." Believing, nevertheless, that we must oppose demonic forms of religion in terms of absolute values,
he says that the only resolution of the dilemma is practical.[73]

Hick tries to avoid a debilitating relativism by regarding ethical norms as
rooted in human nature and as thereby independent of religious belief, so that
these norms can serve as criteria for evaluating the religions in terms of their
fruits.[74] Hick's view of ultimate reality, however, undermines this position. He
says, on the one hand, that morality is derivative from God, or the Real, in the
sense that it is based in our human nature as ethical, which is "an aspect of our
existence 'in the image of God,'" so that living ethically is living "in earthly alignment with the Real." On the other hand, as we have seen, Hick denies that any
of our predicates, including goodness, can apply to the Real in itself,[75] which
implies that the idea of "alignment with the Real" is vacuous. Christian values at
their best can be said to be in alignment with the Real no more than Nazi values
at their worst. Given the fact that Hick's theory has been taken as the paradigmatic example of pluralism, it is not surprising that Race and Gilkey wonder
whether any theoretical avoidance of debilitating relativism is possible.

The question of how to formulate pluralism without relativism has been
uppermost in the minds of Whiteheadian pluralists. In her contribution to *The
Myth of Christian Uniqueness*, Marjorie Suchocki asks whether pluralists can
avoid "religious relativism, which would follow were there no acceptable norms
of discernment to be applied to religious positions." In *Christ in a Pluralistic Age*,
Cobb says that the danger of "the deeper level of pluralism" he is advocating,
according to which "'Christ' and 'Buddha' do not name the same reality," is "an
unqualified relativism." In *Beyond Dialogue*, he says that "thoroughgoing relativism fall[s] outside the boundaries of Christian theology." In his critique of *The
Myth of Christian Uniqueness*, he says that none of the great religious traditions
can find acceptable "a sheer conceptual relativism," according to which a tradition's message "is truth for its believers but irrelevant to others." In an essay titled
"Responses to Relativism," Cobb even uses the same expression as Alan Race,
speaking of the need to avoid a "debilitating relativism." It is noteworthy that

73. Race, *Christians and Religious Pluralism*, 78, 90; Gilkey, "Plurality and Its Theological Implications," 44, 46–47, 50.
74. Hick, *An Interpretation of Religion*, 97–98, 325–26.
75. Ibid., 204, 312, 338.

Race, after pointing to the danger that pluralism can lead to debilitating relativism, says: "The virtue of Cobb's contribution is that he combines fidelity to Christ with unqualified openness to other faiths."[76]

The distinction between God and creativity is at root of the way in which Cobb's version of pluralism differs from Hick's at this point. We saw earlier that, against the kind of allegedly neutral metatheory of religion employed by Hick, Cobb protests in "the name of Christian faith" because of "the implicit relativization and even negation of basic Christian commitments." Cobb elsewhere spells out how the move made by Hick results in this relativization and even negation. "[T]hose who assume that all traditions must be focusing on the same aspects of reality" are led to believe that what Zen Buddhists call Emptying "must be the same as God," which can in turn lead the Christian thinker to "employ the negative theology on the Christian heritage so radically as to dissolve God into Emptying. In that process everything distinctive of the biblical heritage is lost"[77]—in particular, the morality-supporting attributes of God.[78]

One might reply, to be sure, that this criticism would not apply to Hick, because he does not "dissolve God into Emptying" but instead regards both the biblical God and Buddhist emptiness as two phenomenal appearances of the transcendent Real. This reply, however, would not remove Cobb's charge that

76. Suchocki, "In Search of Justice: Religious Pluralism from a Feminist Perspective," 150; Cobb, *Christ in a Pluralistic Age*, 19; *Beyond Dialogue*, 15; *Transforming Christianity and the World*, 67, 68, 102; Race, *Christians and Religious Pluralism*, 98. Cobb's statement about "the deeper level of pluralism," incidentally, provides a basis in his writing for the title of the present volume.

77. Cobb, *Transforming Christianity and the World*, 79; Cobb in Swidler et al., *Death or Dialogue?* 6. Hick defends his negative theology by saying that "all serious religious thought affirms that the Ultimate, in its infinite divine reality, is utterly beyond our comprehension" (*A Christian Theology of Religions*, 58), thereby implying that philosophical theologians who disagree, such as Hartshorne, Cobb, and Ogden, are not really serious thinkers.

78. This problem is illustrated in the thinking of David Tracy, an important religious pluralist who has been influenced by process theism. Tracy agrees with Cobb that God must be understood by Christians as an ultimate that can be trusted and worshiped. But Tracy explicitly rejects Cobb's distinction between God as Ultimate Actuality and creativity as Ultimate Reality, insisting that "if ultimate reality is to be trusted and worshiped, it (he/she) must also be God" ("Kenosis, Sunyata, and Trinity," 139). In retaining the traditional equation of God and ultimate reality, Tracy thereby affirms that what Buddhists call "Emptiness" is the same reality that Christians call "God" (*Plurality and Ambiguity*, 85). Thanks to his involvement in interreligious dialogue with Buddhists, however, he realizes that this equation is very threatening. Trying to think of ultimate reality as emptiness, he says, is "a deeply disorienting matter, for any Christian who holds her/his profound trust in and loyalty to the one God" (*Dialogue with the Other*, 74). It is in the Buddhist-Christian dialogue, he adds, that he has experienced "the full terror of otherness" (ibid., 90). The Buddhist idea of ultimate reality as emptiness has led him, he says, to explore the apophatic neo-Platonic theologies of Meister Eckhart and other Christian mystics (ibid., 91, 103; "Kenosis," 141–42). He "nevertheless remain[s] puzzled whether the Christian understanding of God can receive as radically an apophatic character as Eckhart sometimes insists upon" (*Dialogue*, 91; "Kenosis," 149 [the same sentence is in both writings]). Tracy must pull back from a *completely* negative theology, given his commitment to liberation theology and his faith in God as the one by whom "hope is granted" for "acts of resistance to the status quo" (*Plurality*, 85). But, although he sees the need not to go as far as Hick in negating all positive and thereby morality-supporting attributes of God, the fact that he has felt impelled to go even part way in that direction is due to the fact that he, like Hick, has been unable to relinquish the metaphysical assumption that there must be only one ultimate reality.

the God of the biblical tradition, who has a concern for justice and other particular forms of existence, is dissolved into formlessness. In his early writings on religious pluralism, Hick saw his own distinction—between ultimate transcendent
reality as it is in itself and this reality as it is conceived by us—as parallel to "the
Hindu distinction between *nirguna* Brahman, Brahman without attributes,
beyond the scope of human language, and *saguna* Brahman, Brahman with
attributes, known within human religious experience as Ishvara, the personal
creator and governor of the universe."[79] Adding his own affirmation that "[t]he
infinite God must pass out into sheer mystery . . . and is in this limitless transcendence *nirguna*,"[80] Hick was clearly saying that Advaita Vedanta was right and
Christianity and the other theistic traditions wrong about what the Divine Reality is in itself. Hick later tried to overcome this favoritism by insisting that the
various views of ultimate reality as impersonal, such as *nirguna* Brahman and
Sunyata (Emptiness), are mere *impersonae* of the Real, corresponding no more to
the Real in itself than do the divine *personae*.[81]

The fact remains, however, that what Hick says about the Real is remarkably
similar to what he says about *nirguna* Brahman and *Sunyata*. Hick himself, furthermore, undermines his own attempt at evenhandedness by saying that if *Sunyata* is understood "as referring to the ultimate reality beyond the scope of all
concepts, knowable only in its manifestations, then it is indeed equivalent to
what in our pluralistic hypothesis we are calling the Real."[82] Not flinching from
the implication—which, as Cobb says, is that everything distinctive of the biblical concept of deity is lost—Hick has his interrogator ask: If the biblical God,
which has the attributes of being "good, loving, purposeful," is an authentic
appearance of the Real, must not these attributes "have their analogical counter-
parts in the Real itself?" Hick, while saying that he sees the point of the question,
answers in the negative.[83] This is the main reason why Hick's view of ultimate
reality undermines his own concern that religious beliefs be reformulated to give
more unambiguous support for morality.

Rather than subordinating the personal God to the formless ultimate (as do
Advaita Vedanta, some forms of Buddhism, and Hick) Whitehead—with some
forms of Hinduism and Buddhism—regarded the personal God and formless creativity as equally primordial, with each presupposing the other.[84] Whiteheadian
pluralists can agree with the descriptions, provided by nontheistic Hindus and nontheistic Buddhists, of ultimate reality as formless while still affirming the existence

---

79. Hick, "Towards a Philosophy of Religious Pluralism," 133. (Hick had earlier suggested this
view in *God and the Universe of Faiths*, 144.)

80. Ibid., 134.

81. Hick, *An Interpretation of Religion*, 245, 279, 294–95.

82. Ibid., 292; cf. *A Christian Theology of Religions*, 60–61.

83. Hick, *A Christian Theology of Religions*, 61.

84. I have elsewhere summarized the ways in which Cobb and three other Whitehead-inspired
scholars—Delmar Langbauer, Ernest Simmons, and Gene Reeves—have pointed out parallels to this
Whiteheadian position in Hindu and Buddhist thought (*Reenchantment without Supernaturalism*,
278–81).

of a Divine Actuality with many characteristics in common with the biblical God, including those that support the concern for a just social order.[85] Cobb, on this basis, says not only that he evaluates the various religious traditions in terms of the norm of "[c]ontributing to the indivisible salvation of the whole world" but also that this norm comes from his "hope for what Jesus called the *basileia theou*, the world in which God's purposes are realized."[86] On the basis of this idea of God, likewise, Marjorie Suchocki uses justice—"the normative justice that creates well-being in the world community"—as the norm for evaluating the various religions.[87]

However, although Whiteheadian Christian pluralists, thanks to the distinction between God and creativity, are able to avoid relativism, it may seem as if they can do so only by imperialistically imposing a norm from their own religious tradition, thereby undermining their pluralism. I will look first at the treatment of this issue by Suchocki. Explicitly addressing this issue, she asks whether religious pluralists, who by definition reject "absolutizing one religion as the norm for all others," can avoid the relativistic view that "each religion is governed by norms and perceptions uniquely conditioned by the cultural and historical situation of the religion." Having suggested that justice can provide a norm that expresses a "transcendence of our particularity," she recognizes that the norm of justice that she and other liberationists would employ would not command universal assent. This norm might, therefore, seem imperialistic by virtue of taking "the notion of physical well-being developed in a culture-specific context and appl[ying] it evaluatively to all cultures and religions." Suchocki suggests that this charge could be answered by showing that there is sufficient unanimity in the various religions' ideas of "the ultimately perfect mode of existence" expressed in their eschatological visions to provide a criterion of justice that is "nonimperialistic" because it would be "an internal norm within each religion." She admits, however, that this solution does not completely overcome the charge but only "mitigates" it, because "the norm is hardly culture-free."[88]

Suchocki's own self-critique here can be fleshed out with a point made by Cobb in response to Knitter. While not denying that there are common elements in all the major traditions, Cobb does maintain that "if there are such common elements, they do not constitute what all the traditions regard as most important."[89] This point is relevant to the degree of unanimity that can be found in the images of ideal existence found in the various traditions. Describing her approach, Suchocki says that, valuing well-being, she "look[s] for its traces within that which is given ultimate value in each religion."[90] The relevance of Cobb's

---

85. Having described God as the ultimate in the line of efficient, formal, and final causes, Cobb describes the "other ultimate" as "that which, without possessing any form, is subject to taking on any form. It is the formless" (*Transforming Christianity and the World*, 184).

86. Ibid., 182.

87. Suchocki, "In Search of Justice," 149, 154.

88. Ibid., 154, 156, 158, 159, 160.

89. Cobb in Swidler et al., *Death or Dialogue?* 181.

90. Suchocki, "In Search of Justice," 159.

point is that, even if traces of the valuation of well-being, including physical well-being, that is found in a central strand of the Judeo-Christian tradition—the strand regarded as normative by liberation theologians—can be found in all the other traditions, this fact would not mean that this valuation has the same importance in all those traditions. It would, therefore, be imperialistic for Suchocki to propose "justice that creates well-being" as "*the* fundamental criterion of value and *the* focus of dialogue and action among religions" (emphases added).[91] However, this problem could be overcome, without lapsing into relativism, by changing the definite articles in this statement to indefinite ones. In Cobb's version of Whiteheadian complementary pluralism, this modification is central.

The crucial point is that we can hold fast to the universal validity of our own norms without insisting that these norms are the *only* ones with universal validity. Having said that for him to enter into genuine dialogue with people of other traditions means that he must provisionally bracket his claim that what he as a Christian sees as most important is truly the most important thing, Cobb clarifies his point by saying that what is bracketed is

> neither the content of what I find supremely important, for example, that we transmit a habitable planet to our children's children, nor the conviction that this is important for all, but only the opinion that it is *more* important for all than what others regard as supremely important. *Perhaps* becoming empty is just as important![92]

As Cobb puts it elsewhere, to enter into dialogue "we do not need to relativize our beliefs." Rather, "[w]e can affirm our insights as universally valid! What we cannot do, without lapsing back into unjustified arrogance, is to deny that the insights of other traditions are also universally valid."[93] With regard to Suchocki's question, the implication is that it is not imperialistic for Christians to propose liberative justice as a norm to evaluate the various religious traditions *if* we recognize the equal right of other traditions to propose different norms based on their own sense of what is most important.

In giving this answer, however, it may seem that Cobb has avoided imperialism only by accepting a more subtle form of relativism—one that, rather than saying that *nothing* is of universal truth and validity, has a *plurality* of universally valid norms based on different universally valid truths. The relativism would indeed result, Cobb says, if a Christian came to "recognize that there is a wisdom from which faith shuts one out." Explaining how pluralism of this sort would stimulate the "corrosive acids of relativism," Cobb says:

91. Ibid., 149.
92. Cobb in Swidler et al., *Death or Dialogue?* 11.
93. Cobb, *Transforming Christianity and the World*, 137. Given his affirmation of the universal validity of Christian insights, Cobb's version of Christian pluralism would not be subject to Ogden's criticism of some versions for being "inconsistent with the claim to universal salvific truth that is evidently constitutive of the Christian witness" ("Problems in the Case," 498).

> One recognizes that one's faith, a faith that had previously seemed compre-
> hensive and adequate, has left something out. . . . One realizes that one's
> faith does not have the completeness one had thought, that there are other
> faiths embodying other strengths.[94] One concludes that Christian faith is
> one faith among others.[95]

Such a view would be corrosive, Cobb holds, because it would work against the
wholehearted commitment for which Christian faith calls: "If other movements
seek other ends than the Christian end, and yet have equal validity with Christianity, then how can one give whole-hearted commitment to the Christian
goal?" The problem is intensified by the recognition that although these other
movements are seeking other ends, they can contribute to what the Christian sees
as the Christian goal—"the indivisible salvation of the whole world"—"in ways
that Christianity as now constituted does not and cannot." It is primarily this
recognition, Cobb says, that constitutes him "as a pluralist."[96]

Cobb's solution draws on the twofold idea that Christianity is a living movement, which "should be constantly changing and growing," and that the Christian's devotion should be not to any particular form of Christianity but to "the
living Christ" who "calls us in each moment to be transformed by the new possibilities given by God for that moment." Whereas this perspective "does relativize every form taken by Christianity in time," it "does not relativize the process
of creative transformation by which it lives and which it knows as Christ."[97] The

94. This side of Cobb's position distinguishes it from that of Ogden, who argues "that any other
religion must also be true just insofar as it both confirms and is confirmed by the truth in one's own"
("Problems in the Case," 498). The "just" in his statement seems to mean that he would not be able
to recognize a truth in another religion that is not already contained in Christian faith. This difference between Cobb and Ogden is germane to Suchocki's (mis)description of Cobb as an inclusivist
(in the epistemic sense). Cobb's position is (epistemically) inclusivist, Suchocki argues, "because
Christ as known in Christianity becomes the norm by which other religions are affirmed." Cobb's
affirmation of other religions, she further suggests, is really only "an affirmation of Christianity as
seen in and through other religions" ("Pragmatic Pluralism," 51). Although this description would
be true of Ogden's position (who, as we have seen, accepts the inclusivist label, understood epistemically), it is not, as the discussion in the text shows, true of Cobb's.

95. Cobb in Swidler et al., *Death or Dialogue?* 4. There is a sense, of course, in which Cobb does
believe that Christian faith is "one faith among others," the sense that is part and parcel of his generic
pluralism. What he means by the phrase here is the idea that other faiths would be seen as having
truths and values that could *never* be incorporated within Christian faith.

96. Cobb, *Transforming Christianity and the World*, 44–45. (The phrase "the indivisible salvation
of the whole world" is from Dorothee Sölle, *Political Theology*, 60.)

97. Ibid., 45, 47. In reaction against Hick's version of "theocentrism," according to which we are
urged to center "our attention on the noumenal Absolute" and thereby "away from this world toward
another sphere which alone 'has absolute reality and value,'" Cobb has called his position "Christocentrism" (*Beyond Dialogue*, 45, quoting Hick, "Towards a Philosophy of Religious Pluralism," 147).
What Cobb is calling "Christ," however, is "the incarnation of God in each occasion [of experience]"
or, alternatively expressed, "the universal revealing and saving presence of God in ourselves and the
world" (*Transforming Christianity and the World*, 157; *Beyond Dialogue*, 45). He acknowledges,
accordingly, that "this kind of Christocentrism is really theocentrism [of another sort] after all"
(*Beyond Dialogue*, 45). Cobb also acknowledges that although it is natural for him as a Christian to
use the term "Christ" to name God as incarnate in the world, in attempting to "share Christ" it is

Christian can recognize that other religions have truths and values and make contributions that Christianity, in its present form, does not incorporate, accordingly, without relativizing Christian faith itself and thereby undermining one's wholehearted commitment to it:

> The fullness of Christianity lies in the ever-receding future. One can be a whole-hearted participant in the present movement as long as one believes that the particular limitations to which one is now sensitive can be overcome.[98]

The way for the Christian theologian to be pluralistic without being relativistic, in other words, is to encourage the continual creative transformation of Christian theology in the direction of its becoming a "global theology," in which the truths and values of the other religious traditions have been incorporated. Pointing out that the task of transforming Christianity "in relation to each of the great ways of humankind is a vast one," Cobb says: "We have barely begun to deal with the fundamental changes that must be effected within our Christian faith."[99]

True to his pluralism, Cobb hopes that this work of globalization will occur in the other religious traditions as well, at least those that claim universal validity,[100] adding that if it does, it will result in "a movement toward greater resemblance." Contrary to the hitherto dominant proposals for global theology, however, Cobb advocates "confessional global theologies."[101]

> Global theology in a pluralistic age need not cut its ties to the particularities of [the] religious traditions. Instead it can work within each religion to make the theology of that tradition more global. In the name of what is most sacred, even what is most particular, in each tradition, adherents can be called to more global religious thinking and practice.
>
> My suggestion is that there is no global strategy for developing global theology in a pluralistic age. The strategy is pluralistic. It will be quite different for Muslims, for Hindus, for Sikhs, for Jains, for Buddhists, for Jews, and for Christians.[102]

"not usually best to begin with the name" because "it will be laden with meanings that may distract from matters at hand" (*Transforming Christianity*, 154). Those who do find the term "Christocentrism" distracting can, therefore, call Cobb's position "theocentrism"—a term that, given the usual connotations of "God" or "theos," actually fits his position better than it does Hick's.

98. *Transforming Christianity and the World*, 45.

99. Ibid., 52, 58–60, 84.

100. This qualification reflects Cobb's awareness that there are many religions, such as primal religions, Shinto, and Judaism under one interpretation, that do not claim or aspire to universal validity. Also, the fact that he expresses the "hope" that other universalist religions will move toward greater inclusiveness, rather than simply assuming that they *will* or at least *should*, reflects his awareness that continual creative transformation toward universality is an ideal that may be more important to Christianity than to other universalist religions. For example, having advocated participation in interreligious dialogue as a means to achieve an ever more comprehensive vision, he emphasizes that he "favor[s] this *for Christians*," adding: "Of course, I as a Christian hope that [Muslims and Hindus] will be creatively transformed, but I am open to the possibility that there is no inner impulse within Islam or Hinduism to submit to such transformation" (Cobb in Swidler et al., *Death or Dialogue?* 120).

101. *Transforming Christianity and the World*, 59, 58.

102. Ibid., 59.

If such a process occurs, there could be pluralism without relativism in all the universalist traditions.

Cobb's Christian pluralism, which he has been developing since his 1967 book *The Structure of Christian Existence*, provides one version of Whiteheadian religious pluralism, the version that has thus far been developed most fully and most in dialogue with pluralists of other persuasions. As such it provides a version that other Whitehead-inspired philosophers and theologians, from other religious traditions as well as from Christianity, can learn from and then build upon or modify.

PART TWO
EXTENDING COBB'S BUDDHIST-CHRISTIAN DIALOGUE

Chapter 3

God as Peace-Bestowing Buddha/Christ

An Amplification of Cobb's Contribution to Dialogue between Christianity and Shin Buddhism

Steve Odin

INTRODUCTION

This essay takes up the notion of transpersonal peace as a theme for East-West comparative philosophy and Buddhist-Christian interfaith dialogue in an age of religious pluralism. There is a special focus on the ideal of Peace in Jôdo Shinshû, or True Pure Land Buddhism, based on the teachings of Shinran Shonin (1173–1263), in relation to the organismic process theology and process cosmology of Alfred North Whitehead. The kind of pluralism involved here is a version of the *deep* religious pluralism articulated by process theologians John B. Cobb Jr. and David Ray Griffin, which is rooted in the pluralistic vision of Whitehead's naturalistic process theism, which recognizes at least two ultimates: Creativity and God. These two ultimates function to clarify two major kinds of religious experience—theistic and nontheistic, or devotion to a personal, form-giving God and realization of an impersonal formless reality. From the standpoint of Christian-Buddhist interfaith dialogue, the distinction between the two ultimates of Creativity and God in Whitehead's Christian process theology illuminates both the nontheistic religious experience of *satori* or sudden enlightenment in Zen Buddhism, as realization of formless emptiness, and the theistic religious experience of salvation in Shin Buddhism, through *shinjin* or inward faith in the compassionate Other-power grace of Amida Buddha.

However, although the pluralistic hypothesis of two ultimates in Whiteheadian process theology explicates the formless ultimate of emptiness/nothingness in the nontheistic tradition of Zen Buddhism, it is closer to the theistic position of Shin Buddhism, which holds that the formless emptiness of Dharmakaya is always experienced in and through the divine form of Amida the Sambhogakaya Buddha, just as for Whitehead the formless ultimate of Creativity, which is said to be "without a character of its own," is always experienced through its primordial characterization by God as the source of all forms. In Shin Buddhism, Amida Buddha (Sambhogakaya) is not subordinate to Formless Emptiness (Dharmakaya), just as for Whiteheadian naturalistic theism, God is not subordinate to the formless ultimate of Creativity. The two ultimates of God and Creativity in Whiteheadian process theology, and its correlates of Amida Buddha (Sambhogakaya) and Formless Emptiness (Dharmakaya) in Shin Buddhism, are equal and presuppose each other. The Whiteheadian ultimates of Creativity and God, wherein the formless process of Creativity is primordially characterized by God as the source of all ideal forms, therefore corresponds to the Shin Buddhist position that the Dharmakaya Buddha of Formless Emptiness is itself primordially characterized by the Primal Vow of Amida as the Sambhogakaya Buddha of infinite light and life or wisdom and compassion.

Unlike the nontheistic naturalistic traditions of Buddhism such as Zen/Chan, according to which the emptiness/suchness of events in Nature is all that is, the Shin Buddhist school holds that the dynamic process of evolutionary flux, whereby momentary events co-arise into actuality through harmonic interpenetration of many into one, is itself guided and saved by the operation of a personal deity: namely, Amida Buddha. That is to say, the Shin Buddhist tradition approximates Whitehead's naturalistic process theism whereby all momentary events in the dynamic web of felt value-relations in the aesthetic continuum of nature are influenced by the divine lure of a cosmic mind—Amida Buddha in Shin Buddhism and the dipolar God in Whitehead's process theology.

In this essay, I attempt to clarify that while Amida Buddha and the God of traditional Christian theology are very different, Amida and the God of Whitehead's process theology are strikingly similar. Like Amida Buddha in Shin Buddhism, the God of process theology is not an omnipotent creator of the universe. Like Amida Buddha, the God of Whitehead's process theology is to be envisioned through the image of "care," so that for both traditions reality is compassionate or caring in nature. It is fundamental to Whitehead's process theology that God is "dipolar" and therefore has two natures: the Primordial Nature, which acts as a persuasive *lure* for all events to realize God's divine aims for them, and the Consequent Nature, a repository which acts as the divine memory that saves all events everlastingly in the kingdom of heaven. Whereas the Primordial Nature of God has been compared by John Cobb to the Primal Vow of Amida, the Consequent Nature has been compared by John Shunji Yokota to Dharmâkara/Amida as a personification of the "Storehouse Consciousness." Cobb even identifies the Name of Amida Buddha with Christ as the divine Logos or Word, which is graciously incarnated into each occasion of experience.

After discussing this Buddhist-Christian interfaith dialogue between Shin Buddhism and process theology, I argue that transpersonal Peace is the ultimate spiritual value derived from God in process theology as well as Amida in Shin Buddhism. Peace in Whitehead's process theology is similar to Buddhist *nirvana*, insofar as it is not only a goal of civilization but also an expanded awareness transcending the ego-self whereby one achieves deliverance from the suffering and tragedy inherent in the perpetually perishing nature of impermanent events in the flux of interrelational existence. Finally, I show that for Whitehead's process theology, transpersonal Peace is not achieved through personal effort but comes only as a "gift" of divine grace through the divine immanence of a caring God, just as for the Shin Buddhist teachings of Shinran, rebirth into the Pure Land of Peace is not achieved by "self-power" (*jiriki*), but only through a "gift" (*ekô*) received from the transformative grace of Amida Buddha's compassionate "Other-power" (*tariki*).

I now develop these ideas as a way of amplifying the power of Whiteheadian thought, especially as developed by John Cobb, to promote a deep form of religious pluralism. Although one dimension of Cobb's contribution is the recognition that some religious traditions are radically different from others, I am here amplifying the other dimension—his discernment of deep similarities between Whiteheadian process theology, which originated in the Christian West, and Shin Buddhism, which reflects Indian, Chinese, and Japanese civilizations.

1. AMIDA IN SHIN BUDDHISM AND THE DIPOLAR GOD OF PROCESS THEOLOGY

Various scholars have noted that out of all Buddhist schools, it is Japanese Shin Buddhism that most nearly approximates Christian theism, just as Amida Buddha as the compassionate Savior of all sentient beings comes nearest to the Christian monotheistic idea of God. In response to the question "Is Amida Buddha a Buddhist 'God'?" Kenneth Tanaka has given the following response:

> You could say that Amida is "God," but only if you define God as the dynamic activity of understanding (wisdom) and caring (compassion). But clearly, Amida is not a personal God who is 1) the creator of the universe, 2) a divine, transcendent being, 3) an omniscient (all knowing) being . . . or 4) a judge who decides my final destiny.[1]

As indicated by Tanaka, Amida Buddha has none of these four attributes of "God" as conceived by traditional Christian theism. However, these attributes are also not applicable to Whitehead's revolutionary concept of God. Whitehead in fact said:

1. Tanaka, *Ocean: An Introduction to Jodo-Shinshu Buddhism in America*, 153.

"The notion of God as . . . transcendent creator, at whose fiat the world came into being, and whose imposed will it obeys, is the fallacy which has infused tragedy into the histories of Christianity and of Mahometanism" (PR 342).

To begin with, against the traditional Christian theological conceptions of God, Whitehead argues that "the nature of God is dipolar. He has a primordial nature and a consequent nature" (PR 345). While the Primordial Nature of God is absolute, transcendent, impassible (unfeeling), eternal, and unchanging, God is also relative, immanent, sympathetic, temporal, and changing, these features constituting God's Consequent Nature. The most radical aspect of Whitehead's process theology is that God is not to be understood as divine Creator of the world but as a caring deity that aims to save all occasions in world-process: "He does not create the world, he saves it" (PR 346). There is, to be sure, a sense in which God is the creator of our particular world ("cosmic epoch"), but Whitehead emphatically rejected the idea that the word "God" refers to an omnipotent being who created the universe out of nothing. For him, the ultimate metaphysical category is "creativity" (PR 21), according to which all events in nature are self-creative, in that they arise through a process of *creative synthesis,* a dynamic activity of unifying the dynamic web of interrelationships into a novel event or occasion with beauty and value.

For Whitehead, as well as for Charles Hartshorne, John Cobb, and other leading process theologians, insofar as all events arise though a process of creative synthesis, they are spontaneous, emergent, and unpredictable, so that God cannot be "omniscient" in the sense of an infinite, unqualified knowledge that sees the outcome of all decisions before they have been made.

Finally, Whitehead clearly rejects the image of God as a legalistic judge, lawgiver, or "ruthless moralist" (PR 343). Instead, God is to be envisioned through the image of "care" (PR 346). Hence, while traditional notions of the Christian God might be very different from Amida Buddha, Whiteheadian process theology provides a description of God that resonates deeply with the Shin Buddhist vision of Amida as a peaceful, gentle, and caring deity that operates to forever lure all events toward realizing its divine aims toward value, beauty, goodness, truth, harmony, peace, and salvation. It might be said that the dipolar God of Whitehead's process theology functions like Amida as the Cosmic Buddha, defined as a dynamic activity of wisdom and compassion.

2. THE "PRIMORDIAL NATURE" OF GOD AND THE "PRIMAL VOW" OF AMIDA

The Buddhist-Christian interfaith dialogue between Shin Buddhism and Whitehead's process theology was initiated by John Cobb in his groundbreaking work *Beyond Dialogue: Toward a Mutual Transformation of Christianity and Buddhism.* In this work, Cobb endeavors to show various parallels between the "Primal Vow" as the working of the compassion of Amida Buddha's Other-power and the "Primordial Nature" of God in process theology:

> Whitehead's account of the Primordial Nature of God addresses the same feature of reality as that spoken of by Shinran as the primal vow of Amida. Both of these are remarkably analogous to . . . accounts of the Word of God or Logos or Truth which is Christ.[2]

Cobb then goes on to make the bold declaration:

> The conclusion from the above is that *Amida is Christ.* That is, the feature of the totality of reality to which Pure Land Buddhists refer when they speak of Amida is the same as that to which Christians refer when we speak of Christ.[3]

Here, it should be pointed out, Cobb is in agreement with the view of Nishida Kitarô (1870–1945), founder of the Kyoto school of modern Japanese philosophy, who likewise argued that the Name of Amida Buddha in the Shin Buddhist teachings of Shinran is to be identified with Christ as the divine Logos or Word of God in Christian theology.[4] Cobb's profound insight is that Christ as the divine Logos or Word is itself the Primordial Nature of God, which *incarnates* itself into each and every occasion as the "initial aim" toward realizing maximum harmony and value, while moreover identifying the Logos or Primordial Nature with the Primal Vow of Amida. Whitehead describes the Primordial Nature of God as a "lure" to realize value (PR 344). For Cobb, the lure of God's Primordial Nature is a theological equivalent to the Primal Vow of Amida or, as it were, the "call of Amida."[5] Elsewhere, Cobb refers to Whitehead's idea of the Primordial Nature of God or Logos, in its working as a divine lure prescribing initial aims, as "the call forward" and therefore describes God as "the One Who Calls."[6] For Cobb, the lure from God's Primordial Nature as Logos or Word is therefore a Christian theological equivalent to the Primal Vow of Amida Buddha, or what he otherwise describes as the "call of Amida."[7]

Finally, Cobb argues for another similarity between Amida and the dipolar God, holding that the ultimate metaphysical category of creativity, as an indeterminate formless activity of creative synthesis, is itself conditioned by the determinate forms of harmony provided by the Primordial Nature of God, just as the formless emptiness of Dharmakaya Buddha is conditioned by the Primal Vows of Amida (the Sambhogakaya Buddha) in Shin Buddhism:

2. Cobb, *Beyond Dialogue: Toward a Mutual Transformation of Christianity and Buddhism*, 128.
3. Ibid.
4. Nishida, *Last Writings: Nothingness and the Religious Worldview*, 195.
5. Cobb, *Beyond Dialogue*, 136.
6. Cobb, *God and the World*, 43–66.
7. Cobb, *Beyond Dialogue*, 136.

It is the Primordial Nature which qualifies creativity in a way so strikingly similar to the qualification of the Dharmakaya by the primal vow. Just as the Primordial Nature of God is the primordial decision for the sake of all creatures, even more clearly the primal vow is made for the sake of all sentient beings.[8]

Hence, as developed by Cobb, and further crystallized by David Ray Griffin,[9] Whiteheadian process theology establishes the basis for a genuine religious pluralism with its recognition of *two ultimates,* including both God and Creativity. For Whitehead, the two ultimates of God and Creativity are equally primordial and presuppose each other. These two ultimates function to explain two fundamental modes of religious experience: theistic, or the worship of a personal deity, and nontheistic, or realization of an impersonal formless reality. (For the sake of simplicity, I here leave aside the third ultimate discussed by Cobb and Griffin—the world of finite actual occasions—which provides the basis for a third kind of religious experience.) Furthermore, these two ultimates of Whiteheadian process theology correspond to the Shin Buddhist categories of the Dharmakaya Buddha as Formless Emptiness and the Sambhogakaya Buddha represented by Amida Buddha. According to the pluralistic hypothesis of Whiteheadian naturalistic theism based on the two ultimates of Creativity and God, then, the formless impersonal process of Creativity is primordially characterized by a personal savior God as the source of all ideal forms, just as for Shin Buddhism the Dharmakaya Buddha of Formless Emptiness is itself primordially characterized by the Primal Vow of Amida as the Sambhogakaya Buddha of infinite light and life or wisdom and compassion.

The profundity of Cobb's view of the divine lure of the Primordial Nature of God, or the divine Logos, as the One Who Calls, and its applicability to the Primal Vow of Amida Buddha as the "call of Amida," can at once be seen when considered in relation to the view of leading Shin Buddhist scholars, as well as the views of Shinran (1173–1263), founder of Shin (True Pure Land) Buddhism in Japan. Shinran sums up the Larger Pure Land Sutra by describing its essence as Amida's primal vow (*hongan*) and its embodiment as Amida's divine Name (*myôgô*), as well as the practice-faith of calling the Name of Amida Buddha through the *nembutsu* of NAMU-AMIDA-BUTSU. These two aspects, the primal vow and the *nembutsu,* were stressed to the exclusion of the other by the competing faith and practice factions of the Pure Land school. Shinran, in his interpretation of the teachings, considered the two aspects united in the Larger Pure Land Sutra, thereby avoiding the extremes of the factions.

In the second fascicle of this work, Shinran aims to clarify how *nembutsu* is the one true religious practice assuring birth in the Pure Land. *Namu* means "I take refuge in" (*kimyo*) and indicates the act of turning toward Buddha. Shinran, however, interpreted "taking refuge in" as "the beckoning command of the prin-

---

8. Ibid.
9. Griffin, *Reenchantment without Supernaturalism: A Process Philosophy of Religion,* 247–84.

cipal vow" (*hongan shôkan no chokumei*).[10] The active practice of reciting or calling the Name (*nembutsu*) does not occur by calculation (*hakarai*) of self-power
(*jiriki*), but through the lure, magnetism, or attraction of the primal vow of
Amida's compassionate Other-power (*tariki*), here understood as the divine call
to enlightenment. In Shinran's phrase "the beckoning command of the principal
vow" (*hongan shôkan no chokumei*), the term *shôkan* means to beckon, invite, or
call. Although through the practice of *nembutsu* we call out the Name of Amida
Buddha in order to receive his gift of saving grace through the openness of *shinjin* or faith, it is Amida's call for us to realize perfection, because the *nembutsu* is
not an act of self-power but the compassionate Other-power of Amida.

To sum up this point: Shinran's idea that the primal vow is to save all beings
through the *nembutsu*, as "the beckoning command of the principal vow" of
Amida, is what Cobb describes as the "call of Amida." The "beckoning command" is the imperative and urgent *call* of Amida implanted into each sentient
being to achieve perfection, enlightenment, awakening, and Buddhahood. However, by identifying the Name of Amida Buddha with the Christ as the Logos or
Word of God, and by further identifying both with the Primordial Nature of God
as the divine magnetic "lure" or beckoning *call* to perfection, Cobb has made a
breakthrough contribution to interfaith dialogue, showing how the notion of
Amida Buddha in Shin Buddhism might be comprehended from the standpoint
of Whiteheadian process theology and process metaphysics.

In his book published under the title *Naturalness: A Classic of Shin Buddhism*,
Kanamatsu Kenryo describes the Other-power of Amida Buddha as follows:

> This Unthinkable Power [= *tariki*, the Other-Power of Amida Buddha]
> stronger than ourselves, this persistent urge impelling the self to transcend
> itself, is a *call* to us of the All-feeling Compassionate Heart, the Eternal Spirit
> of Sympathy, who is in his essence the Light and Life of all, who is World-
> conscious. To feel all, to be conscious of everything, is the Spirit. . . . [T]his
> Light and Life, this All-feeling Being is in our hearts.[11]

Kanamatsu's view—that the Other-power of Amida, as the urge of the self to
transcend itself, "is a *call* to us of the All-feeling Compassionate Heart"—rein-
forces Cobb's view of the Primal Vow as the "call of Amida" and hence, by extension, its similarity to the Primordial Nature of God as the "One Who Calls." In
his interpretation of Whitehead's process theology, Cobb emphasizes that the Primordial Nature of God as the One Who Calls is not a coercive but a persuasive
agency, so that even though God inwardly *calls* the arising self-creative occasion
to achieve perfection, the occasion is nonetheless free to accept or reject God's
divine aims for it.

Likewise, Kanamatsu states that "shut up within the narrow walls of our limited self, we . . . turn a deaf ear to the *call* welling up from the inmost depths of

10. Dobbins, *Jodo Shinshu: Shin Buddhism in Medieval Japan*, 34.
11. Kanamatsu, *Naturalness: A Classic of Shin Buddhism*, 3–4.

our heart."[12] Here, it should be further noted, Kanamatsu describes Amida Buddha as the "All-feeling Compassionate Heart" and the "All-feeling Being who is in our hearts." He adds that Amida Buddha is "that *basal, pure, universal feeling* that interpenetrates all objects" and that to achieve enlightenment, the self must "sink into this basal *pure feeling*."[13] Thus, as will be discussed later in this section, Kanamatsu's writings suggest how the striking similarities between the notion of Amida Buddha in Shin Buddhism and the dipolar God of Whitehead's process theology are based on a concept of ultimate reality as *pure feeling*. Just as for Whitehead, all actualities are centers of feeling—and this includes God, as the supreme actual entity who feels all other actual entities everlastingly in their fullness—so in Kanamatsu's classic of Shin Buddhist theology, Amida Buddha is the "All-feeling Compassionate Heart." For both, enlightenment is achieved through perception in the mode of "pure feeling."

The depth of Cobb's penetrating interpretation of the Primal Vow in Shin Buddhism as the "*call* of Amida" can further be established by reference to the writings of Taitetsu Unno, a leading academic scholar and ordained minister of Shin Buddhism. In his introductory book about the Pure Land teachings of Shin Buddhism, Unno develops his understanding of the *nembutsu,* or vocal recitation of the Name of Amida Buddha, as the "Name-that-calls."[14] The *nembutsu* is the Name that calls one to go beyond the ego-self and achieve one's full possibility for enlightenment as an awakened human being.[15] Even though one calls to Amida through the *nembutsu,* the *nembutsu* is recited only through a gift of Amida's compassion, so the *nembutsu* is ultimately to be conceived as the Name-that-Calls. It is the beckoning *call* of Amida to transcend the ego-self through reliance on the compassionate Other-power grace of Amida Buddha. "If I were to translate *nembutsu* into English," says Unno, "it would be the 'name-that-calls,' for it calls us to awaken to our fullest potential to become true, real and sincere human beings," "to take leave of delusion and awaken to reality-as-it-is."[16] Unno further explains that "the saying of *nembutsu* is experienced as a call from Amida, but simultaneously it is our response to that call."[17] Since the *nembutsu* of NAMU-AMIDA-BUTSU is the Name-that-Calls, the central practice of Shin Buddhism is that of "deep hearing" (*monpô*), or "deep hearing of the call of Amida."[18] Unno states:

> Religiously speaking, deep hearing means that we have no choice but to hear and respond to the call of boundless compassion. It is through the Name-that-calls that Amida Buddha gives us the ultimate gift of true and real

12. Ibid., 2.
13. Ibid., 4.
14. Unno, *River of Fire/River of Water: An Introduction to the Pure Land Tradition of Shin Buddhism,* 26–35.
15. Ibid., 31.
16. Unno, *Shin Buddhism,* 25, 257.
17. Ibid., 5.
18. Ibid., 19.

life. . . . Thus, the invocation of the Name, NAMU-AMIDA-BUTSU, is
. . . a voicing of the call that comes from the bottomless source of life itself,
the Buddha of Immeasurable Light and Life.[19]

From Unno's understanding of the *nembutsu* as the Name-that-calls, one can
come to appreciate the profound significance of Cobb's discussion. For it is
Cobb's landmark contribution to have reformulated Whitehead's notion of the
initial aim, or lure toward perfection for self-actualizing occasions derived from
the Primordial Nature of God, as "the call forward" from the power of deity as
the "One Who Calls," while at the same time identifying this with the Primal
Vow of Amida Buddha, understood as the "call of Amida."

From the standpoint of contemplative practice, the great strength of Shin
Buddhism is its practice of *nembutsu*—natural, effortless, vocal recitation of the
divine Name of Amida: "Namu Amida Butsu, Namu Amida Butsu, Namu Amida
Butsu." But I fully agree with the view, stated by the Shin Buddhist scholar Taitetsu
Unno, that the closest parallel to this *nembutsu* practice is the Jesus Prayer as
described in a book called *The Way of the Pilgrim,* which urges people to undertake the effortless practice of ceaseless prayer as a call upon the Name of God:
"Lord Jesus Christ, have mercy on me."[20] Moreover, it must be pointed out that
the divine form of the aesthetic image of Amida Buddha, as depicted in the Man-
dalas of Pure Land Buddhism in Japan, has much in common with the archetypal
image of the sacred artistic icons of Jesus Christ depicted in the Eastern Orthodox
Church, so that one can easily visualize both Christ and Amida as imaginative vari-
ations of the Logos or divine creative Word of God. But it is the notion of the Primordial Nature of God in Whitehead's process theology that most clearly
articulates the reality of the Logos, or divine creative Word, represented by Amida
in Shin Buddhism and Christ in Christianity.

3. THE CONSEQUENT NATURE OF GOD AND AMIDA
BUDDHA AS THE STOREHOUSE CONSCIOUSNESS

Although Cobb analyzes parallels between the Primordial Nature of God and the
Primal Vow of Amida Buddha to save all sentient beings through the working of
compassionate Other-power, he does not find any parallels between the Consequent Nature of God and Amida. Cobb argues that whereas the value-qualities
realized by momentary events arising and perishing in the world of creative
process function to influence and enrich the Consequent Nature of God, he sees
no sense among Buddhists that dharmas contribute anything to Amida: "There
is, in other words, nothing [in Shin Buddhism] comparable to what Whitehead
calls the Consequent Nature of God."[21]

19. Ibid., 52.
20. Unno, *River of Fire/River of Water*, 29.
21. Cobb, *Beyond Dialogue*, 131.

However, the very significant contribution of John Shunji Yokota, a scholar of both Shin Buddhism and process theology, is to have demonstrated the profound relation between the Consequent Nature of God and Amida Buddha. More specifically, Yokota argues for a parallel between the Consequent Nature of God, as the repository functioning to save all perishing events, and the nature of Dharmâkara Bodhisattva/Amida Buddha, as the "Storehouse Consciousness." Yokota rightly asserts: "The tradition [of process theology] is unanimous in its understanding of God as this final and unifying repository of all events. God is the keeper of the past."[22] In Whitehead's process theology, when an event perishes it then becomes a cause influencing all future events, thereby acquiring what he terms an "objective immortality." Yet with the passing of time, the causal influence of each passing event in its objective immortality would become dimmer and dimmer, gradually fading away into oblivion, if not for the functioning of the Consequent Nature of God. The values realized by all events do not fade away with the passage of time because they are retained, stored, and saved everlastingly in their full intensity and vividness as imperishable data in the Consequent Nature of God as the collective repository of the past.

Explicating the relevance of the Consequent Nature of God in process theology to Amida Buddha in Shin Buddhism, Yokota states:

> As the [Buddhist] tradition develops, one encounters the notion of *alayavijnana* or the storehouse consciousness that is comparable to the collective unconscious. It is the storehouse of all karma. . . . It is interesting to note that the Shin Buddhist scholar Soga Ryôjin equated Amida with this storehouse consciousness.[23]

Yokota here makes reference to the insights of the Shin Buddhist scholar Soga Ryôjin (1875–1971), who endeavored to locate Pure Land Buddhism within the mainstream of the Mahâyâna Buddhist tradition by showing how Dharmâkara Bodhisattva/Amida Buddha is the personification of the Storehouse Consciousness, the repository of all dharmas or karmic events.[24] Because of his compassionate Primal Vow, which aims to save all sentient beings, Dharmâkara Bodhisattva was to become Amida Buddha presiding over the Pure Land of Peace and Bliss. In his analysis of the name Dharmâkara, Soga clarifies how the meaning of the Sanskrit word *âkara* is "storage," so that Dharmâkara is the "Dharma storehouse." According to Soga, therefore, "Dharmâkara Bodhisattva of Pure Land doctrine is synonymous with the Storehouse Consciousness, the *âlayavijnâna* of traditional Mahâyâna Buddhism."[25] Furthermore, Soga emphasizes not only that Dharmâkara/Amida is the personification of the Storehouse Consciousness, but that the Storehouse Consciousness is itself the "Buddha Nature."[26]

---

22. Yokota, "Understanding Amida Buddha and the Pure Land: A Process Approach," 91.
23. Ibid., 95.
24. Soga Ryojin, "Dharmakaya Bodhisattva," 221–31.
25. Ibid., 228, 223.
26. Ibid., 224–25.

In my book about the microcosm-macrocosm conception of reality as a dynamic network of interrelatedness, interdependence, and interpenetration, formulated both in Whiteheadian process metaphysics and Hua-yen (Kegon) Buddhism, I myself have developed parallels between Whitehead's Consequent Nature of God and both the Collective Unconscious of Jungian depth psychology and the Storehouse Consciousness of Buddhism.[27] However, Yokota specifically clarifies, from the perspective of Shin Buddhism, how the Consequent Nature of God in process theology relates to Dharmâkara Bodhisattva and his fully realized state as Amida Buddha in his function as the Storehouse Consciousness. Yokota states:

> As the discussion of objective immortality noted, it is in the incorporation into God of the entirety of an occasion in all its vividness and completeness that the evil of perpetual perishing is resolved. Amida too is seen as taking in the entire person in that the karma of that person is taken on by Amida in its entirety.[28]

Yokota's point is that just as for Whitehead's process theology all events in their objective immortality functioning as causes that condition all future events would gradually fade away if not for being fully retained, stored, and saved in the Consequent Nature of God, the karmic influence of all dharmas on future events would also gradually fade away into insignificance if it were not for the working of Dharmâkara Bodhisattva/Amida Buddha, who as the personification of the Storehouse Consciousness functions as the collective repository of the past, which saves all dharmas in their full vividness and intensity.

There is yet a further dimension to the parallel. In Shin Buddhism, persons are saved through the compassionate Other-power of Amida Buddha upon rebirth in the Pure Land. Likewise, in process theology all perishing events are "saved" as they enter into the everlasting divine life of the Consequent Nature of God, explicitly identified by Whitehead as the kingdom of heaven (PR 346). At the conclusion of his final chapter of *Process and Reality*, entitled "God and the World," Whitehead propounds: "Thus the consequent nature of God is composed of a multiplicity of elements with individual self-realization. . . . This is God in his function of the *kingdom of heaven*" (PR 350; italics added). He continues:

> The kingdom of heaven is with us today. The action of [this] phase is the love of God for the world. . . . What is done in the world is transformed into a reality in heaven and the reality in heaven passes back into the world. . . . [T]he love in the world passes into the love in heaven and floods back again into the world. (PR 351)

Here we find yet another convergence between Shin Buddhism and process theology: namely, the idea of salvation through rebirth in Amida's heavenly paradise

27. Odin, *Process Metaphysics and Hua-Yen Buddhism*, 159–71.
28. Yokota, "Understanding Amida Buddha and the Pure Land: A Process Approach," 95.

as the Pure Land of Peace and Bliss, and Whitehead's soteriological notion whereby events are saved by passing into the everlasting life of the Consequent Nature of God as the kingdom of heaven.

Although Taitetsu Unno does not discuss either Whitehead's process theology or the idea of Amida Buddha as the Storehouse Consciousness, he does clarify the deep spiritual meaning of this consequent function of the divine nature from the perspective of the Japanese Buddhist poetics of impermanence. Unno explains how the Buddhist teaching of "impermanence" was depicted through the image of fleeting dewdrops in Japanese poetry of the Heian Period (794–1185). This Heian poetics of impermanence came to be known as *mono no aware,* the "tragic beauty" of perishing events in the flux of becoming. Unno goes on to say: "In this early period the notion of impermanence had a negative tone, carrying a tone of sadness, regret, pathos. But with the passing of time it took on a more positive tone, an encouragement to discover an enduring, unchanging reality beyond the phenomenal world."[29] Unno then illustrates this with a poem by the priest-poet Ryokan (1756–1831), a Zen monk filled with the spirit of the Pure Land who wrote poems on Amida:

> If not for Amida's inconceivable vow
> What then would remain to me
> As a keepsake of this world?[30]

Ryokan encouraged people to follow the path of *nembutsu* to find salvation from the suffering of impermanence, where all transitory events disappear like falling dewdrops, by taking refuge in the everlasting Pure Land of Amida—the Buddha of infinite Light and Life:

> Return to Amida
> Return to Amida
> So even dewdrops fall.

Unno goes on to interpret the above poems from the standpoint of Shin Buddhism as follows: "Everything in our evanescent world constantly reminds us not to rely on passing, unreliable things, but to entrust ourselves to that which is timeless—Immeasurable Light and Life that is Amida."[31]

The closest Western parallel to the Buddhist teaching of "impermanence" and the Japanese poetic ideal of *mono no aware,* or the tragic beauty of impermanence, is to be found in Whitehead's process theology. At the conclusion of his chapter in *Adventures of Ideas* entitled "Peace," Whitehead holds that due to the immanence of God, which provides divine aims to be actualized by events, each occasion realizes some degree of beauty, or aesthetic value-quality. Yet the beauty realized by events is always a "tragic Beauty" (AI 296), in that the aesthetic value-quality of each occasion perishes immediately upon becoming. For Whitehead,

29. Unno, *River of Fire/River of Water,* 164.
30. Ibid.
31. Ibid.

the problem of tragic beauty, arising from the ultimate evil of the perpetual per-ishing of events in the ever-changing flux of becoming, is thus to be resolved through the concept of deity formulated in his process theism, according to which all perishing events are retained, stored, and saved everlastingly in all their vividness and intensity in the Consequent Nature of God. Likewise, the Japan-ese poetic ideal of the tragic beauty of transitory dharmas in the ceaseless imper-manence of universal flux is overcome in the Shin Buddhist tradition through salvation by rebirth into the heavenly paradise of the Pure Land of Amida Bud-dha as the Storehouse Consciousness that saves all dharmas forevermore.

It is indeed remarkable that both Whitehead and Japanese Buddhism have converged upon an organismic process model of actuality as a temporal stream of arising and perishing events, upon a religio-aesthetic vision of Tragic Beauty, whereby suffering, pain, and tragedy are intrinsic to actuality due to the loss of beauty attaching to each arising and perishing aesthetic event in the ceaseless flux of impermanence, and upon a vision in which the evil of perpetual perishing is itself ultimately overcome by the grace of deity as the divine memory.

4. COMPASSION IN SHIN BUDDHISM AND CARE IN PROCESS THEOLOGY

One of the most significant points of contact between the frameworks of White-headian process theology and Shin Buddhism is that both envision the divine nature of God/Amida as a caring or compassionate deity. For Shin Buddhism, the nature of Amida Buddha is that of unconditional "compassion" (*jihi*) work-ing through the call of Amida's *tariki* or "Other-power" as expressed by the "Pri-mal Vow," with its aim, or compassionate intent, to save all sentient beings. Describing the divine nature of Amida Buddha's salvific Other-power as bound-less compassion, Taitetsu Unno asserts: "The working of the Primal Vow, the compassion of the Buddha of Immeasurable Light and Life, is called Other Power."[32] Yokota explains both the compassionate nature of Amida Buddha's Pri-mal Vow, to save all sentient beings through the grace of Other-power, as a call to compassion as well as the centrality of compassionate moral conduct based on a wisdom seeing the emptiness/openness of reality as interdependence:

> The whole point of the Buddhist analysis of reality with its emphasis on impermanence, becoming, openness/emptiness, and dependent arising is that it tells us that reality is like this so that we can act accordingly. . . . [I]n short, we should act compassionately. We act compassionately because a world of openness and dependent arising is a compassionate world. . . . If compassion is the primordial character of existence, then a personal center to existence is undeniable. Compassionate intent (the primal vow) is pres-ent and undeniable as well.[33]

32. Ibid., 36.
33. Yokota, "A Call to Compassion" (2000), 211.

Like the Shin Buddhist tradition, Whitehead's organic process metaphysics articulates a doctrine of concern, care, or compassion based on a metaphysics of interconnected, dependently arisen events that emerge out of a relational web of causal interconnections in the dynamic, creative, undivided aesthetic continuum of nature. Although Whitehead does not use the language of *emptiness*, he does formulate the most comprehensive Western theory of interrelated events arising through *prehensions,* or sympathetic feelings of relations to all other events, which at once calls to mind the Buddhist doctrine of *pratitya-samutpâda*: dependent co-origination, interconnectedness, or relational existence. For Unno, this awareness of reality as a "vast network of interdependence" is itself the core of Shin Buddhism.[34] Emphasizing this point, Unno states: "Interdependence is an elemental truth. When one awakens to this fact, compassion that sustains us strikes us with full force, and we are made to respond to the world with the same compassion."[35]

Whitehead's principle of "universal relativity" functions as a metaphysical category expressing the interrelatedness, interdependence, and interpenetration of all events. The principle of relativity states that "every item in the universe is involved in each concrescence," that "every item of the universe including all the other actual entities are constituents in the constitution of any one actual entity" (PR 22, 148). Indeed, Whitehead's principle of relativity is reminiscent of the Buddhist doctrine of *sûnyatâ*, which is generally translated as "emptiness" but has been alternatively translated as "relativity" and "universal relativity" by the Soviet Buddhologist Stcherbatsky.[36]

In Whitehead's organismic process metaphysics, the Buddhist theme concerning the "indivisibility of emptiness and compassion" is articulated in terms of what Whitehead calls the "concern" structure of causal process and universal relativity, wherein each act of prehension, or "feeling of feeling," is itself understood as an act of sympathetic concernedness. In Whitehead's technical vocabulary, each dependently co-arising occasion or event is a unified *subject* arising through prehension, understood as concern for all multiple *objects* of the past: "The occasion as subject has a 'concern' for the object. And the 'concern' at once places the object as a component in the experience of the subject with an affective tone drawn from this object and directed towards it" (AI 176). Whitehead further states: "It must be directly understood that no prehension . . . can be divested of its affective tone, that is to say, of its character of a 'concern.' . . . Concernedness is of the essence of perception" (AI 180). This concern structure of causal process, whereby events arise through their concern for all prior events, is further clarified by his notion of "sympathy," or feeling of feeling, whereby each occasion arises through sympathetic feelings of its relationships to all prior events (PR 162). Hence, for Whitehead, "concern" is a functional equivalent to compassion (deriving from the Latin verbal root *compassio* meaning "to feel with"),

---

34. Unno, *River of Fire/River of Water*, 141.
35. Ibid., 142.
36. F. Th. Stcherbatsky, *The Conception of Buddhist Nirvana*, 42.

understood as sympathy or feeling of feeling. Like Buddhist compassion, White-head's concernedness involves sympathy with all phenomena arising out of the dynamic network of interrelationships.

It can now be further clarified how the dipolar God of Whitehead's process theology relates to the image of Amida Buddha. In Whitehead's process theology, God is not the omnipotent creator of the universe, just as in Shin Buddhism, Amida Buddha is not understood as a divine creator, since all dharma events naturally emerge from the dynamic web of interrelationships through the causal process of dependent co-arising. According to Whitehead's dipolar theism, God's Primordial Nature functions as a "lure for feeling" (PR 344). God is not an authoritarian deity, who rules by forceful coercion, but a caring deity, who lures events to achieve maximum depth of aesthetic value, beauty, harmony, and peace through gentle persuasion. Whitehead rejects the images of God as an unmoved mover, an imperial ruler, or a ruthless moralist, and instead envisions a patient, tender, and caring God who lures events to realize divine aims. He writes that in contrast to these other images, the origins of Christianity in Jesus suggest an image of deity that "dwells upon the tender elements in the world, which slowly and in quietness operate by love" (PR 343). Describing the divine primordial care operating in terms of the image of *tenderness*, he writes that God's "tenderness is directed towards each actual occasion, as it arises" (PR 105). Again, in his description of the Primordial Nature of God in its function as a lure toward value, Whitehead asserts that God is "the poet of the world, with tender patience leading it by his vision of truth, beauty, and goodness" (PR 346).

In its Consequent Nature, the dipolar God is a caring deity who saves all beauty achieved by creative events as everlasting value-qualities in the divine memory. Describing the cosmological function of God's Consequent Nature, Whitehead thus writes: "The image . . . under which this operative growth of God's nature is best conceived, is that of a *tender care* that nothing be lost" (PR 346; emphasis added).

The parallels with Shin Buddhism are striking. Just as the care of God's Primordial Nature lures all events to actualize the divine aims for them to realize harmony, beauty, and value, the Primal Vow of Amida's compassionate Other-power grace calls out to all sentient beings to achieve enlightenment, nirvana, and rebirth into the Pure Land. And the Consequent Nature of God as the kingdom of heaven is a caring deity who operates like the compassionate nature of Dharmâkara/Amida as the Storehouse Consciousness, which functions to save all sentient beings through rebirth in his heavenly paradise as the Pure Land of Peace and Bliss. Hence, both Whiteheadian process theology and Shin Buddhism envision the divine nature of God/Amida through the image of *care* or *compassion*, just as they view the metaphysical character of ultimate reality itself as caring or compassionate, due to the *concern* structure of existence itself as composed of dependently co-arisen events or dharmas emerging from their sympathy for past events.

5. DIVINE 'SUFFERING' IN PROCESS THEOLOGY
AND SHIN BUDDHISM

In the classical tradition of Christian theology, God is an unchanging absolute, characterized by attributes of transcendence, immutability, and impassibility, completely unaffected by events in process. By contrast, the Consequent Nature of God in Whitehead's process theology is a caring God who feels the feelings of all becoming and perishing events. God is thus forever evolving with the world-process as the creative advance into novelty. Above it was shown how Whitehead's dipolar God is to be conceived through the image of "care," just as the structure of ultimate reality itself is to be described as the "concern" structure of causal feelings. In opposition to the impassibility ascribed to deity by traditional Christian theology, Whitehead clarifies how the Consequent Nature of God is a caring deity who feels both the suffering and joy of all becoming and perishing events. Whitehead therefore asserts: "God is the great companion—the *fellow sufferer* who understands" (PR 351; emphasis added).

Thus far, the interfaith dialogue between Whiteheadian process theology and Shin Buddhism has not yet addressed the importance of this notion of "divine suffering" in both traditions. However, Professor Takeda Ryusei of Ryukoku University, an eminent Japanese scholar of both Jôdo Shinshû and Whiteheadian process theology, has clearly explained the Shin Buddhist notion of *duhka* (suffering) in an article entitled "Pure Land Buddhist View of Duhka" (1985). In this essay, Takeda explicates what he calls "the bodhisattva's compassionate practice of vicarious duhka" in Shin Buddhism.

> This dynamism of the bodhisattva's ceaseless 'de-substantializing' [self-emptying] is embodied as the universal creativity of Dharmakara Bod-hisattva's Primal Vow, whose fulfillment is Amida Buddha's untiring dynamism of saving all sentient beings. The uniqueness of Amida's compassion . . . is the ultimate form of bodhisattva's vicarious duhka.[37]

Like Whitehead's God of care who acts as a "fellow sufferer" who understands, Dharmâkara Bodhisattva/Amida Buddha is a compassionate deity who saves all sentient beings by feeling their suffering as its own through vicarious *duhka*. Although he does not explicitly refer to Whitehead in this essay, Takeda nevertheless shows the unmistakable influence of process theology by his use of Whitehead's distinctive technical term "ingression" when discussing the influx or incarnation of divine grace as a gift of faith from the Primal Vow of Amida Buddha's compassionate Other-power, thereby implying a parallel between the ingression, descent, or incarnation of grace from the divine immanence of the Primordial Nature of God. Takeda writes: "For Shinran, buddha-nature is faith.

---

37. Takeda, "Pure Land Buddhist View of Duhka," 15.

Faith is given by Amida to each being, and through this gift of faith the buddha-nature *ingresses* itself into each being."[38] Again, he states:

> Apart from the bodhisattva's actualization as *ingressing* his will into the actual existence of each being, the 'de-substantializing' [self-emptying] reality turns out to be so abstract that any sort of reference to it falls into delusive attachment to that reality itself, which is none other than its dogmatic sub-stantialization.[39]

6. PEACE IN SHIN BUDDHISM AND PROCESS THEOLOGY

Imamura Yemyo (1867–1932), the Bishop of the first Buddhist temple in America (the Honpa Hongwanji Mission of Hawaii) and one of the earliest missionaries to transmit Shin Buddhism to America, proclaimed a Gospel of Peace grounded in the Primal Vow of Amida to bestow the gifts of peace, happiness, and salvation to all beings. In his essay "Democracy According to the Buddhist Standpoint," he wrote:

> "Peace! Peace!" is the universal cry; for this is the only condition in which we can realize our ideals of truth, goodness, and beauty. But we cannot have a permanent peace unless we have a thorough understanding as to the true signification of peace.[40]

Imamura concludes: "We cannot stop short of propagating the *gospel of true peace* based upon the Will-to-Save [Primal Vow] of the Buddha."[41]

The process theology of Whitehead similarly holds to a vision of God as having a Primordial Nature that out of concern aims to lure all events toward realization of peace, happiness, and salvation. For Whitehead, Peace is the ultimate spiritual value which comes as a gift of God's divine grace. The God of process theology is a poet of the world, luring it toward a vision of beauty, goodness, and truth, along with their unity in the supreme Harmony of Peace. For Whitehead, as for Shin Buddhism, the realization of Peace as cosmic Harmony is an ultimate goal of civilization as well as an expanded transpersonal state of consciousness beyond the ego-self, analogous to resolution of suffering through overcoming attachment to an ego-self in the Peace of *nirvana*. Hence, in this final section, I will clarify how both Whiteheadian process theology and Shin Buddhism culminate in a Gospel of Peace, including both the social ideal of Peace as the

38. Ibid., 21.
39. Ibid., 15.
40. Tomoe, *Yemyo Imamura: Pioneer American Buddhist*, 87.
41. Ibid., 108.

goal of civilization and the soteriological goal of an expanded consciousness transcending the ego-self in a cosmic Harmony of Harmonies.

The imaginative picture of Amida Buddha depicted in the three great mandala images representing the three Pure Land scriptures—as magnificently reproduced in *The Three Pure Land Sutras* by Inagaki Hisao—illustrate the serene countenance of Amida Buddha in his Pure Land of Peace and Bliss. This same tranquil and quiescent visage of Amida Buddha's sublimely calm expression is shown through such great religious art as the famous Daibutsu, or Great Buddha, located in Kamakura. Throughout the Pure Land scriptures, along with the writings of Hônen, Shinran, and other Japanese masters of Shin Buddhism, it is constantly repeated that the Pure Land of Amida Buddha is the realm of Peace, as imparted by a variety of technical Japanese terms in the lexicon of Jôdo Shinshû, including *annyo* (Land of Peace), *annyo jodo* (Pure Land of Peace), *annyo josetsu* (Pure Land of Peace), *annyo kai* (Land of Peace), *anraku bukkoku* (Buddha Country of Peace and Bliss), *anraku butsudo* (Buddha Land of Peace and Bliss), *anraku jodo* (Pure Land of Peace and Bliss), *anraku koku* (Land of Peace and Bliss), *anraku kokudo* (Land of Peace and Bliss), and *anraku sekai* (World of Peace and Bliss)—to give just a few representative examples.[42]

As James Frederiks has noted, for Shinran, Rennyo, and the whole Jôdo Shinshû tradition, "the true sign of saving faith came to be 'peace of mind' (*anjin*)."[43] Shinran's notion of *anjin*, or "peace of mind," is itself the criterion of true *shinjin* or faith—the state of openness and receptivity to the transformative grace of Amida Buddha's compassionate Other-power. In the writings of Shinran, accordingly, the faith-consciousness of *shinjin* is called the "peace-bestowing pure mind."[44]

In *Kyôgyôshinshô* and other writings from his Collected Works, Shinran often quotes from the Pure Land scriptures about the Buddha's teachings on Peace. In *The Sutra of the Tathagata of Immeasurable Life*, Amida Buddha declares: "I will benefit the world, bringing peace and happiness." Again, "Such people as these, hearing the Buddha's Name, will be full of peace and obtain the supreme benefit."[45] For Shinran, these scriptural passages declare Amida Buddha's Primal Vows to bestow infinite Peace on all who call out Buddha's Name, while at the same time guaranteeing the effectiveness of reciting the Buddha's Name through the *nembutsu* for rebirth into the Pure Land of Peace and Bliss. For Shinran, "practicing the saying of the Name alone" leads one to "birth in the Pure Land of peace."[46] Moreover, Shinran underscores how rebirth into the "Pure Land of Peace" (*annyo jodo*) through recitation of *nembutsu* itself sponta-

---

42. Inagaki, *A Glossary of Shin Buddhist Terms*, 3.
43. Frederiks, "Jodo Shinshu's Mission to History: A Christian Challenge to Shin Buddhist Social Ethics," 56.
44. Shinran, *The Collected Works of Shinran*, Vol. I: 171.
45. Ibid., 15, 16.
46. Ibid., 113.

neously, effortlessly, and naturally springs forth as the expression of *shinjin,* faith. It is therefore asserted, "Swift entrance into the city of tranquillity . . . is necessarily brought about by *shinjin.*" Shinran remarks: "We see, therefore, that the realization described above is all the great benefit we receive in the Pure Land of peace, the inconceivable, perfect virtue of the Buddha's [Primal] Vow."[47]

The Primal Vow of Dharmâkara Bodhisattva/Amida Buddha, which aims to bestow Peace on all who recite his Name, is cited by Shinran in such passages as follows: "When I attain Buddhahood, the sentient beings throughout the countless, immeasurable, inconceivable, numberless worlds throughout the ten quarters who receive the Buddha's majestic light and are touched and illuminated by it shall attain peace."[48] For Shinran, the realization of the pure mind of "enlightenment" is characterized by the overcoming of "suffering" and the experience of divine Peace as the "gift" of the saving grace of Amida's compassionate Other-power received in the openness and receptivity of *shinjin,* faith. Shinran cites *The Sutra of Immeasurable Life*: "The peace-bestowing pure mind (is so termed) because (the bodhisattvas) eliminate all sentient beings' pain." Again, "[T]hey follow the gate of compassion. They eliminate all sentient beings' pain and become free of thoughts that do not bring peace." Shinran remarks, "The undefiled pure mind is in accord with the gate to enlightenment. Also: "Enlightenment is the realm of purity that brings peace to all sentient beings."[49] In his commentary on these scriptural passages, Shinran further emphasizes that Amida Buddha's Primal Vows arise from the heart of "compassion" and promise to eliminate the problem of suffering due to impermanence by bestowing Peace on all who recite his Name in the state of faith: "[Concerning compassion (*jihad*)]: 'To eliminate pain is termed *ji*; to give happiness is termed *hi*. Though *ji* one eliminates the pain of all sentient beings, through *hi* one becomes free of thoughts that do not bring them peace." The Pure Land is continually referred to as "the land of peace."[50] Shinran continues: "Thus we clearly know from the Tathagata's true teaching and the commentaries of the masters that the Pure Land of peace is the true fulfilled land."[51]

One of the most neglected categories in Whitehead's thought is his notion of transpersonal Peace. Yet his idea of transpersonal Peace is not only the crown of his process cosmology and theology; it is also the nearest parallel to the ultimate Buddhist goal of *nirvana,* or Peace. The notion of Peace is therefore a central point of intersection between Whiteheadian process theology and the Shin Buddhist idea of rebirth in Amida's Pure Land of Peace and Bliss, as well as its idea of the Peace of *nirvana* as a gift of the divine grace of Amida Buddha.

47. Ibid., 73, 62.
48. Ibid., 117.
49. Ibid., 169, 168.
50. Ibid., 169, 194.
51. Ibid., 202.

It might be said that both Amida Buddha in Shin Buddhism and the dipolar God of Whitehead's process theology represent the Peace-bestowing Buddha/Christ whereby there comes to be the *ingression*, influx, or descent of transpersonal Peace, as the divine aim toward cosmic Harmony in each dharma event through the grace or persuasive agency of divine immanence as the Primordial Nature of God, the Primal Vow of Amida. For Whitehead, Christian theology explains Christ as a revelation of God's persuasive agency in the world as a lure toward the divine aims of peace, love, and sympathy: "The essence of Christianity is to appeal to the life of Christ as a revelation of the nature of God and the world" (AI 167). Whitehead then describes the revelation of the life, person, and teachings of Jesus as occurring through "his message of peace, love, and sympathy" (AI 167). In *Process Theology*, coauthors Cobb and Griffin write, "Christian Peace is an expansion of care for self to care for others."[52] This statement underscores how in process theology there is a deep relation between God's function as bestowing Peace and the divine nature as care, concern, compassion, love, and sympathy.

Whitehead's *Adventures of Ideas* concludes with a remarkable chapter entitled "Peace." According to Whitehead, transpersonal Peace is not only the ultimate aim of civilization; it is also an expanded state of consciousness wherein the self is transcended in a cosmic Harmony. Suffering, pain, and tragedy are intrinsic to the dynamic evolutionary temporal process of creative advance into novelty: "Decay, Transition, Loss, Displacement belong to the essence of Creative Advance" (AI 286). And just as for Buddhism, deliverance from the "suffering" of impermanence is realized only in the Peace of *nirvana,* so for Whitehead, salvation from the tragedy, pain, and suffering of existence, as the perpetual perishing of momentary events, comes only with the immediate experience of transpersonal Peace, the Harmony of Harmonies: "The Adventure of the Universe starts with the dream and reaps tragic Beauty. This is the secret of the union of Zest with Peace: That the suffering attains its end in a Harmony of Harmonies. The immediate experience of this Final Fact . . . is the sense of Peace" (AI 286).

Whitehead further describes his concept of Peace in a manner consonant with Buddhism when he writes: "The inner feeling belonging to this grasp of the service of tragedy is Peace—the purification of the emotions. . . . Peace is the understanding of tragedy" (AI 286). The salvific transpersonal dimension of Peace is then indicated in a manner reminiscent of Buddhist *anâtman*, or no-self: "Peace is . . . the width where the 'self' has been lost, and interest has been transferred to coordinations wider than personality. . . . Peace carries with it a surpassing of personality" (AI 285). The parallel is further shown by Whitehead's assertion that Peace is "a broadening of feeling due to the emergence of some deep metaphysical insight" (AI 285). Whitehead even identifies the immediate experience of transpersonal Peace with the "attainment of truth" (AI 292) and with "extreme ecstasy" (AI 289).

---

52. Cobb and Griffin, *Process Theology: An Introductory Exposition*, 140.

In Cobb and Griffin's *Process Theology*, it is written: "To whatever extent our lives become aligned to God's ever-changing aims for us, we can have 'that Peace, which is the harmony of the soul's activities with ideal aims that lie beyond any personal satisfaction.'"[53] Clarifying that "it is the immanence of deity as a whole, with its Primordial and Consequent Natures, its creative and responsive love, which is the source of Peace,"[54] they quote this remarkable passage from Whitehead:

> It is the immanence of the Great Fact including this initial Eros and this final Beauty which constitutes the zest of self-forgetful transcendence belonging to Civilization at its height. . . . The immediate experience of this Final Fact is the sense of Peace. (AI 381)

Through the caring persuasive agency of God's Primordial Nature as the divine lure, there is implanted in each dependently co-arising event an initial aim toward realizing the harmonic value-qualities of beauty, art, adventure, and truth, as well as their unity in the supreme aim of Peace, the cosmic Harmony of Harmonies. Cobb and Griffin continue:

> The presence of God in us is divine grace. . . . It gives rise to adventure, and to art. To it we owe the beauty we experience. . . . It works at all times in all people. The supreme gift is Peace, which is an alignment of ourselves with God's grace.[55]

As again emphasized here, this aim toward Peace in each occasion derived from God's Primordial Nature as the divine lure is the functioning of grace, and the realization of Peace in each occasion as a result of this grace is itself the gift of God through Christ as the divine Logos, which incarnates into each occasion. Therefore, Cobb and Griffin conclude: "Peace is the gift of Christ."[56]

Whitehead himself writes: "The experience of Peace is largely beyond the control of purpose. It comes as a *gift*" (AI 285; italics added). Again, "Peace carries with it a surpassing of personality. . . . It is primarily a *trust* in the efficacy of Beauty. . . . The trust in the self-justification of Beauty introduces *faith,* where reason fails to reveal the details" (AI 285; italics added). For Whitehead, transpersonal Peace comes as a gift of grace ingressing as the divine immanence of God received through entrustment, or faith in the divine efficacy of God's ideal aims for each occasion.

Thus, we arrive at a most remarkable convergence upon the idea of salvation from the suffering and tragic beauty of impermanent dharma events through a bestowal of transpersonal Peace by God/Amida in the framework of Whitehead's

53. Ibid., 124.
54. Ibid., 125.
55. Ibid., 126.
56. Ibid., 127.

process theology and that of Shin Buddhism. For just as in Whitehead's process theology the realization of Peace is not attained by self-effort, but is only received as a "gift" of divine grace through faith by means of the divine immanence of God, so in Shin Buddhism based on the teachings of Shinran Shonin, one attains salvation, enlightenment, *nirvana,* and rebirth in the heavenly paradise of the Pure Land of Peace and Bliss, not through the efforts of self-power" (*jiriki*), but only as a gift (*ekô*) of the transformative grace of Amida Buddha's compassionate "Other-power" (*tariki*), realized in tranquil inwardness of *shinjin,* faith.

It is in such a manner, then, that we have arrived at this vision of Amida in Shin Buddhism, and the dipolar God in Whitehead's process theology, as the caring and compassionate Peace-bestowing Buddha/Christ that forever guides and saves all events co-arising from the dynamic network of interrelationships in the ceaseless flux of becoming.

Chapter 4

Where beyond Dialogue?

Reconsiderations of
a Buddhist Pluralist

John Shunji Yokota

INTRODUCTORY REMARKS

The context of the Buddhist-Christian dialogue is the foundation for a critical self-understanding of Buddhism's doctrines and its way of life. Moreover, to dialogue with other religious as well as nonreligious ways of knowing and thinking about our world is imperative for a fuller and truer vision of reality. Only in this context of dialogue with traditions of disparate views of our world can there be real understanding of this world we live in. Nevertheless, while the gains, personally, from such an opening up to these other traditions have been central to the growth in my thinking and appreciation of my Shin Buddhist tradition, an inertia has set in that has caused me to question whether I can go any further.

This personal journey to and through dialogue has fortunately taken me far from a formerly unrecognized, parochial, and absolutistic acceptance of my Shin Buddhist tradition. Admittedly, how far it has taken me is a question that needs to be constantly pondered. This transformation has come about less by design than by fortunate or malicious happenstance—I simply do not know which. This ambivalent feeling toward the turn of events that has determined my personal and academic preoccupations derives from the fact, again, that I find myself at an impasse in personally developing my understanding and articulation of my tradition as well as seeming to see the same impasse in others joined in interreligious dialogue. On a personal note, I simply keep repeating myself. Have I gone too far, too quickly, and perhaps too superficially to proclaim "Amida as the Christ"? Do I need to go deeper into the reality of Christianity to see more distinctly a new and fuller reality of Buddhism? Do I need to go deeper into the reality of Buddhism to see more distinctly a new and fuller reality of Buddhism? Obviously, in both cases, the answer is a constant yes. There is no end to this task. Where, indeed, are we headed?

The basic religious assumption I hold is reflected, surprisingly or perhaps not, in my one purely Buddhist studies publication, which summarized my specific concentration in Buddhist studies—the Mahayana Buddhist doctrine of the two-truths (or preferably, twofold reality), with special emphasis on its Chinese Sunyavada development.[1] It reflects a period of study prior to any real knowledge of Christian theology. Again, this understanding of the Buddhist two-truths doctrine, concretely and self-consciously, is the basic intuition that guides my studies in Buddhist studies, Christian theology, and interreligious dialogue. The usual understanding of the two-truths doctrine has a basic similarity to the two-realms doctrine of Christianity. It can and has been used or abused to condone the sociopolitical status quo. The understanding of this twofold reality is that reality is an ever-active coming forth out of itself to embody and reveal itself to us. Reality, if it is indeed reality, must embody itself in the sociohistorical realm and work to transform and enlighten the way things are. There is thus, reality unto itself and reality going forth and actualizing itself in our concrete, everyday lives. The religious ultimate finally is this active, primordially self-actualizing reality. It is reality itself as well as reality for us, reality coming forth to us and for us. The soteriological meaning and intent is explicit.

This is not the orthodox understanding of the doctrine. My active soteriological emphasis may be questioned by more mainline Buddhist studies experts. Indeed, the only major Buddhist studies scholar who explicitly understood the two-truths doctrine in such a manner was Yoshifumi Ueda, who directly influenced my understanding. His argument came from the simple paradox of the usual definition of the two truths declared to be ultimate truth and provisional (or worldly) truth, with the explicit understanding that the latter was ultimately false. It made no sense, he said, to talk of "two truths" when one of them was false. The basis of his understanding was Yogacara-vijnaptimatra ("School of yogic practice toward consciousness-only"), not Madhyamika, and reflected the transforming, soteriological aspect of the Yogacara's distinctive doctrine of the three natures of existence and its emphasis on compassion. Moreover, Ueda was a Shin Buddhist scholar as well, and his Buddhist thought can be described as Mahayanized Shin Buddhism or a Shin Buddhist Mahayana. Cobb notes Ueda's claim that

---

1. Yokota, "Rethinking the Doctrine of Satya-dvaya."

Shinran's thought is the culmination of the Mahayana spirit or quest for universality in its emphasis on salvation for all.[2]

The first part of this paper will restate and summarize my earlier work in Buddhist-Christian dialogue, including the road I took in accepting and finally seeing the necessity for Amida as the Christ. This first section also raises a number of questions or problems involved with seeing Amida as the Christ. The second part of this paper will look into certain specific questions centering on the character of the process God and how they can and should be incorporated in the conceptualization of Amida Buddha and Dharma-kaya, the reality body. This discussion of God will lead to a new synthesis of my work in Christian-Buddhist dialogue.

AMIDA AS THE CHRIST:
THE CHALLENGE OF BEYOND DIALOGUE

Cobb's radical challenge of mutual transformation to both his own Protestant Christian tradition and my Shin Buddhist tradition was what prodded me to attempt to fathom the core issues of my own religiosity and the rationale for interreligious dialogue.[3] This was no simple matter. It forced me to see the other in all its otherness as well as similarity. Perhaps more importantly, it forced me to see my own tradition in a new light as a living tradition with a spiritual and traditional core but, nevertheless, always changing, growing, and ideally open to radical self-transformation. To keep their vitality and power to convince, religious traditions must always be so constituted, but this is anything but an easy or simple task.

To open up truly to the other is obviously difficult, even if one is enthusiastic about such an ideal. While in many ways intrigued and stimulated by Cobb's proposals, I found it difficult to actualize them in my own thinking and articulation of my tradition. I could not accept the notion of Jesus as being the central historical actualization of the compassion of the Vow of Amida Buddha. I thereby could not accept Amida as the Christ. Indeed, the fact that belief in the compassion of Amida Buddha needed a foundation in historical actualization was not fully recognized. Nevertheless, the problem of the myth of Dharmakara Bodhisattva/Amida Buddha as the foundation of our tradition had been a source of intellectual discomfort for me for some time. Cobb's explicit declaration of the problem of myth therefore hit an intellectual sore spot. I had dealt with this problem, as had many Christians, in an existentialist manner by collapsing time into the moment of faith. I remember giving Cobb a copy of the translation of an influential essay by the Kyoto School philosopher Keiji Nishitani, "The Problem of Time in Shinran."[4] Cobb's courteous but ultimately dismissive remarks about

2. Cobb, *Beyond Dialogue: Toward a Mutual Transformation of Christianity and Buddhism*, 123.
3. Ibid., 97–143.
4. Nishitani, "The Problem of Time in Shinran."

this classic interpretive exposition of Shinran's faith-centered, existential notion of time by this student of Nishida and Heidegger baffled me at the time.

THE PROBLEM OF HISTORY

The preoccupation with history did not resonate with my religious way of thinking. I had come upon a Christian presumption that did not make sense to my Buddhist mentality. I tell an anecdote to my students in interreligious/cultural studies courses to illustrate the great difference between our traditions. Enthusiastically returning from Japan to the United States to engage in Shin Buddhist ministry and the study of Christian theology, I looked forward to working again in my native language. I was stunned when I discovered I did not understand the meaning or the premises of the lectures and discussion. I believe that this reverse culture shock lasted for a good two years. Our premises are that different. The historical and ethical preoccupation of Christianity was something that seemed to be dangerously superfluous to the real religious agenda that Buddhism and Shin Buddhism tried to implement: salvation in and through enlightenment and compassion and a centering into the present, the eternal now.

THE PROBLEM OF MYTH

Nevertheless, it was the problem of the central authenticating role in our tradition of the myth of Dharmakara Bodhisattva becoming Amida Buddha that made me open to a resolution of the problem of having one's tradition based solely on a myth. It is to this story that we Shin Buddhists look to see the activity of compassion actualized. The power this myth still holds for many devout believers cannot be denied. It has an emotionally persuasive power that I can understand though not finally accept. The problem of myth should be an issue in today's Enlightenment-influenced culture of Japan as well as in the Western cultures to which Shin Buddhism has been introduced. Nevertheless, I have encountered no expression of uneasiness about the myth. The times I have broached the subject, there is a palpable horror on the part of clergy, in both Japanese and American temples, as well as confusion on the part of the laypeople. The laypeople are not aware of the historical-critical problems involved in the Dharmakara/Amida account in the professed statements of Sakyamuni. The problem of myth and inaccurate historical-critical statements is not perceived as a problem because it is not talked about.

For a variety of reasons, perhaps, there is a little discomfort with this central position of myth within our tradition. One rationale for the basis of our belief in the compassionate activity of Amida Buddha may be as good as any other. Belief in the transcendent reality of the vows of Amida Buddha may need no more than the story of Dharmakara/Amida Buddha. In popular postmodern culture, the power of myth has been duly re-recognized. Myth is a very basic and important way by which primordial, religious reality is revealed and through which religious reality is apprehended. It has been and will always be a fundamental way of expressing and revealing one's deepest feelings in poetic, primordial images. I do not simply dismiss this attitude. However, a story is still just a story and I, personally, have never been convinced by the myth. I do not see how the reality of Amida Buddha and Amida Buddha's compassion are authenticated by the story.

ACCEPTING THE PROBLEM OF HISTORY

Historical events that actualize and express the compassionate intent of Amida Buddha, while initially not deemed essential by me to an expression of the authenticity of Amida Buddha's compassion, slowly came to be seen as a needed concrete remedy to the supraworldly, suprahistorical quality of Shin Buddhist reality and this blind spot in Shin Buddhist studies. Upon reflection, I realized that the one undeniable historical act of actualizing compassion in the Buddhist tradition is Sakyamuni Buddha rising from the seat of his own enlightenment to go forth and proclaim the content of this enlightenment experience to others.[5] I took half of the challenge put forward by Cobb. I could not enter the full adventure that Cobb proposed with "Amida as the Christ."

Nevertheless, this hesitant, uncertain participation in the adventure did yield an important and interesting insight into Shinran's thinking on and articulation of Amida's reality. While a truism, a familiar passage of scripture read from a new perspective yields new interpretations and emphases. Shinran does indeed have a clear and pronounced concern about the historical transmission of the teaching and explication of the compassionate activity of Amida Buddha. He places great emphasis on specific articulations of Amida's compassionate reality by a select line of Pure Land "Fathers" from India (Sakyamuni, Nagarjuna, and Vasubandhu), China (T'an Luan, Tao-ch'o, and Shan-tao), and Japan (Genshin and Honen). Excluding Sakyamuni, these are the seven patriarchs of the Shin Buddhist tradition. Admittedly, this follows a favored precedent of authenticating one's new school of Buddhism by claiming a lineage going back to Sakyamuni. In Shinran's *Shoshin Nembutsuge*,[6] *Jodo Wasan*, and *Koso Wasan*,[7] Shinran, in accessible and popular form, cites various declarations detailing the compassion of Amida Buddha by these Pure Land Buddhist masters, including Sakyamuni. It is apparently very important for Shinran to make clear the historical expression of this spiritual truth. While the spiritual, individual experience of the

5. Yokota, "Sakyamuni within the Jodo Shinshu Tradition."

6. "Hymn of True Shinjin and Nembutsu," the ending verse section of the second chapter of Ken Jodo Shinjitsu Kyo Gyo Sho Monrui, in Shonin Shinran, *The Collected Works of Shinran*, vol. 1, 69–74.

7. "Hymns of the Pure Land and Hymns of the Pure Land Masters," Shinran, *The Collected Works of Shinran*, vol. 1, 319–93.

compassion of Amida Buddha is important if not central to the tradition, there is this obvious need for articulating concrete expressions of this truth/reality by those in the tradition. These historical expressions make the compassionate reality and activity of Amida Buddha real. It may be because of their relative accessibility that the above works are used by the later tradition for liturgical purposes, but it is also because they convey a central message—the message that our tradition is conscious of and holds important these historical expressions of the compassion of Amida. Again, there is this historical emphasis in Shinran's thought. It is important for Shinran to express examples or incidents within the tradition in which there is expression and actualization of the reality and efficacy of Amida Buddha's compassionate activity. There is a sense in which the reality of Amida Buddha is concretized and made effectively real through the citation of the historical articulations or actualizations of the Amida story in the tradition.

There are, obviously, many historical-critical problems in the assumptions upon which Shinran cites the historical validity of Amida Buddha given by the above teachers. One of these problems is that Sakyamuni Buddha, again, did not talk about Amida Buddha, nor in all probability did the other Indian masters, Nagarjuna and Vasubandhu. The notion of Amida Buddha is in all probability the outcome of Buddhism's being influenced by a central Asian Zoroastrian form of faith in a figure or divinity symbolized by light. Thus, in many ways, before "Amida as the Christ" there was "Amida as the Buddha." This point will be highlighted again in the final section. Here, the point is that Sakyamuni did not preach the Pure Land Sutras or talk about Amida Buddha and the establishment of the Western Pure Land. It can be said—and has been said by those responding to the critical-historical criticism of the attribution of authorship of the Pure Land Sutras to Sakyamuni Buddha—that if not Sakyamuni Buddha, a Buddha, an enlightened one, did talk of Dharmakara's practice and its fulfillment and thus the compassion of Amida Buddha. While that may be one way to declare the historicity of the Amida myth, it is far from satisfactory.

I instead, as indicated above, looked at the activity of Sakyamuni itself. The message of Sakyamuni Buddha, while impossible to determine with absolute certainty, can be confidently summarized to encompass an analysis of our present spiritual and physical situation and the practical means to transcend their disabling limitations through certain spiritual practices centering primarily on meditational and ethical discipline. In short, while the ultimately soteriological orientation of the discussion is prominent, it is a salvation that is won, as it were, by the individual practitioner's efforts. There is no indication of a compassionate activity working toward the salvation of believers. Rather, a straightforward message of spiritual discipline leading to spiritual emancipation is enunciated. That this enlightenment experience is anything but simple and easy to realize may not be necessary to state but should be emphasized.

Although the following interpretation is admittedly a reinterpretation, I do see the primordial act of the entire Buddhist tradition to be not the enlightenment experience itself but rather the decision to go forth from the seat of enlightenment to teach and influence others toward their own enlightenment. Without this act there is no Buddhist tradition. It is this act, not the enlightenment experience itself nor the specific teachings, that can be looked at as the activity of enlightenment, the compassionate coming forth of the enlightened one. Moreover, it is this act that is the compassion of Amida Buddha, the compassion of the activity of enlightenment, in its most concrete and understandable form. Reflection on my tradition through the catalyst of Cobb's challenge thus had me recognize the inherent importance of the articulation of the reality of compassion and enlightenment in history and the fact that for Shinran himself this articulation was equally important. While the historical presumptions of Shinran were faulty in the case of Sakyamuni, this reinterpretation provides, in my view, a more credible historical narrative pointing to the primordial act in our tradition. This narrative can be seen, therefore, as the historical articulation of the basically compassionate nature of Buddhist reality. Therefore, I did not see the need to incorporate Jesus as the explicit actualization of love/compassion in this world and thus declare Amida as the Christ.

THE ISSUE OF HISTORICAL-CRITICAL CONSCIOUSNESS AND ACCURACY

A point should perhaps be made that has been dormant in my thoughts for some time but concretized itself in the stimuli involved in working on this review and extension of my thinking on the Buddhist-Christian dialogue. While I understand Cobb's claim that Jesus in and through his ministry talked of the loving grace of God, there is still the historical-critical problem of ascertaining the actual message of Jesus. While this issue is clearly beyond my expertise, the findings of New Testament scholarship, especially radical elaborations, do seem to reflect a deep uncertainty about the actual message of Jesus. While the opinions of the Jesus Seminar may be too drastic a negation of the validity of the Gospel accounts, there is, nonetheless, a real question about how much one can know the authentic and accurate message of Jesus. In short, the existence and authenticity of "Q" or the so-called source tradition of Jesus' teachings itself is being questioned. I realize the fluid nature of biblical studies and the swings in opinion on the veracity of the sayings of Jesus. Yet how much is really certain about the teachings of Jesus? In no way do I infer that the unequivocal negation of Sakyamuni's link with the Pure Land sutras and Jesus' link with the Gospel accounts are any way similar. I just want to point out the relative uncertainty of all declarations of a core teaching of Jesus.

In a parallel fashion, the critique of Pauline scholarship by Kristol Stendahl's questioning whether there really was an explicit message of grace enunciated or even implied by Paul may be radical but is nevertheless the opinion of a respected New Testament scholar. Stendahl's point is that the later tradition, principally Augustine and Luther, had much to do with seeing Paul's rather orthodox Jewish statements in a completely different light.

The problem of historical-critical studies and their conclusions and methodology is a problem for us all. Again, it is important to have historical foundations for one's central beliefs. Nevertheless, how far we can be certain we have an undeniable historical foundation is the question constantly to be pondered.

The above in no way denies the importance of the foundation of historical events. Rather, its unquestioned certainty is never fully possible in terms of our formative religious events. Moreover, while I would personally like to say that this difference in attitude toward history between Buddhism and Christianity is a matter of degree and not of kind, it is, unfortuately, a difference in kind. The lack of any historical anchoring of these formative events in our tradition is really not seen as a problem, and that is the problem. There is a "happy" lack of concern for historical foundations in the Shin Buddhist tradition of scholarship, at least in relation to Sakyamuni's relationship with the story of Amida Buddha.

One way to confront this problem of questionable historical foundation is to look at the larger context of one's own tradition and not just the narrow range afforded by it. Here, interpretation of the tradition and its context is unavoidable and should, therefore, be clearly acknowledged. While acknowledging that it is tainted with subjectivity, I will offer one exploration of our larger traditional context. For my tradition, I think it is imperative to look at Shin Buddhism in the context of the wider perspective of "general" Buddhism as well as other Indian and central Asian religious traditions, in terms not only of theology or doctrine but also of concrete historical and archeological data.

In the same way, I believe, it is important to look at Christianity in the context of the religious traditions of the people of the Book. Judaism and the Jewish Bible as well as Islam and the Koranic tradition must be special dialogue partners. I have been profoundly influenced by Abraham Heschel's notion of the "God of Pathos"[8] in trying to understand the Abrahamic tradition's notion of God and have therefore tried to see the compassion or love of God, in a soteriological as well as in a personal sense, as central to the whole tradition of the people of the Book. My knowledge of Islam is too scant for me to provide a parallel illustration in that tradition, though I am sure it exists. The discussion of the perspective of the larger tradition in the case of both Christianity and Buddhism will be addressed again in the last section.

FROM SAKYAMUNI TO JESUS

I had come to see the importance of centering on the activity of Sakyamuni Buddha to provide a historical anchor for the myth of Amida Buddha. From my fellow Buddhists, however, I met with little acknowledgment of the importance of a historical foundation. The existential, faith-moment transcendence of the

8. Heschel, *The Prophets*, vol. 2.

sociohistorical realm is the basic stance of Japanese sectarian Buddhists, be they Pure Land, Zen, or Lotus Sutra believer/practitioners. Perhaps because of the lack of consciousness of the importance of the sociohistorical context in relation to the symbolic meaning of myth, the central importance of Sakyamuni's act of going forth to expound the insights of enlightenment was never really confronted by my fellow Shin Buddhists. When acknowledged, the problem of actualization in history was, as usual, deflated in the individual, personal awakening to the reality of Dharmakara.[9] I finally made the transition to seeing Amida as the Christ without really having any stimuli, positive or negative, from my fellow practitioners of the nembutsu.[10] This lack of response may be one reason why I took the plunge and asserted Amida as the Christ, just to shock my fellow believers.

In fact, why exactly I made the decision to commit myself to Amida as the Christ was unclear in my memory. Rereading my earlier enunciations of Amida as the Christ, I saw that it was not so much that I asserted Amida as the Christ as that elements of the reality of Christ were what I felt were needed to "improve" or to make "more complete" the articulation of the reality of Amida Buddha. In my dialogue with process theologians, their image of Christ with its similarities and differences became vital elements for improving the image of Amida Buddha. This recognition of the need, through dialogue, to augment and develop one's vision of reality was the agenda set forth by Cobb. Thus, in mature or real interreligious dialogue, one sees the need creatively to adopt elements of the dialogue partner's vision and enunciation of reality to complement and develop one's own understanding and elaboration of a personal vision of this saving power. I should acknowledge that it was and still is a personal, inner traditional task of trying to understand and conceptualize Amida Buddha that prompted me to declare Amida as the Christ. While admittedly guided largely by a process theological hermeneutic, my basic image of reality—as ever coming out of itself to reveal itself—is consciously faithful to traditional sources of general Buddhist and Shin Buddhist writings. I have therefore always tended to look for elements in the tradition that supported this soteriologically active vision of reality.

Thus, the primary rationale for announcing Amida as the Christ was and is the desire to think about and thereby refine and, if need be, redefine the conceptuality of Amida Buddha. It is primarily an endeavor internal to Shin Buddhism, not an endeavor of interreligious dialogue. The explicit message or motive behind Cobb's challenge to Shin Buddhists was to think about Amida Buddha and see whether our doctrinal message was coherent. If not, then we must rethink the doctrinal message by listening to the popular theology of common practice and belief and readjust the doctrine to this practice and belief so they will not be mutually negating. This was and is the task of Christian process theology and

9. Unno, "Review of *Toward a Contemporary Understanding of Pure Land Buddhism*," 213.

10. Yokota, "Amida as the Christ: An Exercise Beyond Dialogue"; "Understanding Amida Buddha and the Pure Land: A Process Approach"; "A Call to Compassion: A Response to Cobb and Kaufman."

should obviously be the task of a Shin Buddhist process theology. In short, to announce Amida as the Christ was and is for me primarily the means for a development of a more tenable doctrine of Amida Buddha and the elaborations of a thus redefined Shin Buddhist worldview. The radical nature of a declaration of Amida as the Christ and the incorporation of Jesus of Nazareth into the Shin Buddhist tradition was only passively acknowledged.

What, then, is the full import of declaring Amida as the Christ? It means that in the person and mission of Jesus of Nazareth we find the pivotal incarnation into history of the message and reality of salvation through a saving other power. We Shin Buddhists can, and more importantly should, see in the person Jesus of Nazareth the central historical actualization of this saving other power. In short, for Shin Buddhists, the reality of Amida Buddha is fully actualized in the person Jesus, who through word and deed actualized the power of the Primal Vow of Amida Buddha. The radical move to Amida as the Christ, in many ways glibly made in order to help me rearticulate the reality of Amida Buddha, carries this heavy baggage that must be recognized and willingly borne. In working on a Shin Buddhist social ethics, in rethinking the doctrines of Amida Buddha and the Pure Land, and in developing a Buddhistic awareness of sociohistorical influences on all social (including religious) phenomena, I, in fact, took the fruits of declaring Amida as the Christ without bearing the consequent religious implications of receiving Jesus-who-is-the-Christ into our tradition.

What, then, are the consequences of receiving Jesus, who is the Christ, the incarnate manifestation of the Christian God, into our tradition? On a very superficial level, the Gospel accounts and the Pauline interpretation of the person of the Christ would have to become part of the sastra or commentative tradition in this transformed Shin Buddhism. We Shin Buddhists would include the "writers" of the Gospels and Paul as new Pure Land Patriarchs alongside T'an Luan, Shan-tao, and Honen. Is this a realistic possibility? I do not know, although I know that this will not come about any time soon. Is it desirable? Again, I do not know, but it would seem that this kind of opening up of our traditions will at least create a viable range of religious choices and worldviews that should ideally and hopefully have the effect of curbing the religious sectarian fanaticism that plagues our contemporary world.

These are peripheral issues that nevertheless indicate concrete actualization of the activity of making Amida the Christ. What then is the meaning of including Jesus and seeing Amida as the Christ?

THE IMPLICATIONS OF ACCEPTING
AMIDA AS THE CHRIST

To see and accept Amida Buddha as Jesus of Nazareth—Jesus who is the Christ, the Son of God, the incarnation of the Word, God as a specific human being who expressed through his existence, words, acts, death, and resurrection the saving grace of God, as well as God's stern and radical demand—is to change radically the reality and conceptuality of Amida Buddha. In recognition of this radical change, I half-consciously (why one does things usually becomes clear only in hindsight) embarked on a two-track exercise in thinking about Shin Buddhism and the conceptuality of Amida Buddha. One preoccupation was the development of a Shin Buddhist social ethics closely related to a revised doctrine of Amida Buddha. The other preoccupation was the development of the doctrine of Amida Buddha where process modes of thought soon became central to the expression of the doctrine.[11]

I had two motives for developing a Shin Buddhist social ethics. In the first place, work on the doctrine of the twofold reality made me sensitive to the problem of social ethics. Thus, the motive was and is an inner Buddhist one. It is simply imperative to think about a Buddhist social ethics, since we are all beings in the world. I developed the discussion of social ethics from an inner Buddhist perspective working from a Buddhist worldview. In the second place, however, it was the vision of Jesus as the Christ and the Judeo-Christian God, which grew out of my work in Christian thought, that was the impetus that guided the development of a Buddhist/Shin Buddhist social ethics. Amida as the Christ means that the image of Amida Buddha must have an ethical core or at least a recognition of the moral imperative that the image of Christ includes.

Moreover, if Amida as the Christ is to be fully accepted with the implications of process theology, the merely soteriological emphasis of Amida Buddha must be expanded to include a vision of Amida Buddha with creative, transformative, uncoercive powers as well as the ability to take in the effects of these activities. This means the inclusion of the primordial nature of God as well as the consequent nature of God. The former is a creating and persuasive power that has concern for the whole of the creative process and of all actual existent forms. The latter is the taking in of the whole of existence and reacting to it. The inclusion of this consequent nature of God was readily developed without too much hesitation. It was the primordial nature of God that was and still is problematic. If incorporated, this would be the most disturbingly difficult change in the vision of Amida Buddha. The psychological barrier to transforming this solely saving power that is Amida Buddha to a more cosmic, creative power is a difficult line to cross for this Shin Buddhist. While I have done such work on this, and though it was, I believe, carefully thought out,[12] I still have hesitation about the results. The line crossed by making a solely soteriological figure, who grasps the faithful to bring them into the enlightenment of the western land of bliss never to let them go, into a figure of creative transformative power is a very critical and problematic line to cross. Granted, this creative transformative power is not an absolute power of *creatio ex nihilo*, and yet God as Creator is being asserted. Can

---

11. Yokota, "A Call to Compassion: Process Thought and the Conceptualization of Amida Buddha."
12. Ibid., 94–95.

this description apply to Amida Buddha? The one distinctive difference between the Christian God and Amida Buddha, who are otherwise quite similar, is that our Amida Buddha is not a creator God. Can or should this taboo be broken and the distinction between our two religious ultimates be so blurred? What do we have left of our tradition if this Christianized, ethical-creator vision of Amida Buddha is forthrightly asserted?

THE GOD OF PROCESS THEOLOGY AND AMIDA BUDDHA

The distinction between the primordial and consequent natures of God in process thought and its application to the conceptuality of Amida Buddha expresses both the clear benefit and the difficulty of conceptualizing Amida Buddha through the process conceptuality of God. For the conceptuality of the Christian God, this distinction is a successful way to reconceptualize the active participation of God in the creative process (primordial nature of God) as well as the responsive, being-affected, and growing aspect of this God (the consequent nature of God), which is a valuable and needed way to conceptualize an ideal not found in the classical conceptuality of God but practiced and believed in the living faith of the tradition. It is with the consequent nature of God that the reality of Amida Buddha can also be coherently conceptualized. Amida, being compassion itself, cannot be anything but that which is open to and affected by the events that occur around it. There is no real problem with articulating Amida Buddha with this characteristic of being open to the world around it. The Buddhist reality of dependent origination implies such an openness. For a variety of reasons it is this open quality in God that is revolutionary in the process conceptuality of God. For Buddhists, I believe, there is really no such problem. Rather, for Buddhists, it is the primordial nature of God that poses certain problems.

The consequent nature of God conceptualizes and enunciates certain assertions about God that are the consequence of holding God to be love. In a similar fashion, the conceptuality of the consequent nature of God can help conceptualize and enunciate certain assertions about Amida Buddha's compassionate character. The sometimes stoic and apathetic notions of the enlightened state, which are found in my tradition, must be overcome. Feelings of the feelings of others, which characterize the consequent nature of God, must, therefore, become a vital and clearly expressed aspect of Amida Buddha, indeed of the enlightened state itself. I have developed this notion of the consequent nature of God with the aid of Heschel's discussion of "the God of pathos" in an elaboration of the compassionate nature of Amida Buddha.[13] Again, the application of this process conceptuality of the consequent nature of God is essential to expressing and comprehending the implications and workings of the compassionate Amida Buddha.

13. Yokota, "Understanding Amida Buddha and the Pure Land," 74–81; "A Call to Compassion: Process Thought and the Conceptualization of Amida Buddha," 92–93.

It is interesting that while I discussed and developed the applicability of the primordial nature of God, with its persuasive power exercised through initial subjective aims, to the conceptuality of Amida Buddha in my 1994 article in *Process Studies*,[14] I do not even hint of this conceptuality in the later, expanded discussion of Amida Buddha.[15] Again, the active side of Amida Buddha is the soteriological activity of a subject compassionately "grasping never to let go." There is no sense that Amida Buddha lures form or thingness upon reality. Amida Buddha is simply not thought of as being a creating activity. It is this problem with the use of the primordial nature of God that hinders a total identity of Amida as the Christ. Can and should we think of Amida Buddha as having powers of creation? This is one of the difficult questions with which I am now struggling. I will address this issue at the end of this chapter in a renewed attempt to articulate Amida Buddha with certain powers of creation.

A TRADITION WITHIN A LARGER TRADITION

I have come to think that the proposal of Cobb to engage in a dialogue between the traditions must be consciously broadened to a dialogue within the various traditions. For Shin Buddhism, this must include the entire history and tradition of Buddhism. For Christianity, this must include not only its history but the history of the other monotheistic traditions as well. In many ways, the former task that I must undertake is much simpler than the latter task for Christianity, with the many suspicions caused by a long and acrimonious history among the three monotheistic traditions. The former task is my task and the following will center upon it, but I feel, as an outsider, a strange responsibility to make at least one point about this latter task as well at the end of the following discussion.

In an essay titled "Nagarjuna, Shinran, and Whitehead," I attempt to show that compassion is the primordial and central characterization of the Buddhist reality of emptiness. In short, I show that Shinran's primordial characterization of Amida Buddha as compassionate wisdom or wise compassion was not just a sop for the spiritually slothful. Beginning with the act of Sakyamuni to step forth from the tree of enlightenment to speak of and embody the reality of enlightenment, one can see the compassionate activity of enlightenment in the entire tradition. The gathering of the early "home-leaving" monks saw compassion as well as wisdom take on importance in certain tales or motifs of the scripture tradition. The Kisa-Gotami tale of a mother who had lost her infant son has multileveled meanings or intentions, but one clear image is of the compassionate concern of Sakyamuni to see the grief-stricken mother realize the real meaning of the impermanence of life, so as to aid her through her sorrow. The

---

14. Yokota, "A Call to Compassion: Process Thought and the Conceptualization of Amida Buddha," 94–95.

15. Yokota, "Understanding Amida Buddha and the Pure Land."

forming of the order of nuns, again, has a multileveled message, but the concern and compassion of not only the Buddha but also the disciple Ananda are vivid illustrations of compassionate wisdom. It also, from another perspective, is a good tale to show how an enlightened one could still harbor gender bias, for whatever reason, in Sakyamuni's initial refusal to allow such an order. Even Nagarjuna's radical negative dialectic, while seemingly a nihilistically absolute denial of reality, is a focused and reasoned attempt to see reality in its stark suchness. Moreover, this suchness is never seen to be neutral or with no characteristics but is always seen as compassionate reality. Bhavaviveka, one of two central classic interpreters of Nagarjuna, clearly understands Nagarjuna as enunciating a fundamentally compassionate character to emptiness. A characterless suchness is negated. His commentaries on Nagarjuna and his own exposition of emptiness emphasize the compassionate characterization of enlightenment and emptiness repeatedly in variously expressed forms with a deep insight into the Buddhism of his time.[16] In Shinran's exposition of the compassionate character of Amida Buddha, he uses images of emptiness coming forth to actualize compassionate activity and compassion coming forth from emptiness.[17] Thus we see in Shin Buddhism a tradition in which emptiness is described as compassionate and compassion as being based on emptiness. The "and Whitehead" in the above essay title represents the philosophical basis of the paper. The incarnational emphasis of process theology, with its refusal to have any element of its theology absolutized and neutrally expressed, was the philosophical incentive of the paper.

Beyond this doctrinal narrative, there is the historical narrative that can bring more understanding to the multiple streams in the one larger tradition. The Shin Buddhist tradition has a self-absolutizing tendency that sometimes leads to seeing itself as being somehow fully formed at its inception. The idea I asserted at the beginning of this paper—that before Amida as the Christ, there was Amida as the Buddha—is a case in point. The whole Buddhist tradition has had a long, vital, and ever-changing and developing history, in which it has borrowed freely from innumerable sources. This figure of infinite light was joined at some point with a figure of eternal life that came to be buddhicized as it made Buddhism more central Asian. Moreover, successively in China, Southeast Asia, Korea, and Japan, and now in the Western world we saw and are seeing Buddhism slowly but steadily changing. Western Buddhists are both Western and Buddhist, and with the rise of certain vital, westernized forms of Buddhism there will be a slow and positive transformation of Buddhism.

One sign that proves this is the interest in Buddhist ethics, ecology, and theology initiated and encouraged by these Western Buddhists. Buddhism changes

---

16. Eckel, *To See the Buddha*, 158–71.
17. Shinran, *The Collected Works of Shinran*, vol. 1, 461–62; 530.

and Buddhism grows. I witnessed one example of this at a forum on Buddhist ecological ethics, where the German Buddhist scholar and practitioner Lambert Schmithausen gave a clear, informed message of a "simple" Buddhist ecological ethic, which spoke from the spirit of Buddhism but also from the analytical and ethical standpoint of Western culture. One of the elders of contemporary Japanese Buddhology responded to this clear and simple message in an obstruse, technical way that did not see, or want to see, the ethical imperative behind the message.

Japanese Buddhist studies is stuck in a strange and petty scholasticism that seems to glory in being out of touch with the world. Moreover, the tragedy of Shin Buddhism in the West is that it is an ethnically centered form of Buddhism that is made up mainly of Americans, Canadians, and Latin Americans of Japanese descent who still have close emotional ties with the mother temple in Japan. Relations are artifically close and efforts are being made to make them closer for the purpose of clerical hegemony in the guise of "doctrinal purity" on the part of the mother temple in Kyoto. I see it as crucial to the very life of our tradition that it open itself up to the whole Buddhist tradition as well as to other traditions. We must not be afraid to have Amida as the Christ as our prescient fore-believers had Amida as the Buddha. Their example may be one way to revitalize our tradition before it is too late.

In the case of Christianity, as stated above, there is an actively negative historical background to real dialogue among the people of the Book. As noted when discussing the consequent nature of God, the influence of Abraham Heschel's insight into "the God of pathos" helped me emotionally feel comfortable with Amida Buddha in terms of the consequent nature of God. The notion of "the God of pathos" was and is central to my thinking on deity and what makes deity worthy of worship. Heschel's book *The Prophets* stands central for me and has deeply and permanently affected my personal and academic religious interests. It beautifully shows what it means to be touched by and permanently affected by the majesty of God and even more effectively shows how God is permanently affected by the activities and thoughts of all creation. What it enunciates is that God is primordially a compassionate, loving God of thoroughgoing relationality with abiding care and feeling for all existence. It is asserting the existence of a "christian" God before Christianity. Looking at old film clips of the freedom marches in the South, you can see Heschel's tall, lanky figure striding alongside Martin Luther King, and one sees both the prophetic and Christian spirits actualized equally in both figures. Here the roots of the entire tradition of the people of the Book are impressively expressed. Christians must look at this prophetic tradition and see themselves before they were themselves. Again, I have no real knowledge of Islam, but, here too there are parallel notions of justice and love so that relations with this third sibling are vital for all three. As an outsider, may I be allowed to say this: you people of the Book had better get along and get to know each other sometime soon, for the good of all of us.

WHERE INDEED BEYOND DIALOGUE?

The dialogue between traditions that Cobb sees as necessary for going beyond dialogue is indeed where we should be headed. I believe that for this dialogue to be truly successful, it must be opened up to the larger tradition of one's own specific tradition. It is in this dialogue that we can hope to see a glimpse of who we really are and who we may become by looking at how we became the way we are and how much we have in common with those fellow believers in the larger tradition we find ourselves in. Personally, I must look not only to the Christianity that I have come to know, but to reaquaint myself with the larger tradition from which my specific tradition has come and to which it belongs. I began my studies of religion concentrating in general Buddhist studies and have come full circle to look upon this larger tradition as where I must start again.

THE PRIMORDIAL NATURE OF GOD LOOKED AT ANEW

The rejection of Amida Buddha as having active engagement with us through the creative activity of the primordial nature of God and initial subjective aims is, I have indicated, a position that I am struggling with. I do not wish simply to return to my earlier inclusion of the primordial nature of God and the "creative" aspect of the initial subjective aims. Nevertheless, there is something to be said for this positive activity (primordial nature of God) and not only the passive activity of being open to the world around it that is the consequent nature of God. It is indeed interesting, though understandable, that for the monotheistic tradition, the "passive" or consequent nature of God is novel and problematic while the active, creative aspect of the primordial nature of God has no such novelty or difficulty. It is the opposite for my tradition. While the consequent nature of God is more easily accessible to us, the more positive and actively creative aspect of the primordial nature of God is anathema to our way of thinking. Nevertheless, the noncoercive aspect of the initial subjective aims, which can help guide us as we are formed and act out our existence, may indeed have some part to play in our way at looking at Amida Buddha and Amida Buddha's relation to us.

Amida Buddha, while solely a soteriological figure promising salvation through birth into the Pure Land of enlightenment, is in that role a figure that constantly "calls to us" to recognize who we are and where we are bound unless we come to see the fault in our condition and in our way of life. In traditional Pure Land imagery, Amida calls us toward a salvific, creative transformation that is birth in the Pure Land. Amida, in short, calls us toward a new birth. While the tradition is admittedly centered upon birth into this transformed state in our next life, there is an equally strong tradition that calls for a true, creative transformation in this life that negates many of the aspects of who we are precisely through the recognition of the truth of who we are. It is this "new birth" of our old selves that is designated as birth in the Pure Land, and this is a transformation into a new being aware of the need for Amida's compassionate power. It is here that the initial subjective aims and the primordial nature of God of process thought may be a helpful way to understand the dynamics of this new birth that is birth in the Pure Land. The constant, repetitive acting out of all our worst fears, difficulties, and complexes can be broken only by a novel insight of true self-realization that comes obviously from within—but not only from within. This call of grace can be a revitalizing experience that can change who we are. Here we can see the spiritual influence of the initial subjective aims provided by Amida Buddha as the cause for this personal creative transformation.

PART THREE
BUDDHIST, CHINESE, CHRISTIAN, HINDU, ISLAMIC, AND JEWISH VERSIONS OF DEEP RELIGIOUS PLURALISM

Chapter 5

Deep Religious Pluralism and Contemporary Jewish Thought

Sandra B. Lubarsky

Although Jews have a great deal to gain from the "pluralistic turn" of Christian theology, engagement with the implications of religious pluralism for Jewish theology and self-understanding has been rather limited. Instead, Jewish thinkers since the Second Vatican Council have been preoccupied with the two cataclysmic events preceding that period: the Holocaust and the founding of the State of Israel. As Rabbi Arthur Green has pointed out,

> Theology has not been the creative forte of the Jewish people throughout most of the twentieth century. We have been too busily engaged in the process of surviving to have had the energy to devote to sustained religious reflection. . . . For the past fifty years the Jewish people as a body politic has been fully and single-mindedly engaged in the task of reconstruction, in our case meaning above all building the State of Israel as a secure national home for the Jewish people. . . . Besides these monumental undertakings, all else seemed to pale.[1]

When Jews have engaged in interreligious conversations, it has often been as participants in discussions about how Christianity might overcome anti-Judaism.

1. Green, "New Directions in Jewish Theology in America," 486.

111

Jewish-Christian dialogue has been appreciated largely for its aim in correcting Christianity's understanding of Judaism and preventing further tragedy. Only recently have the structural consequences of religious pluralism *for* Judaism begun to be considered.

Jewish thinkers who came of age before the Holocaust, several of whom wrote important theological works after the Holocaust, by and large did not affirm the salvific nature of other religions except as they overlapped with Jewish insights. Both Leo Baeck and Franz Rosenzweig developed sophisticated forms of religious inclusivism in which tolerance and respect were given to members of other faiths, but the faiths themselves were not seen as having intrinsic value apart from their relationship either to Judaism or to the Noachide covenant.

Martin Buber and Abraham Joshua Heschel stand out as exceptions to this approach. Acknowledging that Judaism and Christianity differed in doctrine and practice, they nonetheless maintained that both were revelations of the same God and the same truth, differently expressed. Christianity, in particular, was assessed as having value that was independent of Judaism and yet legitimate. Heschel believed that "religious diversity is the will of God" and spoke of the possibility of "mutual enrichment";[2] Buber maintained that the task of religious traditions is "not to tolerate each other's waywardness" but to "acknowledge the real relationship in which both stand to the truth."[3]

I begin this essay with a summary of the views of several of the most significant Jewish thinkers since 1960, each of whom acknowledges his intellectual debt to Buber and Heschel. Irving Greenberg addresses religious pluralism as part of his post-Holocaust theology. David Hartman speaks from the perspective of an American-Israeli, confronting intrareligious dialogue and, by extension, interreligious dialogue. Arthur Waskow, Arthur Green, and Michael Lerner are representative voices from the Jewish Renewal movement. They include questions of religious pluralism in their new configuration of a Judaism that is responsive to contemporary American intellectual and social movements.

It almost goes without saying that the situation of these thinkers is different from that of their predecessors. In addition to the ongoing development of Jewish-Christian dialogue, they face intensified intra-Jewish conflicts between Orthodox, liberal, and secular Jewish communities in both the United States and Israel. Further, Jews remain on guard against continuing patterns of anti-Judaism and negative stereotyping.[4] And while American Jews have earned the reputation of being the most successful minority in the United States, the intermarriage rate among U.S. Jews is now greater than 50 percent. (As I will discuss later, there is still strikingly little consideration given to the impact of this demographic

---

2. Heschel, *Moral Grandeur and Spiritual Audacity*, 243, 254.
3. Buber, *Israel and the World: Essays in a Time of Crisis*, 40.
4. See, for example, Amy Newman's essay, "The Idea of Judaism in Feminism and Afrocentrism." Newman discusses the presence of standard Christian stereotypes of Judaism—including an understanding of "Jewish law" as external and compelled in contrast to Christian morality, described as flowing freely from the heart—in many contemporary feminist texts.

revolution on the issue of religious pluralism.) Likewise, in the last twenty-five years, a disproportionate number of Jews have turned away from Judaism, not simply to become secularists, but to embrace non-Western traditions, particularly various forms of Buddhism.

In light of these events, the question of "other religions" ought to be a high priority for contemporary Jewish thinkers. But because the Jewish encounter with religious pluralism has largely been in the context of Jewish-Christian dialogue, initiated by Christians as part of a rethinking of Christianity—and not as a catalyst for a Jewish rethinking of Judaism—Jewish thinkers have yet to develop a full-blown theology of religious pluralism.[5] Hence the distinction between generic religious pluralism and differential or deep pluralism is rather ahead of the discussion in Jewish circles. But the trajectory is clearly toward a full embrace of religious pluralism and indeed seems to be toward an affirmation of deep religious pluralism. Following a summary and assessment of the current discussion of religious pluralism among these several thinkers, I offer some reflections on a Jewish approach to deep religious pluralism, informed by process philosophy. Such an approach can be seen as consonant with the current discussion.

IRVING GREENBERG

Irving (Yitz) Greenberg is a remarkable figure in contemporary Jewish life. An Orthodox rabbi with a Ph.D. in American history, a former professor at Yeshiva University, where he initiated the teaching of courses on the Holocaust, and an instrumental leader in establishing the U.S. Holocaust Memorial Museum, he has also been accused of heresy by the Orthodox Rabbinical Council because of his advocacy of interdenominational cooperation and interfaith dialogue. In 1974, he founded the National Jewish Center for Learning and Leadership (CLAL) in order to promote intra-Jewish unity. Under his leadership, CLAL has become an important center for discussion and advocacy of Jewish pluralism, based on the principle that the multiple voices within Judaism—liberal, conservative, and Orthodox—are legitimate Jewish voices.

The starting point for Greenberg's activism and intellectual work, including his approach to religious pluralism, is the Holocaust. In the face of the Holocaust, indeed, in the face of "burning children"—Greenberg's now famous standard for post-Holocaust discourse—Greenberg argues that the primary responsibility of all people is to honor and promote the value of every human life. "There is one

---

5. The recent book *Christianity in Jewish Terms*, edited by Tikva Frymer-Kensky et al., is an important exception to this statement. The editors call for a reexamination of both Judaism and Christianity in light of the post-Holocaust reflection on Judaism by many Christian theologians. The volume addresses two main concerns: "[How] to renew our understanding of Judaism today from out of the sacred texts and, then, how to understand Christianity in terms of this Judaism" (xii). Moreover, the editors recognize that this "is a bold undertaking: to be open to thinking seriously about Christianity, let alone about God and religion in a new way" (xiii).

response to such overwhelming tragedy: the reaffirmation of meaningfulness, worth, and life—through acts of love and life-giving. The act of creating a life or enhancing its dignity is the counter-testimony of Auschwitz."[6]

Greenberg's theological project is based on two trajectories that come together in a post-Holocaust covenantal theology. This first flows from the biblical idea that humans are created in God's image; Greenberg asserts over and over again that every individual thereby possesses infinite value and that humanity is involved in a redemptive process and ultimately will be redeemed. "Judaism and Christianity tell of God's love for man and stand or fall on their claim that the human being is, therefore, of ultimate and absolute value."[7] The Shoah is evidence of what happens when this religious orientation is dismissed and human life is devalued.

But it is also "counter-testimony" to assertions about God's love and care. "The cruelty and the killing raise the question whether even those who believe after such an event dare talk about God who loves and cares without making a mockery of those who suffered."[8] In response to suffering as countertestimony to God's love, Greenberg turns to an analysis of power, both divine and human. This is the crucial step in his construction of a post-Holocaust covenantal theology that yet includes a redemptive God. In answer to the question "Where was God at Auschwitz?" Greenberg asserts that God's power is self-limited.

> According to Jewish tradition, God, out of love, self-limits—first to create and sustain existence, then to enable its ultimate perfection. . . . The primordial self-limitation is expressed in establishing natural order/law and being bound by it. . . . Similarly, God does not continuously interfere with history; nor will the divine enter into human lives with constant miraculous intervention.[9]

According to Greenberg, without such divine self-limitation, there could be no covenant, understood as divine-human partnership. As an expression of God's love for humankind, the covenant is a framework within which human freedom is joined to human responsibility. Through the covenant, humans become cocreators with God in perfecting the world. God is present in God's hiddenness; to put it differently, God is hidden in the presence of human freedom.

> The final question for the believer is not: where was God in the Holocaust? The manifest answer is that God was present, being tortured, gassed, shot down relentlessly amidst God's people. Rather the question is: what was God's message when God did not stop the Holocaust? Let us venture to say that God was calling humans to take full responsibility for the achievement

6. Greenberg, "Cloud of Smoke, Pillar of Fire: Judaism, Christianity, and Modernity after the Holocaust," 406.

7. Greenberg, "Judaism, Christianity, and the Partnership After the Twentieth Century," 25.

8. Greenberg, "Cloud of Smoke," 398.

9. Greenberg, "Judaism and Christianity: Covenants of Redemption," 141–42.

of the covenant. . . . As humans take power, they must develop their antenna to perceive God as the Presence everywhere.[10]

Even in the face of overwhelming evil, God declines to intervene in a supernatural fashion, for such intervention, though it may well change the immediate balance of power for the good, will unravel the power relations that enable the covenant. Thus God's commitment to the covenant is evidenced by God's self-restraint in the use of power apart from human agency.

Greenberg writes with tremendous sensitivity to the loss of faith experienced by many Jews after the Holocaust. He continually makes reference to the responsibility of post-Holocaust thinkers to speak with honesty and clarity about the reality of evil. Nevertheless, Greenberg maintains that we can speak of a redemptive God, even amidst the ashes of Auschwitz. Fundamentally, this is because he believes that in our era, God acts in history through the deeds of human beings. He does, however, offer an additional reason why Jews can still speak of God as redeemer: the existence of the State of Israel.

> If the experience of Auschwitz symbolizes that we are cut off from God and hope, and that the covenant may be destroyed, then the experience of Jerusalem symbolizes that God's promises are faithful and His people live on. Burning children speak of the absence of all value—human and divine; the rehabilitation of one-half million Holocaust survivors in Israel speaks of the reclamation of tremendous human dignity and value. If Treblinka makes human hope an illusion, then the Western Wall asserts that human dreams are more real than force and facts. Israel's faith in the God of History demands that an unprecedented event of destruction be matched by an unprecedented act of redemption, and this has happened.[11]

Greenberg does not speak directly about the kind of divine action that was involved in this event. Instead he shifts from theology to anthropology, describing how Jews must accept a "dialectical tension"—between atheism bred by the catastrophe of the Holocaust and faith borne of redemption of a Jewish homeland—and the "moment faith" that follows from living between Auschwitz and Jerusalem.[12] Yet the contrast between Auschwitz and Israel calls out for clarification regarding God's mode of action; in not addressing it as a continuation of the pattern of God's hidden work, Greenberg intimates that in regard to the establishment of Israel, the supernatural God of Exodus replaces the self-limiting God of Auschwitz. At issue is the fact that Greenberg never directly renounces either divine omnipotence or the assumption that power is primarily coercive. In proposing that God acts through human action, Greenberg opens up the opportunity to declare that omnipotence is no longer a meaningful divine attribute. But rather than doing this, he maintains divine omnipotence, yet declares it to

---

10. Greenberg, "Judaism, Christianity, and the Partnership After the Twentieth Century," 35–36.
11. Greenberg, "Cloud of Smoke," 405.
12. Ibid.

be hidden, so that God remains all-powerful in essence though in actuality God's power is severely curtailed.

It is, however, the power of human beings, rather than the issue of God's power, that fuels Greenberg's passion. According to Greenberg, the covenantal claim on human beings is for responsible use of power applied to the perfecting of the world. This means that humans need to practice self-restraint and self-criticism, the one in regard to power, the other in regard to claims about truth. The affirmation of religious pluralism is, for Greenberg, both a necessary response to the Holocaust and a strategy for establishing a balance of power between people. Assertions of absolutism lead to the "delegitimizing" and devaluing of other human beings; power that is not sufficiently distributed leads to conflict and the destruction of weaker members of society. "The practice of pluralism is essential to the exercise of power. . . . Pluralism divides power; this guards against excesses. Pluralism distributes power so more interests are accommodated and fewer feel left out." Furthermore,

> Why should people instructed by God (as they understand it) grant serious weight to other views which are merely human (as they understand it)? Absolutism would answer—they should not. Relativism would answer— they should—because there is no ultimate truth. . . . Pluralism answers that there are real truths and ultimate claims. But humans of good will differ on which of the conflicting views are real and ultimate. Therefore we are left with genuine disagreements. Out of the unity of common goal, then, people pledge not to delegitimize. This self-restraint will contain conflict and not let it tear society and community apart—lest everything be destroyed.[13]

For Greenberg, religious pluralism reins in both theological and political aggrandizement and is instrumental in sustaining both the value of life and actual human lives. It is based on the limited nature of human understanding and the historical evidence that unlimited power, fired by claims of absolute truth, results in great evil.

To support his affirmation of the social necessity of pluralism, Greenberg offers a theory of progressive covenantal relationships established by God. First, through the universal Noachide covenant, God's presence permeates the created world so that all people have access to God's blessings. However, God chooses to establish particular covenants in order "to establish the human scale of redemption and to hasten its pace," as well as to "release the channels of blessing already inherent in the creation." The stages of covenant creation begin with the family of Abraham (and even as the vision of redemption/perfection is revealed to others, Israel continues to play a special role as the people of the original redemptive pattern in which "God's presence is more visible").[14] Because God's goal for humanity is redemption/perfection, "step by step" covenantal relationships are

---

13. Greenberg, "Yizhak Rabin and the Ethic of Jewish Power," 7, 9.
14. Greenberg, "Judaism and Christianity: Covenants of Redemption," 145, 149.

established with other peoples as the "model of perfection itself unfolds in history."[15] In this linear model in which "each stage of the covenant has its own time," a covenant is eventually established with Christianity, itself a "tree of life," able to bear "redemptive fruit."[16]

In regard to Christianity, Greenberg writes, "To reverse a classic image, then, it was God's purpose that a shoot of the stalk of Abraham be grafted onto the root of the Gentiles." Although Christianity is "an organic outgrowth of Judaism," it eventually becomes an "independent religion" with its own "vitality" and "contributions to meaning and ethics around the world."[17] Indeed, it is a "counterpart religion" to Judaism, balancing Judaism's stress on peoplehood with an emphasis on faith community and serving as a "moral/religious balance wheel."[18]

Greenberg's affirmation of religious pluralism is rooted in the idea that there is a "universal divine covenant with humanity" and that, through God's covenantal guidance and human effort, life will be perfected, triumphing over suffering and death. For Greenberg, this constitutes the basis of all religious traditions: the ground of religion itself is a messianic drive toward perfection, understood as the perfection of social relationships and human relations with natural processes. Theistic and nontheistic traditions alike are motivated by the same longing and commitment. Greenberg writes, "I believe that world religions such as Islam and noncovenantal faiths such as Buddhism and forms of Hinduism should be recognized as movements legitimately striving to fulfill the universal divine covenant with humanity."[19]

While Greenberg posits a structure of salvation that all traditions share, he also affirms that "God has many messengers" and speaks of the "full spiritual dignity" of other traditions.[20] Because traditions have their own salvific power and legitimacy as well as their own spiritual dignity, and because they have a common salvific goal, traditions can guide and inspire one another. "Models of faith are what we have to gain from each other. Those models evoke our own deepest possibilities."[21]

Finally, for Greenberg, religious pluralism is a strategy for avoiding the kind of suffering that Jews experienced in the Holocaust and for helping to establish peaceful relations between people. He writes:

> The indivisibility of human dignity and equality becomes an essential bulwark against the repetition of another Holocaust. It is the command rising out of Auschwitz. This means a vigorous self-criticism, and review of every cultural or religious framework that may sustain some evaluation or denial of the absolute and equal dignity of the other. This is the overriding command

15. Greenberg, "Judaism and Christianity: Their Respective Roles in the Strategy of Redemption," 196.
16. Greenberg, "Judaism and Christianity: Covenants of Redemption," 149.
17. Ibid., 149, 155, 154.
18. Ibid., 155, 33.
19. Ibid., 158.
20. Ibid., 155.
21. Greenberg, "Judaism and Christianity: Their Respective Roles in the Strategy of Redemption," 27.

and the essential criterion for religious existence, to whoever walks by the light of the flames. Without this testimony and the creation of facts that give it persuasiveness, the act of the religious enterprise simply lacks credibility.[22]

Religious pluralism is a tool for perfecting the world, helping to eliminate religious arrogance which has resulted in so much human suffering. Greenberg's analysis centers on a balance of power, and religious pluralism helps to ensure such a balance.[23]

DAVID HARTMAN

David Hartman is an Orthodox rabbi and founder of the Shalom Hartman Institute in Jerusalem, which is dedicated to addressing religious, political, and ethical issues facing Israeli society. In 1971, he immigrated to Israel from the United States, and Israel is the geographical and intellectual landscape for his thought.

---

22. Greenberg, "Cloud of Smoke," 407. In spite of Greenberg's passionate cry for vigorous self-criticism as a protection against the misuse of power, he has been criticized for his own lack of critical attention to Israeli policies toward the Palestinians. Greenberg's idea of a progressive covenant in which humans have greater and greater power, and God has less authority, would seem to demand the development of heightened critical sensitivities to the use and misuse of power. Yet Arnold Jacob Wolf pointed out in an early critique of Greenberg's idea of a "voluntary covenant" that Greenberg's complex theological dialectic might be "a cover for the new Jewish chauvinism. . . . The voluntary covenant, I fear, is a product of our natural inclination to evil more than it is a new revelation. *We* are the center of the covenant. *We* have the primary task of self-protection. (Do the Palestinians, too, even if they have not yet suffered a Holocaust?) *We* are the makers and unmakers of the *mitzvot*, since our existence is already a fulfillment of them all. *We* define the terms on which *we* choose, not what God chooses; of course, not what the United Nations or the peoples of the world might expect" ("The Revision of Irving Greenberg," *Shma* vol. 13, no. 254 [May 13, 1983]). Marc Ellis too has reproved Greenberg and other Jewish theologians for their lack of attention to the Palestinian struggle for legitimacy and power in relation to Israel. Indeed, Greenberg has by and large defended "Jewish Power" as abiding by the rabbinic restrictions of "purity of arms" or self-defense ("The Ethics of Jewish Power").

23. Greenberg arrives at an affirmation of religious pluralism by way of the tragedy of the Holocaust. His primary question "How can we prevent suffering?" is framed in terms of the question "How can we balance power so that things don't go awry?" Because his focus is on power relations—the recognition that power is our covenantal responsibility, both to use it and to use it with a critical awareness—his hopes for the level of relationship between different traditions are by and large characterized in terms of mutual "legitimation." He may be described as a theological pragmatist and a passionate, moving defender of covenantal responsibility, analyzing religious structures in terms of their powers to improve human conditions.

Because Greenberg sees the task of religious traditions to advance the use of power for good and prevent its use for evil, he emphasizes power as the dominant mode of relationality and thus offers a picture of the relationship between traditions as primarily external. His metaphor, for example, of Christianity as a "balancing wheel" to Judaism captures this externality. And while Greenberg at times goes beyond this image to say that traditions may in fact be inspired by one another, his overall discussion relies on an understanding of traditions as politically and socially intertwined, but theologically independent (each having its own sufficient covenantal revelation). Interaction tends to be limited to traditions working side by side with one another on the common goal that they share. Viewed this way, interreligious engagement can lack emotional and intellectual depth; Greenberg's language of "delegitimation" describes a less robust relationship between traditions than I believe he intends. An external model does not do justice to the ramifications of evil (and goodness) on all traditions, regardless of how removed they may be from initial, immediate impact.

His overarching concern is the integration of Jewish tradition with modern Israeli society; his goal is the development of a covenantal Judaism that is relevant to the spiritual and political dimensions of Israeli life.

Although Hartman recognizes the importance and legitimacy of Diaspora Judaism, he sees Israel as the place where Judaism can regain its full covenantal integrity. Judaism in the Diaspora has been largely a private affair, confined to home and synagogue; psychologically, it has been shaped by fear and alienation stemming from life as a minority culture in a largely hostile environment. In contrast, Judaism in Israel is part of the public domain and, according to Hartman, this new political reality offers tremendous opportunities. Most important is the chance to develop as a messianic society (carefully nuanced) in which the "guiding principle is to seek to expand the powers of knowledge, wisdom, and love."

> I live with the guarded hope that out of this complex and vibrant new Jewish reality will emerge new spiritual directions for the way Judaism will be lived in the modern world.[24]

What Hartman calls "convenantal consciousness" is shorthand for his efforts to shape the identity of Israeli society in response to political self-determination. He is both optimistic about the spiritual possibilities afforded by the new political entity of the State of Israel, believing that it can be the embodiment of prophetic values, and realistic about the difficulties facing Israeli society, both internally and externally.[25] In regard to both intrareligious and interreligious relations, religious pluralism is central to his theological project. "We can respond 'halakhically' to our past suffering by striving in the contemporary world to discover how the presence of the other can be spiritually redemptive. Thus the attempt to establish a secure framework for religious pluralism and tolerance in the State of Israel is not spiritually tangential to our national rebirth."[26]

Hartman gives special attention to the complex of issues around intrareligious differences. In a beautiful letter to an American Reform rabbi, he acknowledges the importance of heterogeneous forms of Judaism for *klal Yisrael* (the house of Israel), replacing the question "Who is a Jew?" with the question "How [can we] build a people and a nation in the midst of radical ideological diversity?"[27] He deplores the treatment of Reform and Conservative Jews by the Orthodox establishment in Israel. And though he disagrees with the Reform approach to Halakhah, Hartman firmly supports theological diversity, not for its pragmatic effect on relations between Diaspora Jews and Israel, but because he believes that religious pluralism can lead to "a new level of spiritual dignity."[28]

---

24. Hartman, "The Third Jewish Commonwealth," 443, 440.
25. Hartman maintains his optimism alongside a "sober appreciation of [the] political and moral complexities" that characterize contemporary Israeli society. See *A Heart of Many Rooms*, especially "Auschwitz or Sinai? In the Aftermath of the Israeli-Lebanese War" (259–65). His optimism is based on the belief that Sinai—not Auschwitz—is the normative framework for Israel and Judaism.
26. Ibid., 253.
27. Hartman, *Conflicting Visions: Spiritual Possibilities of Modern Israel,* 210.
28. Ibid., 211.

That new level is based on the ancient inheritance of the Sinai event, which Hartman believes is the normative frame for Jewish life, including the rebirth of the State of Israel. Unlike Greenberg, he does not view the Holocaust as revelatory (although he believes that any suffering should result in increased sensitivity). It is, rather, in memory of Sinai, not Auschwitz, that Jews must build a just and moral society that includes efforts to create "a shared moral language with the nations of the world."[29]

Hartman's approach to religious pluralism has both a theological and a psychological dimension. In both ways, his approach breaks new ground in Jewish theology and prepares the community for richer and potentially transformative encounters. Although at this stage in his writings his outline of the psychological and theological aspects of pluralism calls out for fuller treatment and greater systematizing (his argument is scattered over a number of essays in several different books), Hartman has already made important contributions to the discussion.

He argues that "cultural monism is no longer a psychological option" in Israel; the "other" is both the non-Jewish other (Muslim or Christian) and the Jewish other. In coming home from the ghetto to Jerusalem, Jews find themselves face to face with diversity and feel challenged to defend their various structures of identity. Psychologically, religious pluralism leads to a "radical shift" in "human religious sensibility" analogous to the consciousness of death, which awakens "fear, uncertainty, loss of control."[30] Such emotional terrain poses a spiritual challenge: how might encounter with the other generate love rather than suspicion? In answer, Hartman posits a theological shift in which the divine creative-redemptive activity is understood as an ongoing temporal process, marked by novelty and uncertainty.

According to Hartman, the divine name that was spoken to Moses at the burning bush is best rendered, "I will be—I will come in new ways" (*Ehyeh asheer ehtehm,* Exod. 3:14).[31] And he interprets the daily prayerbook's description of God as the one "who in His goodness renews the act of Creation continually each and every day" as "thereby implying that divine creation is an abiding feature of reality and not merely something that happened once."[32] Moreover, "Creation is the affirmation not of the exclusive worth of eternity, but of the value of temporality." God is both the God of history and "a God who says that radical novelty and surprise are possible in a spiritual life in which the covenantal ancestors follow you constantly."[33] Elsewhere he asserts that "belief in radical freedom, in an open future, in surprise and novelty are crucial elements of normative Judaism."[34]

---

29. Hartman, "Auschwitz or Sinai?" (2001).
30. Hartman, "Judaism Encounters Christianity Anew," 70, 80.
31. Ibid., 73.
32. Hartman, *Conflicting Visions,* 246.
33. Hartman, "Judaism Encounters Christianity Anew," 76, 73.
34. Hartman, *A Heart of Many Rooms,* 260. Hartman's halakhic approach parallels this position. He understands the Torah as open to creative possibilities. "[T]he last chapter has not yet been written. That is the meaning of oral tradition in Judaism. We never live by the literal word alone. We live by a word that is open and reinterpreted and recreated" (242).

Novelty and uncertainty, then, are essential characteristics of the process of creation. But there is an additional source of novelty and surprise in the world: human freedom. In this case, however, novelty is corrupted by human imperfection, giving rise to sin and estrangement from God and further uncertainty in the world. God's response is to "repair the rupture" by reaching out to human beings through revelation, covenant, and election. According to Hartman, God, out of love and respect for human freedom, seeks a divine-human relationship that is based on freely chosen commitment to God. "God agrees, as it were, to share the stage with humanity, to limit His own freedom and power so as to sustain human freedom, and to accept the risks of relation to human beings from within the context of history." The consequence of human freedom is divine self-limitation. "God no longer simply speaks and produces results automatically as in the Creation ('And God said . . . and there was . . .'). He addresses human beings without being sure of their response."[35] Uncertainty becomes an aspect of both divine and human experience.

Revelation is the balance to Creation; it is God's lure, as it were, to bring humanity back into relationship with God and to counter individual freedom with community stability. It is "not meant to be a source of absolute, eternal, and transcendent truth," but is rather "an expression of God's love"[36] and of "God's ability to love us in our imperfection."[37] Hartman argues against any claims of universality for either Revelation or Redemption. Revelation is about building community and continuity of structure within history; it is always particular and limited to a specific community.

And about Redemption, he says: "It would be 'bad faith' to advocate tolerance and pluralism in unredeemed history, yet maintain a triumphant monolithic universalism with regard to the End of Days."[38] He maintains instead that the only universal is the sanctity of life, a universal that follows from Creation.

There is, then, a dialectical tension between Creation and Revelation. Creation is the confirmation that all of life is interconnected and sacred. It is the basis for a universal ethics that proclaims that all of life, as the creation of God, is sacred and that all human beings were created in God's image. Revelation is the confirmation that God chooses to enter human history, chooses to establish particular relationships with human communities, and chooses to love humanity in spite of our imperfection. But although Creation is a "metahistorical category,"[39] bearing a universal ethic, and Revelation is in history, hence limited and particular, each affirms "the value of temporality,"[40] including spontaneity, freedom, and ongoing responsiveness. Together they engender the development of multiple communities that have legitimate, responsive relationships to God.

35. Hartman, *Conflicting Visions*, 247.
36. Ibid., 248.
37. Hartman, "Judaism Encounters Christianity Anew," 79.
38. Hartman, *Conflicting Visions*, 249.
39. Ibid.
40. Hartman, "Judaism Encounters Christianity Anew," 76.

By deuniversalizing Revelation and establishing a dynamic between universal Creation and particular Revelation, Hartman argues that faith communities need not be rivals. There is no revelation that transcends the particular, no revelation that is complete, and no revelation that "exhaust[s] the divine plentitude." "Buddhism, Hinduism, Christianity, Islam, and Judaism are distinct spiritual paths, they bear witness to the complexity and fullness of the infinite."[41] Indeed, Hartman maintains that Revelation is not about knowledge of God at all. Rather, "Revelation is God's speaking to human beings for their own sake and not for the sake of uncovering the mysteries of the divine mind."[42]

Hartman celebrates religious pluralism, even proclaiming it to be "spiritually redemptive." It preserves the understanding that God is greater than any single faith community; it frees humans from the mistaken belief that any revelation is universal; and it reasserts the sacredness of all human life, regardless of different truth claims.[43] Hartman recognizes the theological import of religious pluralism and the need to embed it within the religious system as a whole. To that end, he calls on Jews to examine the implications of the ideas of election and covenant and to develop new forms of commitment that rely on neither exclusivism nor absolutism. And because he believes that Judaism is a creative-responsive system, he is confident that it can offer a vigorous spirituality without claiming religious uniqueness, denigrating other traditions, or isolating itself from other ways of being religious. Although Hartman says that "We have not yet built religious communities where acceptance of 'the other' and celebration of religious diversity go hand in hand with intense piety and religious devotion," he clearly believes this to be possible and to be a task in which all religious thinkers must engage.[44]

THE JEWISH RENEWAL MOVEMENT

The Jewish Renewal Movement is a uniquely American movement that developed in response to various cultural shifts in the 1960s and '70s and emerged as an organized movement in the early '80s. Its leading voices are Rabbis Arthur Waskow, Zalman Schachter-Shalomi, Arthur Green, and Michael Lerner. To date, little has been written in a systematic fashion about the movement, and no single thinker has constructed a renewal theology of Judaism that gives adequate attention to religious pluralism. Nonetheless, the movement embraces pluralism as one of its core principles, and its main representatives have addressed aspects

41. Hartman, *Conflicting Visions*, 247, 248.

42. Ibid., 248. By particularizing revelation and confining its value to the community that receives it, Hartman faces the problems of relativism, including undercutting the impetus for any deep appreciation of difference. For if revelation is designed exclusively for a particular community and has limited relevance to any other community, there is little reason for interaction and a dangerous disconnect between communities may arise.

43. Ibid.

44. Hartman, "Religious Diversity and the Millennium" (2001).

of it. In this section, I present some of what has been said in relationship to pluralism, drawing on several of Renewal's leading thinkers for this picture.

In response to the question "What is Jewish Renewal?" Waskow offers a "definition-in-process":

> At the heart of Jewish Renewal is a renewed encounter between God and the Jewish people, and an understanding of Jewish history as a series of renewed encounters with God. These encounters have followed painful crises during which God has been eclipsed; yet each crisis has resulted in the emergence of a more or less deeply transformed, renewed, and joyful version of Judaism.
>
> In our generation, Jewish Renewal is the increasingly joyful, renewing, and transforming response of Jews to the crisis of the Holocaust and the triumph of Modernity in both its creative and destructive aspects.[45]

Waskow points to the neo-Hasidism of Martin Buber, Abraham Joshua Heschel, Zalman Schachter-Shalomi, and Shlomo Carlebach as the spiritual basis of Jewish Renewal. Emphasis is given to direct spiritual experience with divinity and creation, embodied in intimate community life as modeled in the *havurah* movement and in the practice of social justice. The movement draws on Hasidism for its spiritual vitality at the same time that it embraces the Reconstructionist idea that Judaism is an evolving civilization in which the past has a "vote but not a veto." Hence it also shapes itself in positive response to feminism, egalitarianism, environmentalism, and religious pluralism. It sees itself as involved in a "paradigm shift" that requires a reconstruction of Judaism, akin to the major reconstructions in response to the challenges of Hellenism, 70 CE, 1492, and the European emancipation. Renewal recognizes modernity as posing both positive and negative challenges to spiritual life. Such aspects as gender equality, participatory democracy, and religious pluralism are affirmed; the "modern urge to constrict religious expression, to shatter communities, and to conquer the earth" is rejected. Stressing the importance of personal experience with God, often described as "Godwrestling," Renewal encourages people to connect to traditional sources "without getting stuck" in them. Accordingly, the Torah, understood as a wisdom source, a spiritual aid, and record of encounter between God and generations of Jews, is to be augmented and interpreted on the basis of new religious experience and new cultural insights and sensibilities.[46]

---

45. Waskow, "God and the Shoah."

46. Ibid. Moreover, ALEPH, a major Renewal organization, offers the following additional detail on spiritual sources: "Among our guides to interpretation of Torah are the Prophetic, Kabbalistic, and Hassidic traditions as they are now being transformed in the light of contemporary feminist spirituality, process theology, and our own direct experience of the Divine." I am convinced that process theology in fact offers a theological model appropriate to the Renewal movement. However, I have yet to see any application of it thus far. My own intention is to do just this, so I was pleased to discover this recognition of the congruence of process thought with Renewal (www.aleph.org/html/ principles.html).

Beginning with the teaching from Genesis that every human being is made in the image of God and that God's presence is throughout the world, Renewalists value both intra-Jewish and interreligious diversity. Waskow's definition includes "respect for and often learning from other spiritual paths (e.g., Buddhism, Sufism, etc.)," and the Alliance for Jewish Renewal (ALEPH) says:

> We are committed to consult with other spiritual traditions, sharing with them what we have found in our concerned research and trying out what we have learned from them, to see whether it enhances the special truths of the Jewish path.
> . . . We will ourselves treat with respect and open-mindedness those who belong to other peoples and walk other paths than our own, even if we feel compelled to oppose their actions in the world.
> . . . We intend to treat with respect other Jews and other Jewish communities whose approaches to Jewish life differ from our own, even if we feel compelled to oppose their statements or their actions.[47]

Zalman Schachter-Shalomi puts it this way: "We now, on this small planet, bump against each other and discover, God didn't speak at just one Sinai."[48]

The Tikkun Community, headed by Michael Lerner, likewise promotes pluralism, making it clear, though, that pluralism is distinct from relativism:

> [W]e believe that there are many paths to spiritual truth, and we want to honor all of those which are open to an Emancipatory Spirituality. . . . We do not believe that every particularistic tradition must be totally left behind in some new globalized spiritual mush. . . . [W]e do not seek a spiritual melting pot but a world in which plurality and difference can be respected, even as we affirm the Unity of All Being, the interconnectedness of all with all. . . . [W]e want to be clear that we do not embrace a vapid "tolerance" which refuses to make moral distinctions or a deconstructionist logic which sees all forms of discourse as little more than strategies for some group or other to gain power over others.[49]

Clearly, a core principle of Jewish Renewal is the affirmation of generic religious pluralism, including intrareligious diversity.

At this point, there seem to be two prevailing theological approaches undergirding Jewish Renewal. The dominant form is neo-Hasidism, which looks to a Kabbalah-informed metaphysics and practice. Because Jewish mysticism promotes a form of monism—All is One without distinction—differences between traditions are ultimately overcome (either on this plane of existence, once vision of the oneness of all is gained, or on a higher plane where unity overcomes diversity). As Arthur Green has taught,

---

47. At www.aleph.org/html/principles.html.
48. Zalman Schachter-Shalomi, quoted in Kamenetz, *Stalking Elijah: Adventures with Today's Jewish Mystical Masters* (San Francisco: Harper, 1997), 33.
49. At http://www.tikkun.org/community/index.cfm/action/core_vision.html.

> In the insight of Chabad mysticism—sheer nonsense, but also the greatest truth—nothing but God exists. This is the most profound Jewish mystical teaching. . . . [T]he Lord is God on heaven above and on earth beneath—'*Ein od.*' There is nothing else. Patently nonsensical, yet the only truth. We need to train ourselves to this awareness—that there is no separation between human beings. We must know there is only the One.[50]

Although the monistic claim that distinction is an experiential error makes religious pluralism only a fact of nonultimate reality, Green nonetheless believes that Buddhism has much to teach Judaism about the insight of nothingness/oneness. "It's probably the next important philosophical, theological step Judaism will take. . . . When I talk about the move from monotheism to monism and trying to redo Judaism in a nondualistic framework, I'm preparing the way for that kind of dialogue and am already open to that sort of influence."[51] Green believes that the Jewish mystical notion of unification and the Buddhist notion of nothingness are compatible. Because of his commitment to monism, Green posits this at the outset and approaches Buddhism with this expectation in mind. Likewise, Waskow operates with a neo-Lurianic approach, but nonetheless asserts that other traditions are "I-Thou responses" to divinity and thus acknowledges their validity; finally, though, they are only aspects of the "Godwave" and hence not truly distinct creations.[52]

The other theological approach, as yet underdeveloped, is panentheistic. Michael Lerner expresses this approach most clearly, speaking of a "notion of God as the Unity of All Being, in whom everything exists, but who is more than all that exists, yet manifests through all that exists."

> At any given moment we are part of God and God is part of us, but we are not all that there is to God.
> . . . [E]verything is alive, capable of interacting with the rest of the universe in increasingly conscious and self-determining ways as matter organizes itself in greater and greater complexity, and everything is permeated with God's spiritual energy.[53]

Lerner does not relate his panentheism to his stance on religious pluralism, but he does present a metaphysics that supports his recognition of the validity of truly diverse traditions.

There is much within the Jewish Renewal movement that supports a commitment to a deep religious pluralism, though, again, a systematic consideration has yet to be undertaken. Renewalists take seriously direct human intuition of God's presence in the world and thus begin with respect for the religious experiences of others. They also respect the right of individuals to explore other traditions, given both the intensely personal nature of spirituality and the belief that

---

50. Green, quoted in Kamenetz, *Stalking Elijah*, 47.
51. Green, quoted in Kamenetz, *Stalking Elijah*, 281.
52. Waskow, "God and the Shoah."
53. Lerner, "A Jewish Renewal (Kabbalistic-Mystical-NeoHasidic) Approach to God."

God's continuing creative energy is at work throughout the world. The tendency among Renewalists is to talk of God as a "presence" or "source of life" or "breath," and thereby to intimate that God acts in the world in nonsupernatural ways. Indeed, most Renewalists may be described as affirming what David Griffin calls naturalism$_{ns}$, although this is not language they have used. But Renewalists define their task as the reshaping of Judaism and Jewish theism in harmony with *some* of the insights of modernity. Nonatheistic naturalism is one of these. Furthermore, the Renewal movement contends that neither Judaism nor any other tradition is constituted by unchanging truths or is a completed system; God's omnipresence and ongoing creativity, human limitations, and the great beauty, complexity and diversity of the created world undermine such confidences.

TOWARD A JEWISH-WHITEHEADIAN APPROACH TO DEEP RELIGIOUS PLURALISM

The thinkers under consideration—representative of some of the finest thought currently underway in the Jewish community—have embraced a number of key principles that support generic religious pluralism and move toward deep religious pluralism. A brief summary of these principles includes (a) a self-limiting God who makes room for human freedom; and thereby (b) a God who thereby acts in the world through human agency and the ongoing persuasion of revelation; (c) a God who is immanent in the world and responsive to it, expressed by affirming panentheism or pantheism or by simply drawing on the covenantal structure of partnership; (d) redemption as a process that requires humans to work in tandem with God and each other; (e) God's love as overflowing any single "vessel"; (f) God as the source of ongoing creativity; (g) no single tradition as able to claim full and final understanding of God or to claim to be complete in itself and eternal in relation to the world.

It is particularly striking that Greenberg and Hartman, both Orthodox Jews, affirm the notion of a self-limiting God. In traditional covenantal theology, divine omnipotence and human freedom are upheld simultaneously, the tension negotiated by a parenthetical "as if" regarding human freedom; despite God's omnipotence, humans are to act "as if" they made free choices. Although neither Greenberg nor Hartman goes so far as to embrace the strong form of theistic naturalism, as defined by Griffin, they are remarkable in deflating the traditional covenantal tension by proposing a self-limited God as a primary principle of post-Holocaust covenantal theology. Although they maintain that God, ontologically, *could* interrupt the world's normal causal processes, they affirm the weak version of naturalistic theism, holding that God never actually does interrupt these processes. For Greenberg and Hartman, the affirmation of theistic naturalism arises in response to the Holocaust; for the Renewalists, it seems to be related more to the challenges raised by modern science. Indeed, although the Renewalists at this point have the least developed theology, they may be the most open to accepting theistic naturalism in its strong form, both because of their desire to be in sync with certain aspects of the modern world and because of their valuing of personal experience over authoritarian models of truth.

This rethinking of God's redemptive power (even if it continues to be understood as a contingent arrangement) is the basis for proposing a limit on God's revelatory power as well. In a sense, God presents revelatory truths in a graded manner to human communities, attending to the limitations inherent in human understanding. Hartman (following Maimonides) proposes that God limits revelatory truth to the needs and abilities of particular communities. Greenberg imagines a "step-by-step" unfolding of various covenantal relationships over time. Renewalists speak of ongoing encounters with God and multiple "Sinais." All affirm that God continues to act in the world, presenting and responding to novelty. None yet use the language of "persuasive" power to describe God's work, but it is language I believe they would find useful in expressing the notions of self-restraint, hiddenness, and creative Presence.

At this point, "identist pluralism" characterizes the position of this diverse group of Jewish Renewal thinkers. Despite their affirmation of naturalistic theism (in its weak form), their recognition of the complexity of God and the inability of any single tradition to embody God's plentitude, their high regard for other forms of revelation, and their acknowledgment of the limitations of human understanding, they all speak in terms of one and only one ultimate reality. Many paths are celebrated, but all paths are regarded as leading to a relationship with a single ultimate reality. This ultimate is understood as personal and as establishing interpersonal relationships akin to the model of Jewish covenant. (Although covenantal language is used less often by the Renewalists in reference to non-Jewish traditions, it is so deeply a part of Kabbalistic and Hasidic thought that it can be assumed until a noncovenantal option is articulated.) Not only do Renewalists assume a single ultimate, but they also assume the shared goal of perfecting the created order. God is the ultimate reality who establishes appropriate covenantal relations with different communities. Religions, then, are all engaged in some form of the covenantal model and thus involved in a personal relationship with a personal God in efforts to improve present conditions.

In the main, the reasons why Jewish thinkers have not moved toward a differential pluralism are more sociological than theological. As yet, the discussion about religious pluralism among Jewish theologians has taken place almost entirely within the bounds of Jewish-Christian relations or intra-Jewish relations. Apart from these discussions, religious pluralism has simply not been as pressing an issue as the responses either to the Holocaust or to the founding of the State of Israel (and the numerous attendant issues associated with both). For example, although Greenberg participated in the groundbreaking conversations with the Dalai Lama in 1990, his covenantal theology is first and foremost a response to the Holocaust and not to the truth claims of other traditions.[54] In the end, it may

---

54. See Kamenetz, *The Jew in the Lotus.*

be sociological reasons that eventually lead to the development of a pluralistic pluralism. Jewish Renewal is home to many Jews who have explored Buddhism as part of their spiritual journey and who maintain a positive relationship with it, even as they develop their neo-kabbalistic and neo-Hasidic approach to Judaism. As Renewal theology develops, it may respond to the claims of its adherents to recognize Buddhism and Judaism as expressing complementary but distinct truths, based on their experiences as practitioners of both traditions.

Another reason why a differential, deeper pluralism has not yet been considered among this group of Jewish thinkers is the underlying essentialism that characterizes their approaches. Greenberg addresses the increased risk of assimilation that comes with an affirmation of religious pluralism, but he does so by making the "risk" an occasion for "choice." He writes: "We act out of weakness to retain the otherness of others because we are afraid we cannot survive choice. Is not the ultimate message of the covenant that God wants us to exercise choice?"[55] In other words, for Greenberg, religious pluralism calls on individuals to clarify their faith commitments and to choose one tradition over another. He does not address the possibility that pluralism may result in new forms of traditions. Intermarriage and the identity issue raised by the emergence of hybrid religious identities (such as Jewish-Buddhists) have not been addressed as issues related to religious pluralism. Both issues challenge the essentialism of traditions in a direct way, clearly violating boundaries. The fact that these issues have been ignored and that the existence of "other traditions" has not been seen as equally problematic lends credence to the suspicion that, thus far, Jewish thinking about religious pluralism has assumed boundaried entities. Although they all acknowledge the responsive character of the covenantal relationship and the ongoing creative process, as well as the limited nature of human understanding and religious communal understanding, they nonetheless hold to the idea of Judaism as fundamentally a theologically independent and self-sufficient system. Other traditions are pictured as "next to" or side by side with Judaism. A model of external relations makes it less likely that the internal experience of other traditions will be seriously entertained.[56]

Among many Orthodox Jews, pluralism is equated with relativism and thus rejected. For example, Rabbi Marc Angel, a past president of the Rabbinical Council of America and a member of the Orthodox Caucus, writes that "since [pluralism] is generally used as a vague synonym for relativism, the Orthodox find it intellectually and religiously unacceptable." Although he distinguishes between pluralism and relativism, he ends up conjoining the two, concluding that, "[i]n short, pluralism/relativism is one sure way for unraveling the whole-

---

55. Greenberg, "Judaism and Christianity: Their Respective Roles in the Strategy of Redemption," 26–27.

56. Greenberg writes, "How else could multiple models [of covenant] be created except in communities which must have their own inner *élan*, their own procedures, their own hierarchy, and their own standard symbols of participation?" ("Judaism and Christianity: Their Respective Roles in the Strategy of Redemption," 24).

ness of the Jewish people."[57] Greenberg and Hartman clearly oppose this under-standing of pluralism. But they have set up the relationship between traditions in such a way that the accusation of relativism is not groundless. Greenberg's affir-mation of multiple legitimate covenants, all with the same purpose and goal, and Hartman's support for limited revelatory relationships, perfectly tailored to par-ticular communities, increase tolerance but do not contribute to an expanded understanding of the very reality that they believe to be diverse, complex, and only partially experienced by human beings.

Surely there are advantages in proposing a pluralistic ontology, such as the ability to support pluralism without succumbing to either relativism or inclu-sivism. Is there any reason why a Jewish thinker could not do so? Can a monothe-ist affirm the existence of plural ultimates? While it is one thing to imagine that truth is not exclusive, it is another to propose that there is more than one ori-enting principle. Can there be a Jewish affirmation of Cobb's proposition that "in the full complexity of reality . . . 'Emptying' identifies one truly important aspect, and 'God' another"?[58] The inclination, I believe, is to affirm diverse aspects of reality but to treat them as aspects of a single ultimate, God. If God "will come in new ways," as Hartman interprets the divine names, can't one of those ways be impersonal and formless? Can a Jew say about a Buddhist's experience of emptiness that "this, too, is an aspect of God"? In fact, such an interpretation leads to the imposition of theism and the denial of the possibility of nontheistic experience. It has untenable similarities to the grace bestowed on "anonymous Christians." As Griffin and others have pointed out, such a move collapses plu-ralism into inclusivism.

Cobb points to Christocentrism as "the deepest and fullest reason for open-ness to others"[59] and also as the basis of Christian uniqueness. The Jewish notion of covenant may function likewise for Jews and thereby enable the affirmation of plural ultimates to explain the quite different experience of others. In the con-cept of covenant, several values are affirmed that are important for the affirma-tion of genuine religious pluralism: relationality as fundamental, freedom and novelty as qualities of God and the created world, and the demand that humans "choose life" and act in its behalf. Conceived as a pattern for becoming more fully alive by entering into conscious relationships with the profusion of life, covenant can be the means by which Jews affirm truly diverse experiences of reality. For the Jewish thinkers considered in this essay, covenant is central to their affirma-tion of generic religious pluralism; it is possible for it to serve also as the basis for an affirmation of deep religious pluralism.

57. Angel, "Pluralism and Jewish Unity."
58. Cobb in Swidler et al., *Death or Dialogue?* 6.
59. Cobb, *Transforming Christianity and the World*, 71.

Chapter 6

Anekanta Vedanta

Toward a Deep Hindu
Religious Pluralism

Jeffery D. Long

TOWARD A DEEP RELIGIOUS PLURALISM:
A WHITEHEADIAN APPROACH

The goal of this essay is to develop a "deep Hindu religious pluralism." This goal raises the questions: What is a "deep" religious pluralism? What distinguishes a deep religious pluralism from one that is superficial? And what do we mean by "religious pluralism"?

David Ray Griffin defines religious pluralism as consisting of two affirmations, one negative, and one positive:

> The negative affirmation is the rejection of religious absolutism, which means rejecting the a priori assumption that [one's] own religion is the only one that provides saving truths and values to its adherents, that it alone is divinely inspired, that it has been divinely established as the only legitimate religion, intended to replace all others. The positive affirmation, which goes beyond the negative one, is the acceptance of the idea that there are indeed religions other than one's own that provide saving truths and values to their adherents (3, above).

This is the understanding of religious pluralism with which I shall operate in this essay. I shall also presuppose that religious pluralism is a good thing, a correct attitude to hold.

As Griffin has explained, there is an ongoing debate in the contemporary academy over the meaning of religious pluralism and what religious pluralism *should* be. Because this position allows for subvarieties, several distinct forms of it have arisen. The debate is over which of these is the best, the most adequate to the reality of religious diversity.

This, of course, propels me back into the question with which I began: What is a "deep" religious pluralism? The definition of a deep religious pluralism with which I shall be operating is a stipulative one, according to which a form of religious pluralism is *deep* inasmuch as it reflects the real diversity of the religions that actually exist without either reducing that diversity to a single common idea or set of principles (which is different from discerning common themes that might actually unite all religions) or vitiating that diversity by devolving into a debilitating relativism.

The problem with many existing forms of religious pluralism, like that proposed by John Hick, is an *identist* tendency to presume that if many religions are true, then they must, as Griffin puts it, articulate the *same* truths and/or be "oriented toward the same religious object . . . and promote essentially the same end (the same type of 'salvation')."[1] But might there not be, as differential pluralists affirm, many aspects of the one larger truth that the religions express, many legitimate religious objects and ends?

An identist religious pluralism lacks "depth" and adequacy because attention to the particulars of the world's religions reveals at least three basic types of religion, distinguishable in terms of their religious objects, their salvific goals, and the corresponding worldviews that they affirm. Again following Griffin, I define these three types of religion in the following manner:

1. *Theistic religions* are oriented towards a Supreme Being, a personal God, and are productive of *salvation*, or a right relationship between God and the practitioner, which is conceived in various ways, such as loving union or eternal life with God in heaven, and typically have a strong ethical emphasis. Examples include Zoroastrianism, Judaism, Christianity, Islam, Shin Buddhism, and the Hindu Vaishnava, Shaiva, and Shakta faiths.

2. *Acosmic religions* are oriented towards an impersonal Absolute, or Ground of Being, and are productive of *realization* or *enlightenment*. Such religions are typically contemplative in nature, with a strong emphasis on wisdom and on gaining insight and transforming consciousness through meditation. Examples include Jainism, Theravada Buddhism, philosophical Daoism, and, within Hinduism, Advaita Vedanta.

---

1. Griffin, above, 24.

3. *Cosmic religions* are oriented towards the cosmos itself, the cosmic order, and the spiritual beings that inhabit it, and are productive of harmony within this cosmos and right relations with these beings. Examples of these religions include the so-called "animistic," indigenous traditions of the Americas, Africa, Australia, Asia, and of Europe (such as Wicca and the related Druidic and neopagan faiths, and the ancient Norse and Greco-Roman faiths), as well as Shinto, popular Daoism, and Confucianism.

The caveat, of course, must also be entered here that no religion fits exclusively into any of these categories. Rather, these categories mark the dominant trends within the religions included under them. In fact, *some* element of each category is present in nearly every world religion—preeminently, as we shall see, in Hinduism.

As it relates to these three types of religion, the main problem with identist religious pluralism is that it tends to reduce these three to one—most often to an acosmic impersonalism—and to privilege a realization experience over experiences of loving union with divinity or cosmic harmony. So although Hick's position, for example, is that "the Real"—the one transcendent object toward which he claims all religions are oriented—is beyond the categories of "personal" and "impersonal," he describes It in ways strikingly reminiscent of acosmic forms of Buddhism and the Advaita Vedanta school of Hinduism:

> [I]t cannot be said to be one or many, person or thing, substance or process, good or evil, purposive or non-purposive. None of the concrete descriptions that apply within the realm of human experience can apply literally to the unexperienceable ground of that realm [i.e., the realm of the Real, the spiritual realm].[2]

Hick could here just as easily be talking about the Advaitic *Nirguna Brahman*. Similarly, his account of the salvific process—as a process of self-transformation from an "ego-centered" to a "Reality-centered" state—is strongly reminiscent of acosmic religions. The implication that devotion to the "personae" of the Real, the personal deities of the theistic religions, is "really" a way of overcoming our state of ego-centeredness is not unlike Advaitic Hindu claims about the function of *Bhakti*, or devotion to a personal God.

However, the phenomenological evidence, if we take it seriously (which process thought allows us to do), suggests that experiences of a personal God and an impersonal Absolute are not reducible to one another, but are distinct and produce distinct—albeit overlapping—results in the lives of those who have them. To privilege one kind of experience and reduce the others to it is a failure of pluralism. A unified, nonrelativist worldview is needed in which these types of experience can retain their distinctiveness if a more adequate religious pluralism is to be developed.

2. Hick, *An Interpretation of Religion*, 246.

Whiteheadian process thought is just such a worldview. It allows a differential or deep religious pluralism in which all three types of religious object and the salvific experiences that correspond to them can be accepted, and in terms of which the varied worldviews of the many religious traditions can be interpreted not as incompatible but *complementary.*

The legitimate worry that underlies identist religious pluralism is the concern to avoid "debilitating relativism," meaning affirmation of diversity that results in an inability to affirm needed distinctions between truth and falsity, good and evil. Outlining an internally coherent worldview in terms of which the world's religions can be shown to be mutually compatible is a central task of the philosophy of religion. As Griffin writes:

> [T]he problem of the intellectual conflicts among the various religions has provided one of the major objections to the truth of religious beliefs, especially because the claim that religious beliefs reflect genuine religious experience is arguably undermined by the existence of radically different ideas of ultimate reality.[3]

Many religious pluralists—including, but not limited to, Hick—have therefore taken it to be imperative to demonstrate, in their pluralistic models, a convergence of religions. This has met with, at best, mixed success, because convergence has more often than not taken the shape of the *reduction* of several religious types to one. These thinkers have neglected Whiteheadian process thought to the detriment of their own positions. Process thought postulates the existence of a personal God, an impersonal Absolute, and an eternal cosmos of actual entities. All three religious objects and ends can obtain in this internally coherent worldview.

But the fact that process thought can account for the differences among the three *types* of religion does not make it able to account for *all* of the apparent incompatibilities among the world's religions. As Griffin points out, Christianity's "relations to Hinduism and Buddhism involve very different issues from those involved in its relations to Judaism and Islam."[4] Can process thought also be used to address the differences among religions of the *same* type, such as Judaism, Christianity, and Islam?

I would argue that it can. As I have shown elsewhere, process thought shares a number of basic metaphysical affinities with traditional Jain philosophy.[5] On the basis of their relational ontology, Jain thinkers developed, over the course of several centuries, a complex and logically rigorous method for demonstrating the deep compatibilities of seemingly incompatible metaphysical doctrines, using this method to resolve classical Indian philosophical disputes between the Brahmins and Buddhists. It seems to me that a Whiteheadian could use the same logical model.

---

3. Griffin, *Reenchantment without Supernaturalism,* 247.
4. Ibid., 248.
5. Long, "Plurality and Relativity"; "Multiple Aspects and Ultimate Notions."

Taking Whiteheadian process thought as the basis for a pluralistic model of truth also addresses a number of the other major concerns that have been raised as criticisms of the dominant forms of religious pluralism in contemporary Western academic discourse. Prominent among these, as Griffin points out (30–31, above), is the concern that pluralistic models of truth tend to be presented as religiously and philosophically neutral "metaviews" or as value-neutral theories of religion with a "neutral universality."

What emerges from such an approach, as Mark Heim points out, is a modern Western intellectual imperialism, an imposition of the standards of a particular culture—that of Western modernity—on the world's religions. This is an imposition arguably no less destructive in its potential to distort the religions than are the traditional religious absolutisms of which it is a critique.[6] This destructive potential is highlighted even further in an article by Kenneth Surin, in which he points out the affinities between this identist style of religious pluralism and the homogenization of culture under global capitalism.[7]

Another concern is that, in the writings of many pluralists, the desirability of pluralism is more often than not simply assumed, due to a perception of its being conducive to more positive interreligious relations and dialogue. But the urgency of the issues of interreligious violence and misunderstanding seems to be all the more reason to produce nuanced philosophical arguments that can answer potential criticisms of logical incoherence—arguments lacking in the writings of many contemporary religious pluralists.

If one holds a Whiteheadian process metaphysic, one can *expect* there to be the very kind of religious plurality that we actually find—because the universe, as conceived in process thought, lends itself to just such a plurality of interpretations. A Whiteheadian does not embrace religious pluralism as an ad hoc political stance because it is conducive to better interreligious relations (although an imperative to pursue this goal does emerge from process thought). Religious pluralism is a *logical implication* of process thought.

The fact that religious pluralism is a logical extension of a process worldview helps Whiteheadian religious pluralists avoid a debilitating relativism. Because they are already committed to certain propositions about the nature of reality, they are able to engage substantively with the world's religions. They are thus enabled to coordinate and synthesize insights from these diverse traditions into the Whiteheadian worldview, which is itself enriched by the encounter—as are, ideally, the religions themselves. This is one variety of the "mutual transformation" of which John Cobb speaks.[8]

This point addresses another criticism of religious pluralism: the charge, leveled by Paul J. Griffiths, that most pluralist conceptions of interreligious dialogue omit the substantive issues that make such dialogue at all interesting or intellec-

---

6. Heim, *Salvations*, 141–42.
7. Surin, "Towards a 'Materialist' Critique of 'Religious Pluralism.'"
8. Cobb, *Beyond Dialogue*.

tually engaging. Because they typically emphasize interreligious agreement and unity at the expense of the very real diversity and substantive differences that characterize the world's religions, such conceptions of dialogue tend to produce "a discourse that is pallid, platitudinous, and degutted."[9] They leave the adherents of the world's religions very little to talk *about*. What is there to discuss? If your religion is working for you and mine is working for me, we need not attack or seek to convert one another, but there also seems to be little motivation for us to interact at all. As we each go through the process of transformation from an "ego-centered" to a "Reality-centered" state, we may be more inclined to feel compassion for one another and to work for peace and social justice—as many pluralists, like Paul F. Knitter, argue. But can we *learn* from each other?

A Whiteheadian perspective, because it makes substantive claims, is able to engage with the world's religions in the intellectually interesting fashion that Griffiths says can occur only through interreligious *apologetics*, in which both sides are committed to a worldview but are, at the same time, open to learning something from one another.

Religious pluralists fear that such apologetic exercises are likely to degenerate into polemics, which can further degenerate into justifications for interreligious violence and oppression. One might argue that process thought is susceptible to the same misuse.

But given the hypothetical, open-ended nature of process thought, Whiteheadian religious pluralism is not an absolutist worldview, assumed to have all the answers already and hence open to other views only inasmuch as they reinforce beliefs already held. Process thought is open to the claims of the religions themselves, as vast repositories of human wisdom and experience. It does not see itself as offering the *final* answers to any of the ultimate questions. Process thinkers do, indeed, have definite views about the nature of reality, but they are also open to new experiences, insights, and expressions of truth. For while process thought aspires, as its ideal, to the articulation of "a coherent, logical, necessary system of general ideas in terms of which every element of our experience can be interpreted" (PR 3), it also recognizes that

> [p]hilosophers can never hope finally to formulate these metaphysical first principles. Weakness of insight and deficiencies of language stand in the way inexorably. Words and phrases must be stretched towards a generality foreign to their ordinary usage; and however such elements of language be stabilized as technicalities, they remain metaphors mutely appealing for an imaginative leap. (PR 4)

Process thought, therefore, encourages a keen awareness of the limits of language. "In philosophical discussion," Whitehead writes, "the merest hint of dogmatic certainty as to finality of statement is an exhibition of folly" (PR xiv). The

9. Griffiths, *An Apology for Apologetics*, xii.

assumption "that we are capable of producing notions which are adequately defined in respect to the complexity of relationship required for their illustration in the real world" he calls the "Dogmatic Fallacy" (AI 145).

Because of the character of Whiteheadian thought as a "middle path" between the extremes of absolute certainty and absolute skepticism, the Whiteheadian is in a position both to teach and be taught by the world's religions and philosophies. Cobb describes the open and open-ended character that is proper to a Whiteheadian pluralistic approach to truth when he speaks of "the self-relativization of metaphysics":

> It is the nature of process thought to understand itself as in process. There is no certain or irreformable core, however strongly one may be convinced of some formulations. Everything is always open for reconsideration. The expectation is that all of its ideas will some day be superseded, although it expects also that this supersession of ideas will still include the pre-linguistic discernments expressed in particular and imperfect ways in current formulations.[10]

My conclusion is that a religious pluralism expressed in terms of Whiteheadian process thought is an excellent contender for the title of a "deep religious pluralism." It does not reduce the diversity of the many religious interpretations and experiences of reality to one single type. Nor does it refrain from seeking to situate and to coordinate and synthesize these various interpretations and experiences within a larger internally coherent worldview, thus avoiding the potential charge of relativism. At the same time, this worldview is sufficiently open-ended and expansive that it is open to transformation *by* the religions and philosophies with which it comes into contact.

Presupposing this worldview, in the remainder of this essay I shall be developing a Hindu version of Whiteheadian religious pluralism.

ISSUES SPECIFIC TO A WHITEHEADIAN HINDU RELIGIOUS PLURALISM

What are the issues a Whiteheadian Hindu must face in developing a religious pluralism that is both authentically Whiteheadian *and* authentically Hindu? On my analysis, there are two such issues. The first is the pervasiveness of expressions of Hindu religious pluralism that seem to have an *identist* character. A Whiteheadian Hindu must face the hard truth that the identist religious pluralism, which has been so problematic in the Western academy, is essentially a *Hindu* position expressed in the guise of Western—typically Kantian—philosophical terminology.

Identist religious pluralists have essentially been echoing—and in some cases repeating almost verbatim—the claims of major nineteenth- and early twentieth-

---

10. Cobb, "Metaphysical Pluralism," 56–57.

century Neo-Vedantins like Ramakrishna Paramahamsa and Mahatma Gandhi. This fact accounts, in part, for the objection raised against identist religious pluralism that it is not an authentically Christian position. It is not—it is a Hindu position. Does this mean that Hinduism necessarily entails an identist position—in which case a *Whiteheadian* Hindu religious pluralism would be impossible? Or is an alternative Hindu view possible? I shall argue that such a view not only is possible, but already exists.

The second major issue a Whiteheadian Hindu must face is *inclusivism.* Many Hindu assertions often taken to express Hindu openness to other religions, and hence religious pluralism, are actually expressions of religious *inclusivism.* The seemingly inclusivist, as opposed to deeply pluralistic, character of Hindu assertions gives rise to the question: Is a truly Whiteheadian Hindu religious pluralism possible?

Hindus have long prided themselves on the internal diversity and inclusiveness of the Hindu tradition. Indeed, two of the seven points in the definition of Hinduism used by the Indian Supreme Court are (1) "[a] spirit of tolerance, and willingness to understand and appreciate others' points of view, recognizing that truth has many sides" and (2) the "[r]ecognition that paths to truth and salvation are many."[11] A contemporary Hindu creed includes the line, "I believe that no particular religion teaches the only way to salvation above all others, but that all genuine religious paths are facets of God's Pure Love and Light, deserving tolerance and understanding."[12]

This idea is expressed in the most ancient of Hindu scriptures, the *Rig-Veda*: "Reality is one, though the wise speak of it variously."[13] It is also expressed in the well-known *subhashita*, or proverb: "Truth is one, paths are many." A theistic version of this pluralistic approach is expressed in the *Bhagavad Gita* when Krishna proclaims the validity of many paths to salvation, or liberation: "As human beings approach me, so I receive them. All paths, Partha, lead to me."[14]

Such an attitude toward diversity has become especially prominent in the modern period—meaning, in India, since the early 1800s. The nineteenth-century Bengali saint Ramakrishna Paramahamsa, regarded by many as an *avatar*, or divine incarnation, was famous for his openness to a variety of religious practices. He even practiced the paths of several distinct Hindu *sampradayas* (denominations) as well as Christianity and Islam:

> I have practiced all religions—Hinduism, Islam, Christianity—and I have also followed the paths of the different Hindu sects. I have found that it is the same God toward whom all are directing their steps, though along different paths. He who is called Krishna is also called Shiva, and bears the name of the Primal Energy, Jesus, and Allah as well—the same Rama with a thousand names.[15]

---

11. Fisher, *Living Religions*, 126, 127.
12. Subramuniyaswami, *Dancing with Shiva*, 532.
13. *Rig-Veda* 1.164:46c.
14. *Bhagavad Gita* 4:11.
15. Nikhilananda, *The Gospel of Sri Ramakrishna*, 60.

The vivid imagery used by Ramakrishna to describe his conception of the relations among the world's religions continues to be used by many religious pluralists today:

> God can be realised through all paths. All religions are true. The important thing is to reach the roof. You can reach it by stone stairs or by wooden stairs or by bamboo steps or by a rope. You can also climb up a bamboo pole. . . . Each religion is only a path leading to God, as rivers come from different directions and ultimately become one in the one ocean. . . . All religions and all paths call upon their followers to pray to one and the same God. Therefore one should not show disrespect to any religion or religious opinion.[16]

Along similar lines, Mahatma Gandhi writes of the "Equality of Religions":

> Religions are different roads converging upon the same point. What does it matter that we take different roads so long as we reach the same goal? In reality there are as many religions as there are individuals. I believe in the fundamental truth of all great religions of the world. I believe that they are all God-given, and I believe that they were necessary for the people to whom these religions were revealed. And I believe that, if only we could all of us read the scriptures of different faiths from the standpoint of the followers of those faiths we should find that they were at bottom all one and were all helpful to one another.[17]

Hindus, especially in the modern period, have tended increasingly to conceive of Hinduism as something like a pluralistic model of truth along the lines of what many Western philosophers of religion have also been trying to develop. Indeed, Hinduism has been the inspiration and source for many Western pluralistic models—like those of Hick and Aldous Huxley—as well as the imagery in which these are expressed: many names for one God, many rivers flowing into one ocean, and many paths to a common destination.

With the philosophical positions and the writings of many contemporary Western religious pluralists containing echoes of the writings of such prominent figures of the contemporary Hindu tradition as Ramakrishna and Gandhi, one can see why a Hindu could conceivably look at Whiteheadian religious pluralism and say, "Aren't we already there? What need does Hinduism have for Whitehead?" The Whiteheadian answers this question with another: "This may be religious pluralism, but is it *deep* pluralism?"

Some Hindus would say that it is. They can argue that Hinduism already *is* something like a Whiteheadian religious pluralism by virtue of the fact that Hinduism is not so much "a religion" as an architectonic structure incorporating the actual variety of religious paths that exist. This, in fact, is what many Hindus claim.

Empirically speaking, Hinduism is a vast family of faiths that contains many religions that cut across the spectrum of religious types described earlier. There

16. Richards, *A Source-Book of Modern Hinduism*, 65.
17. Ibid., 156, 157.

are theistic religions, such as the Vaishnava and Shakta faiths and some forms of Shaivism. There is acosmic impersonalism, such as that found prominently in Advaita Vedanta as well as in other forms of Shaivism. There is also cosmic religion, of which possibly the most ancient form of Hinduism—that described in the ritualistic Vedic *Samhitas*, or hymns—seems to have been an example, as well as the numerous practices that have been incorporated into Hinduism over the millennia of the Adivasis, the various aboriginal tribal peoples of India.

Hinduism has self-consciously theorized this internal diversity in terms of the four *yogas*, which are all conceived as valid paths to the common ultimate goal of liberation, or *moksha*, from *samsara*, the beginningless—and potentially endless—cycle of birth, death, and rebirth. The basic division of these *yogas* has striking affinities with the division of the world's religions into three types, based on religious object and salvific goal, presented earlier. There is the *karma yoga*, or spiritual discipline of good works, which encompasses the ancient Vedic ritual practices, as well as personal morality, or *dharma*, and so comes close to mapping onto the idea of cosmic religion. There is the *jñana yoga*, or way of realization, the path of acosmic impersonalism. There is *bhakti yoga*, or theistic devotionalism. Finally, there is the *raja yoga*, or royal yoga, the classical path of meditation as outlined in Patanjali's *Yoga Sutra*, which has been adopted in numerous traditions, including some that are usually regarded as distinct from Hinduism, such as Buddhism, Jainism, Sikhism, and even some non-Indian traditions.

As the reference to these traditions suggests, Hinduism has been *productive* of diversity. Three major world religions have emerged from it: Buddhism, Jainism, and Sikhism. According to at least one prominent definition of Hinduism, that used by the Indian Supreme Court, these three religions are actually forms or "branches" of Hinduism. Many regard them as *nastika*, or heterodox, Hindu sects.

Even the perceived "heterodoxy" of these three traditions is often downplayed in current practice. I have observed, at least in the Indian diaspora, that Hindus and Jains frequently make use of the same temple facilities. I have personally visited two "Hindu-Jain" temples in Pennsylvania alone, and am a member of one of them. These temples celebrate Jain holidays with no less fanfare than they do Hindu festivals and *pujas*, and they include images of the Jain *Tirthankaras* alongside those of Hindu deities such as Rama and Shiva.

Finally, in the minds of many Hindus, even Buddhism is assimilated to the Hindu tradition. "Bhagavan Buddha" is regarded as an *avatar* of Vishnu, a divine incarnation. Although historically an anti-Buddhist doctrine, its original polemical intent is forgotten. The influence of Hinduism, via Buddhism, on the cultures of East and Southeast Asia is well known. A number of Chinese and Japanese deities are clearly derived from Hindu originals.[18] In light of these relationships, many Hindus regard Hinduism as the "trunk" of the "tree" of the world's religions and philosophies, the historical, cultural, and conceptual center from which its many branches have emerged.

18. Reader, *Simple Guide to Shinto*, 40, 41.

But many see this internally variegated tree as a unity, with which Hinduism is to be identified—which brings us back to the issue of inclusivism. In the Hinduism installment of the world religions video series entitled *The Long Search*, the following dialogue occurs between the narrator, Ronald Eyre, and a Hindu *pandit*:

> **Eyre:** Do you mean that we're all Hindus really, going various ways?

> **Pandit:** I think at the highest stage there is nobody beyond Hinduism. Everybody is a Hindu.

"Everybody is a Hindu." Is this a deep religious pluralism, or is it the most radical conceivable form of *inclusivism*?

Religious inclusivism is a position of which Western religious pluralists have long been critical. Seeing it as a paternalistic view—an exclusivist wolf in a pluralistic sheep's clothing—they have sought to distinguish it from pluralism. Inclusivism, like pluralism, is a position that has many possible subvarieties, some being more open to other religions than others. In general, though, it can be said that religious inclusivists, like religious pluralists, regard the world's religions in a positive light, as, in accordance with the definition of religious pluralism given earlier, providing "saving truths and values to their adherents."

What is problematic from the religious pluralists' perspective is that religious inclusivists are not inclined to view the world's religions in such a positive light *on the religions' own terms*. Inclusivists tend to take their own religion to be definitive of truth and salvation for all human beings, then judge the adequacy of other religions in terms of the resulting standard.

In these terms, the difference between inclusivism and *exclusivism*—which rejects the legitimacy of all religions but one—is that, whereas exclusivists evaluate other religions in terms of the standards of their own tradition and find those religions wanting, inclusivists do the same thing but with considerably greater interpretive charity. For exclusivists, one could say, the glass is half empty; for inclusivists, it is half full.

From a Whiteheadian pluralist perspective, the problem with both inclusivism and exclusivism is that they do not take with sufficient seriousness the possibility that other religions may teach important truths that are not already contained within their own traditions. Exclusivism and inclusivism are also not incompatible with a denial of the ultimate *legitimacy* of all other religions—with their right to exist *as* other religions. The question here is: Is this account descriptive of Hindu attitudes toward other religions? Is Hindu "inclusiveness" necessarily an assertion of Hindu superiority, a claim that Hinduism *already* includes all the truths of the other religions? Or is it a genuine openness—a deep religious pluralism that is willing to learn from other paths?

Before exploring these questions further, it is necessary to repeat the distinction made by Griffin between two positions that critics of inclusivism frequently conflate: *epistemic* and *soteriological* inclusivism (36, above). Soteriological inclusivism, I would argue, is rightly found objectionable. But epistemic inclusivism is an inevitable outcome of holding any nonrelativist position. Virtually all of us are inclusivists in this sense.

Griffin summarizes the Christian version of *soteriological* inclusivism in the following way:

> It asserts that Christianity is the only religion in full possession of saving truth, so that whatever religious truths are found in other religions are already included in Christianity. And it asserts that although all salvation comes through Jesus Christ, people in other religions can be included in this salvation. (35, above)

This doctrine is well illustrated by the Roman Catholic theologian Karl Rahner's concept of the "anonymous Christian." Like the *pandit* who claims that "everybody is a Hindu," Rahner claims that all people of good faith, regardless of explicit religious affiliation, are oriented salvifically towards Christ—even if only implicitly. This is because faith in Christ, in some form, is *constitutive* of human salvation. Through this ingenious, albeit paternalistic, formulation, Rahner reconciles the Christian insistence on the necessity of Christ for human salvation with the equally central proclamation of God's universal love.

Is Hindu inclusivism of this soteriological variety, which asserts the superiority of Hinduism as the only legitimate way to salvation? Is it the inevitable epistemic variety? Or is it something else? One classic statement of Hindu inclusivism says that

> [a] characteristic of Hindu religion is its receptivity and all-comprehensiveness. It claims to be the one religion of humanity, of human nature, of the entire world. It cares not to oppose the progress of any other system. For it has no difficulty in including all other religions within its all-embracing arms and ever-widening fold.[19]

This position seems not so much to affirm religious diversity as to obliterate it. Hinduism is not the one *true* religion, but the *only* religion! This is an odd claim, since Hindus clearly know of the existence of other religions. What does it mean to call Hinduism "the one religion of humanity"? I shall argue that what is at issue here is ultimately a matter of semantics, albeit one of great importance to the self-understanding of Hindus. But first I shall turn to the issue of the identist character of Hindu pluralism.

ADDRESSING THE MONISTIC OR IDENTIST
ORIENTATION OF HINDU PLURALISM

There is a sense in which a Hindu religious pluralism of any kind will inevitably be identist, albeit an identism that is not finally incompatible with a Whiteheadian religious pluralism. Identism in this sense can be called *minimalist* identism.

---

19. Pandit, *The Hindu Mind*, 30.

This minimal identism is not identist with respect to the ultimate religious object, for it is fully compatible with process thought's three ultimate realities. It is also not an identism with respect to religious ends, inasmuch as it still recognizes the distinct ends of loving union with the Supreme Being, realization of the Absolute, and harmony with the Cosmos—the ends of *bhakti yoga, jñana* and *raja yoga*, and *karma yoga*, respectively.

The identism to which I am referring is identist only with respect to a particular consequence that the Hindu tradition takes to arise from the attainment of any of these three ends, and to which all three of them are believed to lead. I referred above to the fact that the common soteriological goal of all of the four *yogas* is *moksha*, or liberation from *samsara*, the cycle of birth, death, and rebirth. This is a view that is, in my judgment, so pervasive in and so central to the Hindu tradition as to be nonnegotiable.

On the other hand, the ideal of liberation is broad enough that it still allows for considerable diversity in terms of what might constitute it. A Hindu religious pluralism will inevitably be identist in the sense that a Hindu will most likely conceive of the soteriological goals toward which all religions point as involving some kind of liberation from the rebirth process. But answers to the question, "Of what does such a liberation consist?" can and do vary enormously among the numerous schools of thought in Hinduism, and so still allow for considerable diversity. For Advaitins, liberation is an effect of the obliteration of personal identity in the realization of one's unity with the impersonal Brahman—indeed, not an obliteration so much as an awareness that there never was a distinct identity to obliterate in the first place. For theistic Vaishnavas, however, it is eternal life in heaven with Lord Vishnu, a life accompanied by retention of personal identity and memory, and even a quasi-physical form not unlike the glorified resurrection body in the Christian tradition. For Mimamsaka *karma yogis*, it is not *yet* a goal, life *in* the Cosmos being preferable, but for those who are weary of the world and desirous of liberation, the instructions for attaining it are available in the Upanishads.

For a variety of reasons, however, an Advaitic model has dominated recent English-language Hindu discourse, as well as discourse about Hinduism by non-Hindus; hence the tendency of Hindu-inspired Western writers such as John Hick to develop identist models that bear a strong resemblance to Advaita Vedanta. Because of the influence and the predominance of a particular interpretation of Advaita Vedanta in contemporary Hinduism, expressions of Hindu religious pluralism, too, tend to take an identist form, assuming all true religions must lead to an Advaitic realization.

Advaita Vedanta, however, does not reflect the dominant historical consensus, or even the contemporary consensus, of the Hindu tradition regarding the ultimate nature of reality, a point that Griffin and others have made.[20] As Griffin explains, "Most Hindu piety is theistic, being *bhakti* (devotion) to a personal deity."[21]

---

20. Griffin, *Reenchantment without Supernaturalism*, 278–79.
21. Ibid., 278.

Indeed, the practice of Hinduism is overwhelmingly theistic in nature. The kind of acosmic practice and understanding that Advaita Vedanta expresses—that ultimate reality is not a Supreme Person to whom one should be devoted, but an impersonal Absolute to be realized—is typically to be found either among the members of the original Advaita community—the *Dashanami* order of monks founded by Shankara (ca. 788–820 CE) and their lay supporters—or among more modern Western or westernized Hindus.

Theistic practice, of course, is not incompatible with Advaita Vedanta. Indeed, Shankara recommended the path of *bhakti*, the path of devotion to a personal deity, for householders, instituting the practice of *Pañcayatana Puja*, or devotion to the five deities: Vishnu, Shiva, Surya, Ganesha, and Shakti. All five of these deities are regarded in this tradition "as equal reflections of the one Saguna Brahman, rather than as distinct beings." It is this practice that laid the foundation for the modern practice "in which Hindus freely add Jesus, mother Mary, Mohammed, Buddha or any other holy personage to their altars," a practice typically taken to be indicative of Hindu religious pluralism.[22]

But according to Shankara, as Griffin points out, *Saguna Brahman*—Brahman with attributes, the Supreme Being or personal God—is derivative from *Nirguna Brahman*, the formless Brahman that, according to this school of thought, is finally the only true reality. All else, including the personal God, is a projection of *maya* (cosmic illusion) and an effect of *avidya* (ignorance). "Brahman is the reality—the one existence, absolutely independent of human thought or idea. Because of the ignorance of our human minds, the universe seems to be composed of diverse forms. It is Brahman alone. . . . It can never be anything else but Brahman. Apart from Brahman, it does not exist."[23] Even the Supreme Being, God (Bhagavan or Ishvara), is derivative from this impersonal Ground. "Devotion to a personal God, therefore, would involve an inferior relation to ultimate reality."[24] To be sure, such devotion can help one overcome the selfish, desiring ego. But ultimately, according to Advaita Vedanta—or at least according to its dominant interpretation—one must renounce such practices and take up the path of realization.

The *Bhagavad-Gita*, the most popular of Hindu scriptures in the modern period, regarded by many as having an authority on a par with the Vedas, acknowledges the legitimacy and the effectiveness of both practices, theistic and acosmic. But it actually recommends *bhakti*, or theistic devotionalism, as the more appropriate path for most people, due to the difficulty of the acosmic practice, which is essentially a monastic practice, requiring the renunciation of physical pleasures and most human social relations: "The difficulty of the search for the Unmanifest is greater [than that of *bhakti*]. Embodied beings can only attain it by constant striving, the suffering of their repressed senses, self-discipline, and

22. Subramuniyaswami, *Dancing with Shiva*, 779.
23. Prabhavananda and Isherwood, "Introduction to Shankara's Philosophy," 70.
24. Griffin, *Reenchantment without Supernaturalism*, 278.

anguish."[25] This verse, of course, is not incompatible with Advaita Vedanta. Shankara takes it to support his view that the *jñana yoga*, the impersonal path, is superior *because* it is more difficult, hence suited to persons of greater spiritual capacity. But his view is *not* universally held in the tradition and seems contrary to the plain sense of the text.

This brings us to the next point, which is that Vedanta, the larger stream of Hindu thought of which Advaita is a portion, is more internally diverse than the contemporary Western privileging of Advaita might suggest. Among the ten schools of Vedanta (only three of which are typically mentioned in textbooks on Hinduism or Indian philosophy), most are not, in fact, monistic in the same sense that Advaita is. Most, like Ramanuja's Vishishtadvaita Vedanta, seek to coordinate the experienced phenomena of identity and difference, of unity and diversity, into a coherent whole. This is not unlike Whiteheadian process thought, which coordinates unity and plurality, the one enduring reality and the many passing moments, and sees both as integral to human experience. Like process thought, most forms of Vedanta seek to affirm the reality of both the personal and impersonal, temporal and eternal, ultimate realities. Although the predominant tendency of all of these schools is to regard God, Being, and World as aspects of one larger, all-comprehensive Reality or Whole, a real ontological pluralism with an *organic* unity is sometimes affirmed.

This is also true of the Vedanta of the modern period, from which many Western forms of religious pluralism take their inspiration. Swami Dayananda Saraswati (1824–83), the founder of the *Arya Samaj*, made the following affirmation, not unlike a Whiteheadian affirmation of a plurality of ultimate realities:

> There are three things beginningless: namely, God, Souls, and *Prakriti* or the material cause of the universe. As they are eternal, their attributes, works and nature are also eternal.[26]

A Whiteheadian would, of course, reject the *ontological* dualism this quotation suggests between the soul and matter, regarding soul as a personally ordered series of experiencing actual entities and *Prakriti* as an aggregate of such entities experienced as an object. Process thought, in a basic ontological sense, is monistic, but dualistic with respect to the kinds of structures which actual entities can constitute. But Dayananda Saraswati's basic ontological pluralism and his rejection of the Advaitic monism of many of his fellow Neo-Vedantins places him closer to Whitehead than to Shankara, as indicated by his statement: "The *Neo-Vedantists* look upon God as the *efficient* as well as the *material* cause of the universe, but they are absolutely in the wrong."[27]

---

25. *Bhagavad Gita* 12:5.
26. Richards, *A Source-Book of Modern Hinduism*, 55.
27. Ibid.

Ramakrishna (1836–86) also made a distinction between the personal deity—his favored divinity being Kali, the Divine Mother—and the impersonal Absolute, in spite of the identist flavor of his many famous pronouncements about the unity of the world's religions. For his devotees, he is definitive of the virtuoso religious practitioner. In the course of his many famous *sadhanas* (spiritual practices), Ramakrishna is said to have experienced forms of *both* acosmic realization *and* loving union with divinity. In contrast with Advaita, he recommended *both* as salvific and liberating experiences, reducing neither to the other. For his own part, Ramakrishna preferred to remain in *bhavamukha*, a state in which he is said to have been aware *simultaneously* of *both* the one eternal substance at the foundation of existence *and* the ongoing personal presence of divinity.[28]

Another Bengali sage of the modern period, Sri Aurobindo (Aurobindo Ghose, 1872–1950), is also known to have experienced all three kinds of religious object. He developed a system of "Integral Yoga," with affinities to process thought, intended to incorporate all three, without privileging one over the rest.[29]

Finally, Mohandas K. Gandhi (1869–1948) similarly affirmed the validity of both theistic and nontheistic religious experiences and ends, despite the identist implications of many of his pronouncements on religious pluralism. Indeed, what is particularly of interest about Gandhi's perspective is the fact that he drew explicitly upon the Jain doctrines of relativity, mentioned earlier, in the formulation of his view. These three doctrines are *Anekantavada*, the "Doctrine of Pluralism," *Syadvada*, the "Doctrine of Conditional Predication," and *Nayavada*, the "Doctrine of Perspectives." If, as I have argued elsewhere, these doctrines arise out of a relational ontology essentially identical to that affirmed by Whitehead, then Gandhi's willingness to draw upon these ideas suggests a *logical* compatibility, at least indirectly, with process thought.

While Gandhi embraced Advaita in many of his writings, he also spoke and wrote frequently of a personal God and of the importance of discerning and behaving in accordance with God's will—theistic concepts more in line with Vaishnava Dvaita thought, or Judeo-Christian-Islamic monotheism, than with the impersonal, formless Brahman of Advaita Vedanta. This apparent inconsistency was pointed out by a reader of his newspaper, *Young India*, in a letter to the editor. Gandhi's response is revealing and useful in discerning a consistent philosophy underlying his seemingly disconnected pronouncements on religion:

> I am an *advaitist* and yet I can support *Dvaitism* (dualism). The world is changing every moment, and is therefore unreal, it has no permanent existence. But though it is constantly changing, it has a something about it which persists and it is therefore to that extent real. I have therefore no objection to calling it real and unreal, and thus being called an *Anekantavadi* or a *Syadvadi*. But my *Syadvada* is not the *syadvada* of the learned, it is peculiarly my own. I cannot engage in a debate with them. It has been my experience that

28. Tapasyananda, *Sri Ramakrishna: Power and Glory.*
29. Griffin, *Reenchantment without Supernaturalism*, 279.

I am always true from my point of view, and am often wrong from the point of view of my honest critics. I know that we are both right from our respective points of view. And this knowledge saves me from attributing motives to my opponents or critics. The seven blind men who gave seven different descriptions of the elephant were all right from their respective points of view, and wrong from the point of view of one another, and right and wrong from the point of view of the man who knew the elephant. I very much like this doctrine of the manyness of reality. It is this doctrine that has taught me to judge a Musalman [a Muslim] from his own standpoint and a Christian from his. Formerly I used to resent the ignorance of my opponents. Today I can love them because I am gifted with the eye to see myself as others see me *and vice versa*. I want to take the whole world in the embrace of my love. My *anekantavad* is the result of the twin doctrine of *Satya* and *Ahimsa* [truth and nonviolence].[30]

More can be said on this topic, but this brief survey of the tradition should suggest that Hindu religious pluralism, despite the identist shorthand Hindu thinkers often use to express it, is far more Whiteheadian than is generally recognized.

ADDRESSING HINDU RELIGIOUS INCLUSIVISM: *IS* EVERYBODY A HINDU?

But how should a Whiteheadian religious pluralist respond to Hindu assertions to the effect that Hinduism is not merely the only *true* religion, but the *only* religion? Is it truly pluralistic for a Hindu to see religions like Christianity and Islam as forms of *bhakti yoga*, or Jainism and Buddhism as variants of the *jñana yoga*? Or is this a "Hinduization" masquerading as pluralism, turning everyone into an "anonymous Hindu"?

One could argue that this Hindu position does not so much celebrate diversity as obliterate it. Other religions are not accepted as much as their very "otherness" is denied. "Other" religions, in a certain sense, do not even exist. A Whiteheadian Hindu religious pluralist needs to ask whether this inclusivist Hindu stance can be reconciled with a deep religious pluralism. This means asking: When Hindus say, "Everybody is a Hindu" or "All religions are forms of Hinduism," is this actually a version of Hindu triumphalism, the "bad" kind of closed inclusivism that contemporary Western religious pluralists accuse Christian inclusivists like Rahner of perpetuating? Or is it something else? I shall argue that this is ultimately a semantic issue hinging on the meanings of two key terms that are actually foreign to the Hindu tradition—"Hinduism" and "religion."

As Wilhelm Halbfass observes, "It has often been stated that Hinduism is not a well-defined, clearly identifiable *religion* in the sense of Christianity or Islam, but rather a loosely coordinated and somewhat amorphous conglomeration of

30. Gandhi, *Young India: 1919–1931*, 30.

'sects' or similar formations."[31] Indeed, Hindus have historically used not the term "Hindu" but more specific sectarian labels, such as Vaishnava, Shaiva, Shakta, and Smarta.

The same is the case with the term "religion." This term, with all of its various implications, was foreign to the South Asian cultural context prior to extensive contact with the West. Two Sanskrit words come close to meeting the definition of "religion" as generally understood in the West. There is *dharma*, which is often translated—confusingly, I shall argue—"religion," but which actually carries a semantic range that encompasses "personal duty," "way of life," and "cosmic order," the latter meaning a kind of architectonic structure of reality that encompasses the realms of both fact and value. Then there is *sampradaya*, which means "*a* religion," a particular sect or denomination.

"Hinduism" is really an artificial creation, a construct developed first by Muslim and then by European Christian conquerors in order to facilitate their dominion over the Indian subcontinent.[32] The power to define a thing is a power that imperialist forces have utilized throughout history in order to shape the world according to their own ends, as Edward Said's *Orientalism* and Ronald Inden's *Imagining India* have shown. The concept of "Hinduism" has helped enable Westerners for centuries to divest the people of India of agency by teaching them that they are benighted victims of an inescapable prison of superstition and otherworldly spirituality. Hinduism is "'a mysterious amorphous entity,' one that is palpable yet lacks something." What does it lack? "[A] 'world-ordering rationality,'" which the West provides.[33]

One modern Hindu response to this characterization of Hinduism as amorphous, and *not* "a religion" but a collection of sects, has been to accept it. However,

> the weakness or deficiency [this characterization] suggests has been turned into an element of self-affirmation. In this view, the fact that Hinduism is not a *religion* in the ordinary sense does not imply a defect; rather, it means that it is located at a different and higher level. It is something much more comprehensive, much less divisive and sectarian than the 'ordinary' religions. . . . Instead, it is—according to this view—a framework, a concordance and unifying totality of sects. The 'ordinary' religions, such as Christianity and Islam, should not be compared and juxtaposed to Hinduism itself, but to the sects, that is, 'religions' that are contained within Hinduism. Hinduism as the *sanatanadharma* is not a religion among religions; it is said to be the 'eternal religion,' [the] religion in or behind all religions, a kind of 'metareligion,' a structure potentially ready to comprise and reconcile within itself all the religions of the world, just as it contains and reconciles the so-called Hindu sects, such as Shaivism or Vaishnavism and their subordinate 'sectarian' formations.[34]

31. Halbfass, *Tradition and Reflection*, 51.
32. Inden, *Imagining India*, 85–130.
33. Ibid., 86.
34. Halbfass, *Tradition and Reflection*, 51, 52–53.

As Halbfass characterizes it, the Hindu affirmation of the all-inclusiveness of Hinduism is a form of Hindu triumphalism, a reply to those who define Hinduism as amorphous and then denigrate it for being so, a counterassertion that the cohesiveness of other religions is bought at the price of a limited and exclusive vision of truth.

But although this triumphalist dimension of Hindu inclusivism exists and is every bit as unpluralistic as its Christian or Islamic equivalents, is it the entire story? Before one gets caught up in denunciations of Hindu absolutism, it is necessary to examine reasons other than human depravity—*Hindu* reasons—that might shed more light on this stance and the *legitimate* reasons why a Hindu might hold it.

When Hindus call Hinduism "an all-inclusive religion," what is meant by these words, which are, in their origins, foreign to a Hindu self-understanding? Might it be that these terms are being stretched beyond their ordinary meaning to refer to indigenous Hindu concepts? How else could one make sense of the claim that Hinduism is the *only* religion, when Hindus are well aware that other faiths exist?

What does "Hindu" mean to Hindus? First of all, one is not simply a "Hindu" any more than one is simply a "Christian." A Christian is, except in idiosyncratic cases, a Roman Catholic, a Protestant, or a member of one of the Orthodox churches. Similarly, a Hindu is, at least by birth, connected to a subsect of one of the four major Hindu traditions: the orthodox Vedic Smarta tradition or one of the three mainstream theistic traditions—Vaishnava, Shaiva, and Shakta. Again, in premodern times, these religions or "subreligions" within Hinduism were the primary means by which Hindus identified themselves in what a modern Westerner would recognize as religious terms—as devotees of Vishnu or Shiva or Devi, and so on, with appropriate sectarian beliefs and practices.

The more comprehensive term, *dharma*, means, at its broadest, the totality of the cosmic order. In its narrowest meaning, it refers to one's own personal duties within that order—one's *svadharma*—as a member of society born with a specific role in a specific family, in a specific caste, in a specific community, *and* in a specific sect. *Dharma*, though it manifests as many *svadharmas*, is ultimately one.

Dharma is *sanatana*, or eternal. It is the universal law, the foundation of actual existence. Its literal meaning is "that which gives support." If it must be identified with the term "religion," it would mean something like "religion as such," the eternal ideal or "Platonic form" of religion, in which all particular instances of religion participate, rather than any one actual religion (although it has gradually come to take on the latter usage in more recent times). My own preference, however, would be to make a sharp distinction between *dharma* and religion, despite current usage.

In contrast with the unity of *dharma*, the sectarian varieties of the *yogas*, or ways to *moksha*, are numerous. A *sampradaya* is a genus with species, like a "religion" or a "denomination." *Dharma*, however, is not a genus with species but the basic structure of reality. It therefore makes no more sense to talk about "a *dharma*," on the premodern meaning of this term, than it does to talk about "a number four" (contrary to current usage, in which one hears terms like "Hindu Dharma," "Jain Dharma," "Sikh Dharma," and so on). When Hindus affirm that Hinduism "includes all religions," they essentially equate the Western term "religion," regarded as a genus, with the Hindu term *sampradaya*, similarly equating the Western term "Hinduism" with *dharma*.

This is logically distinct from Christian inclusivism, which amounts to saying: "Religion C—a particular member of the genus 'religion'—includes all religious truth." Hindu "inclusivism," on the understanding I am suggesting, amounts to a tautology: "Religion as such includes all religious truth." Indeed, a better formulation would be: "The basic structure of reality includes all religious truth."

Articulating something like the *Sanatana Dharma*—the "eternal religion" in the sense of the all-inclusive worldview of general truths that encompasses all the world's religions and philosophies—is arguably the ideal goal of all pluralistic interpretations of religion: to give expression to the larger vision and structure of reality that underlies all religious and philosophical diversity. But, as we have already seen, one central insight of Whiteheadian thought is that, with regard to the expression of this larger worldview in some historically particular linguistic and conceptual form, there will never be finality.

A question thus arises: Can the historical Hindu tradition, a tradition particular to a specific time and place, be identified with the *Sanatana Dharma*, the eternal truth, the structure of reality as such? Is using the term "Hinduism" to refer to this truth not like the false claim to universal neutrality asserted by identist forms of religious pluralism?

I would say that, triumphalist motives aside, this issue has arisen out of an ambiguity in the meaning of the word "Hinduism," an ambiguity traceable to the word's history. If, in the mind of a Hindu, "Hinduism" means *dharma*, and, in the mind of someone else, "Hinduism" is a *sampradaya*, a particular religion alongside others, then something will definitely get lost in translation—namely, Hindu religious pluralism.

One can discern at least three distinct meanings of the term "Hinduism." Many modern Hindu authors frequently conflate these meanings, or oscillate between them without warning, sometimes even in mid-sentence. Which definition is employed will have a profound effect upon the meaning of statements such as "Everybody is a Hindu," hence determining whether they are compatible with a deep religious pluralism. Clarifying what we mean by "Hinduism" will go a long way toward addressing the issue of Hindu inclusivism and whether Hinduism can truly be deeply pluralistic.

In order to distinguish between these three meanings, I shall use the nomenclature of Hinduism$_I$, Hinduism$_V$, and Hinduism$_{SD}$. These "Hinduisms" are distinguished in the following manner:

1. Hinduism$_I$ refers to Hinduism as the family of religious traditions that are indigenous to the *Indian* subcontinent. "Hindu," on this understanding, basically means "Indian."

2. Hinduism$_V$ refers to Hinduism as the *Vedic* tradition, that family of religious traditions and philosophical schools that take the Vedas to be, in some sense, sacred and foundational. This premodern orthodox Brahmanical meaning is the standard world religion textbook meaning of Hinduism, the one Western scholars of religion typically have in mind when they use this term.

3. Hinduism$_{SD}$ refers to Hinduism as the *sanatana dharma*, the "eternal religion," the "universal religion," the "metareligion" inclusive of all others. This understanding of Hinduism is the most relevant to our concerns. It seems to inform most Hindu writing that can be interpreted as expressing religious pluralism, religious inclusivism, or both.

Whereas Hinduism$_{SD}$ is the most inclusive meaning of "Hinduism" and Hinduism$_V$ the least inclusive, Hinduism$_I$ is the most *problematic*. The logical relations among these meanings of Hinduism can be illustrated schematically in the following way:

Hinduism$_V$—The Vedic Tradition	*Hinduism$_I$—The Indian Tradition*	*Hinduism$_{SD}$—The Sanatana Dharma*
Sampradayas ("Religions"): Smarta	Hinduism$_V$—The Vedic Tradition	Hinduism$_I$—The Indian Tradition
Vaishnava	Jainism	*Non-Indian Theistic Religions:*
Shaiva	Buddhism (Theravada, Mahayana, Vajrayana)	Zoroastrianism, Judaism, Christianity, Islam, etc.
Shakta		*Non-Indian Acosmic Religions:*
Darshanas ("Philosophies"):	Sikhism	Gnosticism, Neo-Platonism,
Samkhya	Lokayata (Materialism)	Philosophical Daoism, etc.
Yoga	Ajivika (extinct)	*Non-Indian Cosmic Religions:*
Nyaya		Shinto, Popular Daoism,
Vaisheshika		Confucianism, Indigenous Religions, etc.
Purva Mimamsa		*Non-Indian Secular Philosophies:*
Uttara Mimamsa (Vedanta—Advaita, Vishishtadvaita, Dvaita, Bhedabheda, etc.)		Modern Science, Marxism, Process Thought, etc.

A simplistic identification or confusion of Hinduism$_{SD}$ with Hinduism$_V$ or Hinduism$_I$ leads to the closed variety of inclusivism. But *some* form of the idea of Hinduism$_{SD}$—ultimate truth or cosmic order, "eternal wisdom (*veda*)"—is as indispensable for a Hindu religious pluralist as is the symbol of Christ for a Christian religious pluralist. What ultimately is at issue is whether Hinduism$_{SD}$ needs to be called "Hinduism" at all; for the very ambiguity of the term "Hinduism" leads to the confusion just mentioned, and so to the problematic type of inclusivism.

The *identification* in many Hindu writings of either Hinduism$_V$ or Hinduism$_I$ with *Sanatana Dharma*, the Eternal Truth, implies an absolutism that is the antithesis of a deep religious pluralism. It restricts truth by identifying a particular historical and linguistic expression of truth with truth itself. It may evidence the same closed attitude that Hindus criticize in others. It also violates Hindu tradition, which teaches that Brahman is *neti, neti*—"Not this, not that"—and so cannot be defined in words.[35]

The ambiguity of the term "Hinduism" is a function of the fact that the very notion of "Hinduism" is a foreign import, an outside imposition. The word "Hindu" is a geographic term, a Persian mispronunciation of the word "Sindhu," the river beyond which, from a Persian perspective, lay "Hindustan," the land of the "Hindus." In other words, "Hindu" simply meant, in its origins, "Indian." The religion of the Hindus—of the Indians—is what I am calling Hinduism$_I$.

Hinduism$_I$, being simply an ethnogeographic term meaning "Indian," is not very useful for the purpose of pointing out a coherent tradition. To be sure, one can argue that there are quite a few common assumptions and issues that give some cohesiveness to what one might call the "Indian tradition," just as there is a similar cohesiveness to the "Western tradition." But this elides significant differences internal to both "traditions." Ideas that unite most of the schools of thought that make up this tradition—Hinduism$_V$, Jainism, Buddhism, and Sikhism—include *karma*, *moksha*, and *samsara*. But Hinduism$_I$ also includes the Lokayata, or Materialist, philosophy, which rejects these ideas.

Hinduism$_I$, being the definition employed by the Indian constitution, serves mainly to distinguish Hinduism from nonindigenous or "foreign" religions: Christianity and Islam. This, however, is a problematic usage because it is precisely such a nationalistic definition of Hinduism that helps the anti-Christian and anti-Islamic rhetoric that has been a major Hindu contribution to the poisoning of interreligious relations in India in the modern period. The logic of the exclusivism based on this definition is that if "Hindu" means "Indian," then the "Indianness"—and the patriotism—of those who do not define themselves as "Hindu" can be called into question.

Christians and Muslims in India can thus be viewed with suspicion, as outsiders and invaders. This thinking can also fuel questions about the "loyalty" of Hindus who reach out to other communities—hence the assassination of Mahatma Gandhi by a fellow Hindu for his alleged "treason" against Hinduism in seeking Hindu-Muslim unity and unity amongst the castes of Hinduism.

This definition also has a significant impact on non-Indian converts to Hinduism, such as myself; for the "Hinduness" of those of us who hold Hindu beliefs

35. Brihadaranyaka Upanishad 4.5:15.

and engage in Hindu practices but are not ethnically Indian is problematized by this same logic.

The identification of Hinduism$_I$ with Hinduism$_{SD}$ essentially amounts to a nationalistic assertion that India is the fountain of all primordial wisdom. Such an identification issues in a closed inclusivism, a restrictive understanding of truth, for the fairly clear reason that it can, like all forms of nationalism, slide easily into an assertion that no other culture has ever done anything worthwhile, that India has much to teach the rest of the world but nothing to learn.

As a definition of Hinduism, Hinduism$_I$—rooted in the *Hindutva* ideology of V. D. Savarkar—is just inclusive enough to be so vague as to be useless from a scholarly point of view. At the same time, it is just exclusive enough to promote interreligious violence, marginalization, and hatred. I personally think it should be jettisoned.

Because of the ambiguities inherent in Hinduism$_I$, this definition has, in fact, been largely abandoned by scholars of religion, who primarily employ Hinduism$_V$, a definition that does point to something fairly specific and that also seems to have more foundation within the tradition itself. Hinduism$_V$ is rooted in a Brahmanical understanding of what is now called "Hinduism." On this understanding, one is a Hindu if one recognizes, in some sense, the authority and sanctity of the Vedas (which usually, though not always, implies membership by birth in the *varna* or "caste" system as well). This is, in one sense, a restrictive definition of Hinduism; but it is also a strikingly liberal and inclusive one. Historically, as the schematic above suggests, it has allowed for an enormous variety of internal diversity within the Hindu, or Brahmanical, tradition.

This inclusiveness is a function of the fact that Vedic literature does not present a single coherent worldview. Views as divergent as monistic idealism and ontological pluralism are thus able to claim Vedic authority. It is also the case that, as the tradition developed historically, the actual Vedic texts became more and more remote from many of the tradition's central concerns. Allegiance to the Vedas eventually became more of a political statement, a way of locating oneself within the Brahmanical hierarchy of views, than a substantive indicator of one's philosophical position. The term "Veda" came to refer to an unspecified, widely revered primordial wisdom. Authors claiming allegiance to the Vedas could, and still do, articulate positions with little or no relation to the views laid out in any actual Vedic text.

The religious paths and systems of philosophy in the Vedic tradition include, at the most orthodox end of the spectrum, the explicitly Veda-based Purva Mimamsa and Vedanta *darshanas*. Then, within the broad mainstream of the Vedic tradition, there are the various Hindu theistic paths, which nominally acknowledge the Vedas, but give far greater emphasis, in practice, to their own sectarian literatures.

But this tradition also includes Samkhya and Yoga, which can hardly be called even nominally Vedic. Although these two systems do not *deny* the authority of the Vedas, they are based on the enlightenment experiences of their sage-founders,

Kapila and Patañjali. It is not obvious from examining their root-texts, or *sutras*, that the Vedas historically had any relevance to them whatsoever, with respect to their origins (though they do share certain ideas and vocabulary with the Upanishads). Perhaps they were later incorporated into the Vedic fold because of their widespread followings, an incorporation made possible because they were not explicitly *opposed* to the Vedas. Some speculate that these two schools (along with Jainism) are remnants of a pre-Vedic culture.

In what sense, then, is Hinduism$_V$ a restrictive understanding? This has to do with the premodern, authoritarian, and supernaturalist character of orthodox Brahmanical epistemology. If a path explicitly rejects Vedic authority, then even if it is substantially *identical* with some Vedic path, it is regarded by orthodox Brahmins as beyond the pale of legitimate practice and belief. Jainism and Buddhism, therefore, are regarded by orthodox Brahmins as being on the same level as the Lokayata or Materialist system and are designated by the same term of opprobrium—*nastika*, or "denier," often translated today as "atheist," the closest Hindu term that there is to "heretic."

Therefore Hinduism$_V$, because it bases itself not on common human experience and reason but on the authority of a set of texts, is basically a *premodern* understanding of Hinduism. It is also an *exclusivist* understanding; for rejection of the Vedas removes even those with substantively Vedic views from the pale of religious legitimacy.

In terms of its basic logic, this is not much different from Christian exclusivism, which regards even religions with essentially the same worldview and ethical norms as Christianity to be beyond the pale of salvation if they do not accept Jesus as Lord and Savior. According to orthodox Brahmins, those who reject the authority of the Vedas are beyond the pale of eligibility for the saving knowledge that alone can lead to *moksha*. *Nastikas* can aspire to liberation only if they accept the authority of the Vedas or if they are fortunate enough to be reborn in a Brahmanical household. Hinduism$_V$ is therefore not an understanding of Hinduism that is conducive to religious pluralism, or even to religious inclusivism in its wider sense, as "including" traditions from beyond the Vedic fold. We are not yet in the realm of "Everybody is a Hindu."

However, modern Hindu writers, in contrast with more orthodox authors, base their claims ultimately, in keeping with the modern epistemic shift, on the authority of human experience and reason. They reconcile their commitment to the Vedas with their modern epistemology through an interpretation of the Vedas as recording the *experiences* of enlightened sages, or *rishis*, who discerned the *sanatana dharma*, the fundamental structure of reality, while deep in meditation. Such experiences are conceived as being available, in principle, to all who undertake the requisite yogic practices. Hinduism is, in the modern writings of the tradition, extolled as a supremely rational religion that has an empirical basis in meditative experience, and its scriptures are regarded as firsthand accounts of the fundamental structures of existence. "[T]he sages . . . in concentrating on consciousness itself . . . found they could separate strata of the mind and observe its workings as objectively as a botanist observes a flower. . . . Brahmavidya . . . is, in a sense, lab science."[36]

This is the Hindu version of the shift Griffin describes among Western thinkers from a *supernaturalist* to a *naturalist* worldview (13–21, above). The Vedas are seen by the premodern, orthodox Hindu tradition as "eternal," as existing outside of time and space and not subject to analysis by human reason. The Vedas are, on this premodern view, basically "supernatural." But with the modern shift, they become repositories of wisdom, available, in principle, to everyone—"natural" wisdom, not unlike scientific knowledge.

This is where Hinduism$_{SD}$, the all-inclusive metareligion, comes into play. If the Vedas articulate a worldview available, at least in principle, to human beings of all cultures and at all times, then that worldview becomes discernible, in principle, in the sayings of great wise people and mystics of *all* religions, not just Vedic religions. On this understanding, "Everybody is a Hindu" because everybody has access to the same truths that are recorded in the Vedas. Hinduism$_V$ is universalized, becoming Hinduism$_{SD}$.

In the modern period, therefore, one begins to find prominent Hindu thinkers such as Rammohan Roy, Ramakrishna, Vivekananda, Gandhi, Swami Prabhavananda, Paramahamsa Yogananda, and Sarvepalli Radhakrishnan extolling the virtues of figures like Jesus and the Buddha. The Hindu tradition becomes a universal tradition, *including* the wisdom of all the world's religions. To what extent this universalism amounts to a "closed" inclusivism of the kind Halbfass describes (which "finds" Vedic ideas latent in the teachings of the world's other religions) or is an "open" pluralism (incorporating into Hinduism$_V$ *new* understandings and insights from other religions) varies from author to author, and even from text to text by the same author. But it is clearly in the modern period, with the emergence of Hinduism$_{SD}$, that something like a deep Hindu religious pluralism becomes conceivable: Hinduism as an open-ended worldview.

But the question still remains: Why use the word "Hinduism"? Why *identify* the historical Vedic tradition—Hinduism$_V$—with the universal truth to which it points and in which it participates—the *Sanatana Dharma*—if, as so many modern Hindus claim, *all* traditions point to and participate in this truth? Is such a usage at all legitimate from a pluralistic perspective? In a world where, in the minds of most people, the word "Hinduism" refers to *a* religion alongside others, a particular way of life and worldview, this usage sounds absolutist and imperialist and is no less problematic, from the perspective of a religious pluralist, than are Christian or Islamic identifications of Christianity or Islam with the ultimate, absolute truth, the one true religion.

On the other hand, if one thinks not in English, but Sanskrit, and bears in mind the distinction between *dharma* and *sampradaya* discussed above, the picture changes. It is not only compatible with a deep religious pluralism, but is precisely the *point* of a deep religious pluralism, to affirm a more profound structure

---

36. *The Upanishads* (trans. Easwaran), 16.

of reality or cosmic order, aspects of which are manifested by the worldviews and practices of the various religions.

But what is the relationship of this order, or *dharma*, to Hinduism$_V$? If Hindus, even pluralistic Hindus, have a prior commitment to an understanding of the Vedic tradition as disclosing fundamental truths and as a reliable *guide* to truth, then, when they encounter the insights of other traditions, they will of course attempt to incorporate those insights in a way that will be coherent with what they already hold to be true from the Hinduism$_V$ tradition. This is the sense, mentioned earlier, in which an *epistemic* inclusivism is inevitable for anyone who is open to other views and yet is not a relativist. It is compatible with deep pluralism to evaluate other traditions in terms of one's own, provided one is also open to new truths that, though they may need to be *compatible with* what one already holds, will not necessarily be *identical to* it.

Significantly, not all Hindu thinkers automatically make the move from epistemic inclusivism to an inclusivist deployment of the term "Hinduism" as referring to the eternal religion—or better, to *dharma*. Gandhi, not unlike Whitehead, articulates a postmodern understanding of truth as transcending its historically or linguistically particular formulations, including Hinduism$_V$: "The one Religion is beyond all speech. It is not less real because it is unseen. This religion transcends Hinduism, Islam, Christianity, etc. It harmonizes them and gives them reality."[37] And Swami Vivekananda, rather than saying, "Everybody is a Hindu," articulates a position that anticipates Cobb's idea of the mutual transformation of religions through dialogue: "The Christian is not to become a Hindu or a Buddhist, nor a Hindu or a Buddhist to become a Christian. But each must assimilate the spirit of the others and yet preserve his individuality and grow according to his own law of growth."[38]

I, for one, would certainly prefer to think of myself as an adherent of *Sanatana Dharma*, the eternal religion—as living an authentic existence based on the universal structure of reality—than as Hindu, as long as this term has exclusive geographical and ethnic connotations. Even many Indian Hindus share this sentiment. But the word "Hindu," despite its many ambiguities, still communicates more about our beliefs and practices than any other term in widespread current usage. Hindus, it seems, are stuck with "Hinduism." Hence I hope that my distinction between Hinduism$_I$, Hinduism$_V$, and Hinduism$_{SD}$ will catch on.

I believe it is perfectly legitimate for a Hindu to refer to the *Sanatana Dharma* as Hinduism, but with the self-relativizing understanding that a Christian can, with equal legitimacy, call it Christianity—much as Augustine does when he writes, "For what is now called the Christian religion existed of old and was never absent from the beginning of the human race until Christ came in the flesh."[39] Similarly, if by "Islam" a Muslim means obedience to the will of God

37. Richards, *Source-Book of Modern Hinduism*, 156.
38. Ibid., 89.
39. Ogden, *Is There Only One True Religion or Are There Many?* 1–2.

and holds that all human beings who follow the will of God, inasmuch as it is known to them, are thereby "anonymous Muslims," I have no objection. If this is what "Islam" means, then I *want* to be a Muslim. If "Christianity" means the primordial truth that "was never absent from the beginning of the human race," then I *want* to be a Christian. And if "Hinduism" means the *Sanatana Dharma*, the eternal order underlying all religions, then please, call me Hindu! But would it not be better—both simpler and less politically problematic—simply to call the truth the truth?

In conclusion, the interpretation of Hindu inclusivism along deeply pluralistic lines is a possibility, if one takes the term "Hinduism" in proclamations about all religions being parts of Hinduism to refer to an eternal truth *beyond* "religions," to the basic architectonic structure of reality pointed out by the Sanskrit term *dharma*. The term "Hindu," however, is unfortunate, inasmuch as it is bound up with a history and with ethnic and religious traditions that are *not* universal, but are highly particular and localized in scope. It is also problematic because of its ambiguity. It is natural for Hindus to use the term "Hinduism" to refer to the cosmic order. But if, in the minds of others, this term refers to a specific religion, then one's proclamations sound like Hindu triumphalism and may even slip into a deliberate triumphalism, if one ends up simply identifying an historical tradition or "ism" with ultimate truth. "Hinduism," then, is probably best replaced with a more specific indigenous term with less political and cultural baggage, like *Sanatana Dharma*, or truth, which was Gandhi's preferred term.

CONCLUSION: *ANEKANTA VEDANTA*—TOWARDS DEEP HINDU RELIGIOUS PLURALISM

Hinduism, as I understand it, entails a position that is fundamentally identical to a Whiteheadian religious pluralism. On this understanding, if one is a Hindu, then one is also a religious pluralist. One is a religious pluralist *because* one is a Hindu.

It is not, however, a perfect tradition—for there is no such thing. As Cobb says of process thought, Hinduism is—and will always be—"in process." The identification of Hinduism with the *Sanatana Dharma* runs the danger of slipping into an absolutism no less closed to the truths of others than the most rigid forms of religious exclusivism; and the identist understanding of Hindu pluralism that arises from Advaitic interpretations has the same problems as identist Western models, though closer readings of Shankara may alter this. But there are also strong affinities, as we have seen, between process thought and the dominant Hindu worldview, and there is a way of interpreting Hindu inclusivism as truly pluralistic.

Much more work clearly needs to be done in terms of coordination and synthesis between Hinduism and process thought. But by showing the affinities between these two systems and the ambiguities of the term "Hinduism," I hope

I have at least begun the task of developing a deep Hindu religious pluralism, a pluralistic or *Anekanta Vedanta*.

The ultimate hope, of course, is that such a pluralistic understanding of Hinduism, and of all religions, might lead to the kind of harmony among human beings envisioned by the Vedic sages: "United your resolve, united your hearts, may your spirits be at one, That you may long together dwell in unity and concord!"[40]

40. Panikkar, *The Vedic Experience*, 863.

Chapter 7

Islam and Deep Religious Pluralism

Mustafa Ruzgar

INTRODUCTION

This essay consists of four sections. In the first section, I describe how Islam has related itself to other religions in the sociological and political sense. Considering the intolerant situation in the West, especially in the Middle Ages, the Islamic approach to other religions is an important issue to be explored, because Islam treated them with a significant amount of tolerance and freedom. In the second section, I focus on some theological issues, especially the question of salvation. I argue that Islam's understanding of itself as the final, most perfect, and self-sufficient religion has, for the most part, prevented Muslims from engaging in dialogue with other religions. Throughout most of Islamic history, Muslims have generally not thought that they could learn and benefit from other religions. If we ignore some individual exceptions, this attitude has generated an exclusivist approach towards other religions. In the third section, I argue that some leading contemporary Muslim thinkers have challenged this exclusivism. The emergence of a more pluralistic consciousness has led some Muslims to reconsider their position towards non-Muslims. I explore the views of a leading Muslim thinker, Seyyed Hossein Nasr, who belongs to the school of thought generally called the *perennial tradition*. In the

158

final section, after pointing out some shortcomings of Nasr's version of religious pluralism, I argue that the position of Mohammed Iqbal, a Whitehead-inspired Muslim philosopher, provides the basis for a more plausible Islamic pluralistic position.

ISLAM AND OTHER RELIGIONS

In order to understand Muslim attitudes towards other religions, we need to look at some Islamic principles and consider their effectiveness in the history of Islam. The most important principle Muslims have accepted and employed in reference to this issue throughout Islamic history states that there is no compulsion in religion. The Qur'an says: "Let there be no compulsion in religion: Truth stands out clear from error: Whoever rejects evil and believes in Allah hath grasped the most trustworthy handhold, that never breaks. And Allah heareth and knoweth all things" (2:256).[1] At another place, the Qur'an says: "Say, 'the truth is from your Lord': Let him who will, believe, and let him who will, reject (it)" (18:29). The Qur'an emphasizes this point once more: "If it had been the Lord's will, they would all have believed—all who are on earth! Wilt thou then compel mankind, against their will, to believe!" (10:99).

The basic point that can be drawn from these verses is that Islam does not ask Muslims to try to convert the followers of other religions into Islam by the use of force. The prophet Mohammed was the chief example of one who actualized this principle. One example is provided in a story narrated by the famous Muslim historian Tabari, according to which

> a Muslim named Al-Husayn had two sons, who having been influenced by Christian merchants, converted to Christianity and left Medina to go to Syria with these missionary merchants. Al-Husayn pleaded with the Prophet to pursue the convoy and bring his sons back to Islam. But the Prophet . . . said, 'There is no compulsion in religion,' that is let them follow the religion of their choice, even though it is not Islam.[2]

The meaning of the principle that there is no compulsion in religion was not limited to freedom of individuals to choose their own religion. Islam also provided non-Muslims with considerable economic, cultural, and administrative rights. Islam, in other words, has guaranteed that under the rule of Islamic governance, non-Muslims could have autonomy in all their internal affairs, not only religious matters. That is why during the Ottoman Empire, for example, non-Muslims had their own jurisprudential courts for cases among themselves.

Another application of this principle occurred when Mohammed migrated to Medina in 622 to build a new community. In Medina, Mohammed's first aim

---

1. The first number refers to the chapter, the second to the verse. All references to the Qur'an are quoted from Abdullah Yusuf Ali's translation of the Qur'an: *The Meaning of the Holy Qur'an.*
2. Aslan, *Religious Pluralism in Christian and Islamic Philosophy,* 191.

was to create a community within which every religion could contribute to the society as an integral part of it. For this purpose, Mohammed signed a treaty with non-Muslims, mainly Christians and Jews, agreeing on some basic principles. According to this treaty, everybody in the city, regardless of religious, racial, gender, and other differences, was considered a distinct part of the community. Some articles of the treaty illustrate this point:

> *Article 1*: They are a single community (*ummah*) distinct from (other) people.

> *Article 16*: Whoever of the Jews follows us has the (same) help and support (*nasr, iswah*) (as the believers), so long as they are not wronged (by him) and he does not help (others) against them.

> *Article 25*: The Jews of Banu 'Awf are a community (*ummah*) along with the believers. To the Jews their religion (*din*) and to the Muslims their religion. (This applies) both to their clients and to themselves, with the exception of anyone who has done wrong or acted treacherously; he brings evil on himself and on his household. [Articles 26 to 31 repeat this rule for six other Jewish tribes of Medina at that time.]

> Article 37: It is for the Jews to bear their expenses and for the Muslims to bear their expenses. Between them (that is to one another) there is help (*nasr*) against whoever wars against the people of this document. *Between them is sincere friendship and honourable dealing, not treachery.* A man is not guilty of treachery through (the act of) his confederate. There is help for the person wronged.[3]

As these articles show, Mohammed's aim was to create a single community within which citizenship for and cooperation with non-Muslims were essential. Jews and Christians were asked to help protect the city against outside attacks. Moreover, Mohammed accepted Judaism and Christianity as distinct religions that were indispensable constituents of the community. This document also illustrates that Muslims and non-Muslims had equal rights and responsibilities. According to some Muslim thinkers, this treaty can be taken as a model for Islamic governance. For example, one Turkish intellectual, Ali Bulac, argues that because Mohammed created a pluralistic society in Medina, an Islamic community or state should essentially be pluralistic, without allowing any kind of religious, legal, or cultural oppression.[4]

One may argue that Mohammed performed such an action because he needed the help of other religions in order to protect the Muslim community. Although this argument has merit, tolerant Muslim attitudes did not disappear in later Islamic history. Even when Muslims possessed enormous power, as was the case in the Ottoman Empire, they did not act against this principle.

At the root of such tolerance lie some other religious convictions. According to Islam, all revealed religions have the same origin, being derived from the same

---

3. Ibid., 197.
4. For more information, see Ali Bulac, *Islam ve Demokrasi* [Islam and Democracy], 161–75.

God. Allah has sent many prophets to guide various peoples to the true path. Moses, Abraham, Noah, Christ, Mohammed, and many other prophets are mentioned in the Qur'an as being sent by the one God. For example, the Qur'an endorses the same moral principles the Torah announces. Among those principles are worshipping one God, praying, almsgiving, and treating parents, relatives, orphans, and the needy well (2:83). The Qur'an also says that the Torah contains guidance, light, and grace (5:44, 6:154). The Christian Gospel is also mentioned in the same manner. After referring to the Torah as a holy book containing guidance and light, the Qur'an says that the Gospel also possesses guidance and light.

The Qur'an refers to the followers of these two religions, Judaism and Christianity, as "the People of the Book."[5] In several places, the Qur'an reminds us that Islam and the other Abrahamic religions share the same origin. The Qur'an commands that Muslims should not dispute "with the People of the Book, except with means better (than mere disputation), unless it be with those of them who inflict wrong (and injury)" (29:46). The verse continues by urging Muslims to declare: "We believe in the revelation which has come down to us and in that which came down to you; our God and your God is one; and it is to Him we bow (in Islam)" (29:46).

The fact that the Qur'an calls Christians and Jews the People of the Book does not undermine the importance of other religions, such as Buddhism, Hinduism, Native American religions, and so on. According to the Qur'an, Allah has sent a messenger to every nation and community. This means that there is not a single community or nation that has not received the message of God. Although this is the case, the Qur'an does not mention the name of every messenger. As Adnan Aslan argues, "Muslims receive a Qur'anic sanction which enables them to expand an Islamic account of prophecy in such a manner that it could include those messengers who are not mentioned in the Qur'an, including Gautama the Buddha and the avatars of the Hindus."[6] The Qur'an repeatedly emphasizes that the divine messages sent through all prophets emanate from a single source. In several places, the Qur'an uses the terms "the mother of the book" (43:4, 13:39) and "the hidden book" (56:78), thereby referring to the single source from which the divine revelation originates. More importantly, all Muslims are required to believe in the prophets and their messages. This belief constitutes one of the six items that are compulsory for being a Muslim. Therefore, the unity of the divine message is not limited to the Western religions. Eastern and indigenous religions are included in this unity as well. It is also worth mentioning that some Sufi poets, after encountering Hinduism and Buddhism in India, experienced and described a mystical unity with them.

We can summarize this section by stating that throughout Islamic history, encountering non-Muslims has always been a practical, sociological, and political

5. Osman, "Monotheists and the 'Other': An Islamic Perspective in an Era of Religious Pluralism," 359.
6. Aslan, *Religious Pluralism*, 188.

issue. In other words, Muslims have paid attention to living together with non-Muslims in a peaceful way within the same community. The norms that determined the attitudes of Muslims towards non-Muslims have been derived from the Qur'an itself and Mohammed's applications of the Qur'anic teachings. In the following section, I will focus on the theological side of the issue in terms of salvation.

ISLAM AND OTHER RELIGIONS FROM A THEOLOGICAL STANDPOINT

Although Islam has shown a considerable amount of tolerance towards other religions, this does not mean that Muslims have been affirming a position that can be identified as "religiously pluralistic." In his first chapter in this volume, David Ray Griffin defines religious pluralism in the generic sense as the acceptance of the idea that "there are indeed religions other than one's own that provide saving truths and values to their adherents" (3, above). Given this definition of religious pluralism, it is important to examine the issue in terms of exclusivism, inclusivism, and pluralism. The decisive question here is: To which of these three positions has Islam generally adhered?

When we look at the history of Islam, the relations of Muslims with non-Muslims have dominantly been a matter of Islamic jurisprudence. As Aslan argues, Muslims have not seen this as an issue of faith or theology.[7] The absence of a theological consideration of the issue, according to Aslan, lies in the Muslim conviction that "only God can know who has a genuine faith in God, and therefore deserves salvation."[8] But I think that Aslan's view on this second matter is incorrect. It is true that Muslims believe that only God is able to know who deserves salvation. But traditionally, the content of this conviction was not extended to include non-Muslims. According to Islam, except for Mohammed and a few of his companions, no Muslim can know whether he/she will be saved. Being a Muslim does not mean that one will be saved. Accordingly, Muslims do not think that sheer belief in one God and Mohammed will be sufficient for salvation.

This point deserves more elaboration. In Islamic theology, the relationship between faith and practice has been a significant subject for discussion. What is the situation of those who claim to be believers in God without showing any religious concerns whatsoever and without organizing their lives at least somewhat according to Islamic teachings? One of the main Islamic sects, called Mu'tezila, fought against the distinction between belief and works. Without reducing belief to works, they stressed that there is an indispensable relationship between belief and works. Accordingly, if some people claim to be Muslim believers without showing any religious concerns whatsoever, the Mu'tezila concluded that their claim to believe is not credible. They, in fact, have neither belief nor nonbelief.

7. Aslan, *Religious Pluralism*, 186.
8. Ibid., 186.

As Fazlur Rahman explains, "on the question of the relationship of faith to deeds, whereas the Kharijites [another sect in Islam] regarded a grave sinner as an outright infidel and the main body of Muslims considered him a 'sinner-Muslim,' the Mu'tezila held that he was neither a Muslim nor a non-Muslim."[9] This shows that sheer utterance of belief does not make one a Muslim.

The important point, which Aslan overlooked, is that the principle that only God knows who will be saved is only about Muslims, not also non-Muslims. A Muslim cannot know even if he or she will be saved. It logically follows that no Muslim can make a claim about another Muslim's salvation. But this says nothing about the status of non-Muslims. It is true that Muslims were reticent to make claims about non-Muslims. But the reason for this reticence was not the conviction that even a non-Muslim can be saved. It was the assumption that some people, while publicly announcing that they are non-Muslims, might secretly accept Islam as the true religion.

If we ignore a few exceptions, it is fair to say that throughout Islamic history, until recently, this exclusivist attitude towards non-Muslims was the Muslim view. What is the religious basis for this exclusivism? It lies, of course, in some verses in the Qur'an, or at least in the way they have traditionally been understood. The Qur'an announces: "This day have I perfected your religion for you, completed my favour upon you, and have chosen for you Islam as your religion" (5:3). Elsewhere the Qur'an says: "The religion before Allah is Islam (submission to His will)" (3:19). Another verse says, "If anyone desires a religion other than Islam (submission to Allah), never will it be accepted of him; and in the Hereafter he will be in the ranks of those who have lost (all spiritual good)" (3:85).

The main point emphasized by these verses is that Islam is the final religion and is self-sufficient. However, although this might at first glance seem straightforward enough, there is an ambiguity running through these verses. Although Islam generically means "submission to the will of God," including such submission in all revealed religions, it can also refer to the specific historical religion that was revealed to the prophet Mohammed. The majority of Muslims have understood the word "Islam" in these verses to refer to Islam as this specific religion. Therefore, according to most Muslims, these verses mean that Islam, in its specific meaning, is the final religion. There will be no more revelation after Islam. Mohammed is the last prophet and Islam is the last religion.

The claimed self-sufficiency of Islam is closely related to the idea that it is the final religion. During the classical ages of Islam, Muslims believed that Islam did not need to learn anything from other religions in terms of religious matters.[10] This conviction has had a positive effect on Muslims in two respects. First, the belief in the self-sufficiency of Islam has led Muslims to preserve the authenticity of Islamic sources, especially the Qur'an and the hadith, throughout history.

9. Rahman, *Islam*, 88.
10. Mehmet S. Aydin, "Islam 'in Evrenselligi" [Universality of Islam], in *Islam 'in Evrenselligi* [Universality of Islam], 13.

The second positive aspect of this belief appeared in the struggle of Muslims in coping with foreign elements. In order to prove that Islam represents and includes all the positive aspects of foreign elements, such as ancient philosophy, socialism, and democracy, Muslims paid considerable attention to those foreign concepts and developments. This attention led them to take knowledge and science more seriously, perhaps, than most other civilizations.

However, the concept of self-sufficiency has also resulted in a lack of dialogue with other religions. Throughout Islamic history, most Muslims have not regarded other religions as sources that might make contributions to Islam. The notion that Islam is the final and self-sufficient religion, along with the belief that the textual authenticity of Western religions has been contaminated by human intervention,[11] is the main reason why Muslims have been exclusivist towards other religions. It can be argued, however, that this exclusivist conviction contradicts several verses in the Qur'an. For example, the Qur'an asserts: "Those who believe (in the Qur'an), and those who follow the Jewish (scriptures), and the Christians and the Sabians[12]—any who believe in Allah and the last day, and work righteousness, shall have their reward with their Lord; on them shall be no fear, nor shall they grieve" (2:62). At another place, it says: "Whoever works righteousness, man or woman, and has faith, verily, to him will we give a new life, and life that is good and pure, and we will bestow on such their reward according to the best of their actions" (16:97).

When these verses are taken seriously, it is not easy to claim that the Qur'an encourages an exclusivist approach towards other religions. The Qur'an seems to put more emphasis on being just and righteous than on doctrinal correctness. This emphasis can be seen very clearly in these two verses. However, it is usually claimed that these verses are cancelled by later ones. The concept of cancellation is technically known as "nesh." But some Muslim scholars do not accept the idea of cancellation. I, in any case, think that these two verses are closer to the essence of the Qur'an than the exclusivist approach.

SEYYED HOSSEIN NASR AND RELIGIOUS PLURALISM

In this section, I will explore the pluralistic position of Seyyed Hossein Nasr, which is a type of identist pluralism. After briefly analyzing his views, I argue that Nasr's pluralism is subject to the criticisms put forward by Cobb and

---

11. Harold Coward argues that since the thirteenth and fourteenth centuries, Muslim scholars have held that although the legislative parts of the Bible are true while their exegeses are in error, the historical narratives have been altered by human intervention. See Harold Coward, *Pluralism in the World Religions*, 69.

12. Abdullah Yusuf Ali says that it is difficult to identify those who are called Sabians. There are several views on the issue. I hold the view that the term "Sabians" refers to people who worshipped the Sun, the Moon, and Venus. For more on this issue, see Abdullah Yusuf Ali, *The Meaning of the Holy Qur'an*, 33.

Griffin. Because of the deficiencies of identist types of pluralism, I will suggest, in the final section, that a more plausible position can be built on Iqbal's philosophy.

In his article "To Live in a World with No Center—and Many," Nasr gives several reasons for a pluralistic world and briefly introduces his position. According to Nasr, the very existence of human life requires living with a meaning-giving center to which all aspects of human life are related. For Nasr, the existence of such a center is necessary for avoiding a life of chaos. Only through orienting our lives towards a meaning-giving center can we eliminate the dangers of nihilism, atheism, and other ideologies that threaten the sacred aspect of human life.

Nasr argues that Western civilization created a center that underlay all aspects of human life during medieval times. In Nasr's words: "The theology, philosophy, and cosmology, the ethical norms and laws, architecture, painting, and music, as well as nearly every other realm of human life, reflected the realities of the world of faith with its theocentric character, which in the Christian context was naturally also Christocentric."[13] Although this homogeneous worldview has been challenged in many respects since medieval times, ethical life, Nasr argues, survived until recent decades without being challenged seriously.[14] However, during the past few decades, even "the very foundations of the ethical norms"[15] have been challenged. Other developments, such as "new nihilistic philosophies, various attempts at the revision of history, and the deconstruction of sacred scripture and well-known works of literature,"[16] have helped create a chaotic and centerless world where our absolute values have lost their ultimate point of reference.

Nasr explains that pluralism has been widely considered the only alternative to this centerless worldview. One of the most important reasons why pluralism has been so important, especially during recent times, is the fact that, given the present world situation, we can no longer isolate ourselves from exposure to other religious, cultural, and ethnic diversities. This exposure helps us understand and appreciate the true nature and value of the other.

According to Nasr, several developments, especially in America, have prepared the ground for a more pluralistic appreciation of the other. In today's America, one can easily see that there are multiple religions, along with diverse cultural and ethnic identities. Thanks both to migration and conversion in the American continent, there are numerous kinds of religious people, such as Muslims, Buddhists, Hindus, Sikhs, Native American Shamans, and Mormons.[17] Accordingly, Nasr argues that diverse religious and philosophical currents and ethnic groups have helped strengthen a more pluralistic consciousness. Given the pluralistic context of the present world, he says that "[o]n the religious level, it becomes [even] more

---

13. Nasr, "To Live in a World with No Center—and Many," 319.
14. Ibid., 319.
15. Ibid., 319.
16. Ibid., 319.
17. Ibid., 320.

difficult to assert the truth of only *our* religion while denying any truth to the religion of others."[18]

Although Nasr affirms the value of pluralism, he is very concerned about the loss of the notions that give meaning and value to our lives. He says:

> But what about the question of truth? And what about the principles of human action, the ethical norms by which we must live as individuals and also members of a human collectivity? Can we simply affirm pluralism with total disregard for the truth and falsehood of things or have a view of the world or a *Weltanschauung* without a frame of reference? And on the practical level, can a society survive if, for many of its members, there are no ultimate ethical values since there is no ultimate reality which would bestow ultimacy upon those values?[19]

In Nasr's view, any pluralistic position that will encourage the loss of our values is deeply problematic. Such a loss would bring about the most destructive consequences.

According to Nasr, since the reality of diversity cannot be ignored, we can no longer live in a nostalgic world where there will be only one center. Considering the dangers of a centerless world, relativism and nihilism are likewise not real options.[20] But, he says: "There is also another possibility, which is to be able to live in a world with many centers while confirming the reality of the center of our own traditional universe."[21]

For Nasr, every religion and culture is based on a center from which moral, social, intellectual, and artistic values stem.[22] The real task before us, therefore, is to live in a way that appreciates the value and importance of these various religions and cultures without falling into the dangers of sheer relativism and nihilism. How is this possible? What is the constructive part of Nasr's argument that will make it possible to live in the midst of such multiplicity and diversity without falling into sheer relativism?

Contrary to those who see diversity as an inevitable cause for "the clash of civilizations," Nasr argues that diversity does not necessarily imply such a clash.[23] The reason for this lies in the considerable similarities among various traditions. In Nasr's view,

> there is a remarkable unanimity in the various traditional religions and philosophies, which provide the guiding principles and presiding ideas of various traditional civilizations and cultures, concerning the meaning of human life, the significance of the good as the principle of human action, and the presence of a transcendent dimension to human existence.[24]

18. Ibid., 321.
19. Ibid., 321.
20. Ibid., 322.
21. Ibid., 321.
22. Ibid., 321.
23. Ibid., 322.
24. Idem.

"[T]he reality and presence of the Ultimate,"[25] says Nasr, is the most important notion that is common to all religions. Nasr argues that although there are many theological differences among these religious traditions, those differences are "overshadowed by the reality and presence of the Ultimate."[26] Therefore, those differences possess a secondary importance.

It is clear that Nasr's main concern lies in his insistence on the importance of keeping our traditions, with their ultimate values, alive. As indicated above, he strongly rejects a centerless world in which sheer relativism and nihilism would become dominant. For him, such a world constitutes the greatest danger for the present and future generations. The only solution, for Nasr, is to live in terms of one's own tradition while realizing the value and importance of other traditions. He also strongly suggests that any kind of "eclecticism or superficial mixing of various sacred forms and moral imperatives" will not provide a plausible solution.[27]

It is important to emphasize that Nasr's main reason for holding a pluralistic position lies in his consideration that a centerless world possesses the greatest danger for future generations. In order to overcome such a situation, he puts enormous emphasis on the unanimity of different religions. He insists that there is only one ultimate reality and that the existence of such an ultimate carries utmost importance.

Nasr's views on the similarities among religions stem from his conviction that there is an everlasting wisdom, which is called the *sophia perennis*. According to Aldous Huxley, the perennial philosophy is

> the metaphysics that recognizes a divine Reality substantial to the worlds of things and lives and minds; the psychology that finds in the soul something similar to, or even identical with, divine Reality; the ethic that places man's final end in the knowledge of the immanent and transcendent Ground of all being—the thing is immemorial and universal.[28]

Nasr strongly argues for the truth of this perennial philosophy. According to him, the *sophia perennis* is the "everlasting truth which contains all truths of all religions."[29]

In order to clarify Nasr's views, we need to know how he defines the term "tradition." Nasr states that tradition "comprises all the distinctive characteristics and principles or norms that are hereditary and contribute substantially to the main ingredients of civilization."[30] Most importantly, Nasr holds the view that a tradition possesses both an exoteric dimension and an esoteric dimension. The *exoteric* dimension refers to a given tradition's rites, rituals, and laws. The *esoteric* dimension refers to the inward dimension of the tradition. While this esoteric

25. Idem.
26. Idem.
27. Ibid., 323.
28. Quoted in Aslan, *Religious Pluralism*, 43.
29. Aslan, *Religious Pluralism*, 50.
30. Ibid., 48.

aspect comprises "the essence and the core of tradition itself," it is "not accessible to everyone, but only to those who are able to appreciate the inward dimension of tradition."[31]

Nasr's conviction of the truth of the *sophia perennis,* along with its distinction between the exoteric and esoteric dimensions of a religious tradition, provides the basis for an identist form of pluralism. Nasr, as we have seen, argues that there is enormous unanimity among the religions. The real solution to the issue of pluralism, he further holds, lies in accepting "the transcendental unity of religions at the level of the Absolute, endorsing the fact that 'all paths lead to the same summit.'"[32] He believes that his version of pluralism, according to which there is only one Absolute and all manifestations of the Absolute are relatively absolute,[33] can do justice to all the traditions.

Although Nasr holds that the esoteric dimension of religion can be known only by "those who are prepared for it" or those "who are chosen [for it],"[34] he nevertheless, in Aslan's words, claims that "the Divine Essence is beyond any human categories and is totally ineffable."[35] He also believes that "the 'gods' of religion are not different 'entities'" but "different names of the same Reality which reveals itself in different ways within the context of a different religious universe."[36]

Although I fully agree with Nasr's concerns about the dangers of sheer relativism and nihilism, I find his insistence that there is only one ultimate problematic. On this basis, he is not hesitant to say that it is irrelevant to argue that "one particular religion is better than others, since they are all generated from the same Origin."[37] That is a positive consequence of his position. However, as Griffin points out, to say that personal and impersonal religious experiences are experiences of the same ultimate reality, and yet are equally true, amounts to saying that each resulting type of religion "is equally mistaken" (45, above).

I will clarify this point further by briefly exploring the Whiteheadian version of pluralism, which is developed by Griffin as well as John Cobb. Whitehead's panentheism provides a distinction, albeit a close relation, between God and creativity. Whitehead's term "creativity" "refers to the power embodied in all actual things—both God and finite actualities."[38] According to this view, finite actualities have their own self-determining power. In Whitehead's view, creativity "points to the twofold power of each occasion of experience to exert a degree of self-determination in forming itself and then to exert causal influence on the future."[39]

---

31. Ibid., 50.
32. Ibid., 117.
33. Ibid., 117–18.
34. Ibid., 89, 91.
35. Ibid., 156.
36. Ibid., 156.
37. Ibid., 118.
38. David Ray Griffin, "Panentheism and Religious Pluralism," 9.
39. Ibid., 10.

Whitehead's understanding of the relation between creativity and God is crucially important for a Whiteheadian pluralism. According to Whitehead, as Griffin puts it, "God and creativity are equally primordial."[40] This means that "our world was created . . . out of a primeval chaos. Although our particular world is a contingent divine creation, there has always been *a* world, in the sense of a multiplicity of finite actualities embodying creativity."[41] It is clear that Whitehead does not accept the dominant doctrine of *creatio ex nihilo* and the widespread view that creative power belongs only to God. More specifically, Whitehead strongly rejects the traditional view according to which God voluntarily chose to create a world of finite entities (although he holds that God did choose our particular world).

Whiteheadian religious pluralism is not of the identist variety, which fails to do justice to the radically different conceptions of ultimate reality held by theistic and nontheistic types of religion. Cobb, applying Whitehead's system to the issue of religious pluralism, suggests that, in Griffin's words, "the distinction between God and creativity provides a basis for speaking of two ultimates."[42] According to this view, "different religions . . . have seen different truths and have offered different paths to salvation."[43] According to Cobb, one ultimate, which has been called "'Emptiness' ('Sunyata') or 'Dharmakaya' by Buddhists, 'nirguna Brahman' by Advaita Vedantists, 'the Godhead' by Meister Eckhart, and 'Being Itself' by Heidegger and Tillich,"[44] corresponds to Whitehead's "creativity." This is a *formless* ultimate. The other ultimate, which has been called "'Amida Buddha' or 'Sambhogakaya,' 'saguna Brahman,' 'Ishvara,' 'Yahweh,' 'Christ,' and 'Allah,'" is the "*Supreme* Being" who is the "source of all forms, such as truth, beauty, and justice."[45]

According to this account of pluralism, therefore, there is no need to maintain, as does John Hick, that God and emptiness are "two names for the same noumenal reality."[46] Nasr's view is similar. Although he does not use the word "noumenal," he does claim that, in Aslan's words, "the 'gods' of religions are not different 'entities'" but rather "different names of the same Reality."[47] But this account of pluralism cannot overcome the problem that both Cobb and Alan Race have called "debilitating relativism," because it cannot really affirm the truth of any given religion. In other words, if "God" and "emptiness" refer to the same ultimate, then it follows that the ultimate reality is neither personal nor impersonal. Therefore, neither type of religious experience is correct. This, as Griffin argues, amounts to saying that each type of religion is equally mistaken (45, above).

40. Ibid., 10.
41. Ibid., 10.
42. Ibid., 10.
43. Ibid., 10.
44. Ibid., 11.
45. Ibid., 11.
46. Ibid., 10.
47. Aslan, *Religious Pluralism*, 156.

IQBAL AND WHITEHEAD

Given the problems involved in Nasr's position, I now turn my attention to the possibility of a more adequate pluralistic position in Islam. For this purpose, I will analyze Iqbal's philosophy and argue that if it is interpreted in a certain way, his position can lead to a more promising form of pluralism than Nasr's identist position. Following this interpretation, I argue that Iqbal's position in particular, and hence Islam in general, allow for a position that does not involve the problems of identist pluralism.

As we have seen, the main problem in Nasr's pluralism is his assumption that all religions are aimed towards the same ultimate. The essence of all religions, being oriented toward this one ultimate, is the same, while their external forms differ. Nasr holds that these external differences are of secondary importance. However, given the evidence that not all religions are oriented towards the same ultimate, this identist position cannot do justice to some religions, and perhaps not to any.

In order to clarify this point, I will look at Iqbal's views, arguing that if Iqbal's philosophy can be carried forward in a certain way, it allows for a conception that postulates the possibility of more than one ultimate. While doing so, I am not arguing that Iqbal clearly accepted this view. On the contrary, some of his notions, if made central, would show him not even to be a genuinely pluralistic thinker.

Iqbal clearly holds the view that Mohammed is the final prophet. He also does not give up the notion of *creatio ex nihilo*. The rejection of the notion of *creatio ex nihilo* has crucial importance for the type of pluralism articulated by Cobb and Griffin, which I find illuminating and otherwise helpful. Iqbal's political attitudes towards certain religions, which resulted from his conviction of the finality of Mohammed, suggest that he did not hold a pluralistic position. It would involve a distortion of his views to claim otherwise.

My whole argument, however, is that if Iqbal's metaphysics can be reconstructed along more Whiteheadian lines, it can provide the ground upon which a more plausible Islamic pluralism may be built. I think that Iqbal's views possess enormous possibilities for such a turn. As Iqbal left the elaboration of his views to later generations, it is my conviction that a more Whiteheadian interpretation of Iqbal does not contradict his major project, which is to reconstruct Islamic thought without rejecting the positive aspects of modern science and philosophy.

Given the fact that Islamic thought had been in an unproductive state for a long period of time, Iqbal tried to return to the basics of Islamic teachings without being blind to the philosophical, social, and cultural developments of his time.[48] His major project was to reinterpret Islam so that it would no longer seem alien to modern people. He tried to do this without compromising his basic

---

48. Sir Mohammed Iqbal, *The Reconstruction of Religious Thought in Islam*, 9–10.

Islamic convictions. At the same time, he did not prevent himself from employing many modern ideas that may seem very radical to conservative Muslims.

In my explorations of Iqbal's views, I will rely heavily on Mehmet S. Aydin's interpretation. According to Aydin, Iqbal argued for a world that is in constant change and creation.[49] Therefore, Iqbal's conception of the universe is that of a dynamic creation. Iqbal rejected philosophies of substance devoid of experience and dynamism.

In Iqbal's view, God did not create the universe arbitrarily. As the Qur'an says, God did not create "the heavens, the earth, and all between them, merely in (idle) sport" (44:38). Another verse asserts that God "adds to creation as he pleases" (35:1). These two verses constitute the starting point for Iqbal. In Iqbal's view, the universe "is not a block universe, a finished product, immobile and incapable of change."[50] Thus, Iqbal did not base his philosophy on substances but on events. Furthermore, instead of speaking of matter, he described his philosophy, as did Whitehead, as a philosophy of organism.[51]

In order to clarify this, I will analyze Iqbal's position in regard to one important Islamic school, the Ash'arite. Iqbal argued that the Qur'anic conception of the universe does not allow conceptualizing a fixed universe. He suggested that the event-based dynamic universe is closer to the true essence of the Qur'an. The implications of such a universe can easily be found in the Ash'arite School.

Iqbal strongly rejected the Aristotelian idea of a fixed universe. According to him, "The rise and growth of atomism in Islam" represents "the first important indication of an intellectual revolt against the Aristotelian idea of a fixed universe."[52] The philosophy of atomism is developed by Ash'arite scholars. According to them, "the world is compounded of what they call *jawahir*—infinitely small parts or atoms which cannot further be divided."[53] The reason why Ash'arite scholars developed such a theory is that they wanted to protect the ceaseless activity of God in the universe.[54] As Iqbal put it, "Since the creative activity of God is ceaseless the number of the atoms cannot be finite. Fresh atoms are coming into being every moment, and the universe is therefore constantly growing."[55] This understanding of the universe is more adequate to the Qur'anic description of it, since the Qur'an states that "every day in (new) splendour doth He (shine)!" (55:29). Therefore, God is constantly creating.

Iqbal drew two conclusions from Ash'arite thought: "(i) Nothing has a stable nature. (ii) There is a single order of atoms, i.e., what we call the soul is either a finer kind of matter, or only an accident."[56] Iqbal argued that the first proposition

---

49. Aydin, "Iqbal'in Felsefesinde Allah-Alem Iliskisi" [The God-World Relation in Iqbal's Philosophy], 156.
50. Iqbal, *The Reconstruction*, 13.
51. Aydin, "Iqbal'in Felsefesinde Allah-Alem Iliskisi," 156.
52. Iqbal, *The Reconstruction*, 93.
53. Ibid., 95.
54. Aydin, "Iqbal'in Felsefesinde Allah-Alem Iliskisi," 156.
55. Iqbal, *The Reconstruction*, 95.
56. Ibid., 97.

has an important element of truth, since it includes a continuous creation, which is what the Qur'an asserts. He strongly opposed the second proposition because of its allowance of pure materialism.

Iqbal's conception of the universe can be called "spiritual pluralism."[57] According to this doctrine, the Ultimate Reality is conceived as an Ego. This Ego creates other egos, which are of various levels. In Iqbal's words:

> The creative energy of the Ultimate Ego, in whom deed and thought are identical, functions as ego-unities. The world, in all its details, from the mechanical movement of what we call the atom of matter to the free movement of thought in the human ego, is the self-revelation of the 'Great I am.' Every atom of divine energy, however low in the scale of existence, is an ego. But there are degrees in the expression of egohood. Throughout the entire gamut of being runs the gradually rising note of egohood until it reaches its perfection in man.[58]

These egos are not like Leibniz's monads, which are closed to each other. On the contrary, Iqbal's egos are organisms that are in constant relation with each other.[59]

According to this general picture, Iqbal's universe can be seen as a cosmos whose main character is constituted by mutual relations. In Iqbal's view, as Aydin argues, the material world is related to the biological one, while the biological world is related to the psychological one. They cannot be isolated from each other. The whole universe, including the material, biological, and psychological worlds, is related to God. Therefore, God is not an element of opposition to the universe; on the contrary, God is highly friendly to it.[60]

Time and God's Knowledge

Iqbal's views about time give important clues to his understanding of God's relation to the world. According to mainstream Islamic thought, God, as the most perfect being, is able to know the future in all its details. Any lack of such knowledge would be considered as detracting from God's perfection. This idea, of course, creates significant problems for the idea of human freedom. Because of the mainstream affirmation of God's knowledge of the future, the problem of human freedom has been at the center of the thinking of several Islamic sects.

In his explanation of time, Iqbal again starts with the Ash'arite theory. According to the Ash'arite view, Iqbal pointed out, time "is a succession of individual 'nows.' From this view it obviously follows that between every two individual 'nows' or moments of time, there is an unoccupied moment of time, that is to say, a void of time."[61] Iqbal finds this theory of time absurd, because it cannot properly explain the relation of God to the world.

57. Aydin, "Iqbal'in Felsefesinde Allah-Alem Iliskisi," 157.
58. Iqbal, *The Reconstruction*, 99.
59. Aydin, "Iqbal'in Felsefesinde Allah-Alem Iliskisi," 157.
60. Ibid., 157.
61. Iqbal, *The Reconstruction*, 101.

Iqbal then considers another theory of time, which was developed by the Sufi poet Iraqi. According to Iqbal's account of Iraqi, "there are infinite varieties of time, relative to the varying grades of being, intervening between materiality and pure spirituality."[62] According to this account, the time of gross bodies is divisible into the past, present, and the future. "The time of immaterial beings is also serial in character, but its passage is such that a whole year in the time of gross bodies is not more than a day in the time of an immaterial being."[63] However, in the case of divine time, says Iraqi, there is no "divisibility, sequence and change." Accordingly, "[t]he eye of God sees all the visible, and His ear hears all the audibles in one indivisible act of perception."[64]

According to Iqbal, this second theory of time is less obscure than the previous one.[65] However, when it is carried through with all its consequences, it leads to a closed system in which there would be no future and hence no constant creation.[66] In order to preserve the importance of creation, Iqbal developed his own theory of time. According to this theory, "the time of the ultimate Ego is revealed as change without succession, *i.e.*, an organic whole which appears atomic because of the creative moment of the ego."[67] Thus, Iqbal's theory of time is an organic whole. The importance of this theory lies in its assertion that the future is not created or determined in advance.[68]

According to Iqbal, God knows both past and the future. However, the nature of God's knowledge of the future differs from God's knowledge of the past. God does not know the future in the same manner as the past. God knows the future as a possibility that is not yet actualized. Otherwise, there would be no creation in the world and everything would be determined in advance.[69]

Iqbal rejected the theory of omniscience according to which it is "a single indivisible act of perception which makes God immediately aware of the entire sweep of history, regarded as an order of specific event[s], in an eternal 'now.'"[70] Such a theory of time "suggests a closed universe, a fixed futurity, a pre-determined, un-alterable order of specific events which, like a superior fate, has once for all determined the directions of God's creative activity."[71] According to Iqbal, "The future certainly pre-exists in the organic whole of God's creative life, but it pre-exists as an open possibility, not as a fixed order of events with definite outlines."[72]

It is clear that Iqbal's views on time essentially contradict the mainstream Islamic conception of time. According to many Muslim scholars, God knows the

62. Ibid., 104.
63. Ibid., 104.
64. Ibid., 104–5.
65. Aydin, "Iqbal'in Felsefesinde Allah-Alem Iliskisi," 158.
66. Ibid., 158.
67. Iqbal, *The Reconstruction*, 106.
68. Aydin, "Iqbal'in Felsefesinde Allah-Alem Iliskisi," 158.
69. For more information, see Aydin, "Iqbal'in Felsefesinde Allah-Alem Iliskisi," 161.
70. Iqbal, *The Reconstruction*, 108.
71. Ibid., 108.
72. Ibid., 109.

future the same way God knows the past.[73] But this view is not necessarily Qur'anic. Aydin concludes that, contrary to the mainstream Islamic thought, "the view of a determined future cannot easily be attributed to the Qur'an."[74]

Divine Power

Having explained Iqbal's consideration of God's knowledge, I now turn to his understanding of God's power. According to Iqbal, every creature has some self-determining power.[75] God, in other words, has created finite egos that possess self-determination and freedom.[76] At this point, it is important to ask whether Iqbal attributes any limitations to God. This question is crucial for the purpose of this essay, because it is related to the issue of religious pluralism developed through Whitehead's philosophy.

The question, in particular, is whether Iqbal's position allows for an acceptance of two ultimates. As we have seen, Whitehead's position regards creativity as equally primordial with God. In his view, God cannot voluntarily decide whether to have a world, because God has always existed in relation to a world with entities embodying creativity. Iqbal, however, does not accept this view. In his discussion of the limitation of the Ultimate Ego, Iqbal said that if God had wanted to do so, God could have chosen not to create the world. More specifically, he said that

> the emergence of egos endowed with the power of spontaneous and hence unforeseeable action is, in a sense, a limitation on the freedom of the all-inclusive Ego. But this limitation is not externally imposed. It is born out of His own creative freedom whereby He has chosen finite egos to be participators of His life, power and freedom.[77]

Elsewhere, Iqbal argued that the finite ego "shares in the life and freedom of the ultimate Ego who, by permitting the emergence of a finite ego, capable of private initiative, has limited this freedom of His own free will."[78] It is clear from these expressions that although God now has limited freedom because of the existence of finite egos, God originally had the power to choose not to create a world.

Another point on which Whitehead and Iqbal appear to differ, according to Aydin's interpretation, is whether any change can be attributed to God. According to Aydin, Iqbal's system does not allow us to attribute any finitely conceivable type of change to God. More precisely, our conception of time and change, as measurable and serial, depends on a finite point of view, so it cannot be attrib-

---

73. Mehmet S. Aydin, *Alemden Allah'a* [From Cosmos to God], 84.
74. Ibid., 86.
75. Ibid., 91.
76. Ibid., 92.
77. Iqbal, *The Reconstruction*, 110.
78. Ibid., 151.

uted to God.[79] According to Aydin's account of Iqbal's position, we can attribute to God the kind of change that is *within* perfection—as distinct from change that is moving *towards* perfection.[80] However, Aydin argues, this does not mean that God has a changeable nature, because God stays unchanged throughout the whole process.

However, there is another possible interpretation of Iqbal that is, I believe, more accurate. As shown above, Iqbal held that the future preexists in the organic whole of God's creative life as an open possibility.[81] In order to clarify this point, Iqbal gave this illustration: A person comes to know an idea with many possible applications. This means that all the possibilities of this idea are present in this person's mind. "If a specific possibility, as such, is not intellectually known to [that person] at a certain moment of time, it is not because [his/her] knowledge is defective, but because there is yet no possibility to become known. The idea reveals the possibilities of its application with advancing experience."[82] When applied to God's knowledge, this illustration suggests that God's knowledge of the future as a possibility grows with the actualization of these possibilities. However, as Iqbal says, this is not a defect in regard to God's omniscience.

In fact, Charles Hartshorne's distinction between God's "abstract essence" and the "concrete states" is implicit in Iqbal's illustration. According to this distinction, as Griffin explains, Hartshorne argues that "[o]ne attribute of God's abstract essence . . . is omniscience, the characteristic of knowing everything knowable at any given time."[83] Distinct from this, "God's concrete *knowledge* grows, insofar as new events happen which add new knowable things to the universe."[84] Accordingly, Hartshorne does not think that God has a "nature" that changes. The only change that can be attributed to God occurs in God's concrete states. Incorporating this distinction into Iqbal's conception of God provides an understanding of how God's knowledge changes by the actual events while God's abstract essence or nature remains the same.

Given that Iqbal held the view of *creatio ex nihilo*, it is not easy to say that Iqbal's position allows us to consider creativity in the same manner Whitehead conceptualizes it. In other words, it seems that Iqbal's philosophy does not leave much room for accepting two ultimates. The fact that Iqbal does accept *creatio ex nihilo* shows that any attribution of a second ultimate to Iqbal will be a distortion of his view.

However, I believe that Iqbal's position carries significant possibilities that can lead to the reconstruction of a more plausible Islamic pluralism. On many issues, Iqbal differs from the orthodox interpretation of Islam. As I have explained earlier,

79. Aydin, "Iqbal'in Felsefesinde Allah-Alem Iliskisi," 160–61.
80. Ibid., 161.
81. Iqbal, *The Reconstruction*, 109.
82. Ibid., 109–10.
83. Griffin, *Reenchantment without Supernaturalism*, 158.
84. Ibid., 158–59.

his views on God's knowledge and power differ from the mainstream Islamic conceptions. Iqbal's solid insistence that God's power is limited by the power of the creatures, and that God can know the future only as a possibility, strongly contradicts the traditional Islamic conception of God.

Given these views, it seems to me to be possible to take one more step, through which an Islamic pluralism based on two ultimates could be constructed. Although Iqbal held the doctrine of *creatio ex nihilo*, one may argue that this doctrine is neither biblical nor Qur'anic. For instance, two leading Western scholars, Jon Levenson and Gerhard May, both independently argue that the doctrine of *creatio ex nihilo* cannot be found in the Bible.[85] Among Muslim scholars, the doctrine of *creatio ex nihilo* has long been a subject of scholarly debate. As Barry S. Kogan argues, by the latter half of the twelfth century, there were mainly two opposing views on creation in the Islamic world. "The *Mutakallimun* or speculative theologians of Islam, particularly those of the Ash'arite school, had argued for and elaborated the doctrine of creation *ex nihilo*," whereas "the *Falasifa* or philosophers of Islam . . . rejected the doctrine of creation *ex nihilo*."[86] For instance, one can argue that the theory of emanation developed by al-Farabi and Avicenna significantly differed from the doctrine of *creatio ex nihilo*.[87] Averroës, another Muslim philosopher, criticized the views of Mutakallimun on the issue of creation by rejecting *creatio ex nihilo*.[88]

Given the views of these Muslim philosophers in conjunction with some recent Western scholarly discussions, I suggest that the issue of *creatio ex nihilo* needs to be readdressed by Muslim intellectuals. I believe that this point can be developed further to conceptualize a more plausible Islamic metaphysics. It seems that such an undertaking is possible and more illuminating in relation to both the problem of evil and the problem of religious pluralism.

SUMMARY AND CONCLUSION

In the first section, I argued that Islam has historically been tolerant towards the members of other religions. However, I argued that because of the acceptance of the self-sufficiency and finality of Islam, the majority of Muslims have held an exclusivist position on salvation. It is only recently that some Islamic thinkers have focused on this issue theologically. Nasr is one of the leading Muslim thinkers who have done so.

85. For more information, see Levenson, *Creation and the Persistence of Evil: The Jewish Drama of Divine Omnipotence*, and May, *Creatio ex Nihilo: The Doctrine of "Creation out of Nothing" in Early Christian Thought*.

86. Kogan, "Eternity and Origination: Averroes' Discourse on the Manner of the World's Existence," 203–4.

87. For a brief discussion of this point, see Netton, *Allah Transcendent: Studies in the Structure and Semiotics of Islamic Philosophy, Theology and Cosmology*, 162–67.

88. For more information, see Kogan, "Eternity and Origination," esp. 230–32.

After explaining Nasr's views, I argued that he holds, like Hick, an identist version of pluralism. After discussing some problems in identist pluralism, I argued that the Whiteheadian pluralism suggested by John Cobb provides a better approach. As a start toward constructing a more Whitehead-inspired Islamic pluralism that will do justice to the differences among the religions, I then analyzed the views of Mohammed Iqbal.

Iqbal's views are very similar to Whitehead's in many respects. In insisting on the importance of change, event, and process; in saying that God cannot know the future precisely because future events are not yet realized; and in holding that God's power is limited by the power of the creatures, he held views that were similar to those of Whitehead and may have even been inspired by them. Several times Iqbal either directly quoted Whitehead or pointed to his work to support his own ideas (the two books he quoted are *Science and the Modern World* and *Religion in the Making*). Although it is not clear whether Iqbal was actually influenced by Whitehead or whether he had come to similar views on his own and then simply quoted Whitehead for support, Iqbal's positive references to Whitehead's work show that he at least found agreement with him on several issues. However, on some other major points, Iqbal differed from Whitehead. Among them are his acceptance of *creatio ex nihilo*, his correlative idea that the ultimate Ego is the only ultimate, and his hesitation to attribute any change to God. Given these differences, Iqbal himself did not provide the basis for accepting a Whiteheadian version of pluralism. However, I do believe that Iqbal's views can legitimately be taken as a starting point for reconstructing a more plausible and adequate Islamic pluralism by carrying out more consistently his agreement with many Whiteheadian ideas.

Chapter 8

Liberating Truth

A Buddhist Approach to Religious Pluralism

Christopher Ives

With his ecumenical commitments and magnanimous approach to religious difference, John Hick deserves praise. All of us who reflect on religious diversity are indebted to his sustained efforts to formulate a thesis whose "practical upshot . . . is that people of the different religious traditions are free to see one another as friends rather than as enemies or rivals."[1] Yet I wonder whether his identist pluralism passes the test of adequacy to Buddhism. Relative to Buddhist epistemologies, truth claims, and soteriological schemes, Whitehead's process thought, especially in the hands of John Cobb, offers a more adequate framework for articulating a Buddhist approach to religious diversity. For several decades Whiteheadian and Buddhist thinkers have found much to discuss, and their exchange has illuminated complementary truths, highlighted differences, and, as John Cobb would have it, mutually transformed the participants.

As a scholar of Buddhism who in recent years has been mainly sitting on the sidelines of interfaith dialogue and debates about pluralism, and whose understanding of Whitehead is limited at best, I offer here a short critique of Hick's

1. Hick, *God Has Many Names*, 49.

approach and a heuristic angle on Buddhism and religious diversity with an eye toward promoting collaborative efforts to formulate a "deep" religious pluralism. Specifically, given the preponderance of Japanese Mahayanist representations of Buddhism in formal interfaith dialogue, I consider it expedient to bring the perspectives of early and Theravadan Buddhism more into the discussion; Theravadan concerns suggest an approach to religious diversity that focuses less on metaphysical ultimates and more on views of our basic religious problem(s). Specifically, the soteriological bent of Buddhism, especially its focus on diagnosing human religious "suffering" (in Pali *dukkha*; Skt. *duhkha*), points to what I will call, clumsily, a "religio-diagnostic" approach to religious diversity. In viewing all religions as offering valuable insights into existential suffering, this approach can complement more metaphysical approaches and, when expanded to cover other types of suffering, may help Buddhism learn further from Whiteheadian thought, the "soteria" approach of Paul Knitter, and other resources for addressing "suffering" in its various forms. In addition to being more adequate to Buddhism, this approach may, at this point in time, be more mutually transformative—and politically relevant—than our continuing to compare Emptiness with God, and (Buddhist) Nothingness with (Western) Being.

As a means of charting the expanse of religious traditions, Hick's ontologically and soteriologically identist pluralism founders in Buddhist waters. Hick orients his paradigm around the "basic conviction, common to all the great traditions, that religious experience is not simply human projection but is at the same time a cognitive response to a transcendent reality."[2] Hick construes that transcendent reality, which he terms the Eternal One or the Real, as "pressing in upon the human spirit";[3] and with his revamped Kantian epistemology, he argues that the Eternal One is "being perceived within human cultures under different forms."[4]

While perhaps applicable to facets of Pure Land and Tibetan Buddhism, this conception of the Eternal One as the singular object of religious experience does not necessarily hold for other types of Buddhism. For example, Zen thinkers have represented their religious "experience"[5] not as a perception of a special object of experience but as a shift in their mode of experience (from a subject-object mode to a "non-dual" mode), through which the discriminating, self-conscious experiencer "drops off," leaving no sense of being a subject over against the experienced object. If, for the sake of Hick's argument, one were to specify the object of Zen "experience," it is ordinary reality, including, as traditional Zen accounts would have it, the sound of a pebble hitting bamboo or the feeling of being hit by a staff. The key thing "experienced" here is not the Eternal One, or even the "plunk" of the pebble, but the sense of existing profoundly connected to—or *as*—everything else.

---

2. Hick, *A Christian Theology of Religions: The Rainbow of Faiths*, 78.
3. Hick, *God Has Many Names*, 48.
4. Ibid., 59.
5. While I recognize the range of issues surrounding the construct of "religious experience," I am using it here for lack of a better expression.

Though one might criticize this portrayal of Zen experience as hairsplitting and argue that, in a certain nonobjective sense, "satori" or "awakening" is what Zen practitioners experience, the tradition is consistent in arguing that satori, as that mode of experiencing, cannot be objectified in any way. Hence the metaphors about how a sword cannot cut itself or a mirror cannot reflect itself— the key is to do (or "be") the cutting and reflecting. What one might objectify, reflect on, or talk about later is the traces of the experience, a lingering "felt sense" of what the experience was like.

Given the bramble of claims about satori and the methodological problems in talking or writing about something that many portray as "ineffable" or "lost" the instant one starts trying to talk about it, we might be advised to focus on nirvana. Hick construes "Nirvana" as "the nonpersonal awareness of the Eternal One," equivalent to the "Brahman of advaitic Hinduism . . . and the Sunyata of Mahayana Buddhism"[6] (not to mention such odd bedfellows as Allah, God, and Krishna, which Hick regards as that same Eternal One experienced through theistic lenses). Yet virtually no early discourse in the Pali canon portrays nirvana as some noumenal Real, special level of reality, or literal place of peace and tranquility.[7] Rather, as indicated by its etymology, nirvana is the "extinguishment" of the fire of clinging. It is the cessation of suffering that emerges when one has eradicated basic clinging or entanglement in the form of such defilements (Pali *kilesa*) as the Three Poisons of ignorance, greed, and hatred, and by virtue of this eradication no longer clings to impermanent things or conditions and hence does not cause further *dukkha*. Accordingly, what "nirvana" connotes is less a metaphysical presence than a psychological absence. As Rupert Gethin observes, from the perspective of such early Buddhist schools as the Sautrāntikas, "one should not say more than *nirvāna* is the absence of the defilements."[8] And as Paul Williams puts it, "Nirvāna . . . is *not* 'the Buddhist name for the Absolute Reality' (let alone, God forbid, 'the Buddhist name for God'). Nirvāna is . . . an occurrence, an event (not a being, nor Being)."[9] And resisting the urge to conceive of an "object" of experience in that event, scholars like Peter Harvey prefer to construe nirvana as an "objectless consciousness"[10] (whatever that might entail).

In short, most Buddhists regard satori and nirvana not as experiential objects with a special and elusive ontological status like the Eternal One, but as modes of experience or, so to speak, psychological states (of course with huge soteriological import and purportedly accompanied by such feelings as joy and tranquility). And

6. Hick, *God Has Many Names*, 53.

7. Granted, those inclined to construe nirvana as a special place or dimension of reality can find *sutta* passages supportive of this portrayal, especially in the "inspired utterance" (*udāna*) passages. But most Buddhologists agree with Paul Williams, who through his analysis of these and other passages about nirvana concludes that "there is no positive ontological commitment implied at all" (*Buddhist Thought: A Complete Introduction to the Indian Tradition*, 51–52).

8. Gethin, *The Foundations of Buddhism*, 78.

9. Williams, *Buddhist Thought*, 48.

10. Harvey, *An Introduction to Buddhism: Teachings, History, and Practices*, 64.

as I will argue below, *śūnyatā* ("emptiness" or, better yet, "emptying"), while having more of a metaphysical connotation than either satori or nirvana, eludes the grasp of Hick's paradigm as well, despite the reification of the construct by Hick and even certain Buddhists.[11] As John Cobb astutely points out, "Emptiness is not an object of worship for Buddhists" and "it is not illuminating to insist that Emptiness and God are two names for the same noumenal reality."[12]

Hick's paradigm, especially in its earlier expressions, also falters in its representation of indigenous religions. In *God Has Many Names* (1980) Hick argues that "[p]rimitive religion seems to have been a sense of an inscrutable environing power to be feared, or of unpredictable and often ruthless beings to be placated";[13] and in this "primitive," "natural religion, or religion without revelation,[14] lasting from the beginnings of human history down to the spiritual dawn which occurred about three millennia ago,"[15] people had, relative to the "spiritual masters"[16] who founded or developed world religions, "a dim and crude sense of the Eternal One, an awareness which took what are, from our point of view as Jews or as Christians, at best childish and at worst appallingly brutal and bloodthirsty forms, but which nevertheless constituted the womb out of which the higher religions were to be born."[17] Hick also notes that in his theory of pluralism he is "speaking of what we commonly call the great world faiths, not of primitive religion, not of religious movements that have perished," and he claims that there "is a law of the spiritually fittest that simplifies the religious scene."[18]

In response to Hick, one might argue that some of those "primitive religions" have not "perished" but are still around, and quite fit, as the Ooldea in Western Australia and Navaho in Arizona would heartily agree. (Where are their voices in our conferences on religious pluralism? Do we have monotheistic or monistic biases in our approaches that preclude sustained dialogue with polytheistic or animistic others?) Insofar as some "primitive" religions are not very fit, one might wonder whether the survival of the religiously fittest, or the perishing of the least fit, is determined less by religious factors (such as "dim and crude" senses of the

---

11. That being said, Hick's approach is far preferable to those of Langdon Gilkey and Wilfred Cantwell Smith with their talk of a plurality of "revelations" and a God "inspiring" us. While Pure Land Buddhists might concur with Gilkey's notion of revelations, most forms of Buddhism (especially early and Theravadan Buddhism) say nothing about a divinity or higher anything that reveals itself, though perhaps I am reading a transitive connotation into "revelation" that Gilkey did not intend. And Smith seems even wider of the mark, insofar as one is hard pressed to find many Buddhists who see themselves or their religion as having been "inspired" by "God."

12. Cobb, *Beyond Dialogue: Toward a Mutual Transformation of Christianity and Buddhism*, 43; cited by Griffin, 28, above.

13. Hick, *God Has Many Names*, 43–44.

14. I think most adherents of "primitive" religions would view their visions (whether on a vision quest or in shamanistic trance) as revelations, though not necessarily of the kind of monotheistic deity that fits Hick's paradigm best.

15. Hick, *God Has Many Names*, 44.

16. Ibid., 43.

17. Ibid., 44.

18. Ibid., 56.

absolute) than by historical factors, such as the imperialism and cultural conquest pursued by countries that historically have professed Hick's "higher" religions. And rather than "our" Jewish or Christian points of view, the worldview of "primitive" religions, focused on natural forces and patterns, seems from certain Buddhist perspectives to offer a truer picture of the way things are than does the doctrine of a transcendent, eternal God advanced by "spiritual masters" and their "higher" religions.

To his credit, by 1995 Hick had shifted his position on "primitive religions." In *A Christian Theology of Religions* he switches his wording from "primitive religion" to "primal religion," and he writes that primal religions, while not being "salvific in the sense of seeking a radical human transformation, . . . are communal rather than individual responses to the Real."[19] And though Hick proceeds to echo a common stereotype in asserting that "in so far as they [primal religions] are effective, individual ego-transcendence is not called for because in traditional societies the autonomous ego has not become detached from the unity of the social organism,"[20] he ends his exposition by stating that "there are immensely valuable aspects of primal religion that we in the individualistic industrialized world must try to recover—the sense of unity with nature, the awareness of the other animals as our cousins, a sense of responsibility towards the earth as the mother of all life."[21] From 1980 to 1995 Hick has thus tempered his scheme of religious evolution, though the problems with the fit between his identist pluralism and Buddhism remain.

Griffin and Cobb's Whiteheadian approach to religious pluralism, their "differential" and "complementary" pluralism, is significantly more adequate to Buddhism. Griffin writes, "*Differential* pluralism, by contrast [with Hick's identist pluralism], says that religions promote different ends—different salvations—perhaps by virtue of being oriented toward different religious objects, perhaps thought of as different ultimates" (24, above). Further, "It belongs to complementary pluralism to assume that every great tradition is based on some deep insight into, some revelation about—whichever language one prefers—the nature of things" (44, above), and that religions offer "insights arising from profound thought and experience that are diverse modes of apprehending diverse aspects of the totality of reality."[22]

While Cobb and Griffin's approach moves beyond Hick's identification of nirvana with the Real, it still advances what one might call an "objectist" pluralism,[23] insofar as the concern is to discern the special "objects" or ultimate(s) apprehended by various religions. As indicated earlier, many Buddhists would ques-

---

19. Hick, *A Christian Theology of Religions*, 109.

20. Ibid., 109–10.

21. Ibid., 110.

22. Cobb, *Transforming Christianity and the World*, 74; quoted by Griffin in this volume, 47.

23. As opposed to what Cobb refers to as "objectivist views" of heaven and hell as actual places, the passage to which is determined by the presence or absence of confessed faith in Jesus Christ (Swidler et al., *Death or Dialogue?* 13).

tion whether their religious experience—satori and nirvana—is ever *of* some ulti-mate "religious object," whether through sense perception, prehension, cogni-tion, or some sort of "mystical" consciousness. Perhaps in the above statements Griffin does not mean to imply that "religious object" refers to a special reality with distinct ontological status apart from the person, though I do find John Cobb's wording preferable when he notes that the Buddha opened "a different path to a different goal, a different name of a different aspect of reality, a differ-ent language through which something quite different from communion [with the ultimate] is sought."[24] (Granted, the difference between "religious object" and "aspect of reality" may be negligible.)

Nevertheless, "differential" and "complementary" pluralism, especially as grounded by Cobb and Griffin in Whitehead's distinction between two ulti-mates, God and creativity, is preferable to Hick's approach. As many have noted, Whitehead's notion of two ultimates has constructed a much-traversed bridge between Christianity and Buddhism. Building on Whitehead, Cobb argues for three ultimates: God, creativity, and the cosmos or universe, "the totality of [finite] things."[25] Griffin summarizes Cobb's view: "What exists necessarily is not simply God, as in traditional Christian theism, and not simply the world understood as the totality of finite things, as in atheistic naturalism, but God-and-a-world, with both God and worldly actualities being embodiments of cre-ativity" (49, above). Griffin further states—and I would agree—that Cobb's formulation "gives us a basis for understanding a wide variety of religious expe-riences as genuine responses to something that is really there to be experienced" (51, above).

Insofar as Buddhism engages in metaphysical inquiry, its primary focus, espe-cially in the Theravada tradition, is on Cobb's third ultimate, the cosmos as char-acterized by conditioned arising (*pratītya-samutpāda*) or emptying (*śūnyatā*).[26] This "cosmos" on which Buddhism focuses diverges from the cosmos in most "cosmic religions" (to use John Hutchison's typology), for the Buddhist cosmos is not necessarily some sacred realm of nature, a polytheistic universe, an ani-mistic world accessed by shamans, or the natural cycles with which a "nature mys-tic" accords. Rather, the cosmos here is simply the realm of psychological, physical, sociocultural, and natural events, what we experience through the five sense organs and certain nonsensory experiences.

In viewing conditioned arising and emptying in this way, I resist Hick's and Cobb's equations of "Emptiness" with Nirguna Brahman, Being Itself, or the

---

24. Ibid., 81–82; quoted by Griffin in this volume, 28.
25. Cobb, *Transforming Christianity and the World*, 185; quoted by Griffin in this volume, 49.
26. A reader might regard my focus on the cosmos qua conditioned arising as a conflation of the cosmos and creativity insofar as he or she equates creativity and emptying. But, while Whitehead "regarded the personal God and formless creativity as equally primordial, with each presupposing the other" (Griffin, above, 61), I would find it difficult to regard "the personal God and conditioned aris-ing as equally primordial, with each presupposing the other." In fact, rather than presupposing a per-sonal God, conditioned arising brackets if not negates the existence of such a deity.

Godhead.[27] Indeed, not all Buddhists would agree that *śūnyatā* is "the *formless* ultimate reality" (see Griffin above, 47), or some formless ultimate that "is subject to taking on any form."[28] Rather, as indicated by the locus classicus in the *Heart Sutra*, "[f]orm is none other than emptiness; emptiness in none other than form," *śūnyatā* is the mode of the arising and ceasing of all "forms" (events), not some reality apart from those "forms," despite Abe Masao's talk of the "bottomless depth of Sunyata."[29] Nor is it something that has agency or can do certain things, despite Abe's frequent statements about "emptiness emptying itself"[30] and "freely taking form."[31] Though Nargajuna advanced *śūnyatā* primarily as another way of expressing conditioned arising (*pratītya-samutpāda*), most Theravadan Buddhists would have a hard time recognizing the early Buddhist construct of conditioned arising in Abe's statement, "Sunyata remaining with itself, without turning itself into a vow, is not true Sunyata. . . . [I]n and through self-emptying, Sunyata always ceaselessly turns itself into vow and into act, and then dynamically centers itself in a focal point of this dynamism."[32]

In short, for most Buddhists, *śūnyatā* or *pratītya-samutpāda* is not some mysterious ultimate like the Godhead *behind* God but the mode of reality *in front of* God (or, if you will, the principle that characterizes reality "down here"). With this view of *śūnyatā*, and lacking Abe's desire to delineate the ultimate of ultimates that lies deeper than anything else,[33] I feel less inclined to ask a question that Abe asks, namely: "How can Sunyata, as agentless spontaneity in its boundless openness, incorporate a personal deity as the ultimate criterion of value judgment?"[34] If I were to answer this question, though, I would say that "Sunyata" doesn't incorporate any deities, at least not eternal ones with unchanging essences, and it may be presumptuous of Buddhists to assume that it does.

Many forms of Buddhism, especially early and Theravada Buddhism, thus are forms of cosmic religion, not what Hutchison terms "acosmic" religion, especially insofar as the "aspect of reality" on which their metaphysical speculations focus is *śūnyatā*, the conditioned arising that constitutes the cosmos or, more specifically, the fact that all things are impermanent, "empty" of any unchanging essence or soul (*atman*). And the fact that an insight into conditioned arising can eradicate the clinging that causes suffering is for many Buddhists, to use Griffin's

27. Cobb writes, "My view is not that what Buddhists name as Emptiness has played no role in other traditions. On the contrary, it is the same reality that Hindus call Nirguna Brahman, and this is sometimes referred to as Godhead or Being Itself in the West" (Swidler et al., *Death or Dialogue?* 116).

28. Cobb, *Transforming Christianity and the World*, 184; quoted by Griffin in this volume, 62, n. 85.

29. Masao Abe, "Kenyotic God and Dynamic Sunyata," in Cobb and Ives, eds., *The Emptying God: A Buddhist-Jewish-Christian Conversation*, 56.

30. Ibid., 58.

31. Ibid., 28.

32. Ibid., 58.

33. Abe mentions this project at numerous points in his writings. In his introduction to *Zen and Western Thought*, he writes that he is "profoundly concerned with providing a spiritual foundation for future humanity in a global age" (*Zen and Western Thought* [London: Macmillan, 1985], xxiii).

34. Abe, "Kenyotic God," 38.

expression, "universally valid salvific truth" (57, above). This insight into the "aspect of reality" termed conditioned arising or emptying is the sort of thing on which Cobb is focusing in his stance that, as Griffin summarizes it, "different religions can each be seen as proclaiming universally valid insights, which can be synthesized" (48, above). Cognizant of this Buddhist insight, Cobb recognizes that "to be enlightened is to realize the fundamental nature of reality."[35]

In the spirit of complementary pluralism I might add that while it may not necessarily be the case that "to be enlightened is to realize *the* fundamental nature of reality," at a minimum it may be true that "to be enlightened is to realize *a* fundamental facet of reality." That is to say, Buddhists cultivate an insight into the ever-changing process of conditioned arising called the cosmos, and into how people usually experience, and cling to, parts of that process; and through Buddhist practice they can achieve liberation from the suffering that derives from that clinging. At the same time, people in other religions may be cultivating insights into other "aspects of reality," including permanent ones, that transcend (at least partly) the cosmos, and on the basis of those insights and religious practices (or faith) they too may achieve liberation from "suffering" as they understand it—whether sin, disobedience, idolatry, or something else. Simply put, just as religions attend to multiple "facets of reality," they also focus on multiple religious problems and pursue multiple paths to multiple solutions. In terms of traditional Buddhism and Christianity, both premortem psychological release *into* impermanence "right here" and postmortem ontological release *from* impermanence "down here" *to* permanent existence "up there" may be "salvific" and based on complementary and equally valid insights into two key "aspects of reality."

Someone might question here whether this way of affirming Cobb's complementary and differential pluralism squares with Buddhism. My heuristic argument—that Buddhism is a cosmic religion offering a soteriological scheme that is not incommensurable with those of other religions, even religions with a transcendent, eternal God—may appear to be Buddhistically illegitimate. In principle, a zealous member of the sangha, faithful to the doctrine of impermanence, could take a hardline Buddhist approach to religious diversity and reject truth claims about a permanent God (or eternal consequent nature of God) as delusive, as dangerous "wrong views" that reflect ignorance of the fact of impermanence and hence conduce to clinging and suffering. But logically such a rejection would constitute overreaching, for it could be the case (and may very well be the case) that there are several ultimates—or simply several "aspects of reality"—on which religions focus and in congruence with which they offer "salvific" schemes, and not all of these ultimates are characterized by impermanence, emptying, and conditioned arising. These Buddhist doctrines, while offering a fairly accurate representation of the cosmos in and around us, may not apply to all facets of reality.

That being said, one might still wonder what might be the *most genuine* Buddhist approach to religious diversity, that is, the approach that is most faithful to

---

35. Cobb, *Transforming Christianity and the World*, 140; quoted by Griffin in this volume, 48.

the tradition. But which Buddhist tradition? The earliest suttas (*ostensibly* the standpoint of the historical Buddha), Theravadan approaches, Tibetan teachings, Pure Land Buddhism, the Nichiren tradition, or Zen? Despite frequent representations of a singular "Buddhism" with *śūnyatā* as its purported essence, the religion is, not surprisingly, anything but monolithic. Different strands of Buddhism take different stances on religious diversity, even if those stances are not explicitly articulated. For example, despite Abe Masao's claim that Buddhism displays compassion and tolerance, in contrast with what he regards as a judgmental and intolerant tendency in biblical traditions, especially in their concepts of justice,[36] the Buddhist tradition has exhibited its fair share of intolerance, too. Nichiren (1222–82) infamously declared, "Those who practice invocation to Amitābha are due to suffer continuous punishment in Hell; the Zen sect is the devil; the Shingon sect is the ruiner of the country; the Ritsu sect is the enemy of the country."[37] And one does not need to go all the way back to the thirteenth century to encounter this sort of Japanese Buddhist approach to other religious traditions. In the late nineteenth century, nationalist Buddhist leaders assailed Christianity as a foreign, subversive creed, a false if not evil religion, and exhorted Buddhists and government officials to engage in the "refutation of the wicked" (*haja*[38]) and "extermination of Christianity" (*Yaso taiji*).[39] Well aware of claims that Buddhism, in contrast with biblical traditions, is tolerant and presumably more ecumenical, Zen social critic Ichikawa Hakugen (1902–86) writes in his assessment of wartime Buddhist collaboration with the militarist government, "Of what has Japanese Buddhism been tolerant? Of those with whom it harmonizes. Of its own responsibility for the war."[40]

Yet even if we limit our gaze to the more magnanimous approaches of recent representatives of the Dharma, not all Buddhists would sign on to their approaches. Those of a more Theravadan persuasion, heretofore less represented in conferences on pluralism and interfaith dialogue, might question the main approach to date: comparative metaphysics. Much of the Buddhist-Whiteheadian, Buddhist-Christian, and Buddhist-Jewish dialogue has privileged discussions of metaphysical ultimates, whether God, Amida, creativity, *śūnyatā*, the Godhead, or suchness. And most of this dialogue has been with East Asian Mahayana Buddhists

36. Abe writes, "The standpoint of justice, humanistic or divine, cannot be a proper basis for our coming to terms with the Holocaust, because the notion of justice is a double-edged sword. On the one hand, it sharply judges which is right and which is wrong. On the other hand, the judgment based on justice will naturally cause a counter-judgment as a reaction from the side thus judged. Accordingly, we may fall into endless conflict and struggle between the judge and the judged" (Abe, "Kenyotic God," 51).

37. Quoted by Joseph Kitagawa, *Religion in Japanese History*, 120.

38. The character "*ja*" of "*haja*" has such connotations as falsehood, heresy, and evil. The title that True Pure Land thinker Inoue Enryō (1858–1919) crafted for one of his anti-Christian works was *Haja shinron*, "a new treatise refuting the wicked [religion]." See Notto R. Thelle, *Buddhism and Christianity in Japan: From Conflict to Dialogue, 1854–1899*, 97.

39. Thelle, *Buddhism and Christianity in Japan*, 91.

40. Ichikawa Hakugen, *Ichikawa Hakugen Chosakushū*, vol. 2, 86–87.

and their theistic formulations of Amida and "kenotic" representations of *śūn-yatā*, in some cases with a substantialist nuance foreign to most Theravadan Buddhists.[41] This metaphysical orientation can be ascribed to any number of factors, whether the central project of Whitehead to replace substantialist metaphysics with a process perspective, or Abe's quest to elucidate the "foundation" beneath all religions. This orientation is deepened to the extent that consideration of the relationship between religion and science enters the dialogue.

Granted, most Buddhist thinkers do consider the nature of reality, whether in terms of *pratītya-samutpāda*, dharma theory in Abhidharma treatises, or *śūnyatā*. But while these constructs may refer to how things *really* or *ultimately* are, they are not necessarily denoting an "ultimate reality" or *the* Ultimate; and the "conditioned arising" or "emptying" on which they focus does not play any soteriological role (as an impinger [Hick], revealer [Gilkey], or inspirer [Smith]).[42] But more importantly, are these metaphysical "facts" the central concern of most Buddhists, of "ordinary" Buddhists, not Buddhist thinkers ("Buddhalogians") or scholars of Buddhism?

Avoiding questions that "do not edify," many Buddhists, as I stated above, would take less of a metaphysical orientation in their religious life. Members of the Theravadan sangha are more likely to direct their energies to mental cultivation (Pali *bhāvanā*) in conjunction with giving (*dāna*) and ethical precepts (*śīla*). Their ultimate concern is stopping *dukkha*.[43] And early Mahayana thinkers like Nagarjuna regard even the doctrines and techniques deployed in Buddhist practice as conventional, not ultimate, truth, as *upāya*, skillful means of eradicating the causes of suffering. Even *śūnyatā* is seen as a corrective solvent, a "upayic" technique, for dissolving views that promote clinging. In short, soteriology, not metaphysics, is the central concern.

Most Buddhists would agree with Griffin that "[t]he question of the truth of a given worldview must be settled by appeal to the normal rational-empirical criteria

---

41. Hakamaya Noriaki, Matsumoto Shiro, and other advocates of "Critical Buddhism" (*hihan-bukkyō*) in Japan have argued that Buddhist doctrines took a substantialist turn when they encountered Chinese constructs like the Tao, the Great Ultimate, and Original Nothingness. East Asian Buddhist thinkers supplanted "critical" early Buddhism with a "topical" Buddhism, which, on the basis of interpretations of the Indian Buddhist doctrines of Buddha-nature (Skt. *buddha-dhātu*) and the matrix of enlightenment (Skt. *tathāgata-garbha*), and such homegrown doctrines as "original enlightenment" (Jap. *hongaku*), offered a more substantialist, monistic characterization of reality. That is to say, Hakamaya and Matsumoto claim that in such Chinese works as the *Awakening of Mahayana Faith* (Chin. *Ta-sheng ch'i-hsin lun*; Jap. *Daijō-kishin-ron*), "topical" thinkers formulated doctrines of a unified topos or ground existing beneath and prior to particular phenomena in the world; by making these philosophical moves, these thinkers contravened the doctrines of conditioned arising, temporal causality, and no-self in earlier "true" Buddhism.

This critique by Hakamaya and Matsumoto, which is not without problems of its own, has led me to talk on several occasions with Abe Masao about his representation of *śūnyatā* as Emptiness (a noun with an uppercase E), as the foundation of all religions, and as something that "empties itself" as opposed to simply being a way of saying that no entity has any enduring core or soul, that all of reality is processive and all things arise interrelationally.

42. The Pure Land tradition would, I assume, take a different stance on this issue.

43. Granted, most lay Buddhists are concerned with securing good merit through alms, ritually promoting success in daily life, or having priests perform proper funerals and memorial services.

of self-consistency and adequacy to the facts" (15, above). In the worldview of early and Theravadan Buddhists the key facts are that nothing is permanent and that a clear recognition of impermanence is liberating. In formulating their worldview, zeroing in on notions of what the key facts might be, and cultivating insight into those facts, Buddhists are not simply trying to pin down the exact nature of reality. Like most religious thinkers, their metaphysical ruminations serve soteriological aims, and for them the crucial "test of adequacy" is what works to liberate, not merely what worldview is most adequate to the "facts," to the Ultimate or ultimates. That is to say, building on his recognition of the "fact" of impermanence, the historical Buddha set forth the Four Noble Truths, and these four "truths" are "universally valid salvific truth." Importantly, most Buddhist thinkers regard this "truth" pragmatically, as instrumentalist "conventional truth," as a skillful means effective in the same way that sand is when used to scour dirty pots. Buddhism thus privileges a pragmatic notion of truth as opposed to a correspondence theory of truth.

In these respects, for many Buddhists the most genuine Buddhist approach to religious diversity would focus on soteriology. It would regard soteriological *teloi* and the various religious practices leading to those goals as complementary. And perhaps the most fruitful and genuinely Buddhist approach would be to look less at the different goals and paths and more at different formulations of our "basic problem(s)" or "human condition(s)." The central focus here would be on the plurality of diagnoses of our problem (and its causes), on such issues as suffering (*dukkha*), ignorance, disobedience, sin, original sin, unrighteousness, a break in our communion with others, idolatry, impurity, or disharmony with cosmic forces.

As *a* genuine Buddhist angle on religious diversity, the approach that I'm advancing here would complement more metaphysical approaches with their investigation of differing views of ultimate reality (whether the Eternal One, à la Hick, or several ultimates, such as God, creativity, and the cosmos, à la Cobb). Complementing Cobb's "pluralistic metaphysics"[44] and its focus on "diverse modes of apprehending diverse aspects of the totality of reality,"[45] this approach would constitute, for lack of a better expression, a "pluralistic religio-diagnostics," or, to put it even more awkwardly, a "dukkhic" approach that would, to borrow and adapt Cobb's wording, focus on "diverse modes of apprehending diverse aspects of the totality of existential anguish." Granted, this approach has not been completely overlooked in past dialogue or treatments of religious diversity, but pursuing it further could provide another avenue for the mutual transformation that Cobb champions. In fact, Cobb takes such an approach in a remark about Christians and Vedantist Hindus: "through dialogue Hindus may come to appreciate the importance of sin in human life and the urgency of finding forgiveness. . . . And Christians may in turn realize how deeply we are all mired in

---

44. Cobb, *Transforming Christianity and the World*, 88; quoted by Griffin in this volume, 47.
45. Cobb, *Transforming Christianity and the World*, 74; quoted by Griffin in this volume, 47.

illusions, how they distort all our thinking, and how valid and valuable it is to realize that they are just that, illusions."[46]

This approach could also broaden participation in interfaith dialogue and reflection on religious diversity and pluralism, for it might prove more interesting to the majority of religious people, who, unlike those of us who are professorial elites, might not have the time, resources, or inclination to reflect on metaphysical issues; to grapple with the doctrines of *śūnyatā*, Nothingness, God, the Godhead, or the two or three Whiteheadian ultimates; to explore connections to science; to search for a possible "empty" ground of all religions; or to attend academic conferences. This approach might also bring more *nonreligious* people into the discussion, including those who raise issues of verification.[47]

It is not without ulterior motive that I advocate this religio-diagnostic approach, for it can transform Buddhism by nudging Buddhists to look at how Gustavo Gutierrez, Paul Knitter, James Cone, Rosemary Ruether, and other liberationist theologians have gone beyond spiritualized soteriologies and outlined the sociopolitical dimensions of "sin" and "salvation," especially in terms of justice (in a much broader sense than Abe's limited construal of justice as judgment and punishment). Specifically, this approach can help Buddhists develop their diagnostics and ethics into a systemic analysis that links *dukkha* with "mundane" sociopolitical suffering.[48] Of course, some Buddhists might argue here that the *dukkha* with which Buddhism has traditionally concerned itself exists in a "vertical" religious dimension, not on the horizontal plane of "mundane suffering," and that nirvana goes far deeper than, for example, Paul Knitter's *soteria*. Regardless of how we might respond to that argument,[49] I would argue that even though Buddhists might have much to teach about the psychology of *dukkha*, sin, and other existential issues, they have much to learn about the sociopolitical facets of *dukkha*. And Buddhists *need* to learn from thinkers like Knitter, whose "soteriocentric" model focuses on "the welfare of humanity and this earth, the promotion of life and the removal of that which promotes death"[50] and lifts up "the

---

46. Cobb in Swidler et al., *Death or Dialogue?* 13.

47. While God and *śūnyatā* elude public verification, religious problems (experienced anguish) and their solutions (the nature of a person's transformation) are more empirically available for debate and adjudication. Of course, psychological states still pose verifiability challenges, especially in light of claims of ineffability at one end of the discussion of religious experience to rejection of the category of "religious experience" at the other end. This challenge may lead some to focus on the moral effects of religious faith and practice, as Hick does with his "broadly ethical criteria" for determining when people have genuinely shifted from self-centeredness to being centered on the Real, as opposed to something else. See Hick, *A Christian Theology of Religions,* 77.

48. I would argue that *the* crucial project for constructive Buddhist thinkers (Buddhalogians or, as Roger Corless might put it, Dharmalogians) who take Buddhist ethics seriously is to clarify the connections between universal existential suffering (*dukkha*) and sociopolitical suffering and, in response, between seeking awakening and seeking peace and ecojustice.

49. I have come to question the vertical-horizontal model for the relationship between religion and society/history. Though *dukkha* may describe a universal problem, the genesis, tenacity, and resolution of this problem are very much influenced by sociopolitical factors. Expressed differently, *dukkha* is not caused or exacerbated solely by some "original ignorance" or innate human tendency to cling.

50. Knitter, "Interreligious Dialogue: What? Why? How?" in Swidler et al., *Death or Dialogue?* 37.

'salvation' or 'well-being' of humans and Earth as the starting point and common ground for our efforts to share and understand our religious experiences and notions of the Ultimately Important."[51] Dialogue with Knitter and other liberation theologians (as well as Cobb and his recent writings on "economism," globalization, and sustainability) might be the *most transformative* dialogue for Buddhists at present. To some extent this dialogue has begun, with "engaged Buddhists" like Sulak Sivaraksa, Thich Nhat Hanh, and the Dalai Lama frequently discussing sociopolitical suffering with religious and nonreligious thinkers.

To their credit, these Buddhists have recognized the significance of Buddhism's encounter with nonreligious systems of analysis. In the past Buddhists have often deemed those systems not as a resource but as a challenge, if not a threat. While agreeing with Whitehead that religions in modernity have had to face the challenge of "the rise of the third tradition, which is science,"[52] Abe has also construed Marxism as a challenge, as one part of a major crisis for religion: "the problem of religion versus irreligion."[53] Abe writes, "Scientism, Marxism, traditional Freudian psychoanalytic thought, and nihilism in the Nietzschean sense all deny the raison d'être of religion, not merely on emotional grounds but on various rational or theoretical grounds. Not stopping with criticism of particular religions, these ideologies negate the very being of religion itself. The most crucial task of any religion in our time is to respond to these anti-religious forces by elucidating the authentic meaning of religious faith"[54] and developing "a new paradigm beyond the religion-negating principles of scientism, Marxism, traditional Freudian psychoanalytic thought, and nihilism in the Nietzschean sense."[55] It is ironic that Abe sees Marxism as a crisis, a problem Buddhism must confront and somehow overcome, for despite his professed interest in developing Buddhist social ethics through dialogue, he overlooks the fact that in the early-Shōwa period (1926–45) Marxist intellectuals were virtually the only people who criticized Japanese Buddhist leaders for their collaboration with Japanese militarists, with the architects of the imperial ideology that was central to State Shinto, and with propagandists in the Home and Education Ministries.[56] Buddhists with ethical concerns about the political stances of their tradition in Japanese history might find that Marxist modes of analysis are less a problem for Japanese Buddhism than a welcome resource for grappling with the issue of traditional Buddhist symbiosis with the Japanese state and economically powerful interests. Dialogue with liberationist analyses could help Bud-

51. Paul F. Knitter, *Jesus and the Other Names: Christian Mission and Global Responsibility*, 17.
52. Whitehead, *Religion in the Making*, 146; quoted by Griffin in this volume, 41.
53. Abe, "Kenyotic God," 4.
54. Ibid., 3.
55. Ibid., 4.
56. For treatment of these issues, see Ives, "The Mobilization of Doctrine: Buddhist Contributions to Imperial Ideology in Modern Japan" and "Ethical Pitfalls in Imperial Zen and Nishida Philosophy: Ichikawa Hakugen's Critique." Also see Victoria, *Zen at War*.

dhists confront their past—especially the nationalist skeletons in their historical closet—as well as their present, including the numerous and usually ignored issues of class and gender.

An expanded religio-diagnostic approach to religious diversity could also promote intrareligious dialogue among Buddhists by prodding them to reflect critically on past formulations of Buddhist social ethics that were influenced by other traditions. Whitehead is unaware of these influences when he writes about Christianity and Buddhism, "The self-sufficient pedantry of learning and the confidence of ignorant zealots have combined to shut up each religion in its own forms of thought. Instead of looking to each other for deeper meanings, they have remained self-satisfied and unfertilized."[57] While Buddhism and Christianity may not have looked to each other for "deeper meanings," and Christianity may have "remained self-satisfied and unfertilized" over the centuries (a claim I doubt), fertilization characterizes much of Buddhist history. That is to say, Buddhism did not become "shut up . . . in its own forms of thought" and languish in a vacuum as it spread across Asia, for it retained the "flexibility of adaptation" that Whitehead inaccurately denies historical Buddhism when he claims that "neither of them had retained the requisite flexibility of adaptation."[58] For example, since it was introduced into East Asia nearly two thousand years ago, Buddhism has been engaged in relationships of mutual transformation with other traditions, including, at different points in time, Confucianism, Daoism, Shinto, and even Christianity. It has been fertilized by all of these traditions and has fertilized them in return.[59] And in some cases this "fertilization" of Buddhism has germinated weeds, at least relative to certain early Buddhist teachings and Mahayana ideals. For example, one can argue that the Zen assimilation of Confucian ethical and political constructs has in certain respects contravened the Mahayana bodhisattva ideal.

I am not sure how the religio-diagnostic approach I have been sketching here would accord with Whitehead's thought. As he wrote at the beginning of *Process and Reality*, Whitehead's concern was Speculative Philosophy, "the endeavor to frame a coherent, logical, necessary system of general ideas in terms of which every element of our experience can be interpreted" (PR 3). In this endeavor Whitehead did consider broadly soteriological issues, and in their analysis of *dukkha* Buddhists can learn from his discussions of enjoyment, Peace, the Harmony of Harmonies, perpetual perishing, the divine aim, and God's responsive love. Yet from my limited study of Whitehead's writings, Whitehead's explicit treatment of soteriology may be limited, at least insofar as being prehended by God and achieving objective immortality in God's consequent nature does not

57. Whitehead, *Religion in the Making*, 146; the second of these two sentences is cited by Griffin in this volume, 40.

58. Ibid.

59. As Kuroda Toshio has argued, for many centuries the dominant Japanese religion was not Buddhism or Shinto but a Buddhist-Shinto amalgam.

strike me as offering that much solace to those who are wrestling with death as the ultimate problem of interpretability.[60]

In expanding their treatment of suffering beyond *dukkha* to sociopolitical pain and injustice, however, Buddhists can learn much from Whitehead and process thought. Whitehead's ideas about creativity, prehension, novelty, complexity, and beauty provide a rich resource, especially insofar as Buddhists might draw from them to clarify how, for example, conditioned arising allows for novelty, teleology, or simply the envisioning of possibilities beyond the collective ignorance and suffering that characterizes much of the world in these first few years of the new millennium.

---

60. David Griffin and others have reflected on how Whitehead's system might allow for the continuation of some sort of individual consciousness after death (*Reenchantment without Supernaturalism*, chap. 6), and he and other process theologians have developed Whitehead's soteriology beyond the notion of objective immortality.

Chapter 9

To Whom Belong the Covenants?

Whitehead, Wesley, and Wildly Diverse Religious Traditions

Michael Lodahl

for Marjorie Hewitt Suchocki, mentor and inspirer

This chapter itself is mildly, if not wildly, diverse: its three sections will explore three different paths for reflecting upon the reality of the plurality of religious traditions in the world. In the first section, I will set forth the general contours of the process metaphysic as it creates a backdrop for thinking about this issue. In the second section, I will move to the thought of the founder of Methodism, the eighteenth-century Anglican priest-evangelist John Wesley, in the confidence that (of all people!) Wesley contributes a unique, and perhaps somewhat surprising, perspective on religious diversity. Finally, in the third section I will explore some of the particularly Jewish contributions to this issue as I discover them in the Bible and the Talmud.

If there is a consistent, connecting theme among these three paths of thought, perhaps it is best captured in the concept of *covenant.*

I

God works with the world as it is in order to lead it toward what it can be.

Marjorie Hewitt Suchocki

This is the promise and genius of the process vision of God and the world. In her writings Marjorie Suchocki repeatedly has offered this proposition as a kind of programmatic statement about the nature of reality. Sometimes she explicitly associates it with Whitehead or process thought,[1] and sometimes she does not.[2] Nonetheless, the proposition's pedigree is obvious; in this process-relational vision of things, God is *always and everlastingly* laboring with the world as it is, in this moment and in the next, in order to lead the world toward the better world that it might become.

The question is, What are the implications of this vision of things for our attempts to understand the vast number and variety of religious traditions in the world?

So much depends upon how one thinks about God in relation to the world, and the world in relation to God! For the process model of thinking, God always works with the world as it is, in any and every given moment—precisely because there always has been, is now, and always will be a *world*, a "that-which-is-not-God," with and through which God works. Whitehead was not hesitant to put the point bluntly: "It is as true to say that God creates the World, as that the World creates God" (PR 348). The point at which this vision of things becomes irksome to most traditional religious thinkers is in its elucidation of the doctrine of creation; generally, the process model jettisons the abstract idea of a worldless God who, at some undefinable point in eternity, began to create the world out of nothing. Instead, as Whitehead's maxim suggests, the process portrayal of reality offers an everlasting God working with an everlasting world—a world of *some kind or another*, of varying degrees of harmony and complexity, of various possibilities for growth and development. God always labors with this world toward greater measures of harmony and beauty, but must always work with the world that is given to God in any and every given moment. As John B. Cobb Jr. has argued the point, "God in every moment works with and upon the world that is given to him in that moment. If at any point we imagine God's willing something into being in a way not conditioned and constrained by what is already given, it must be wholly mysterious to us why he willed into being a universe so difficult to persuade into the achievement of high forms of order and significant intensities of value."[3] We have here a vision of things that is inherently and ever-

---

1. As she does, for example, in *God-Christ-Church: A Practical Guide to Process Theology*, 94.

2. As is the case throughout her popularly written book, *In God's Presence: Theological Reflections on Prayer*.

3. Cobb, *God and the World*, 91–92. (This early [1969] book still employed language that did not reflect Cobb's later feminist sensitivities.)

lastingly *relational*—and therefore is shot through with all of the ambiguities necessitated by a true relation. The world is not under God's "control," especially if control means tightfisted rule. Further, the nature of truth is not unilateral decree or pristine and eternal ideal unsullied by the mire and muck of the world as we know it; instead, truth truly does emerge as a function of the give-and-receive dynamic *between* God and world—and *among* the innumerable interactions of events within the world—occurring billions upon billions of times in every millisecond throughout our vast and wildly diverse universe.

How does God labor with this world? Essentially, in this vision of things God works by *being present* to each and every occasion of the world. God's presence, however, is clearly not an obvious or overwhelming determinant of each, or of any, occasion. God *cannot* be such a unilateral determinant, since the world itself with all its energies contributes a great deal of momentum to each occasion's becoming. Further, in this vision of things each occasion exercises a measure of self-direction, even if that measure is minuscule. Nonetheless, God is also working: God is present as the offer from a Future that the occasion, in and of itself and its past, could not and would not have striven for. So God is *always* working with the world as it is, and is working in this way *everywhere*. At all times and in all places, God is present as the subtle calling onward, as the whisper of something better than what is in this moment. God has always worked in this way, is always working with the world as it is—for God receives each moment of experience, for what it is, into the incomprehensible abyss of divine knowing. God *receives* what the world *offers*—and out of the sheer facticity of that offering of the world, God weaves something new, a new vision for what could be, what might yet become. In Whitehead's words, "Every act leaves the world with a deeper or a fainter impress of God. He then passes into his next relation to the world with enlarged, or diminished, presentation of ideal values" (RM 152).

We understand that, in this vision of things, the world's vast variety of experiences and experiments are really, truly *the world's to give to God*. We need not be burdened by the misconception that everything happens in accordance with some divine blueprint, for the world in all of its varieties of creaturely response to God's evocative presence truly does make much of its own history—but always in response to ever-new, ever-renewed divine aims for every creature in the world. Both God and the world, then, are sources of novelty; by all appearances, God is well pleased—or at least willing—to labor creatively and redemptively with the novelties the world offers. God does have a will for the world, but it is a will that is pliable, flexible, buoyant, ever-fitted to newly emerging conditions; it has to be so, in order to take into account all of the peculiar contributions of every creature to the world, and thus to every other creature's becoming, and thus also to God. The divine will is always fitted to the particularities and history of each and every creature "with each passing moment" (to quote an old "process" hymn!); or, to draw on the ancient Hindu/Buddhist metaphor, God carefully weaves and wends among all creatures in every moment—each and every creature being (in)securely knitted to all others in the interconnected webbing of Indra's net.

Some critics object that this vision of things is too far removed from the biblical description of God's relation to the world to be of much theological help. However, for starters, one need not stretch the opening creation passage of Genesis very much, if at all, to accommodate the process model. Process thinkers are far from alone in arguing for a less tidy interpretation of the Hebrew text in its opening lines.[4] Rather than the traditional insistence on a clean-cut, clear-cut *creatio ex nihilo* in the very opening of the Torah—a reading which would, of course, yield a deity who, ultimately, works alone—it appears likely that Genesis draws back its opening curtain to reveal a formless, watery chaos with which God begins the labor of creating. If this is correct, then Genesis does not begin with the pure omnipotence of divine fiat, but with God's evocative, alluring call to deep, unformed possibilities that swirl in the darkness.[5] Of course, even before God speaks a word, there is the divine *ruach*, the breath/wind of God, that "hovers" or "broods" upon the face of the deep.[6] Here we encounter a truly pregnant image of the blowing, whispering gift of the life-giving Spirit, stirring and troubling the dark and threatening waters, brewing up a world.

It is toward, and into, this chaotic abyss that God outpours the life of the Spirit; it is toward these unfathomable depths that the Maker faces and speaks the creative word. And what is the nature of the word that God speaks? In Genesis 1 this divine speech repeatedly is *let there be*; it is a word that allows for, makes room for—indeed "creates space" for!—the creatures of sea, sky, and land. It is not so much a word of command as it is a word of hopefulness, a word that offers promise and evokes possibilities. This becomes all the more apparent in the Hebraic wordplays lurking within the divine invitation to the earth and the waters: the earth is invited to "put forth" (*tadse*) vegetation (*dese*) and the waters are called upon to "bring forth" (*yisresu*) living creatures of the sea (*seres*). In other words, God's creative activity is expressed precisely through the appropriate creaturely contributions; God's creating fits, and is fitted to, specific creaturely capabilities.

Then there is that marvelous refrain reverberating throughout the opening chapter: *and God saw that it was good.* The fact that, for Genesis 1, God "sees" that various creatures of the world are good after they have been produced by the earth and the waters—rather than God's simply pronouncing or announcing or simply knowing that they are good de facto—implies a real and timely interactivity between the Creator and the developing creation. God does not "already know from eternity" that the creatures are good; God *sees* their goodness, their fittedness to God's creative purposes. God, in other words, responds with approval to the world's own response to the divine invitation to *let there be*. There is on the opening page of the Bible something of a call-and-response relation that we who are shaped by biblical traditions have learned to call *covenantal*.

4. See, for example, Levenson, *Creation and the Persistence of Evil*; on a more popular level, see Karen Armstrong, *In the Beginning: A New Interpretation of Genesis*, 9–14.

5. For a provocative and eminently creative tour de force on the opening verses of Genesis, see Catherine Keller's *Face of the Deep*.

6. See ibid., especially chapter 5, "The Sea of Heteroglossia."

God "calls"—in process parlance, God offers "initial aims"—and each moment of creaturely experience—each "actual occasion"—includes in its transitory becoming some measure of response to that calling. In this covenantal (Lat., *co vene*, "to come together with") understanding of creation, the particular and peculiar energies that each creature has contributed to the making of this world are respected by God, lovingly received and cherished by God, and help to create new possibilities for the world as it continues to come to being, to become. *Covenant*, understood precisely in this way, necessarily characterizes God's interactivity with all of creation, everywhere, at all times. Every creature's own striving and struggle, its own yearning to be, to persist and perdure—indeed, to survive—is taken seriously in this process vision of things. In thinking of the world in this way, we find help for appreciating the vast number of experiments in living, in surviving and thriving, that the evolutionary history of our world has included. These experiments, of course, continue into this present moment. Creatures of all sorts continue to seek niches in which to grow, thrive, and reproduce themselves.

The pressing question is, How might this vision of things help us to interpret the variety of religious traditions, practices, and experiences of our world? Let us return to the epigram for the opening section of this chapter: *God works with the world as it is in order to lead it toward what it can be.* The process vision of things holds that there has never been a time or place where this has not been true. Because the way in which God works is the way of covenantal colaboring, the world is teeming with difference and diversity. It can be no other way than this, because the complex, interrelated histories of all creatures, throughout all time, inevitably lend themselves to a virtually countless number of ways for beings to be. The world hosts an unimaginable plurality of creatures, all working to carve out a niche for themselves. Correspondingly, among the human species there is a vast variety of cultures, languages, modes of life and of thought, of customs, and of dress—and certainly, intertwined with all of these has been a variety of ideas, intuitions, institutions, experiences, and social practices. Human beings, like the rest of the world, make their own responses to the subtle calling of God.

Since all creatures, including human beings, participate with God in their own making, God never begins with a clean slate: *God works with the world as it is in order to lead it toward what it can be.* God's call, then, is always shaped by previous creaturely responses, and while all creatures offer their own novel experiences, responses, and ways of being, it is human agency in particular that has contributed new twists in our world's becoming in the past fifty thousand years or so. God is always working with those twists, attempting perhaps sometimes to turn those twists in a different direction, other times to reinforce and to build upon them. Real diversity is inevitable in such a world as process-relational thinkers imagine, and perceive, our world to be. We need only see that this diversity very obviously must include the diversity of religious traditions in human history, including the present, as indicative of the covenantal nature of divine activity in the world.

I have attempted in this opening section of my essay to offer a broadly stroked portrait of God and the world as construed in the process vision of things. This is the metaphysic that has inspired and grounded Marjorie Suchocki's theological reflections and clearly has important ramifications for thinking about religious diversity. My intention now is to add a new wrinkle to this process vision of things—a Wesleyan wrinkle.

II

Conscience . . . varies exceedingly, according to education and a thousand other circumstances.

John Wesley

Any estimation of, or appreciation for, Marjorie Hewitt Suchocki's thought and life is incomplete without acknowledging the role of the writings of John Wesley (1703–91), the Anglican founder of the Methodist movement, in her theological development. She explored that role autobiographically in her essay "Coming Home: Wesley, Whitehead, and Women,"[7] making explicit the ready connections among Wesley's theology, Whitehead's cosmology, and feminist sensibilities. A personal reminiscence may help to make this point: in the mid-'90s I was part of a conference on Wesley studies in which Marjorie was the keynote speaker. Our assignment was to wrestle with the question, "What is missing in our Methodist and Wesleyan churches?" In her plenary address Marjorie answered the question simply, "John Wesley is!" She then proceeded in a compelling, rapturous retelling of Wesley's little classic, *A Plain Account of Christian Perfection*, arguing that the book deserved careful study in Methodist churches everywhere. What was so memorable about her address was that she really made Wesley alive by reading him through a new lens—her feminist and Whiteheadian lens. Thus, it seems appropriate to ask whether Wesley, as a looming figure in the undoubtedly always-evolving mix of Suchocki's theological growth, may contribute some element to the issue of how we might interpret the fact of religious diversity. Further, by utilizing Wesley as a guide, we are moving from a general cosmological framework as provided by the Whiteheadian vision and attempting now to think in more consciously and particularly Christian ways about religious diversity.

In the opening section I suggested that the inviting, interactive, and responsive nature of God's evocative "speaking" and satisfied "seeing" in Genesis 1 goes a long way toward softening the more popular traditional notion of unilateral divine fiat. In this section, we shall see that such a reading of Genesis 1 also corresponds nicely with Wesley's ideas about the loving, noncoercive, and responsive nature of God's interactions with human beings. I am not suggesting that

---

7. The essay, which appeared originally in *The Drew Gateway*, has been reprinted in Stone and Oord, *Thy Nature and Thy Name Is Love: Wesleyan and Process Theologies in Dialogue*.

Wesley can be read as some kind of proto–process thinker. Nonetheless, it is readily arguable that the proclivity of so many Methodist theologians of the second half of the twentieth century toward the process vision of things is no mere coincidence. Wesley's practical, preachable theology spun a heritage of Methodist thought that has a history of taking with great seriousness the real lives and contributions of all creatures, to say nothing of the real agency of human beings, in relation to their Maker.

Further, as it is for contemporary process thinkers, so also it was for Wesley: God's creative and sustaining activity in the world is predicated upon God's immediate presence—and yet this presence does not overwhelm or negate the creaturely integrity and energies. God works, speculated Wesley, by "every moment superintending everything that he has made; strongly and sweetly influencing all, and yet without destroying the liberty of his rational creatures."[8] It is fitting to argue, beyond Wesley, that if God is concerned not to destroy or negate *human* agency (or "liberty"), then there is likely a corresponding integrity and energy for *all* of creation in its vastly complex relations to the Creator. We are far less likely than Wesley and his contemporaries to suppose that human agency could be a simple and grand exception to everything else in the world. Granted, Wesley seemed most concerned that the "liberty" of God's "rational creatures" (i.e., human beings) be upheld and sustained, so that, significantly, the "influencing" (or *inflowing*) divine presence does not displace or dispel human energies and agency. It is incumbent upon us, nonetheless, to broaden Wesley's concern to include the creaturely integrity and real contribution of *all creatures* to the ongoing creative activity of God.

In the past two centuries since Wesley, the ecclesial tradition his preaching and practices spawned has argued cogently that human agency—our wondrous capacity to do evil against ourselves and one another, as well as to do good—is consistent with the convictions that *God is love* and *God acts in love*. In order that love might have opportunity to flourish in creation, God has painstakingly nurtured responsible agency in homo sapiens. God's creative power, in Wesley's phrase, "continually co-operates with" God's wisdom and goodness, laboring in a fashion expressive of a love that bestows, encourages, and evokes a response of love from the creature. Having embarked upon the divine adventure of calling forth creatures of responsible freedom, God "cannot deny himself; he cannot counteract himself, or oppose his own work"[9]—and God's work is to allow the creaturely elements "room" to *be*, to *grow*, to *exercise creaturely freedom for the sake of the possibilities of love.*

> Were it not for this [God] would destroy all sin, with its attendant pain, in a moment. He would abolish wickedness out of his whole creation, and suffer no trace of it to remain. But in so doing he would counteract himself, he

8. Wesley, "On the Omnipresence of God," in *The Works of John Wesley*, vol. 7.
9. Wesley, "On Divine Providence," *Works*, vol. 6, 317.

would altogether overthrow his own work, and undo all that he has been doing since he created man upon the earth. . . . Were human liberty taken away men would be as incapable of virtue as stones. . . . God . . . [wills] to assist man in attaining the end of his being, in working out his own salvation—so far as it can be done without compulsion, without overruling his liberty, . . . without turning man into a machine.[10]

In Wesley's cosmological reflections, this grace that is none other than *God laboring in and with the world* is of the greatest intimacy. In his 1786 sermon "On Divine Providence" Wesley explicitly connects God's other-empowering omnipresence to omni-*science*, or God's *knowing* of all things:

[A]s this all-wise, all-gracious Being created all things, so he sustains all things. . . . Now it must be that he knows everything he has made, and everything he preserves from moment to moment. Otherwise he could not preserve it: he could not continue to it the being which he has given it. And it is nothing strange that he who is omnipresent, who "filleth heaven and earth," who is in every place, should see what is in every place, where he is intimately present. . . . Especially considering that nothing is distant from him, in whom we all "live and move and have our being."[11]

This last phrase above, of course, is a quotation from Paul's Athens discourse in Acts 17. It is noteworthy that Wesley insists that "nothing is distant from [God]," for it underscores the notion that God's creative and intimate presence somehow actually *makes each creature possible*—and thus that the mode of God's activity is in, with, and through the actual and authentic contributions of all creatures. In fact, just as the Paul of the Athens sermon could quote pagan poets as testifying to the radical immanence of God, so Wesley is bold enough to cite Virgil's *Aeneid* in describing God as "the all-informing soul, that fills, pervades and actuates the whole."[12] Thus, Wesley's understanding of God's knowing and sustaining of creation is that God labors in and for the world by immediate presence, as "the omnipresent Spirit," and not as a distant, objectifiable "deity." "God," Wesley writes in his third discourse on the Sermon on the Mount, "by his intimate presence holds [heaven and earth and all that is therein] in being, who pervades and actuates the whole created frame, and is in a true sense the soul of the universe."[13]

Wesley, then, offers a surprisingly *immanent* and *intimate* God whose everlasting love and sustaining presence encompass the entirety of creation. In reality, of course, it could be no other way; if for Wesley all human beings are *graced*, it is equally true that all human beings are creatures who share inextricably in the complex webs of creaturely existence as a whole. Thus, there can be no sharp arbi-

10. Ibid., 317–18.
11. Ibid., 315.
12. "On the Omnipresence of God," 240.
13. Wesley, "Upon Our Lord's Sermon on the Mount, Discourse III," *Works*, vol. 5, 283.

trary line drawn between God's loving, sustaining presence offered graciously to humans and God's presence offered graciously to all of creation, since it is the one God "who pervades and actuates the whole created frame." In other words, Wesley anticipates process theologians in their insistence upon God's actual and active presence among, in, and through every element of creation; everywhere, at all times, God is at work.

It is, however, precisely at the point of God's evocation of the *human* response that Wesley offers a viable contribution to our reflections upon the reality of religious diversity. This moment of divine calling, according to Wesley, is experienced by human beings most often as *conscience*. He repeatedly insists that "natural conscience" is *not* "natural," that is, not simply a creaturely phenomenon reducible to social and cultural factors. Instead, for Wesley conscience is "supernatural"— which for Wesley, it must be noted, does not require a miraculous, unilateral activity on God's part, but in fact suggests the dynamic interaction of God with human beings in their actual, concrete sociocultural circumstances.[14] In the Methodist tradition, this is prevenient grace, which is thought to be the *sustaining nearness of God* to all human beings in their situatedness, their concretely historical settings. In fact, in his comments on Acts 17:28 ("in God we live and move and have our being") Wesley writes, "We need not go far to seek or find [God]. He is very near us; in us. It is only perverse reason which thinks [God] is afar off."[15] It is important for our purposes to keep in mind that Wesley, staying true to the intent of the text of Acts 17, is not meaning only Christian believers, nor even just religious people, when he writes that God is "very near us," even "in us." This is the God who, in the imagery of the Qur'an, is nearer to each of us than is our own jugular vein!

For Wesley, accordingly, the human conscience is a *con-fluence*, a flowing together: there is the influence, the inflowing, of all of our experiences, education, and relationships; there is also the inflowing of God's own Spirit to quicken, to address, to call, to convict. In practice, indeed in reality, these influences are inseparably intertwined. We find this notion particularly clearly in Wesley's sermon "On Conscience," where he points out that the term's etymology is "to know together with" another. He takes this "other" to be God—but *not* "none other than" God! Hence, on the one hand he rejects the phrase "natural conscience" because "properly speaking, it is not natural, but a supernatural gift of God, above all his natural endowments."[16] On the other hand, conscience "is that faculty whereby we are at once conscious of our own thoughts, words, and actions, and of their merit or demerit. . . . But this varies exceedingly, according to education and a thousand other circumstances."[17]

14. Wesley, "Working Out Our Own Salvation," *Works*, vol. 6, 512.
15. Wesley, *Explanatory Notes upon the New Testament*, 466.
16. Wesley, "On Conscience," *Works*, vol. 7, 187–88.
17. Ibid., 187.

Education and a thousand other circumstances! There are undoubtedly more than just a thousand such circumstances: events significant and not so; memories (often at least half forgotten); countless conversations; habits of thought and behavior; political, religious, and moral authorities; all kinds of relations with others, and so forth. These all contribute their presence, their effects, their energies into our psyches and bodies. But Wesley of course intends the number of "a thousand" not as a limit, but as an exorbitant and wild gesture toward the infinitely incalculable particulars of each of our lives. If *con-science* is on the one hand a "knowing with" the Spirit of God who searches our hearts and all things, it is on the other a "knowing with" those numberless particulars. Thus, according to Wesley, because God does not negate or cancel the contributions of those "thousand other circumstances,"[18] conscience is not a stable, unvarying universal standard. Indeed, it "varies exceedingly"! Is there a seed here that might grow into a full-branched religious pluralism?

And yet!—on that other hand, *it is God* who calls, who moves, who draws and woos us from within "the boundaries of [our] habitation" (Acts 17:26 RSV). *It is God* who respects the inflowing of those "thousand other circumstances" in their felt presence in our lives—for that is the inevitably covenantal mode of divine activity. Wesley finds further support for this idea by drawing upon the familiar words of Micah 6:8: "So that we may say to every human creature, 'He,' not nature, 'hath showed thee, O man, what is good.'"[19] For Wesley it is significant that the one addressed in the text is "O man" (or, much more faithful to the point, "O human")—and *not* "O Christian" or "O Jew." In Wesley's reading of the Micah text, God labors in the world to show all human beings the good path on which to walk. We must keep in mind, however, that God, working with the world as it is, offers a good path to real human beings of particular times and places, dwelling as they do within "the boundaries of their habitation"—which means that in actual creaturely experience God's good path must be many paths.

Further, Wesley notices that "Balak king of Moab" and "Balaam the son of Beor" are mentioned a few verses earlier (Micah 6:5); thus, not without some justification he assumes that this "beautiful passage" is given "a peculiar force" when we "consider by whom and on what occasion the words were uttered." Wesley suggests that Balaam the pagan prophet was "then under divine impressions," and that "probably Balak too, at that time, experienced something of the same influence. This [divine in-flowing] occasioned his consulting with, or asking counsel of, Balaam,—his proposing the question to which Balaam gives so full an answer."[20] In other words, Wesley assumes that this classic prophetic text calling

18. Of course, while Wesley believed that God *does not* negate or cancel the "education and a thousand other circumstances" of every human life, in the process vision of things God *cannot* do so. Although I suspect that the process vision is closer to the truth, I hope that Wesley is not incorrect. In other words, I still hope for a way to avoid this impasse.

19. "On Conscience," 188.

20. Ibid.

its hearers to "do justice, and to love kindness, and to walk humbly with your God" was originally and long ago the answer given by the pagan prophet Balaam to King Balak's tortured query, "With what shall I come before Yahweh?" (Micah 6:6–8). Wesley's is a fascinating reading, for it implies that this well-known and well-loved text is essentially a textual fragment of prevenient grace, an ancient testimony to a gracious divine presence faithfully laboring among people outside the people and practices of Israel.[21]

Indeed, following the moral philosophy of Francis Hutcheson (1694–1746), Wesley recognizes both a "public" and a "moral" sense as included under the rubric of conscience; the public is roughly equivalent to what we experience in the phenomenon of *empathy*, while the moral is essentially what we would mean by our desire for *justice*. Wesley reiterates that "both the one and the other is now a branch of that supernatural gift of God which we usually style, preventing [or prevenient] grace."[22] Indeed, even to exercise the most intimate of capacities associated with conscience—that of self-knowledge, or "discerning . . . [one's] own tempers, thoughts, words and actions"—"is not possible for [one] to do," insists Wesley, "without the assistance . . . and the continued influence of the Spirit of God."[23] The crucial point to grasp here, though, is that this "continued influence"—we might construe the phrase as *continuous inflowing*—of God's Spirit does not undo the identity, negate the agency, or squelch the energies or education (e.g., religious formation) of the human creatures; after all, "conscience . . . varies exceedingly, according to education and a thousand other circumstances."

In his sermon "On Faith," Wesley pursues similar themes. As he surveys the various kinds of faith that he purports to observe in the world, he writes that he prefers the faith of "Heathens" over that of the mild, rational English deists. He proceeds to associate his category of heathen faith with that of Muslims because "they are rather to be pitied than blamed for the narrowness of their faith."[24] Even while we grant the condescending and undoubtedly largely ignorant tone of his writing on this topic, let us also note his magnanimity:

> It cannot be doubted, but that this plea will avail for millions of modern Heathens. Inasmuch as to them little is given, of them little will be required. As to the ancient Heathens, millions of them likewise were savages. No more therefore will be expected of them, than the living up to the light they had. But many of them, especially in the civilized nations, we have great reason

21. The reading of Micah 6:6–8 as a "conversation" between the pagan ruler Balak and the pagan prophet Balaam bears yet another tantalizing possibility. Balak asks how he is to come before *Yahweh*, the God of Israel, in worship; Balaam replies that *Yahweh* requires of the human being ("O mortal"), who on this reading is of course not an Israelite, that "you . . . do justice, love kindness and walk humbly with your" *elohim*. A likely interpretation of *elohim* throughout the Hebrew Bible is "local god(s)," the god(s) with whom one (or one's people) most directly relates and has to do. At the risk of placing too much theological freight on this one passage, reading it along these lines yields an interesting kind of inclusivism!

22. "On Conscience," 189.

23. Ibid., 189–90.

24. "On Faith," *Works*, vol. 7, 196–97.

to hope . . . were quite of another spirit; being taught of God, by his inward voice, all the essentials of true religion.[25]

Wesley apparently has a penchant for large numbers, as well as for the optimism of grace! After all, *"millions of modern heathens"* will find a measure of grace in Jesus' dictum that people are answerable only for what they actually have been given—in this case in the glimmerings of prevenient grace, "the light they had." Again, even while we grant the thinly veiled superiority complex of colonialism in his allusion to heathen in "civilized nations," let us not miss the finer point: Wesley harbors hopes that these people—context suggests he is referring primarily to faithful Muslims!—"were quite of another spirit; being taught of God, by his inward voice, all the essentials of true religion." But why would those in "the civilized nations" be more likely to be so "taught of God"? Even while Wesley can signify "[God's] inward voice," is it not clear that at some level he assumes the critical role of (an Islamic or, equally, in this case, a "civilized") "education and a thousand other circumstances"? In other words, one is never "taught of God" apart from those thousand-plus circumstances. Further, it is obvious that Wesley, by adopting such an understanding of the nature of divine evaluation of human life and character, is implying that God's "general manner of working" is precisely within those wildly variable circumstances, that is, within the particulars and contours of every human life within its particular social, religious, and cultural contexts.

The Jewish tradition is the next item under Wesley's sermonic consideration of the varieties of faith. Though he had been relatively kind to so-called heathen faith, Wesley states that "it is not so easy to pass any judgment concerning the faith of our modern Jews."[26] Let us be frank: on the issue of Judaism, Wesley undeniably stood in the long and shameful heritage of Christian anti-Jewish bias. Not surprisingly, he cites negative judgments from both the apostle Paul and the book of Acts regarding the predominantly negative response of Jews to the gospel of Christ. Nonetheless he concludes his brief reflections upon Judaism, rather tantalizingly, with this caveat: "Yet it is not our part to pass sentence upon them, but to leave them to their own Master."[27] Of course "their own Master" is, for Wesley, none other than the God and Father of our Lord Jesus Christ; nevertheless, as *the Jewish people's own Master* God is addressed and obeyed—the experience of God is shaped, the perception of God framed—by an education other than Christian teaching, and surely by "a thousand other circumstances" than those of the typical Christian. God is "their own Master" as the God of the Torah, the God who liberated a slave people out of Egypt and called them to become God's own covenant people. This is *their own Master*, one who has become their own Master through a particular historical (rabbinically formed) "education and a thousand other circumstances" uniquely a part of Jewish memory and identity.

25. Ibid., 197.
26. Ibid.
27. Ibid., 198.

Obviously, "heathen" (whoever they are) and Muslims and Jews do not believe the same things regarding God as do Christians, nor or course do they believe the same as each other. They walk on differing paths. *Saving faith* is not affirming the items on a creedal list, in any case. Rather, Wesley draws on the story of Peter at the home of Cornelius (Acts 10) to define faith as

> a divine conviction of God, and the things of God, as, even in its infant state, enables every one that possesses it to 'fear God and work righteousness.' And whosoever, in every nation, believes thus far, the Apostle declares, is 'accepted of [God].' He actually is, at that very moment, in a state of acceptance. But he is at present only a *servant* of God, not properly a *son*. Meantime, let it be well observed, that 'the wrath of God' no longer 'abideth on him.'[28]

The remarkable insight of Peter, in responding to the fledgling testimony of the Gentile God-fearer Cornelius, is not lost on Wesley. In the words of a surprised Peter, "in every nation anyone who fears [God] and does what is right is acceptable to [God]" (Acts 10:35). Indeed, Wesley mildly chastises his own Methodist preachers of a half-century prior who, when they "began to preach that grand scriptural doctrine, salvation by faith, . . . were not sufficiently apprized of the difference between a servant and a child of God" such that people with no conscious assurance of divine forgiveness were condemned as "child[ren] of the devil."[29] Wesley, now older, wiser, and presumably kinder, is far more willing to take into account the "education and a thousand other circumstances" of every human being as the real context and material of God's laboring in the world for salvation.

There may be a host of reasons why a person does not consciously experience divine mercy through Christ, including of course the education of a differing religious tradition. God does not—indeed, according to the process vision of things actually *cannot*—unilaterally overcome or overwhelm those concrete variables that, in fact, help (God) to make us what we are. Nonetheless, for Wesley, God's intention for every person is *salve-ation*—a salving of life in every dimension, a healing of heart and affections toward the image of God, a being "renewed in love"[30]—through living faith in Jesus Christ. Thus salvation is a deliverance from the presence and effects of sin—and a healing toward the truly human life of love for God and neighbor. "And, indeed, unless the servants of God halt by the way, they will receive the adoption of sons," Wesley confidently proclaimed. "They will receive the *faith* of the children of God, by his *revealing* his only begotten Son in their hearts."[31]

Within the confines of the typical set of rubrics, Wesley's thinking about people of other religious traditions is, at best, inclusivist. Yet his respect for the

---

28. Ibid., 199.
29. Ibid.
30. Wesley, *A Plain Account of Christian Perfection*, 30.
31. Wesley, "On Faith," 199.

"education and a thousand other circumstances" of every human life gives us a little room to think more seriously about the real and irreplaceable role that distinct, particular religious traditions contribute to the labors of God in the world. Further, his willingness to believe that (at least some) Muslims are "taught of God . . . all the essentials of true religion" and that, finally, Jews should be "[left] to their own Master" moves us, if only slightly, toward a pluralist rendering of God's salving work. Finally, if we push even harder on his recognition of the importance of "education and a thousand other circumstances" in the formation of human conscience *alongside* and *in concert with* the presence of the divine Spirit, then— particularly with Whitehead's help—we arrive at the conclusion that God and world together have constructed many very different paths on which humans may walk with, and toward, the Soul of the world.

III

Rabbi Yehoshua rose to his feet and said: "It is not in the heavens."

Bava Metzia 59*b*

What was it, again, that Wesley had preached regarding "the faith of our modern Jews"? Interestingly, he suggested that "it is not our part to pass sentence upon them, but to leave them to their own Master." *Their own Master*, indeed! In the Talmudic passage that provides the epigraph above, God does not behave much like a "Master"! Further, it would be difficult to find a more fitting passage with which to begin our reflections upon the Jewish covenantal consciousness, as it provides a complement to our thinking about the wild diversity of religious traditions in our world.[32]

In this famous rabbinic story, a certain Rabbi Eliezer is attempting to persuade a group of his colleagues in a debate on certain purity laws. As the story proceeds,

---

32. There are several reasons for taking this third path of Jewish reflection in this essay. First, I believe that Christian theologians who wrestle with the challenge of religious pluralism are best served by beginning with the traditions of Judaism, since it is very likely that any sustained reflection upon the real differences, as well as undeniable relationship, between the Jewish and Christian traditions may in fact shed some light on how Christians might reflect upon their relationship to other religious traditions as well. Second, Jewish theological reflection has historically begun its labor *textually*, attempting to reflect upon the faith community's holy writ, often in remarkably creative ways, in order to provide that community with persuasive rationales for thinking and behaving in new ways. I believe that Christian theologians, in order to be persuasive to the great bulk of Christians believers, must also allow their thinking to be grounded in, and responsive to, the tradition's canonical texts. If some manner of religious pluralism is to be persuasively argued, it must be discovered and nurtured from *within* the tradition. Jewish sources can help Christian thinkers to learn how to engage their community's authoritative texts seriously and creatively at the same time. Third, the particularly Jewish sensibilities regarding the theme of *covenant* do offer some especially inviting possibilities for thinking about religious pluralism—and, of course, also connect well with the process-relational and Wesleyan themes explored in the first two sections of this essay.

Eliezer tries to convince his fellow rabbis that he is right, and they are wrong, by performing all kinds of miracles and wonders. When his opponents are unmoved, Eliezer finally appeals to heaven. "Suddenly a heavenly voice comes forth and says to the sages, 'Why are you disputing with Rabbi Eliezer? The Halakhah [legal ruling] is in accordance with him in all circumstances.'"[33] Such a phenomenon might be expected to have been just the trump Eliezer needed to win the argument, but the narrative turns out otherwise; instead of conceding the argument to Eliezer, Rabbi Yehoshua stands to his feet and quotes from Deuteronomy 30:12, "It is not in the heavens." What is not in the heavens? *The Torah!* The word or commandment of God—the *lure* of God?—is not out of reach, not beyond human comprehension or application. "No, the word is very near to you; it is in your mouth and in your heart for you to observe" (Deut. 30:14). The word, *God's* word, dwells in the human realm; it is fitted to, and relevant to, the capabilities of the people of Israel.

Yehoshua's reply, in other words, appeals to Moses' own description of the Torah as being the divine word entrusted to the people of Israel to read, to interpret, to apply, to carry out. No further appeals to heaven can be made, precisely because *it is not in the heavens!* Equally interesting is the follow-up story, in which Rabbi Natan encounters the prophet Elijah, long a resident of the heavenly realm, and asks him, "What did the Holy One, blessed be He, do at that time?" The heavenly charioteer's reply is classic, for it suggests a good-natured sense of humor and respect for Yehoshua's bold argument: God, reports Elijah, "laughed, saying: 'My sons have defeated me, My sons have defeated me.'" Contemporary Israeli philosopher David Hartman writes that this Talmudic passage "signifies God's self-limiting love for the sake of making His human covenantal partners responsible for intellectually developing the Torah," such that "students of the Torah are called upon to exercise human initiative and creativity."[34]

This is a surprising sort of Master, one who entrusts to the teachers of Israel this way of walking called the Torah and is certainly not unhappy to be defeated in Talmudic disputation! Of course, one of the purposes of the text is to downplay (if not deny) the validity of miraculous events as somehow signifying God's presence, activity, or sanction. The rabbinic impulse, instead, is to turn to a text and to undertake the hard labor of arguing over that text in order to discern the divine call. How much easier would it be simply to seek, or at least to hope for, a secure sign from God! We can speculate at length as to the power dynamics that would inspire rabbis to tell this story, but we should not overlook its implicit realism. Miracles and signs—divine evidences that would imply a purely divine inbreaking, a unilateral act—are not available. Ambiguity is available, and in great abundance.

33. The Talmudic text, along with a masterful bit of theological commentary, can be found in Hartman, *A Living Covenant: The Innovative Spirit in Traditional Judaism*, 32–34.

34. Ibid., 33, 34. We should add, to be sure, that where Hartman, like Wesley, writes of God's "self-limiting love," in the process vision of things God absolutely, metaphysically, can do no other than to work in such a noncoercive way.

It is not in the heavens! It is noteworthy that in his letter to the Romans the apostle Paul quotes the same Deuteronomic text that Yehoshua does in this Talmudic tale. For Paul, the divine word that "is not in the heavens" is "the word of faith that we proclaim," and it is not in the heavens because it is "on your lips and in your heart . . . because if you confess with your lips that Jesus is Lord and believe in your heart that God raised him from the dead, you will be saved" (Rom. 10:8, 9). Where for Yehoshua and the rabbis the divine word is the Torah entrusted to Israel, for Paul and the apostles the divine word is the gospel of Christ. As New Testament scholar Richard Hays observes, "Both [the rabbis and Paul] . . . presuppose the legitimacy of innovative readings that disclose truth previously latent in Scripture."[35] Yet Hays appears to overlook a more fundamental point: it is precisely *because* "it is not in the heavens" that both the rabbis and Paul can *rightly* presuppose the legitimacy of their innovative readings! God does not "step in and settle the argument" between the rabbis and Paul, or between the Jewish and Christian paths that would flow from their writings, any more than God settles the dispute between Eliezer and his opponents. Instead, the covenantal nature of the divine word, the divine calling and wooing, allows for a great variety of responses. Because God's presence/activity/word "is not in the heavens" but rather enmeshed in the particulars of creation within the boundaries of our habitation, it is and shall always be ambiguous, multivalent, and utterly diverse in its manifestations. God's *covenantal* activity in the world opens up the possibilities for a vast number of "covenants"!

Indeed, in his same letter to the Romans, Paul makes a tantalizing statement about his "kindred," the people of Israel, writing that "to them belong the adoption, the glory, the covenants" (9:3, 4). Though he writes in the light of his faith in Jesus as the Messiah, he does not relegate the biblical covenants with Israel to the past. To them belong, even now, the covenants. These covenants are framed by Paul as a present reality—and they are (of course) plural. Surely it is significant that Paul apparently did not consider these covenants to have been rendered obsolete by the "new covenant in [Jesus'] blood" (1 Cor. 11:25)—the covenant, we might suggest, that "belongs" to Christians. Of course Paul had not thought through the idea of a plurality of covenants, Jewish *and* Christian, to the point of arriving at some kind of religious pluralism. That is the task for Christian theologians, building upon Paul as well as other sources.

The point here, essentially, is that Scripture's testimony to a variety of covenants between God and various groupings of people (or creation as a whole) bespeaks a covenantal deity, a God whose essential being and activity are covenantal, relational, dialogical. If this is the case, then the process view of things explored in the first section of this essay receives significant biblical and theological support. For in that view, God always is working with the world (including all of its peoples and cultures) where it is, and for what it is in this moment, in order to lead it to

---

35. Hays, *Echoes of Scripture in the Letters of Paul,* 3–4.

where it can be. Adding Wesley to the mix, we are reminded that for every human being, in any and all times and places, God's working is always inseparably entangled with "education and a thousand other circumstances."

All of this makes it all the more important that the first covenant mentioned in the Jewish and Christian Bibles is one made "with every living creature . . . a covenant . . . for all future generations" (Gen. 9:10, 12). God in this covenant truly *co-venes*, convenes, comes together with the world as a whole and all of its creatures, for God's covenantal promise is that "never again shall there be a flood to destroy the earth" (9:11). The significance of this promise for our purposes is that it underscores the notion that God is on the side of sustaining the otherness, the utter unpredictability (cf. Gen. 6:6), the real *power* of creatures to make a difference in the world and (therefore also) to God. In light of the overcoming of the watery chaos of the flood that thereby ushers in a new creation, it is clear that this covenant is a reaffirmation of the divine wooing of Genesis 1 to "let there be" real and vital creatures who emerge from land and sea and who flit and soar in the air. It is fascinating to mull this over: it is *a single covenant* that God is making, and yet it is a covenant God makes *with every living thing.* There is something irreducibly and unavoidably *plural* about this universal covenant, especially as we move to consider those living things that are human, contoured and formed as they are by "education and a thousand other circumstances." God's creative relationship with all of creation is fundamentally covenantal—and thus inevitably plural.

Once more, this means that the God of the Jewish and Christian Scriptures works with the world as it is to lead it to what it might become. At one place and time in the world, that working produces, in company with the world, a figure like Gautama; in another place and time, a Confucius emerges; in another, someone like Nanak. And we trace their teachings and influence as their disciples and heirs branch out into a host of subtraditions in differing times and places, all of which continue to evolve under the constraints of history and God's working. "Education and a thousand other circumstances" become magnified and multiplied, creating ever new streams of response to grace that become embodied in a dizzyingly grand diversity of doctrines, practices, and institutions. These are very different paths with quite distinct goals and values. But if these words of Deuteronomy that are cited by both Yehoshua and Paul, "It is not in the heavens," can find application beyond both the Torah and the Gospel (a bit of real pluralism already, to be sure) and can be embraced as a general principle describing the nature of divine presence and activity, then all of these dramatically diverging paths are nonetheless the real fruits of a radically covenantal God. If God is like this, then God's working in the world unavoidably must spawn a variety of ways of being, of praying, of living faithfully in the divine presence.

Chapter 10

Toward an Integrative Religious Pluralism

Embodying Whitehead, Cobb, and the *Yijing*

Chung-ying Cheng

A religion has three components: it has a history and hence is founded in some past events of particular concretion; it has a goal and is directed toward its future realization, whether it delivers the individual or a nation from a human condition or finite fatality or promises a state of grand benediction or eternal bliss for a community of people; it is also presently active in terms of theoretical justification, doctrinal conversion, and institutional organization. All three aspects combine to reflect how the human person and human society are constituted and serve a human purpose of transforming humanity (in life) or transcending humanity (in death). Based on this working definition of what religion is, one can immediately identify in any religion a core of subjectivity, which is the self-identity of what it says it is destined to achieve. One can further identify how a religion perceives its origination and the ways it offers to achieve the goal that it promises.

It is clear that, despite the fact that a world religion has a historical beginning and development, its futurity is not bounded by its historicity. It instead embodies a universal claim, which is to be applied to all people to vindicate its message of final deliverance and spiritual conversion. It is intent, in this sense, on transcending time and space in establishing a power of being at any present. It was inevitable, therefore, that Christianity, Buddhism, and Islam would all establish institutions to spread their doctrines.

Although each world religion makes its universalistic claim, it finds its doctrine being contradicted or rejected by other religions. In this regard, conflicts of religions must take place, insofar as each lays an exclusive claim on truth. This situation of religious conflict is, in one respect, like the conflict between philosophies. In another respect it is different, because it is linked to a populace and thereby can claim a power over society and share an interest in politics. Religious conflict can, therefore, lead to wars, because it can involve claims to power and possession of resources and people.[1] In speaking of religions, accordingly, we must recognize not only their rootedness in history but also their vital interests in the present. This recognition makes religious understanding and religious harmony especially important. If all major religions would find that they could peacefully co-exist, have mutual respect for each other, and honor the right of the others to preach their own vision of truth, there would be no worry about violent clashes between them. They might even learn to assist each other toward better development. They might also cooperate with each other to play a big role in serving humanity when there are calamities.

For such circumstances to arise, each religion would need to see the other religions as equally valid, so that each could consider the others as equal members of a free association or a great council of religious faiths. This development would not mean that the world religions would not compete with each other. They could still compete as they actually do in terms of their persuasive powers.

My own hope is for a comprehensive harmony of world religions founded on the principles of integrative religious pluralism, which would recognize the following propositions:

1. Each religion has its own history and is rooted in a time or location of limited scope.
2. Each has its own view of the origins of the world and the origins and conditions of humanity, particularly in reference to the meaning and value of life and death, which could be formulated in universalistic terms.
3. Each has its own universalistic teaching of salvation and self-discipline and self-transformation of people and the world.
4. Each has its own vision of transcendence, whether in the form of a personal God or Buddha or in the spirit of an impersonal Nirvana or Dao.
5. Each has its own community of preachers, teachers, and believers.
6. Each agrees to recognize and respect the same rights of others to persuade and to preach.

---

1. Without this side, religious conflict could be reduced to philosophical conflict. One notices that seldom if ever are wars caused by mere philosophical differences.

7. Each agrees to resolve its differences of beliefs and its conflicts of interest with other religions through reasonable and peaceful means.
8. Each agrees to refrain from attacking, abusing, defaming, or distorting the others orally or in writing, even though philosophical argument and ethical critique are allowed.
9. Each agrees to try to understand the others to acquire additional wisdom or at least to eliminate bias.
10. Each agrees to cultivate interreligious harmony and the common good.

Given such a scenario—which we may, with Confucius, call "Harmony Without Sameness" or, as I would put it, "Let Being Different Lead to Harmonization"—my question is whether the teachings of the religions may be justified in terms of a comprehensive theory of religious truth that is directed to understanding humanity, the human condition, human deliverance, and reality in general. In other words, once we have religious pluralism, we need to ask philosophical questions about the truth-value of the various religions. This is how the philosophy of religions becomes most relevant for today, because we do have a de facto scene of religious diversity. This I also take to be the task Whitehead set himself to achieve in facing the diversity of two world religions, Christianity and Buddhism: how to relate them or how to transcend them in light of an emerging understanding on what the world is and what human beings are. Whitehead provided his own framework of accommodating all religions against a background understanding and a new interpretation of being and human being. I interpret his purpose in terms of three levels of understanding pluralism:

1. To see the theoretical and practical differences of existing religions such as Christianity and Buddhism
2. To see the theoretical and practical complementarity of different existing religions in light of an underlying philosophy of being and becoming
3. To see all religions as steps toward a comprehensive philosophy of being, becoming, humanity, and the world

Given these three levels of understanding, we may say that there are three forms of religious pluralism: *differential pluralism,* which is set on recognizing the differences between religions; *complementary pluralism,* which is set on seeing all religions as complementary forms of religious practice and belief; and *integrative pluralism,* which is intent on showing that all religions are to be regarded as integral parts of a holistic developmental process of humanity and its understanding of the world. This integrative form of pluralism is important because it provides a philosophical basis for different religions in terms of their histories while also providing an open and creative vision for relating their differences to a creative whole. The various religions can then see their differences and be encouraged to develop further and learn from each other to achieve their ultimately proper places in light of an overarching vision of human understanding and human practice. In this light, I wholeheartedly appreciate John Cobb's and David Griffin's work in developing *complementary pluralism,* but I also wish to stress how this complementary pluralism must, in light of the Whiteheadian philosophy of creativity, go one step further toward *integrative pluralism,* to avoid relativism while preserving uniqueness, to embrace the whole while achieving the part, to realize the global while enjoying the local.

In the remainder of this essay, I discuss four interrelated topics for understanding the importance of developing an integrative pluralistic view of religious truth and beliefs: (1) how the Whiteheadian philosophy of creativity could be integrated with that of the *Yijing* to provide the basis for a global religion; (2) how relativism could be both overcome and allowed in a global religion; (3) how the integrative harmonization of Confucianism and Daoism provides a historical model for the possible integrative harmonization of Christianity and Buddhism; and (4) why Confucianism and Daoism are important for achieving a future transformation of the world religions into a state of integrative harmonization.

1. INTEGRATION OF CREATIVITY: WHITEHEAD AND THE *YIJING*

How do we understand Whitehead's notion of "creativity"? The primary understanding is that creativity is the ultimate that makes any and all things possible or in virtue of which actuality realizes itself in a world of actual things. If creativity is an ultimate category for describing the world, it has to describe the continuous formation and transformation of things in the world, which no doubt includes production of new things, such as new plants and new human babies. Hence creativity must pertain to the ceaseless productivity of things in all times and places. As to how the production of new things takes place, is it a matter of coalescing many into one? Or of differentiating one into many? Observations show that both are common ways for producing new things, which we may refer to as *fusion* and *fission,* respectively. Oftentimes the production of a new thing involves both fission and fusion. For example, the formation of an embryo is a fusion of egg and sperm, but it immediately involves a fission of cells to grow into what it is. In this sense, creativity can have many modes of being and becoming. It is interesting to note that for Whitehead creativity is the principle of novelty, which consists in the formation of a unifying entity from a diversity of many entities. He says:

> Creativity is the universal of universals characterizing ultimate matter of fact. It is the ultimate principle by which the many, which are the universe disjunctively, become the actual occasion, which is the universe conjunctively. It lies in the nature of things that the many enter into complex unity. (PR 21)

> Creativity is the principle of novelty. An actual occasion is a novel entity diverse from any entity in the many which unifies. Thus creativity introduces

novelty into the content of the many, which are the universe disjunctively. The creative advance is the application of this ultimate principle of creativity to each novel situation which it originates. (PR 21)

However, there is no reason why a novel thing may not be an entity resulting from differentiation of an existing entity in the first place. In fact, to mark out this fission as a distinct mode of creativity is extremely important, because we have to see how creativity, as the ultimate of all things and the universal of the universals, is related to the originating agency of all finite things, which is God. We do not have to identify "God" by any historical account of any world religion. We can instead identify "God" entirely by God's creativity and creativeness, which consists in the creation of things by modes of fission or fusion. We could equally well use the word *dao* or *tian* or even, better still, *qianyuan,* the powerful originator in the *Yijing* (the Book of Change). In this sense, God is the embodiment of creativity and the initial and actual fulfillment of creativity as a principle. Whitehead has given the following description of God's relation to creativity:

> The true metaphysical position is that God is the aboriginal instance of this creativity, and is therefore the aboriginal condition which qualifies its action. It is the function of actuality to characterize the creativity, and God is the eternal primordial character. But, of course, there is no meaning to creativity apart from its creatures, and no meaning to the temporal creatures apart from creativity and God. (PR 225)

With God so conceived, it is clear that God is a oneness ever arising, as an infinite power of determination, motivation, inspiration, and efficient causation, from a background that is both itself and not-itself. In its arising as a *sui generis* power of being and becoming, this divine mode of creativity may be conceived as a fission or separation from itself, which may also be described as being for itself in being not for itself. In so conceiving it, we may think of God as both being and nonbeing because God transforms being into nonbeing and transforms nonbeing into being.

In this light, we can see how the Whiteheadian view of creativity and God approaches the view of the onto-cosmology of the Great Appendix (Xici) of the *Yijing* and the *Taiji Tushuo* (Discourse on the Diagram of the Taiji) of the great neo-Confucian philosopher Zhou Dunyi (1017–73). Without going into great detail, I will cite two fundamental insights from the *Yizhuan* (of which Xici is a part), which would lend a base for claiming the complementary plurality of things in the world and their underlying universal oneness.

In section 5 of the Xici, we read: "One *yin* and one *yang* is called the Dao." This statement is based on a comprehensive observation (*guan*), which takes account of both the outer universe and the inner human condition. This comprehensive observation may be regarded as the most comprehensive induction of human experiences, as well as a rational intuition on what any process of change would have exhibited.[2] The key notion here is the Dao; the key assumption is that the world is a process of change (*yi*). The change in the world is observed to move from one state to another, with the two states being different yet connected in terms of time. What becomes visible and explicit is the *yang*, whereas what remains invisible and implicit is the *yin*. Insofar as change is concerned, one must see the transformation of the explicit into the implicit, and vice versa. There are many degrees of such change in terms of the degrees of explicitness and implicitness, which can be related to degrees of brightness and darkness, firmness and softness, motion and rest. To see changes in these dimensions and their relatedness requires common experience and perception. The experience of observation (*guan*) is not limited to sensory perception, but can involve intuitive and reflective apperception.

With this experiential basis, one can see how the Dao as the whole and universal process of change must be an alternation of *yin* and *yang*. The world includes a great diversity of things, many of which are found to be related side by side in a *yin-yang* relationship. The relationship of the cosmic heaven and earth is an example. This suggests that the *yin-yang* conception can be used as a metaphor to understand all kinds of relationships relative to different contexts or conditions sharing the basic pattern of a dynamic contrast. It can be seen, therefore, that the *yin-yang* relationship forms a dynamic field of forces, which can be seen as related in simultaneous opposition and support, interdependence, mutual stimulation, and reciprocal enrichment. It is in light of these experiences that we can see *yin-yang* relationships not only as phenomenologically open but also ontologically allusive: they form open clusters of percepts and concepts that can apply to things and events on different levels in different contexts. As ontological concepts, they define not only dynamical wholeness but also complementarity in a whole process.

The *yin-yang* relationship constitutes a whole field or a whole reality that can be seen as complying with our primary experiences of change. In other words, the *yin-yang* relationship defines a wholeness and a unity or oneness in which the *yin-yang* dynamics can be said to be meaningfully observed. The *yin* and *yang* also constitute those basic elements that, when linked in an appropriate way, would lead to the emergence or creation of novelty or new entities. This shows the *yin-yang* relationship to be a creative process and gives meaning to the assertion that *yin-yang* creativity consists in the production and transformation of all things in the world. It also gives meaning to the notion of complementarity: *yin* and *yang* are complementary in so far that they find each conducive to the change of the other and together are conducive to the production of novelty due to their interaction and merging. This sense of creative complementarity is different from the

2. See Cheng, "Philosophical Significances of *Guan* (Contemplative Observation): On *Guan* as Onto-Hermeneutical Unity of Methodology and Ontology."

whole-producing or holistic complementarity, which involves the coming into existence of diversity and novelty. Creative complementarity, by contrast, is found in many structurally organized phenomena of physical nature, such as the famous wave-particular dynamics of light.

Regarding holistic complementarities, the *Yizhuan* says: "The *yi* (change) has the *Taiji* (the Great Ultimate), and *Taiji* produces the two norms (*yin* and *yang*), two norms produce the four forms (*old yang/young yang/young yin/old yin*), the four forms give rise to eight trigrams" (Shang 11). The so-called eight trigrams *(bagua)* are also forms standing for large clusters of natural phenomena just as the four forms stand for still larger natural phenomena. The two norms of *yin-yang* would underlie these two levels of phenomena as the basic structure of dynamic change, which would lead or create these differentiation of forms.[3]

The processes of differentiation and integration are both observable, but they can be projected as metaphysical principles of the formation and transformation of reality. Thus the difference between *yin* and *yang* works both ways: It leads to the positing of the unity of Taiji, to which both *yin* and *yang* belong, and it also leads to the positing of the diversity to result from the interactive dynamics of *yin* and *yang*. Hence we find that the *yin-yang* principle leads to an ontology of the power of being in oneness, which is Taiji, and a cosmology of many things generated from *yin-yang* processes on different levels and throughout different periods of time. Since both the ontology of being and the cosmology of things are pivoted in the creative integrating/differentiating process under the agency of the *yin-yang*, we have an onto-cosmology of *Taijie-yin/yang*-diversity of forms. The whole world is seen as a procession and process of creativity, working in both the direction of integration into oneness and differentiation into diversity. The positing of the Taiji (the Great Ultimate) can be related to an observation in the *Duan Commentary*, which posits the great creative force, called the Creative *(qian)*, and the great receptive force, called the Receptive *(kun)*, which work together to produce the world. Taiji as the great unity and source of the *qian* and *kun* serves as both the efficient and material cause of all things, which in the process of its production of things also endows things with different forms and subjective aims (teloi). Hence the Qing Critical Confucian Dai Dongyuan (1724–77) says: "To be creatively creative is the source of transformation; to be creatively creative and yet at the same time provide patterning and ordering is the flow of the transformation."[4]

With both integration and differentiation we have a creativity that is creative in both ways. This is referred to in the *Yizhuan* as the process of creative change, or change by creative creativity (*shengsheng*). It is said that "[t]he creativity of creativity is to be identified as the *yi*" (Shang 5). From this it can be seen that the

---

3. All the quotations from the *Yizhuan* are from the standard *Yijing* text under Zhu Xi's commentary.

4. See Dai Dongyuan, *Yuan Shan* [Inquiries into Goodness] and "Mengzi Ziyi Suzheng" [Commentaries on Words in Mencius].

principle of creative unity or wholeness leads to the principle of oneness in Whitehead, whereas the principle of creative diversity leads to the principle of manyness. Both "one" and "many" are principles of creativity, which are exhibited, respectively, in the process of the integration of the many into one and the differentiation of the one into the many. God is the ultimate one, whereas there are no ultimate many, because creativity is an open process that has its sources in the ultimate one, which is Taiji and God.

Here I identify Taiji with God. There is no reason why Taiji, when endowed with personal traits other than pure creativity, may not be called God. This renaming in fact involves a process of onto-hermeneutical interpretation: one interprets something abstract and philosophical from a historical, social, or religious point of view, which is often rooted in experiences of a particular concretion. But it is equally important to hold that one must become aware of the possible reference in light of an understanding of reality. In this sense, Whitehead and the *Yijing* together provide a framework of reference, reidentification, and onto-hermeneutical reinterpretation in light of our new experiences and new insights learned from other traditions.

There are other important messages conveyed in the onto-cosmology of creative change of the *Yijing* that would give a clear sense of complementarity. Complementarity implies wholeness to which complementary parts belong as parts related in an organic way. It also implies creativity that gives rise to novelty and new development in an open future. Whitehead's view of Christianity and Buddhism as complementary would imply both, even though he did not clarify the contents of either in detail. But in the title of his 1926 book, *Religion in the Making*, we could see implied the idea of a new religion arising from the interaction of old religions, inspired by a new view on ontology and cosmology. His 1929 book, *Process and Reality*, was clearly intended to provide this new ontology and cosmology.

In light of the above, it is clear that the *Yijing* philosophy of creative change would lead the complementary plurality of truths or things into an *integrative* plurality of truths and things.

For the onto-cosmology of the *Yijing*, the sense of time and temporal process is important, because creativity is creativity in time and thus is related to the sense of becoming and transformation. The *Yijing's* onto-cosmology presents a creative unity of ontology and cosmology in time and change, in which one and the many, *yin* and *yang,* and being and nonbeing become dynamically one. Understanding this process requires an insight into the creativity of time and the unity in time. At any given time, one needs to see all differences as resolved in a harmony of complementary forces without necessarily losing their individualities. This quality of harmonization in time is also a feature of Whitehead's thought, as we can see in the following quotation:

> The doctrine of the philosophy of organism is that, however far the sphere
> of efficient causation be pushed in the determination of components of a
> concrescence—its data, its emotions, its appreciations, its purposes, its

phases of subjective aim—beyond the determination of these components there always remains the final reaction of the self-creative unity of the universe. (PR 47)

The "self-creative unity of the universe" is regulative of the creative advance of the world in which differences will be harmonized in the sense of a creative unity of the world, if we keep in mind the creativity of time.

Buddhism has a tendency to reduce time to timelessness, so that harmony could be realized in an enlightened understanding of mind. But for the onto-cosmology of the *Yijing*, what is realized in a timeless perception of the self-creative unity in the source has to be realized in a temporal process of ceaseless harmonization of the world. This point is important because the pluralistic differences of the religions must be resolved in the creative evolution of the religions themselves in a process toward harmonious unity and integration. The self-imposed universalism in a religion is merely abstract and needs to be given meaning in a concrete process of creative adaptation and dependent coorigination and codefinition.

Although I do not have the space to argue this point here, I believe that the basic propositions of Whiteheadian metaphysics are reinterpretable in the onto-cosmology of the creative change of the *Yijing* and could receive a clearer meaning with regard to the concepts of Cosmic Epoch, Concrescence, Novelty, Creative Advance, Actual Occasions, Prehension, Complementarity, Dipolarity, Creativity and God, God and World, Primordial and Consequential Natures of God, One and Many, Being and Nothing. On the other hand, it is equally possible to show that the *Yijing*'s concepts, such as the *dao* and *yin-yang*, can also be given a reinterpretation in terms of Whitehead's organismic philosophy of being and becoming. In light of this implicit reciprocal reinterpretation of each other, a comprehensive framework for understanding the creativity of reality and human life could be presented as an East-West philosophy of religion.

2. OVERCOMING RELATIVISM IN INTEGRATIVE PLURALISM

I will now address John Cobb's efforts to overcome relativism in his complementary pluralism of religions. Based on what has been described in the lucid essays on Cobb in this volume by David Griffin, it is obvious that Cobb has shown great insight in seeing the equal relevance and importance of both God (from Christianity) and emptiness (from Buddhism) in describing Ultimate Reality and in thereby affirming the universally claimed truth of both religions as equally valid. His point is that the Ultimate Reality that a world religion has made efforts to embody can enjoy many characteristics, which can be realized or revealed individually or severally to different world religions, perhaps due to their differing historical origins.

Because different religions could yield different insights into Ultimate Reality, dialogue among religions can increase the width and depth of the self-understanding of a religion. Dialogue may also enable religions to enrich each other in the way Cobb calls "complementarity." Cobb has thereby moved from a Christianity-centered point of view to one that puts any two religions on an equal basis to see how they may enrich one another.

Although it is not immediately clear how different religious claims of truth can be reconciled, Cobb has suggested that one way to do so is to find reasons to see two different and apparently contradictory assertions of religious truth as complementary. It seems to me that there are two steps involved in this process of transformation. The first step is to see contradictories as contraries by saying that they do not completely describe the ultimate reality. The second step is to see that contraries are in fact subcontraries, being descriptions of different properties of Ultimate Reality. In this process of transformation, one has to develop a concept of Ultimate Reality with regard to which one can transform contradictories into contraries and then transform contraries into subcontraries. What Ultimate Reality enables Cobb to make these transformations is his understanding of Ultimate Reality, which is based on the notions of Creativity and God suggested in Whitehead's philosophy of organism.

I agree with Cobb's idea of the two ultimates (Creativity and God) or even the three ultimates (Creativity, God, and the World), insofar they are integrated. If they were not holistically integrated, we would not be able to see how the Buddhist truth of Emptiness and the Christian truth of God could be related as parts of a whole. But then the question of integrating the three ultimates is an urgent task, which needs to be confronted. This is an important task of philosophy of religion, which is implicit in Whitehead's philosophy but which has been brought to the surface by Cobb.

Given Whitehead's framework reinforced by the onto-cosmology of the *Yijing*, one can have a sense of complementarity deeper than simply recognizing particularity in a universal whole. One can also see how complementarity could be the condition for further creativity, producing novelty and renewal of the cosmos. For we have to see the rich suggestiveness of the paradigm of the *yin-yang* interaction and inducement in order to see how different religions could learn from each other, renovate each other, and then bring out their own fruits of innovation. It is in this sense that a religion could receive a new life and have a new content based on integration of its old content and new experience of the world. The interaction between emptiness and being, just like the interaction between God and the World, is the fountainhead for the transformation of our beliefs and concepts of World, God and ourselves. In reference to the statement by Whitehead from PR 225 quoted earlier, Griffin notes (49, above) that Cobb has said that "without a cosmic reality there can be no acosmic one and . . . without God there can be neither. Similarly, without both the cosmic and acosmic features of reality there can be no God."[5] The interdependence of the three features demonstrates

---

5. Cobb, *Transforming Christianity and the World*, 121.

an integrative creativity, which is only to be realized in the ongoing creative advance of the world in which everything has a creative role to play.

In the process of recognizing the need for integrating religious differences into a creative totality or whole, what is independently meaningful as a term or concept must inevitably be modified in the context of the whole. One must recognize, therefore, that to hold that Buddhist and Christian truths could be reconciled in a holistic theory of creativity is to hold that each must accept such a transformation of meaning. The method of recognizing independent contributions leads to the method of integrating differences and affirming meaning in a context of the whole. This is the method of moving semantic clarification of specific features to onto-hermeneutical reinterpretation. What is referred to here as "onto-hermeneutical" reinterpretation involves finding a framework of the Ultimate Reality in which every worthwhile feature would be accommodated in a self-consistent way.

One difficulty of relating one religion to another, even in a complementary or an integrative pluralism, is that one usually does not wish to give up one's own religion's standard of truth. There is also the problem of understanding what religious truth could mean in a pluralistic framework. The fundamental problem is that one wishes to accept a pluralistic position without giving up an absolutist standpoint! The reason is that pluralism often leads to relativism, and relativism, with its loss of universal standards, leads to insulated complacency. The result is the failure to proclaim universal values—ones that all human beings should cherish. The problem, therefore, is how to maintain an open system of religious pluralism without diminishing the universalistic values of one's own religion.

As a theoretical and philosophical issue, pluralism need not lead to relativism in the sense that universal standards and universal values need to be given up. It is quite possible that all members of a free association can be subject to the same standard of objective merit and organization while differing in their practices of implementation, evaluation, and development. The problem of recognizing a common core of truths and values need not conflict with different styles of expression or different strategies of achieving secondary goals. As the Confucian motto indicates, there can be harmony and difference at the same time. Of course, genuine harmony may require some creative unity, which binds all different parts into one, and each part has to contribute to maintaining the central harmony as its universal principle and value. In this case, one can have both plurality and unity. This point underscores the importance of identifying the right core values and universal standards.

In order to maintain this unity in plurality, one needs to distinguish the ideal goal of understanding from the actual understanding one presently has with regard to the Ultimate Reality. If this distinction is made, one may see how differences in the other religion may be stimuli and lessons for one to improve oneself, so that one may get closer to the ideal goal of one's religious standard of perfection. This is not to say, of course, that one need not hold one's own self-understanding as authentic and genuine and as a basic standard of identifying truth. But to focus on this as the exclusive standard and the source of all inspiration will close one's mind to the possibility of novel truth about the Ultimate Reality. The very concept of the Ultimate Reality must be maintained in an open and creative manner, so that one can derive openness from it and thus learn from others or come to see one's prejudices in reflection. This also means that one must maintain oneself in an open manner that makes learning from others possible. With this said, the universal claims of one's truth can be modified and enriched in the course of the creative advance in time and new encounters with the other religions of the world. In this sense, there is an *intentional* universal truth and a realized yet still enrichable universal truth in accordance with temporality. The *Yijing*'s motto that one should grow with time (*yu shi juxing*) applies here as a way of reconciling universal claims with specific encounters.

In some of these encounters, one may find the truth of one's own religious teaching confirmed by that of another religion. This is the possibility emphasized by Schubert Ogden, as discussed in Griffin's second essay. But in encounters in which one cannot at least for the moment find such reciprocal confirmation of truth, the differences between two religious truths could be seen as contributions to a redefinition of one's truth and the enrichment of one's belief. This would be the thesis of Cobb, who believes, as shown by a statement quoted by Griffin (65, above), in a process of growth in an ever-developing theology.[6] It is in reference to this possibility of overcoming the present limitations of one's faith by incorporating new truths that Cobb speaks of "fundamental changes" to be effected within the Christian religion.

In China, such fundamental changes were effected within the Buddhist religion in the sixth century. These changes led in turn to other fundamental changes in Confucianism and Daoism. Indeed one may regard globalization as a process of religious change and religious reform in the present era. Cobb is also correct to recognize that when religions become more globalized, their teachings will become both global and local. On the one hand, they must face universal issues. On the other hand, they must still deal with the needs of local cultures and peoples, so that they will also continue to belong to particular communities, informing particular forms of life.

In speaking of complementary and integral pluralism, we are open to the possibility of transformation based on new insights into the Ultimate Reality. We therefore avoid relativistic complacency. But we may also be led to reject experiences and insights from other traditions, thereby becoming enclosed. An enclosed universalism would be as problematic as an complacent relativism.

To avoid both complacent relativism and enclosed universalism, a religious tradition needs to see what it has in common with other religious traditions while also recognizing those elements in other traditions that are different, which may represent genuine insights. Both tasks provide incentives for religious reform.

6. Ibid., 45.

The idea that two traditions are incommensurable often results from looking at things from a static, substance point of view. The seemingly incommensurable can become commensurable if we relate to things in a processive and interactive manner. We have to find mediation in order to see and realize complementariness between two religions. That is why the onto-cosmological philosophy provided by Whitehead and the *Yijing* is extremely important.

For relating two different religious traditions, one may have to work with two basic principles of understanding: the principle of achieving common ground by creating a maximal view of what both religions share in common; and the principle of achieving common ground by creating a minimal understanding of their radical differences. The first principle, which is one of intersection, I call the Principle of Maximal Signification. The second principle, which is one of union, I call the Principle of Minimal Comprehension. My assumption is that we should desire the least difference and the most significance in a coherent system of understanding. We need both principles for an onto-hermeneutical interpretation, so that we can move on from a common ground to a greater and more enriched vision of the Ultimate Reality. This vision will in turn increase the cohesiveness and congruence of the two different religions in a unified whole. The theoretical and philosophical model that exemplifies a combination of these two principles is precisely the *Yijing*-Whitehead-Cobb system of onto-cosmology.

3. THE RELATION BETWEEN CONFUCIANISM AND DAOISM: A HISTORICAL MODEL OF INTEGRATIVE PLURALISM

To recapitulate: There are two principles at work in integrative pluralism: the principle of integration, in terms of which an integrative philosophy of dipolar creativity (being and becoming) will function as a basis for integrating two different religions in the same ontological paradigm; and the principle of differentiation, in terms of which the differences of the two religions are realized as two complementary polarities. The philosophical inspiration of this methodological approach is derived from the *Yijing* philosophy itself, which is well illustrated in Whitehead's philosophy of the God-World dipolarity. But can we cite any factual or historical example of this theory of integrative pluralism to show how it works? Yes, because we can point to the working relationship of Confucianism and Daoism.

Without getting into details, it can be shown that Confucianism and Daoism have accepted the basic philosophy of creative change in the *Yijing*. Even though this point of common heritage may not have become clear until later times, their ways of thinking point to the same ontological grounding. This became obvious in a comparison of the underlying views of Ultimate Reality in the major classical texts of classical Confucianism (*Yizhuan, Zongyong,* and even *Lunyu*) and classical Daoism (*Daodejing* and *Zhuangzi*). These two Chinese schools of philosophy have come to share the same ontology and cosmology in the onto-cosmology of creative change of the *dao* and *tian*. This view became even more systematized in the Song Ming neo-Confucianism of *li/qi and taiji/wuji* in the writings of Zhou Dunyi, Zhang Zai, the Cheng brothers, Zhu Xi, and Wang Yangming. But to say that Confucianism and Daoism and, later, Li Qi and neo-Confucianism shared a common core of onto-cosmology and accepted the same canonical texts is not to deny that they had somewhat different interpretations of the underlying philosophy and somewhat different readings of the same texts. In particular, it is not to say that they have shared the same moral and political philosophies. They have not.

If one takes what Confucius and Laozi have taught, respectively, about how human beings should live and behave, or compare what Mencius and Zhuangzi have said about self-cultivation and government, one will be struck with the vast differences. This would hold with regard to the moral philosophies of the Cheng brothers and Zhu Xi, on the one side, and Lu Xiangshan and Wang Yangming, on the other. Despite their differences and their mutual criticisms, they do appear to have respected each other and gradually to have formed a sense of complementarity. From an objective point of view, one can see how each side has influenced the other even without knowing or acknowledging it. We can see influences and enrichments as well as remaining differences. In this context of dynamical interaction, differences become complementary and complementary differences become sources for novelty and creative advance—for adventures of new ideas, in Whitehead's sense.

With this integrative pluralism based on complementary integration, one can see how its exemplification in Confucianism and Daoism is of great benefit to people in practice. Why cannot a person be a Confucian in public life and a Daoist in retired privacy, when there is time to enjoy more mountains and rivers? It appears that there are different times, different tasks, and different challenges in a person's life, which invite different goals, each of which fulfills the creativity of the central onto-cosmology of the *tian/ren/dao/de*.

With science and technology now well developed, there are different skillful professions, which yield different stations and require different roles for a person, apart from different times and stages, to perform one's duties and demonstrate one's abilities. It is not only necessary but also desirable to have different and even incompatible forms of professional life and professional ethics for social and community life so that humanity may continue to thrive and flourish in division of labor and in cooperation or competition for excellence. But with an underlying onto-cosmology of creativity and creative change, these forms of professional life and professional ethics would learn not to contradict each other but would rather come to cherish and complement and enrich each other and even communally lead to an achievement of the common good. This central core philosophy would become an ever-refreshing source for one to go back for repose and an inspiring stimulus to move on to future. This is what a philosophical or religious globalization should be: a will to integrate, with a willingness to transform differences into complements without yielding one's rightful place and identity in the process of doing so. The ideal goal should be: *Harmonize without being the same.* The ideal norm to follow is: *Let being different lead to harmonization.* A great religion needs this Confucian insight and will have achieved it by reflecting on the essence of creativity in the ultimate reality and process of life.

4. CONFUCIANISM AND DAOISM AS RELIGIONS

One might argue, however, that Confucianism and Daoism are not religions, so their integrative and harmonious complementary differentiation may not apply to established and organized religions such as Christianity and Buddhism. It is true that Confucianism and Daoism are not quite the same religions as Christianity and Buddhism, but their moral and spiritual values and their embodiment in personal practices have sustained vast numbers of people for thousands of years, as early as Buddhism and as solidly as Christianity. There are no Confucian churches and priests, but there are Confucian temples and Confucian scholars. In the case of philosophical Daoism, the Daoist teachings do get absorbed in religious Daoism, and Daoist temples were built and Daoist priests flourished. The whole point of this description is that we could identify the religious sides of Confucianism and Daoism apart from their philosophical sides just as we also need to identify the philosophical sides of Christian and Buddhist thinking apart from their religious sides. I believe that this is precisely what Whitehead has intended to do, with his process philosophy of organism embodying his vision of an integration of Christianity and Buddhism. I do not know whether he had any idea of the integrative harmonization of Confucianism and Daoism in China, but the historical fact of their integrative harmonization does provide a hopeful example for the development of such integration among other world religions.

If Confucianism can be interpreted as leading to Christianity, as by James Legge in his translations of the Confucian classics, Christianity can also be interpreted as leading to Confucianism. Theoretically there is no reason why there could not be mutual and equal interpretation of ancient texts in different religious schools. The possibility of achieving a meeting ground and fusion of horizons via dialogues and reflective understanding is emphasized in the philosophical hermeneutic of Hans-Georg Gadamer. In my own onto-hermeneutics, which is developed in light of both Gadamer's insights and the *Yijing's* onto-cosmology, a mutual but creative recognition of each other's ontological assumptions and reflective understandings of creative change will lead to creative sharing of insights and enlargement of onto-cosmological visions in two different systems of beliefs.[7] A comprehensive and profound understanding of significant differences in one single Ultimate Reality could be developed subsequently. In the

---

7. See my "Confucian Onto-Hermeneutics: Morality and Ontology." See also my articles (in Chinese) in Chung-ying Cheng, ed., *Benti Yu Quanshi* [Ontology and Interpretation], 15–62, and *Benti Quanshi Xue* [Onto-Hermeneutics], 1–14, 25–30.

spirit of both philosophical hermeneutics and onto-hermeneutics, we can see how Confucianism and Christianity could achieve a consensus on the personalization of Heaven and God as well as the formation of a virtue ethics of self-cultivation and self-sanctification in the context and in the spirit of the *Yijing*-Whitehead onto-cosmology of creativity and creative change.

Similarly, Daoism and Buddhism could be mutually interpreted by each other. In fact, when Indian Buddhism was introduced in China in the third century, it was by way of a Daoist interpretation that it became understood and accepted in China. In later times, there were Buddhist monks who undertook a Buddhist interpretation of the Daoist texts. This mutual interpretation and interaction between the two finally led to the formation of the great school of Chan Buddhism, which has combined the Daoist freedom of creative spirit and the Buddhist wisdom of nonclinging into one onto-enlightenment philosophy of the ultimate and the ultimateless.

With such philosophical and hermeneutical alignment for both Confucianism-Christianity and Daoism-Buddhism, we can see how a well-developed integration may also take place between Christianity and Buddhism. In this integration, Christianity and Buddhism will become truly complementary and interrelated in a holistic unity of creative understanding, as have Daoism and Confucianism. The spirit of harmonization and integration, while retaining complementarity, will pass on to the relationship between Christianity and Buddhism. There is no need to worry about differences in ethical norms arising from such differences in styles of life. Insofar as they are harmonized and justified in light of the onto-cosmology of creativity and creative change, they should maintain their distinctive identities, which will be the basis for future creative transformation.

With the model of Confucian-Daoist harmony in view, we shall find a Christian God more humanized under the influence of a Confucian view of life and a Buddhist emptiness more naturalized under the influence of the Daoist natural philosophy. Under Christian influence, we shall also find Confucian individuals more rights-oriented than were Confucians under a purely virtue-oriented ethic. Under Buddhist influence, we shall see a Daoist recluse more compassionate and world-caring than Laozi. In different ways, but with the same insight and spirit of creativity, we come to a consummation of integrative pluralism among the four religions, which would pave a still wider road toward integration and harmonization of all the religions in the world.

Chapter 11

An Asian Christian Approach to Religious Pluralism

Wang Shik Jang

One of the main problems associated with religious pluralism in East Asia is the fact that the so-called Abrahamic religions (i.e., Christianity, Judaism, and Islam) and traditional East Asian religions (i.e., Confucianism, Taoism, and Buddhism) are in conflict philosophically. The idea of religious plurality has been salient in the history of East Asian philosophy, and religious pluralism has been emphasized in the recent theologies of some Abrahamic religions. Why is it that, despite these facts, the East Asian religions and the Abrahamic religions are not well harmonized with each other philosophically?

Some people would say that the reason for the failure of interreligious dialogue lies primarily in the Abrahamic religions' exclusivism. I absolutely endorse this perception. It should not be forgotten that the first impediment to interreligious dialogue in Korea, for instance, has been the tendency of Christians to hold an absolutist view of Christianity's truth.

Although I agree that this is one reason, another reason for the failure of interreligious dialogue is rooted in a philosophical position of the East Asian religions. Apart from the fact that the Abrahamic religions are basically exclusivistic to other religions in their theological positions, some scholars have interpreted the East Asian religions in a radical manner so as to make them seem intransigent in their philosophical positions.

What kind of radical interpretation has given rise to problems in interreligious dialogue between Abrahamic religions and East Asian religions? My thesis is that among the various types of religious pluralism derived from some Asian philosophies, a philosophical understanding of religious pluralism that is not conducive to dialogue with the Abrahamic religions has still been influential in the mainstream of East Asian philosophies. That is to say, a religious pluralism arising from what I call "absolutizing relativism" is partly responsible for the failure of interreligious dialogue in East Asia. By "absolutizing relativism," I mean the position that since all things are so relative, every aspect of everything derives entirely from its relations. In my opinion, this position of relativism has brought about many problems in the philosophy of religions in East Asia and has resulted in unsuccessful interreligious dialogue.

Above all, the tendency of absolutizing relativism in East Asian religions gives rise to many conflicting truth claims in the philosophy of religions. In recent interpretations of traditional East Asian religions, notions of the ultimate—that is, *Tao* in Taoism, *Tian* (the Heaven) in Confucianism, and *Sunyata* (Emptiness) in Buddhism, which are all based on the doctrine of relativism—have been construed by some philosophers in the West as well as in the East as referring to something nontranscendent or unreal. In my opinion, this interpretation is not appropriate in two perspectives. First, this is not how these notions have traditionally been understood in the history of religions in East Asia. Why and how the notions of the ultimate as nontranscendent or unreal may not be an obvious fact in the East Asian religions will be explained later. Secondly, given such notions of the ultimate, it is obvious that the East Asian religions are very different from Abrahamic religions, which usually construe God as transcendent and real. Therefore, this leads to a massive problem in communication and mutual understanding and makes interreligious dialogue unsuccessful.

Considering this, I am sure that an ideal way to formulate a genuine religious pluralism cannot arise unless the problems inherent in absolutizing relativism are solved. In what follows, employing Whitehead's philosophy, I will attempt to show how we can solve this problem. In fact, Whitehead brings a strong type of relativism into his own philosophy. At the same time, however, he offers a philosophical methodology able to go beyond the problems inherent in some relativism.

After showing how and why relativism has been problematic in the philosophies of East Asian religions, I will try to elucidate the way in which a Whiteheadian philosophy of religion can help to develop an ideal type of relativism that solves the problem of religious pluralism in East Asia.

THE RELATIONSHIP BETWEEN RELIGION
AND RELATIVISM IN EAST ASIA

Relativism is essential for the establishment of religious pluralism, because relativism is based on the equal validity of all religions. In other words, the heart of relativism is that "since there is nothing absolute, everything is relative." This easily leads to the idea that since "everything is relative, all is equally valid." This is why relativism is necessary for forming the framework of religious pluralism.

Relativism has been a dominant factor in the philosophy of East Asian religions, because a relational worldview has been the core characteristic of East Asian philosophies. A relational vision insists that a thing does not exist independently of relationships with other things. Therefore, a relational vision easily leads to relativism, in which everything is said to be relative. Both Taoism and Confucianism have always been based on yin-yang thought, which is obviously the expression of a relational vision. Also, the core of Buddhist thought has been derived from a relational worldview based on the doctrine of *prititȳa-samutpada* (dependent coorigination). If this is the case, it is quite natural for religious pluralism to arise in East Asian religions.

This, however, has not been the usual result, because every religion is not only dominated by its philosophy; it is also ruled by its system of faith. The system of faith is an important feature of religion. Since the system of faith is usually dogmatic, it is not easy for a religion to be tolerant of other religions. This can be discovered even in Buddhism, which has historically been noted as one of the most tolerant religions. Many people think that historically Buddhism has always sided with religious pluralism, but this has not always been the case. On the contrary, Buddhist religions have often taken a kind of exclusive attitude to other religions. In the *Lotus Sutra*, one of the most influential Buddhist Scriptures, this is expressed as follows:

> In the Buddha-lands of the universe
> There is only the One-vehicle Law,
> Neither a second nor a third,
> Except the tactful teachings of the Buddha.
> But by provisional expressions
> He has led all loving creatures,
> Revealing the Buddha-wisdom.
> In the appearing of buddhas in the world
> Only this One is the real fact,
> For the other two are not the true.[1]

Of course, here we do not see any kind of strong exclusivism. For it is said that the Buddha accepts all other small vehicles as a provisional way. However, not only is it eventually emphasized that there is only "One" which is "the real fact," but it

---

1. *The Threefold Lotus Sutra*, 64.

is also stressed that all others are "not the true." As this illustrates, Buddhist religions have not always been pluralistic. However, is there any other faith in the history of religion that has been more tolerant of other faiths than Buddhism? It is hard to deny that Buddhism has been one of the most "inclusive" religions, in which the plurality and multiplicity of faiths is recognized. This has been possible simply because the heart of Buddhist philosophy has always been associated with the doctrine of dependent origination and Emptiness, which leads to relativism.

It can easily be assumed, then, that the relativism in Buddhism has enabled Buddhism to make interreligious dialogue very successful in East Asia. Nevertheless, we have to be very cautious, because relativism does not always make interreligious dialogue successful in East Asian religions, including Buddhism. Indeed, my argument in this essay is that an inadequate interpretation of relativism has been an obstacle to achieve the reality of pluralism in East Asian religions. This is to say that the misuse of relativism has caused a lot of trouble to the interreligious dialogue among religions in East Asia. I call this misuse "absolutizing relativism." When absolutizing relativism was introduced, relativism began to be problematic in East Asia. This position of relativism is found in some philosophers of Zen Buddhism, but before articulating how this particular position of relativism was developed in Zen Buddhism, I would like to unpack what I mean here by the term "absolutizing relativism."

As we saw above, by relativism we usually refer to the philosophical position that "since there is nothing absolute, everything is relative." However, relativism can imply two different meanings.

First, by the term "relativism" we may mean that everything is conditioned, or limited. To say that everything is relative is simply to say that the existence of an entity is dependent upon others in the sense that it is conditioned by them. Such an interpretation of relativism is very helpful for the spirit of religious pluralism. For it can be emphasized that, since one religion's truth is limited, there is no "one and only" true religion, and, therefore, every religion has its own distinctive value. However, a second meaning of relativism is that because there is nothing absolute, nothing has its own agency. Thus, if everything is relative, it is impossible for us to affirm the existence of something independent. The denial that anything is independent, because the existence of every entity is subject to others, leads many thinkers to conclude that everything fails to have its own agency. When this is applied to the doctrine of the ultimate in East Asian religions, it is said that the ultimate does not have its own unique existence. Furthermore, the agency of creatures is not affirmed.

One example of this line of thought can be found in Francis Cook, a representative of Hua-yen Buddhism in the West. When he talks about the existence of the ultimate, he refers to this second type of relativism. "The true ultimate must be one which is exactly and literally identical with the nonultimate."[2]

---

2. Cook, "This Is It: A Buddhist View of Ultimate Reality," 139–40.

Another example of this thinking can be found in Seung Sahn, a Korean Zen master and scholar. According to him, the existence of the Buddhist ultimate is so empty that the ultimate must be killed, otherwise we would not understand the true notion of the ultimate. He articulates this as follows:

> Some say "throw away God and all things." This style of speech resembles Zen, but one more step is necessary. If you have God to throw away, you still have God. . . . True God has no name or form, no speech or words. Many people make God in their minds, so they cannot understand true God. You must kill your God; then you will understand true God.[3]

Now we are in a position to understand why their notions of the Buddhist ultimate are based on what I call "absolutizing relativism." This is not only because the existence of the Buddhist ultimate is said to be derived from its relations, but also because it is denied to have its own unique existence.

Although both Francis Cook and Seung Sahn do not allude to this relativism in relation to religious pluralism, it is obvious that their philosophical position causes some problems when it is applied to interreligious dialogue. For instance, when Cook asserts that the existence of the ultimate, which is infinite, is identical with the finite, his claim becomes problematic, because his philosophy of religion cannot be harmonized with that of the Abrahamic religions. This is why I claim that such relativism is not appropriate for setting up the ideal type of religious pluralism in East Asian religions.

Such a relativism is discoverable not only in Buddhist thinkers; it is also pervasive in the mindset of many thinkers in other Asian religions. For example, according to David Hall and Roger Ames, who have published many books concerning the philosophy of East Asian religions, the notion of transcendence is irrelevant for interpreting the philosophy of religions in East Asia. Based on this assumption, they argue that the notion of world order in East Asian religions is altogether this-worldly. According to Hall and Ames, *Tian* (Heaven), which has been traditionally regarded as an ultimate in Confucianism and Taoism, is both what our world is and how it is. The myriad things are not the creatures of *Tian* or disciplined by *Tian*, which is independent of what is ordered; rather, they are constitutive of it. *Tian* is simply the field of creatures.[4]

In my opinion, such an interpretation, based on absolutizing relativism, is not only irrelevant to the interpretation of the philosophy of religion in East Asia, but also problematic in achieving successful interreligious dialogue. For this reason, this type of relativism cannot be recommended for bringing about an ideal type of religious pluralism.

So far, I have attempted to show how absolutizing relativism has been introduced into the philosophy of religion in East Asia. At the same time, I have argued

---

3. Sahn, *Only Don't Know: The Teaching Letters of Zen Master Seung Sahn*, 119.
4. Hall and Ames, *Thinking from the Han*, 242.

that such a relativism is problematic for promoting religious pluralism. Later I will articulate an alternative type of relativism. Before doing that, however, I will clarify some other aspects in which absolutizing relativism is problematic.

THE PROBLEMS OF ABSOLUTIZING RELATIVISM IN THE INTERPRETATION OF TRADITIONAL EAST ASIAN RELIGIONS

The central characteristic of absolutizing relativism in the interpretation of traditional Asian religions is that it usually leads to the denial of transcendence. In my opinion, this is the root of all its problems. Therefore, let us look at the problems created from the denial of transcendence.

In some Buddhist cases, the denial of transcendence is expressed by claiming that there is no difference between the ultimate and the nonultimate. This is based on the principle of universal relativity. The relativism rooted in this principle, such as that of Francis Cook, insists that if everything is relative, then the principle of universal relativity must apply to the dimension of the ultimate. With this assumption, it is further asserted that there is no difference between the ultimate as the transcendent and what it transcends.

If the differentiation between the ultimate and the nonultimate is denied, then we are eventually confronted with the denial of the differentiation between good and evil. This problem arises because the denial of a transcendent dimension gives rise to the denial of the existence of good, as such, finally making the differentiation between good and evil ambiguous. Let us see why this happens.

Francis Cook says that he sees the ultimate even in his cat, Leo.[5] This is because he, like most Buddhists, is able to employ the doctrine of Emptiness when he wants to see an ultimate dimension. In other words, based on the doctrine of Emptiness, which is also the principle of universal relativity, Cook identifies the cat as the finite with the ultimate as the infinite. Of course, I agree with the fact that we can experience a case in which the finite can be identified with the ultimate. If, in accordance with Buddhist doctrine, we have an ability to discover Emptiness, which is the ultimate dimension for Buddhists, then we may see the ultimate in all sentient beings. Therefore, the finite can in one sense be identified with the ultimate. However, there is also a sense in which the finite cannot be identified with the ultimate. In other words, although it is possible to say that an immoral sentient being who committed an unnecessary crime may be identified with the ultimate in one sense, it would be much more reasonable to say that he cannot be identified with the ultimate in most senses. Therefore, we should say that the complete denial of differentiation between the transcendent and nontranscendent is not recommended ethically.

5. Cook, "This Is It," 139.

Considering this problem, some philosophers of East Asian religions concede that the existence of transcendence may be affirmed in traditional East Asian religions, but they insist that its existence should be confined to the category of immanence. This is exactly what David Hall and Roger Ames have insisted on.

According to Hall and Ames, a "strict" transcendence does not exist in the East Asian religions. All we can find in them is "immanent" transcendence, which means that transcendence in the East Asian religions exists only in relationship with what it transcends.[6] I agree that what has been prevalent in the mainstream of East Asian religious thought is exactly an "immanent" transcendence. However, it is equally true to say that transcendence in what is called the "strict" sense has also been strong. This fact can be verified in the *Book of Shijing* and the *Book of Shujing*, both of which have been very influential as Confucian scriptures in East Asia. Chu Hsi's neo-Confucianism is another example. Even in the Pure Land Buddhist tradition, which has been very powerful as a Buddhist religion in Korea and Japan, we can discover the idea of such a strict type of transcendence.

The greatest problem created by an overemphasis on immanent transcendence is that it may lead to the denial of any kind of transcendence. For there is no significant difference between the statement that the existence of transcendence can be denied and the statement that there is no "strict" sense of transcendence. This is because both statements eventually entail the same result, namely, the denial of the reality of transcendence. Denial of a "strict" transcendence implies the denial of a difference between the transcendent and what is transcended. The main reason for not making this differentiation comes from the relativist's philosophical assumption that the reality of transcendence cannot be verified. However, in my opinion, if we do not affirm the reality of transcendence, then we are faced with many problems. A case can be found in some Buddhists.

Of course, there are many reasons why some Buddhists are not sure of the reality of transcendence. However, according to Don Cupitt, who has called himself a Buddhist Christian or a Christian Buddhist, one of the most important epistemological reasons for claiming the nonrealist interpretation of religion is that it is impossible for him to predicate that which transcends human reasoning. He insists that since the reality of transcendence cannot be affirmed or denied, all we can affirm is that it is nonreal.[7]

However, although a nonrealist interpretation of the transcendent might be appealing in a sense, it is not persuasive religiously. If, due to the impossibility of predication, all we can affirm is the nonreality of transcendence, then this is simply saying that we cannot apply human categories to the transcendent. And, if so, there is no basis for assuring that there exists a transcendent reality that is able to care about what is happening in this world. Furthermore, as David Griffin has said, "if the ultimate reality does not have the property of being good, then we

---

6. Hall and Ames, *Thinking from the Han*, 13, 193.
7. For the discussion of this case in nonrealism, see Cupitt, *Taking Leave of God*.

have no reason for assuming that it would be interested in bringing all sentient beings to fulfillment."[8]

Of course, again, it goes without saying that with regard to the issue of interreligious dialogue, such a relativist position is sometimes worthwhile, in the sense that it may make some contribution to relativizing one's dogmatic position and, therefore, may break the shackles of absolutist thinking. However, it can also give rise to demeaning the positive value of one's perspective. This easily leads to undermining the religious passion of sincere believers. Therefore, as John Cobb points out, when we misuse relativism, we can encourage disengagement from all commitment, instead of eliciting strong convictions.[9]

So far, I have made an attempt to show how absolutizing relativism can cause many problems for a philosophy of religions. The problems caused by absolutizing relativism for the philosophy of religion are an obstacle to the interreligious dialogue in East Asia. As we have seen, the denial of transcendence, the denial of differentiation between the ultimate and nonultimate, and the philosophy of nonrealism, which have all been the product of absolutizing relativism, cannot be harmonized with the position of Abrahamic religions. Therefore, if we want to formulate an ideal type of religious pluralism, we first have to suggest an alternative to absolutizing relativism. Now let us turn to this issue.

A WHITEHEADIAN SOLUTION TO THE PROBLEM OF ABSOLUTIZING RELATIVISM

We live a world in which relativism is unavoidable. Some would even say that relativism has been proved not only as a cultural fact but also as a philosophical truth. I can also agree with this in some sense. Especially when applied to interreligious dialogue, relativism has been regarded as unavoidable, because it is obvious that it promotes the realization of religious pluralism. Therefore, although we need to find an alternative philosophy to the absolutizing relativism discussed above, it should not be inferred that the alternative is to reject relativism altogether. On the contrary, the first condition for setting up an adequate alternative is to include relativism.

Whitehead is one of the most provocative figures in the history of Western philosophy to have internalized a type of relativism. For him, to be an actual thing is to be a unification of many other things. In technical terms, each actual occasion can be analyzed into its prehensions of antecedent occasions, which themselves can be analyzed into prior antecedent occasions and so on. Therefore, a thing cannot be conceived without reference to other things. In a word, it is conditioned by others. Up to this point, his philosophy seems to be merely one of the ordinary types of relational worldview. However, his relational worldview,

---

8. Griffin, *Reenchantment without Supernaturalism: A Process Philosophy of Religion*, 276.
9. Cobb, *Transforming Christianity and the World*, 96–98.

when it is reinforced by his theory of process, turns out to be a stronger form of relativism.

The core of Whitehead's theory of process is his recognition that as soon as an occasion achieves its own reality, it perishes, losing its "subjective immediacy." This implies that an occasion is never given a chance to get its own being. When it is coming into existence, it is not yet a being. When it obtains its existence, its own subjectivity is already gone. This is not to say that it does not possess any kind of "being." However, according to Whitehead, all an occasion can have with regard to its own being is its function as a datum for other occasions. This is why we can say that Whitehead's philosophy offers a strong kind of relativism. It is a strong relativism, since it not only emphasizes that everything is conditioned by others, but it also recognizes that nothing has its own being.

There is another philosophical element that makes his relativism more intensified, an intensification that might appear to be similar to the problematic relativism discussed above. As we have seen, if relativism is to be called "extreme" with respect to the philosophy of religion, it must do more than emphasize the relativity of mundane things. It must also relativize the transcendent.

Above all, in Whitehead's philosophy, God is relativized in terms of God's relationship with the world. In traditional Christian theology, God, who is all-powerful and noncontingent, is said unilaterally to control the world, which is wholly contingent. Whitehead criticizes this traditional theism for introducing "an entirely static God, with eminent reality in relation to an entirely fluent world with deficient reality" (PR 346). In Whitehead's philosophy, therefore, God's creative activity is to be shared with the world. The interaction of God and the world is, in his technical expressions, described in the following manner.

In God's primordial nature, God is depicted as a lure for the actual occasions of the world. The lure of God functions to offer the possibilities that can serve as ideal aims for the occasions that are in the process of becoming. The possibilities offered by God can be called "ideal," not only because they have ideal rather than actual existence, but also because they are the best options for the occasions to choose. However, according to Whitehead, God's ideal aim can be influential only in the initial phase of the process of becoming. In other words, although the process of becoming in an occasion is instigated by God, God does not dominate the whole process of becoming. Therefore, all the occasions of the world are free from God's control. The creative power belonging only to God in traditional theism is now ascribed to the world as well. Furthermore, these worldly occasions, having exercised their self-creative power, influence God. This side of the divine nature is called God's "consequent nature." For this reason, we can recognize that Whitehead allows real contingency into God's nature. In this sense, God is contingent upon the world, just as the world is contingent upon God.

So far, we have seen how God, as a transcendent ultimate, is relativized in Whitehead's philosophy. An interesting thing to note here is that what we have seen with respect to the nature of God is totally different from how the transcendent ultimate has appeared in the history of Western philosophy. In Whitehead's relativistic philosophy, God is no longer the only one that is ultimate. This fact is described in the framework of Whitehead's metaphysics in the following manner: " '[C]reativity,' 'many,' 'one' are the ultimate notions. . . . These three notions complete the Category of the Ultimate and are presupposed in all the more special categories" (PR 21). In another place, Whitehead even claims that, in his philosophy, the ultimate is termed creativity and "God is its primordial, non-temporal accident" (PR 7).

As we can guess, the reason why the notions of "creativity," "many," and "one" are involved here, with respect to the category of the ultimate, is that these notions are employed as metaphysical tools for explicating not only how this universe is constituted by interrelationship among things, but also how God shares ultimacy with other ultimates. In this way, Whitehead produces a strong model of relativism. Some may understand why I say that his relativism looks similar to the radical relativism that we discovered above, since it too emphasizes that all things in this universe, including even God, are so relative that they are contingent and conditional. Now that we have seen how Whitehead internalizes relativism into his philosophical system, let us see how Whitehead's philosophy can provide us with an ideal model of relativism that solves the problems of absolutizing relativism. This has been suggested by two notions already discussed, namely, subjective immediacy and the primordial nature of God.

In order to solve the problems of absolutizing relativism with regard to the issue of religious pluralism, I have suggested that a philosophy of religion should provide at least three things. First, it should provide a philosophical method that emphasizes the existence of subjective agency. This is needed because some relativists' idea that everything is conditioned, as we saw, tends to lead to weakening the uniqueness of one's own perspective. Second, it should provide a philosophy of religion in terms of which we can avoid both the denial of the reality of the transcendent and the denial of the differentiation between the ultimate and the nonultimate. Third, it should explain how the different doctrines of the ultimate arising from the conflicting truth claims between Abrahamic and non-Abrahamic religions are to be harmonized. Let us see how these three conditions are to be met in Whitehead's philosophy.

First, how does Whitehead's philosophy provide the kind of relativism in which the existence of subjective agency can be emphasized?

One of the most innovative ideas derived from Whitehead's concept of process is that the standpoint of relationality and the standpoint of creative advance go together. In other words, an emphasis on the relational worldview based on the analysis of process is always complemented by an emphasis on the concept of creative advance. Therefore, in Whitehead's notion of relativism, to be a thing is to be relative by means of two features: a conditional feature and a creative feature. On the one hand, based on the conditional feature, a thing is related to other things as being internally influenced by them. Here, the relativism recognizes that everything is conditioned by others. Based on the creative feature, on the other hand, the thing is not only the unification of other things, but also the modification of them from the perspective of the thing itself. Here, the relativism emphasizes the fact that a thing also conditions other things. In Whitehead's words, this is expressed as "the many become one, and are increased by one" (PR 21).

By virtue of this creative feature, Whitehead's relativism is able to affirm that although an occasion in the process of becoming is produced by the unification of antecedent occasions, it completes the process by entailing "subjective immediacy," which functions as a condition for subsequent occasions. Of course, what we have here with regard to the notion of "subjective agency" differs from the subjectivity posited by the traditional model of Western philosophy. However, the real issue is not so much whether we have a subjectivity that has its own "substantial identity," but, rather, whether we have a unique agency that can function as a condition for others. If this is the case, then Whitehead's relativism is successful in affirming such an agency.

Now we are in a position to see how Whitehead's relativism can be an alternative to absolutizing relativism. As we have seen, one of the most significant problems associated with absolutizing relativism is that since it tends to diminish one's own subjective agency, it is very difficult for it to have any philosophical tools with which it can affirm the positive value of one's own religion. This tendency easily leads to undermining the religious passion of sincere believers.

If we apply Whiteheadian relativism to interreligious dialogue, we can recognize the uniqueness of one's own religion, while still acknowledging the conditionedness of all religions. Instead of debilitating one's own religious conviction, we can encourage people to be proud of the particular value of their own religion, while acknowledging the particular value of other religions too.[10]

The second condition to be met for establishing an ideal kind of relativism is learning how to talk about transcendence without denying the reality of the transcendent or the differentiation between the ultimate and the nonultimate. This condition is met easily when we return to the doctrine of the primordial nature of God.

Owing to the primordial nature of God, Whitehead never gives up the notion of transcendence in a positive sense. This is because the primordial nature of God is said to transcend the world absolutely in some senses. The primordial nature of God transcends the world in the sense that the world will never be able to do what the primordial nature of God uniquely does. According to Whitehead, the primordial nature of God consists in God's entertainment of pure possibilities, which are ready for the sake of occasions to be actualized in the world. Because these possibilities include possibilities that have not yet been actualized in the world, it is by definition impossible for the world to contain them. This is why the nature of God is called "primordial." God thus transcends the world absolutely.

God's primordial nature also transcends the world absolutely in the sense that it intransigently occupies its own position in the process of an occasion's becoming. As we said before, the possibilities offered by God's primordial nature are

---

10. For a similar discussion of relativism, see Cobb, *Transforming Christianity and the World*, chap. 6.

called "ideal," because they are the best options for the occasion to choose. This means that it is necessary for an occasion to consider the ideal option given by God, though this option is influential only in the initial phase of the process of the occasion's becoming. Although the process of becoming in an occasion is not totally determined by God, God is highly determinative of the first phase of the process. In this sense, God's position and status in the process of the becoming of the world are steady and firm. Therefore, although all the occasions of the world are free from God's control in a sense, God's role as the transcendent is unshakable too. This second sense in which God is absolutely transcendent is the basis for a third: God transcends the world in the sense that the ideal aim provided by God, usually called the "initial subjective aim," is to be distinguished from the subjective aim as such, which is determined by the finite occasion's own creative power. God's absolute transcendence is the basis for our ethical distinction between the ideal and the actual, is and ought, good and evil.

This understanding of God's transcendence can provide an alternative to the absolutizing relativism involved in nonrealist interpretations of the transcendent. The primordial nature of God shows how God can function as transcendent in a strict sense. As Whitehead said, "it is as true to say that God transcends the World, as that the World transcends God" (PR 348). Strangely enough, even David Hall and Roger Ames in one place recognize that Whitehead's concept of God can be used to talk about transcendence in a strict sense: "The world as this actual world transcends God in a rather Pickwickian sense since it needs God for its actualization, while God needs only some actual world, not necessarily this one."[11] In recognizing that God exists independently of our present world (cosmic epoch), they acknowledge that God transcends the world in a strict sense.

If this is the case, then is it not obvious that Whitehead's doctrine of God, based on such a realist interpretation of transcendence, cannot be harmonized with East Asian religions interpreted in a nonrealist way?

This is why I said that the third condition, discovering how to reconcile conflicting truth claims of Abrahamic and non-Abrahamic religions, must be met if we want to provide an ideal type of relativism. Whitehead's doctrine of the ultimate meets this third condition too. As we saw above, in Whitehead's metaphysics we discover another ultimate in addition to God. Of course, there have been many different interpretations with regard to the issue of what Whitehead's concept of the ultimate really is. However, recently many Whiteheadian philosophers of religion, such as John Cobb and David Griffin, have agreed that the correct interpretation of Whitehead's position on this issue is that there are two ultimates, creativity and God.[12] I also agree with this interpretation. If we employ this interpretation of the ultimate, it is easy for us to meet the third condition.

---

11. Hall and Ames, *Thinking from the Han,* 202.
12. For discussions that deal with this issue, see Cobb, *Beyond Dialogue: Toward a Mutual Transformation of Christianity and Buddhism,* chaps. 5 and 6, and Griffin, *Reenchantment without Supernaturalism,* 264–84. In what follows, my discussion heavily depends on their discussion.

As we have seen, with regard to the issue of the ultimate, Abrahamic religions and East Asian religions have appeared to be in serious conflict. From the perspective of East Asian religions, the Abrahamic religions' concept of the ultimate, arising from a realist interpretation of transcendence, may seem to be off base. Furthermore, in East Asian religions, the personal God arising from Abrahamic religions has also been widely taken to be inferior to the impersonal Deity rooted in Asian religions, since it is believed that the personal God is derivative from the impersonal Deity. How is this apparent conflict solved by Whitehead's notion of two ultimates?

According to David Griffin, the central argument associated with the Whiteheadian idea of two ultimates is that the relationship between the two ultimates, creativity and God, is not subordination. This is because in Whitehead's metaphysics, creativity and God mutually presuppose each other. On the one hand, God is said to be an embodiment of creativity and, as such, an "instantiation" of the ultimate reality.[13] In this sense, creativity as an ultimate is presupposed by God. However, on the other hand, God is not simply one instantiation of creativity among others but "the aboriginal instance of this creativity" (PR 225). According to Griffin, this can be interpreted as saying that creativity itself is primordially characterized by God. Therefore, as Griffin insists, "creativity has never existed neutrally, without being shaped by God's primordial aim toward value-realization."[14] In this sense, God is also presupposed by creativity, entailing that both are equally ultimate.

Once we accept this Whiteheadian interpretation of two ultimates, this idea can serve to solve the problem of conflicting religious truth claims. If God as an ultimate is to be construed as actual, creativity as an ultimate is to be construed as nonactual. Furthermore, while the former can be said to be personal, the latter can be said to be impersonal, which may mean that while the former is the product of the mainstream in the history of Abrahamic religious experience, the latter is the product of the mainstream in the history of East Asian religious experience. The problem of conflicting truth claims is resolved by saying that whereas they are all equally ultimate, the Abrahamic and East Asian traditions involve complementary emphases, not irreconcilable opposites.

If this is the case, we are once again in a position to understand how this solution overcomes the weakness of absolutizing relativism too. Absolutizing relativism creates significant problems because it favors only one notion of the ultimate, and therefore should not be construed as a genuine type of relativism. In other words, since the position of absolutizing relativism is based on the principle of universal relativity, it tends to deny the differentiation between the transcendent and nontranscendent, and the ultimate and the nonultimate. Hence, the Abrahamic religions, which focus on the differentiation between the transcendent and the nontranscendent, and between the ultimate and the nonulti-

---

13. Griffin, *Reenchantment without Supernaturalism*, 267.
14. Ibid.

mate, are regarded as inferior to East Asian religions. By contrast, if we apply the Whiteheadian type of moderate relativism to the theory of religious pluralism, both kinds of religious experience can be regarded as equally valid. This type of religious pluralism can be construed as more genuine in the sense that it recognizes the plurality of religions in a complete manner.

CONCLUDING REMARK

I am a Christian theologian. However, I see deep problems in traditional Christian theology, insofar as it is not free from the shackles of absolutistic conceptions of truth. Therefore, I believe that as far as interreligious dialogue is concerned in East Asia, it is Christianity that first has to incorporate the relativistic understanding of truth. With this understanding, Christianity must admit the fact that all religions, including Christianity, are relative and limited. This is what Christianity can learn from the truth of relativism.

Nevertheless, while I have been involved in the interreligious dialogue between Christianity and East Asian religions in Korea, I have realized that some scholars' interpretation of East Asian religions is also a stumbling block that hinders the development of interreligious dialogue in East Asia. One of the most significant reasons why some East Asians are not successful in their dialogue with Abrahamic religions is based on their philosophy of relativism, which has turned out, in this essay, to be too extreme to harmonize with the theistic religions. Therefore, although I agree with the fact that most of the East Asian religions have a depth of insight into the principle of relativism, some scholars' interpretation of relativism inherent in the East Asian religions should be transformed in some respects.

This is why I have introduced a Whiteheadian philosophy of relativism. If we apply the Whiteheadian type of relativism to the philosophy of East Asian religions (as well as to the Abrahamic religions), we can get an ideal methodology for establishing a better type of religious pluralism. The new perception of religious pluralism based on this Whiteheadian relativism will be able to push our consciousness toward the insight that all religions are equally valid. I believe that with this perception, we will be able to make some contribution to resolving the conflict between Abrahamic religions and East Asian religions.

PART FOUR
FINAL REFLECTIONS

Chapter 12

Some Whiteheadian Assumptions about Religion and Pluralism

John B. Cobb Jr.

I have expressed my views about "religious pluralism" in many different ways. David Griffin has reviewed my position admirably. In considering how I might say something a little different, it has occurred to me that I might identify what I take to be basic assumptions, negative and positive, underlying these views. If I am right that most of my more specific views flow from these assumptions, together with historical judgments, then putting the assumptions together in one place may make it easier for others to know whether they agree or disagree with me.

Obviously all of us assume many things. I am not trying to formulate all the logical assumptions shared with most writers on religious pluralism. I am discussing only those assumptions, bearing directly on the topic, that some others, and in some cases *most* others, seem not to share. I will begin with some negatives.

I NEGATIVE ASSUMPTIONS

1. We should avoid reifying "religion."

When I first encountered criticism of the noun "religion" in John Dewey, I reacted negatively. The word seemed to be needed as a way to identify Judaism,

243

Christianity, Islam, Hinduism, Buddhism, and other traditions. Each was frequently called a religion, and I thought they could be compared as such.

But the more I thought about it, and the more I saw where the use of that noun led, the more I saw Dewey's point. Categorizing these traditions as religions often misdirects the investigation and discussion. The word is so frequently used and so entrenched in our language, that we may not be able to avoid it. But even if we continue to use the term, as in most of the essays in this volume, we need to be careful not to reify "religion." The term can be useful if we understand that the various traditions grouped under it are related in terms of family resemblance rather than by participating in a common essence. This is important for several reasons.

First, this is not a term that any of the traditions classically used about itself. The term developed in Christendom and gained its meaning from standard features of Christianity. The first two meanings given in my dictionary still speak of a superhuman creator. Clearly this excludes some forms of Buddhism. The use of the term to classify other traditions has typically been one more expression of Western intellectual imperialism. It is we who decide what counts and what does not.

Now it can be correctly pointed out that, over a period of time, scholars have developed definitions of religion that are less biased to the West. We no longer identify "religion" with worship of a "supreme being," for example, or with beliefs about the supernatural. Historians of religion are now doing much more careful phenomenological work to determine what types of practices are common to the traditions they identify as religions.

Even when the Western bias is reduced, however, another problem arises. If "religion" is defined as what is common to all the traditions that are thought of as religions, each tradition's more distinctive elements tend to be depreciated. Consider for example the relation of the cultic and the prophetic in Judaism. Phenomenological study is likely to show that cultic practices are common all over the world; so these are likely to be regarded as part of the essential core of religion. But the prophetic tradition in Israel, one that was often sharply critical of cultic practice, is not common to all the "religions." It is not likely to be given equal status in the definition of "religion." As a result, when Judaism is studied as a "religion," this aspect is neglected or minimized. If it is recognized that, nonetheless, the prophetic tradition is of central importance to Judaism, then Judaism will be understood as partly religious, partly secular.

More broadly, there is a strong tendency, when an essence of religion is sought, to emphasize the sacred. Phenomenologically, this can be found in all the traditions we call religions, as well as in some we do not. Yet the traditions that arose in what Karl Jaspers called the "axial period" all had elements of desacralization. The monotheistic emphasis in all the Abrahamic traditions emphasized God's care for the profane world. It introduced a tendency, never fully carried through, toward viewing only God as sacred and, therefore, doing away with the focus on sacred times and places and practices, to which much of the phenomenological study of religion is devoted. The shift from the distinction between the clean and the unclean to that between righteousness and unrighteousness is also part of this desacralization.

Buddhism went further than any of these through its doctrine that Nirvana is Samsara, culminating in the Zen teaching that if one meets the Buddha one should kill him. I do not mean that any tradition frees itself wholly from the sacred. Obviously, even in the Zen form of Buddhism, the sacred continues to play a large role. I mean only that if we take the sacred to be of the essence of "religion," then we must recognize that in many of the traditions we call "religions," there is an "antireligious" tendency.

Since the prophetic tradition is central to my understanding of Christianity, this point is personally important to me. I participate regularly in the liturgical life of the congregation. But when "religion" is understood with reference to sacred times, places, and practices and cultic observance, then those of us who stand in the prophetic tradition are marginalized when Christianity is identified as a "religion." To acknowledge that cultic practice and attention to the sacred play a role in Christianity is, of course, unobjectionable, and these features relate it to many other traditions. But in my view they do not constitute the heart of Christian faith and practice.

Of course, there are other ways of defining "religion" that do not have this result. We may appeal to the Latin root, which means "binding together." A religion may then, by extension, be understood to be a way of binding everything together. In that case, the definition is open to the real variety of ways that things can be bound together. As one who believes that there is a deep human need to have a comprehensive understanding of one's reality and a coherence of thought and action, I consider religion in this sense to be very important.

But when we define "religion" in this way, what are included and excluded from "religion" are quite different from ordinary usage. For most Protestants in the past two centuries, Christianity has not bound everything together. It has bound a few things together, whereas science and political loyalties have bound other things together. Hence Christianity has not been a religion for most Protestants.

In China and Japan, similarly, Buddhism has bound things together for very few. Most Buddhists have also been Confucianists, and many have been Taoists or Shintoists. What has bound things together for most Chinese has been being Chinese; for most Japanese, being Japanese.

I am quite open to moving in this direction. We can compare the various ways in which people have attained an overview that informs their whole way of being in the world. But we must then be prepared to consider a very different range of topics from those generally treated in academic departments of religion. We must recognize that, in the modern West, churches have functioned only marginally with respect to "religion," thus understood, for most of their members, and that what we call Eastern "religions" are so for only a few. Islam would probably have the best claim among the traditions generally recognized as religious to function as a religion for many of its adherents.

One implication of these observations is that there is no *true* definition. This is, of course, widely recognized but also commonly ignored. Definitions are more or less useful, not true and false. In general, they should point to what is commonly intended by the use of the word, although highly specialized, and even eccentric, definitions can be justified in some circumstances. Since ordinary usage is multivalent and vague, explicit definitions are needed to clarify for the hearer or reader the way a speaker or author has chosen to use a word that is central to the argument. Providing a definition makes it easier to determine whether one is consistent or whether one is slippery in the use of terms.

I often make this point by saying that I do not believe that there is an essence of religion. There is a variety of related phenomena that the word evokes in common usage. It is usually better to use it in relation to those phenomena. But if one makes clear that one is using it in another way, is consistent in doing so, and draws no conclusions about the phenomena usually designated by the term, that procedure is acceptable also. Sometimes it may prove highly illuminating.

Hence I do not say that it is wrong to use the noun "religion." I only say that the usual consequences are disturbing and that few of those who use the term succeed in consistently avoiding these negative consequences.

Perhaps one follows Tillich and defines religion as "ultimate concern." Historically, the meaning of the phrase derives from the Jewish-Christian-Muslim family of traditions. The connotations of "ultimate concern" are related to monotheism. But the term is intended to abstract from theism and be open to nontheistic ways of expressing such concern. That is admirable. But, in fact, it remains misleading to say that Buddhists are ultimately concerned about Nirvana. It would be equally accurate to say that they are ultimately concerned about having no ultimate concern. But such twists and turns only serve to show that this is an alien concept forced on the discussion by the West.

Because of the problematic history of the use of the word "religion," I would like to find other terminology. I have tried speaking of the traditional Ways, meaning, of course, the ways in which communities have tried to integrate thinking and living normatively for themselves. I think this is a more neutral and open approach and makes connection with the language used in many of these traditions about themselves. Others propose that we speak of them as "paths." The problem, of course, is that much explanation is needed each time such substitutions are given.

Since it is not practical to replace the word "religion," I propose that we understand "religions" to be traditional "ways" that have extensively overlapping characteristics, including attention to the sacred and cultic practices, which can well be labeled "religious." We can also emphasize that what is most important to some of these ways may not be the features that lead us to characterize them as religions. In this case, the term can be useful and harmless. I believe that in the essays in this volume "religion" can be understood in this way.

2. There is no common goal.

The most important reason for raising questions about the use of the term "religion" is that often people derive from their definition of religion a norm by which to evaluate what they call the religions. Clearly, if we recognize that there is no essence of religion, this procedure will be avoided. But there may still be a tendency to think that the various religions have a common goal. If we can correctly identify that goal, some suppose, then we can ask how well the several traditions achieve it.

John Hick has made the best proposal of this kind. He suggests that all the "higher" religious traditions aim to transform people from being centered in themselves to being centered in "the Real." He undertakes to define "the Real" in a way that is neutral among the traditions. His effort to find a neutral way to identify a common center in all religious traditions is not, however, a promising project, and calling this center "the Real" creates more problems than it solves. But that is not my concern here. The question in this context is whether success in transforming people away from self-centeredness can be seen as the common goal.

I do believe that it is empirically the case that all the religious traditions of humankind undertake to overcome egocentrism in their adherents. Hence, to ask how well they succeed is to bring to bear *a* norm that may well be common. Hence, I see real value in Hick's proposal.

Formulated in this negative way, however, this is not a norm that distinguishes religious traditions from others. No society could ever have survived if children were not led to care about a greater good than their own ego-satisfaction. What is clearly common to all the religious traditions does not distinguish them from other forms of socialization.

Hick, of course, knows this. That is why he goes on to specify that the *religious* norm is to move people from egocentrism to centeredness on "the Real." This distinguishes the religious goal from that which is required for social functioning. The higher religions, he teaches, seek to orient us to something beyond any limited social grouping, something universal and ultimate, whereas ethnocentric religions and secular movements often prefer more limited loyalties.

There is a certain circularity here. If we define the higher religions as those that are universalistic, then it follows that their goals will have a universalistic character. But this still does not mean that all of them aim to center persons on "the Real," however open-endedly this is defined. We have here another case of generalizing from the monotheistic traditions. In these it makes sense to speak of centering our lives in God rather than in ourselves. In Buddhism it does not make sense to speak of centering in emptiness rather than in ourselves. The realization of emptiness is better understood as decentering.

Even among the monotheistic traditions, in which this ideal has meaning, by no means all serious believers place the same weight on the attainment of this goal. Other goals loom large. For some, the assurance of being accepted by God is primary. For others, growth in love of neighbor may be more meaningful than becoming centered in God. For still others, the primary goal is defined in socio-historical ways rather than as personal transformation. And for some, the goal may be thought of as perfect obedience to God's law. One can find leading thinkers who regard the goal of a theocentric life as unattainable and who recommend, instead, acceptance of our creaturely finitude and constant need of forgiveness.

The Zen Buddhist Masao Abe agrees with John Hick that there is one goal or norm for all the higher religions. He disagrees with Hick as to how this should be identified. His candidate is enlightenment or *satori*. He is convinced that, although this goal has been clarified chiefly in Buddhism, there are tendencies in all religious traditions to move in the direction of this mode of realization. In his view, this is what is truly authentic in all the traditions. It would be very difficult, however, to understand the biblical writers as focusing on this goal. It may be generous of Abe to see that they have in some ways contributed to this attainment, but few biblically oriented Christians can identify the quest for, or realization of, *satori* as the heart of their faith.

My point here is that any statement of *the* goal of all the religions, even of all that one judges to be "higher" religions, involves imposing personal judgments. These judgments may be shaped within one or another tradition. Or they may come from some nontraditional source.

There is no objection to someone announcing her or his personal views as to what religion should contribute to the world and then examining the several religious traditions to determine whether, and how well, they make this contribution. But one should not present this work as an objective explanation and evaluation of the religions.

3. Seeking to identify an essence of Christianity is unwise.

In opposing the idea that there is an essence of "religion," I have spoken of individual religious traditions in ways that leave open the possibility that they have essences. Whereas there is no religion in general, since it exists only in particular manifestations, this is not true of Christianity and Buddhism and other religious traditions. Many people identify themselves as Christians and as Buddhists, and they believe that this identification involves beliefs and practices in important ways. Hence one might be able to identify a set of beliefs or practices essential to being a Christian or a Buddhist and define Christianity or Buddhism accordingly.

However, at least in the case of Christianity, this is not a fruitful approach. The situation with respect to Buddhism may be different, and I leave it to Buddhist colleagues to decide whether essentialist thinking is helpful for them. As Whitehead noted in *Religion in the Making*, Christians draw forth their teachings by responding to a particular person or event. Such responding is an ongoing process throughout history, such that attempts to state once for all, for all Christians, what is to be believed or practiced by all, function to divide rather than to unify. The meaning of the event for believers is, in fact, different at different times and in different circumstances. What is essential for one community in one time and place differs from what is essential under other circumstances. Great harm has been done by trying to limit the freedom of Christians to respond as they judge best.

Accordingly, I define Christianity as that sociohistorical movement in which participants intend to derive their norms from the Christ event. If by the "essence" of Christianity is meant only that which one employs to distinguish Christianity from other phenomena, in this case from other sociohistorical movements, then I can use the term. As noted above, definitions are not true or false but more or less helpful or useful. My intention is to define Christianity in a way that would be acceptable to most people, whether they are Christian or not. Almost all who call themselves Christian attribute some normativity to the Christ event. I can then say that it is the essence of Christianity to try to derive its norms from the Christ event. Communities that seek their norms in other traditions do not consider themselves Christian, even if Christians approve the norms to which they commit themselves.

Of course, this leaves many uncertainties about boundaries. How much weight must a community give to the Christ event, in comparison with the weight it gives to other events or norms, in order for it to be Christian? There can be no precise answer. However, a useful definition need not provide decisive answers to such questions. There are communities that are partly Christian and partly not. There are certainly many individuals who participate in Christian churches but who in fact derive most of their values from other sources. The definition I have provided corresponds closely with the way most people discuss the question of who is Christian and to what extent they are Christian when they are making descriptive judgments.

Christians derive a variety of norms from their encounter with the Christ event. When people speak of an essence of Christianity, they usually refer to some set of these norms. It is this second step that I am opposing in denying that there is an essence of Christianity. As long as this is avoided and talk of the "essence" of Christianity is used only to clarify how the word is being used, the dangers I associate with essentialist thinking are avoided. Typically, however, people who enter dialogue with the belief that there is an essence of Christianity are convinced that some beliefs, practices, attitudes, or orientations are essential to their being Christian. This conviction inhibits their response to other traditions. They have difficulty listening nondefensively to the criticisms directed toward their tradition by others. They can make concessions on other points, but not with respect to what is essential. Or if they do make changes there, too, they feel themselves to have betrayed their heritage.

The belief that there is an essence of Christianity is usually closely bound to the view that Christianity is good. We Christians typically identify being Christian as ideal, or at least desirable; so we identify an essence that we see as purely good. We can then say that those who do evil in the name of Christianity are not truly Christian. If villagers engage in a pogrom against the local Jews on Good Friday, we want to say that they are not Christian. If imperial nations conquer less technologically advanced people, justifying their actions by their duty to convert them to Christianity, we want to say that they are not Christian. If inquisitors torture people's bodies in order to save their souls, we want to say that they are not Christian.

There are certainly normative meanings of "Christian" by which most people who call themselves "Christian" in our time would agree that those who acted in these ways were not behaving in a Christian way. I strongly support this use of "Christian," but I find that according to it there have been, and still are, few "Christians." Further, Christians disagree among themselves as to just how to understand what it means to be Christian in this normative sense, although, fortunately, within most churches and even ecumenically, during a given period, there are areas of agreement as well. Today, for example, there is widespread agreement that racism is not Christian, although until recently many Christians were unapologetically racist, some defending racism on biblical grounds. Both agreements and disagreements remain important.

Like many Christians, I have strong convictions as to what kinds of behavior are truly appropriate to Christian discipleship. But I am also convinced that as a Christian I should respect the sincerity of those other Christians with whom I disagree. I should not so define Christianity as to deny that they are Christians, even if I believe their behavior is not Christian in terms of my normative understanding. I also expect that the time will come when much of the way I live today will be recognized as not Christian because of its participation in ecological destruction, the extreme inequities of global capitalism, and American imperialism, and no doubt for other reasons to which I am not now sensitive.

People who genuinely identify themselves as Christian have done and now do terrible things as expressions of their understanding of Christianity. Christianity has done great harm in human history as well as great good. It is extremely important to formulate Christian teaching in such a way that it will direct devotion and energy to good rather than to evil. Determining what the true meaning of the Christ event is for us is a matter of utmost urgency. However, I am opposed to introducing the conclusions to which my normative reflections have led me into the definition of Christianity. Within the Christian community we can and should take part in an ongoing discussion of the best formulation of theology. We should not use our personal conclusions on that point to define Christianity. I should myself hold these conclusions tentatively, open to transformation as I encounter other ideas.

Those Christians who assume there is an essence of Christianity have put forward various proposals. All of them inhibit real openness in interreligious discussion. If the essence of Christianity is defined by the classical creeds, the restriction on learning from others is obvious. If Christians follow Harnack in identifying the essence as "the Fatherhood of God and the sonship of man," there is much greater openness to diverse theological formulations, but the problem is not fundamentally different. There are many other ways to define essential beliefs, but the fact that there are so many approaches raises doubts that any one of them far transcends the historical context from which it arises.

Today the essence is sometimes identified in terms of orthopraxis, rather than orthodoxy. This may seem to remove the limits on learning from dialogue, but this is not the case. Any particular formulation of orthopraxis will come under criticism from those whose view of orthopraxis is different.

We may derive one norm from the descriptive definition I have offered. If Christianity is a movement that tries to derive its norms from the Christ event, then doing that well is better than doing it poorly. Accordingly, one can recommend to Christians critical study of the source of their norms and the ways in which they have been derived from the source. However, to be part of the Christian movement does not require even this. All too many members of the movement simply follow the leadership of those they suppose speak with authority. As long as these leaders turn to Christian sources for their norms, their followers remain part of the Christian movement. But if the leaders cease to claim to learn from the Christ event and appeal to some other source as decisive norm, they will no longer be Christians, whether the other source is good or bad.

Many Christians are responding to the multifarious opportunities and challenges of our time by tightening boundaries and shutting out new possibilities. Often they understand this to be the Christian response required to protect the purity of the faith. But this is not the only, or the best, response. A better response to the challenge of new ideas and the wisdom of other religious traditions is to reengage our originating event in new ways. The resulting beliefs and practices will be different from those that arose when we were not aware of these other forms of wisdom.

It is also possible that some Christians who respond creatively to new challenges will leave the Christian fold. That is, some may decide that reengaging our originating event is not the way forward in a pluralistic age. Perhaps another tradition will seem superior. Or perhaps they will decide that a syncretistic stance is better today than a stance within the Christian community. The descriptive definition I propose is not designed to do away with boundaries and the possibility of crossing them!

The theology affirmed in this volume does, however, show that one reason many sensitive and thoughtful people consider giving up their Christian identity can be overcome. It demonstrates that remaining firmly Christian should in no way close us to being transformed in our encounter with the wisdom of other traditions. The descriptive understanding of Christianity that I employ recognizes the fact that many Christians will respond defensively to the new opportunities of the changing world situation. We deplore this. It is our intention in this book to show that Christians can and, indeed, should so understand their faith that it requires openness to the wisdom of others. We believe that, in a variety of ways, a process perspective can help other traditions to achieve similar results.

4. There is no neutral position.

My critique of John Hick and Masao Abe was based on my negative assumption that there is no neutral position from which to pronounce on the goals of religions or any other important matter. Hick and Abe have done as well as one could do. But each betrays a particularity of standpoint. I certainly do not object to people speaking from particular standpoints. On the contrary, I am convinced there is no other way of speaking. I only object when what is spoken in this way is presented as an objective and neutral account.

Both Hick and Abe assume that if one speaks as a Christian, one will not be neutral or objective. Christians speak from "faith." But Abe believes that Buddhism appeals only to experience, that Buddhist experience demonstrates the possibility and the final value of enlightenment. Hence, he thinks, to point to this form of human realization does not depend on a particular standpoint that can be relativized by others. Buddhist experience leads to what he calls the "positionless position."

This Buddhist claim should not be trivialized. I have no doubt that Buddhist disciplines have led some people to a radical transformation of experience that is of extreme value. I think it erroneous, however, to say, on this basis, that this is the one goal at which all religious traditions aim or should aim. A group of people may feel called to work for peace and justice in the world rather than to attain personal fulfillment. This may be an inferior goal from some points of view—but not from all. There are also forms of mystical experience that differ from Buddhist enlightenment. They too may be inferior, but those who experience them may judge them superior. Sri Aurobindo, for example, had a series of diverse religious experiences. One of these he considered Buddhist enlightenment. Much as he affirmed this, it was not his climactic experience. Again, he may be wrong and Abe right, but it is difficult to see just how this would be demonstrated.

This means that I view Abe as speaking from the Zen Buddhist perspective. From that perspective, he makes a very important contribution to the whole community of religiously concerned people. But this is not a neutral perspective. The claim that it is neutral hinders, rather than advances, the movement toward fuller understanding.

Hick seeks a neutral perspective by turning to philosophy. He supposes that a philosophical perspective allows him to view all the religious traditions fairly and to make neutral judgments among them. The self-understanding of philosophy as the open-minded quest for wisdom encourages that kind of claim. Nevertheless, it is extremely questionable. Hick's philosophy clearly reflects the Western tradition in philosophy, and within that tradition he selects some sources and rejects others. It also, as I have suggested, reflects the influence of Christianity. It is certainly not a philosophy on which all practitioners of the discipline now agree.

To relativize philosophies means only that the thinking of philosophers is deeply affected by their location in the history of thought, as well as the broader history, in which they stand. Beginning with Descartes, they have made many efforts to find an unconditioned ground on which to stand and then to build on that foundation in uncontestable ways. No one has succeeded. John Dewey long ago criticized this quest for certainty. Many today reject the "foundationalist" approach. Every philosophy is an expression of historically conditioned thought, which is the only form of thought there is. Obviously that applies to Whitehead and to all my assumptions as well.

Of course, Hick, working from his particular standpoint, may have achieved the finally correct philosophy. But it is impossible not to be skeptical. Indeed, Hick would not want to make any such claim. We should welcome those who enter into the discussion of religion from the side of philosophy, but we should recognize that they are not free of particular points of view. Philosophy does not provide a neutral perspective from which to view religions.

The most influential claim to have a neutral perspective comes not from Buddhists or philosophers but from scientists. Science can rightly claim to have developed methods that lead to reliable results that are not as relative as those of theologies and philosophies. People all over the world, coming from many cultural perspectives, can perform the same experiments and attain the same results.

We now know that even in physics the direction of research and the interpretation of data are perspectivally conditioned. The line between what may be regarded as fully established and what is open to reformulation is not easy to establish. Nevertheless, the claim of the sciences to have found ways of achieving relatively objective knowledge must be taken seriously.

Accordingly, those who approach religion "scientifically" seem, on the surface, to have some claim to neutrality. Unfortunately for this claim, repeatable experiments can play a very small role in their study of religion. The "scientific" study of religion is more likely to take the categories of a particular psychology, sociology, or anthropology as given, and then interpret religious phenomena in these terms. These social scientists can certainly throw important light in this way on what is studied. But the categories in which scientific theories are formulated are the least neutral aspect of the sciences. Especially in the social sciences, they are all contested.

The neutrality breaks down in another way. Modern Western science in general and overall is based on a highly questionable worldview. It came into being partly through the exclusion of final causes from its purview. When it studies such highly purposeful activity as religious practices, this exclusion may prove radically distorting. Also, by the twentieth century, the denial to God of any causal role in the world became a cardinal principle of science. To approach the study of theistic religious traditions and practices with the a priori conviction that there is no God, or that God has no effect in the world, is hardly neutral.

Again, atheistic materialists may contribute richly to the study of religion. They, and they alone, may turn out to have the correct worldview. But to assume that this is so is not neutral, and the conclusions that follow from this assumption are not neutral. The "scientific study of religion" is just as perspectival as the philosophical or theological or Buddhist approach.

II POSITIVE ASSUMPTIONS

The distinction between negative and positive assumptions is certainly not a sharp one. In my exposition of negative assumptions, I have made many positive assertions. Nevertheless, what I have tried to do above is to push aside some habits of mind that have, in my view, blocked an adequate approach to issues of religious pluralism.

Much of what I have said in these negations agrees with those who have made the "linguistic turn" in one or another of its forms. These thinkers often go from these negative assumptions to a quite thoroughgoing relativism. They may, for example, see each tradition as having its distinct cultural-linguistic system, incommensurable with other cultural-linguistic systems. The words and symbols of this system may be understood to refer to one another but not to any world outside the system.

I could formulate my differences with this relativistic view in terms of additional negative assumptions. But this approach would result in double negatives, such as, I do not believe that language has no reference beyond language. It seems better to make this point positively. One of my assumptions is that language has a referential element and that this is as true of religious language as of any other. Hence I turn to what I consider the positive assumptions underlying my understanding of religious pluralism.

1. The world is vastly more complex than our thoughts can grasp.

I believe that the world is vastly richer and more complex than any human scheme of thought has ever grasped or will ever grasp. I find Whitehead's vision of this complexity convincing as far as it goes. But Whitehead was very sensitive to the limitations of any scheme of thought in finally grasping the whole. My belief that the complexity of the world exceeds any current or even possible human grasp does not arise simply from Whitehead's authority, but it is reinforced by his agreement and clarification.

Every scheme of thought that has any hold on thoughtful minds highlights some features of this complexity and obscures others. When these schemes of thought, or cultural-linguistic systems, become well entrenched in a society, they deeply shape the sense of what is real and what is not real within that society. People's self-understandings and judgments of importance follow from these visions of reality. When they encounter beliefs arising from other cultural-linguistic systems that do not fit into their understanding of what is real, they are likely to consider them false.

I like to illustrate my understanding of the complexity of things by pointing to the history of healing practices. The dominant form in the twentieth century in the West (and increasingly around the world) is allopathic medicine. It is based on modern scientific knowledge of physiology and chemistry. It has developed a definite picture of the human body. Few of us doubt that this picture accurately describes many features of our bodies and that the practice of this medicine has been brilliantly successful.

There have, however, been groups who have viewed the body differently and have practiced different methods of cure. Chiropractic is a good example of this alternative. It focuses on the way in which lack of alignment of the bones, especially the backbone, causes stresses throughout the body that lead to many problems whose symptoms are treated by standard medicine. I have no doubt that chiropractors have relieved patients of much pain from back problems and that, when the alignment they seek is achieved, there are general health benefits.

Still other practitioners view the body primarily in terms of the food and liquids that are consumed. Far more problems than the dominant medicine has recognized occur because our bodies are allergic to particular foods and need others. Viewing the body in these terms has led to many successful cures.

Christian Science illustrates a more radically different approach. This religious tradition, which is based on philosophical idealism, takes seriously the idealist doctrine that the physical world exists only for thought. This doctrine has led to concentrated attention on how mental states affect physical health. Many other groups, religiously and psychologically oriented, support the judgment that there are such effects, although most regard the body as having partly independent reality as well. Most religious people pray for the sick, supposing that such prayer has some beneficial effects. Some of those who participate in these communities have stories to tell of remarkable successes.

The dominant allopathic community as a whole was long skeptical of all other approaches. Today there are remarkable changes. The hostility toward chiropractic has softened. The importance of diet is recognized. And courses on "religion and healing" have found their way into the curricula of some medical schools. These developments reflect the recognition by the medical profession that the human body is more complex than the traditional scientific depiction recognized.

The success of diverse approaches to human health indicates that the human body is very complex. Each approach focuses on some real features of this body, neglecting others. Even if all are combined, other important elements in the body will continue to be ignored.

The most striking development is the encounter of Western and Eastern medicine. Chinese acupuncture is an excellent example. This medical practice is based on a detailed study of the body over many centuries that discovered patterns of connection in the body of which Western medicine was unaware. The first reaction to the claim that there are such connections could be expected to be denial or, at best, skepticism. But Western doctors were admirably open to the evidence. The evidence is that acupuncture is effective. The maps of the body employed by acupuncturists depict something quite real about the body, even though they are hard to integrate with Western physiology. Clearly, two cultures, approaching the body with different systems of thought, have both learned much about it. An integration of the two schemes of thought should provide a more adequate depiction. But there is no reason to suppose that this integration will capture the full complexity of the human body.

It is my assumption that the human body is not the only part of the world whose complexity exceeds all that we can now think or imagine. I fully expect that advances in physics and cosmology will continue to reveal aspects of reality that astonish us. I also fully expect that, as in the case of the human body, the purely objectifying mode of modern Western science will neglect or omit other dimensions of the totality of reality apart from which the fullness of reality is not understood.

2. Our language refers beyond itself to a real world.

That language refers to a nonlinguistic world is, of course, a practical assumption underlying daily life. If we tell a child to eat vegetables or to avoid taking cocaine, the practical assumption is that vegetables and cocaine are real things that are really beneficial and harmful to the body, respectively, independently of our beliefs. That the human body exists is assumed by all the approaches to healing mentioned above except Christian Science. Most people, even those who have made the linguistic turn, are distressed when Christian Scientists refuse to seek standard medical care for sick children.

Since, practically speaking, almost everyone assumes that language has a referential aspect, it seems hardly necessary to make a point of this as an important assumption. However, especially in the field of religious thought, a large part of the scholarly community rejects this assumption. It is important to understand why this is so.

There are two reasons. One is the history of recent Western philosophy, which has cut strongly in an antirealist direction from Hume and Kant to the present. The second has to do with the way religion has been understood. I will consider the former in this section, the latter in the next.

Western thought has overwhelmingly supposed that knowledge of the external world is mediated exclusively by sense experience. For a long time it was assumed that this sense experience provides a basis for affirming the substantial reality of the physical world. But more sophisticated philosophical analysis showed that this is not the case. Vision gives us only patches of color that we cannot reasonably suppose to exist "out there" where they are seen. The phenomena undoubtedly exist in the experience of the one who sees, but they surely "exist" only in this sense. We cannot deduce from them the existence of material substances underlying them and causative of them. The idea of efficient causes, which had played so large a role in earlier philosophy and science, cannot be justified when we suppose it must be derived from sense data.

Kant "saved" science by theorizing that what sense experience in itself cannot provide us is given as the necessary forming of that experience by the human mind. The resulting experience, being created by the mind, tells us nothing about what is really there independent of our experience. But it does tell us that the only world about which we can have knowledge is a world constructed by our minds. In dealing with that phenomenal world, the sciences are free to proceed. But these scientific investigations tell us nothing about reality, that is, the world as it is in itself.

In general we can say that continental European thought to the present time is Kantian. That means that if language refers beyond itself, it is to the phenomenal world, not to a real one. But within this broad sphere of Kantian antirealism, there have been many creative developments. One of them is the linguistic turn.

Instead of attributing the order of the phenomena to the universal structuring activity of the human mind, one can pay attention to cultural differences. One finds that different cultures have constructed their worlds in different ways. They have done so through language and the broader processes of symbolization. There is no way of speaking of a common world, even a common phenomenal world, that is ordered in these diverse ways. One cannot go behind the diversely constructed worlds to anything else.

To respond to this currently dominant form of antirealism, one must return to the origins of that antirealism in Hume and Kant. One must challenge the fundamental assumption they share with most of the Western tradition, namely, that our knowledge of the external world derives exclusively from sense experience. If that assumption were correct, then the conclusions that have been drawn from it would, indeed, follow.

Most phenomenologists have accepted this standard Western assumption. But we can be grateful that one of the greatest, Maurice Merleau-Ponty, in openmindedly examining experience, recognized that our experience of our bodies cannot be understood exclusively in this way. True, we know something about our bodies by seeing them and touching them. But the body enters into our experience in a more direct way as well. Merleau-Ponty wrote about the "lived body."

Although Whitehead did not call himself a phenomenologist, he did careful phenomenological work. This led him to go beyond the position reached by Merleau-Ponty. He saw, above all, that a major part of every experience was the inclusion of past experience. If each momentary human experience includes both one's body and one's past experience, it is by no means cut off from the reality of other actualities. These are known immediately, not merely by inference from sense experience. When we speak, we can refer to our past experiences and to our bodily feelings. Through these we have access to a wider world about which we can also think and speak. Whitehead's doctrine of what he called "prehensive" relations is his greatest philosophical contribution. It opens the door to the renewal of realism.

At the same time, what is real is now found to be events that are both mental and physical in their constitution. When "realism" is taken to mean the objective existence of enduring substances, Whitehead is certainly not a "realist." But I think it is far clearer to say that this is a different kind of realism than to seek a new term to name it.

3. Religious experience also has a realistic dimension.

I want now to state a more practically controversial conviction. I assume that the experiences talked about in the great religious traditions also have a realistic element. Of course, I do not assume that all the statements by practitioners of all traditions are true. But I assume that just as the medicine of West and East analyzed different features of the human body, so the great religious thinkers of West and East have apprehended real features of a real world.

In the previous section, I said that, in practice, virtually everyone is a realist. The denial of realism in general is a kind of bad faith that intellectual history has imposed on much of the intelligentsia. But this is not necessarily true of the rejection of realism in the sphere of religion. The antirealist view need not express bad faith, especially when applied to divine beings or a divine being. One may believe that natural things are real and even that human experience is real and still doubt the reality of the divine beings about which religious people often speak.

We need to consider some of the reasons that, in the modern world, skepticism has focused especially on religion. First, whereas the antiquity of ideas or writings long gave them special authority, since the Enlightenment the modern has superseded the ancient in authority. Religious traditions, however, have continued to appeal to ancient texts. Often their authority has been associated with the claim that the events or persons whose work they recited were in some way supernatural. This claim has increased modern skepticism about religious assertions.

Second, the claims of various religious traditions are in conflict. To whatever extent these claims are made in absolutist terms, such conflicts necessarily rule out all but one. By far the greater likelihood, the modern mind says, is that they rule out all the conflicting claims.

Third, many religious beliefs are about a putative reality inaccessible to ordinary experience. The arguments given for this reality are unconvincing. Everything then seems to rely on the reality of some type of extraordinary event, such as a revelation, the occurrence of which is not evident.

Fourth, the major argument for the reality of God was the need for a creator of the world. This argument presupposed the reality of efficient causality. But Hume denied that we have any experiential basis for speaking of a "cause" that necessitates an "effect." We can responsibly mean by cause only priority in a regular series of phenomena. God is not a phenomenon at all, and certainly no regular succession can be observed between God and the world. Hence, the implication of Hume's analysis was that the question of God as cause of the world cannot even arise.

Kant's response to Hume also limited causality to a relation in the phenomenal world. For both Hume and Kant, God cannot be a cause of any phenomenon. Accordingly, there is no basis for thought to move from the world we know, or any aspect of that world, to God.

Fifth, standard teachings about God's power and God's love were incompatible with the vast reality of evil and unmerited suffering in the world. The responses given by theists were, for the most part, unconvincing to thoughtful and sensitive people.

I believe that, given much of the content of dominant Western teaching about God, and given the assumption that we know the external world only through sense experience, the skepticism that came to dominance in the intellectual community was well founded. If I am to justify the assumption that, nevertheless, the religious traditions are sources of valid knowledge about the totality of reality, I must explain how I evade these two "givens."

Much of the religious history of humankind has focused on matters that are much more experiential than what is rightly viewed with such skepticism. If we begin with Indian and Chinese religious thought, rather than eighteenth-century Protestantism, this experiential basis for religious thought becomes clear. There are many dimensions of Indian and Chinese thought, but much of it is directly connected to meditational experience of one kind or another. It explains that certain types of practice affect experience in certain ways. To a large extent it is repeatable, much as modern science is. It includes profound analyses of experience in its immediacy. It describes the broader character of experience and life in ways that locate the meditational discipline and explain how it can occur and affect the rest. It connects with Eastern medicine in ways that are mutually reinforcing.

The experience in question is certainly not "ordinary" experience, and what is experienced is not the objects of ordinary experience. But meditative experience is not disconnected from ordinary experience. One can understand it, in some cases, as a highly focused intensification of specific features that can be found also in ordinary experience. Even when this approach breaks down, one can have some understanding of the transformations that occur. To deny all validity to what is learned in these ways expresses the dogmatism of the denier rather than the implausibility of the idea that features of reality unnoticed in ordinary experience may be manifest under these circumstances.

When one turns from Indian and Chinese religious experience to the Bible, one finds very little about special meditational disciplines and what can be learned through them. One finds, instead, a focused attention on human relationships, moral issues, motivation, and the interpretation of history. In these, the working of God is discerned. God is "heard" calling, directing, judging, and encouraging. This awareness of God is not gained through special disciplines and often comes unsought, but it is compelling, all the same. It is not an inference from what is known through sensory experience.

Obviously, those committed to a nontheistic explanation of all phenomena can undertake to explain all these experiences. I am not proposing that one can prove that they are wrong. I am suggesting that if one approaches the matter open-mindedly, the scientistic accounts of moral and religious experience are likely to be less convincing to many of those for whom these experiences are intense than the idea that in those experiences one is affected by a reality that transcends the experience. The scientistic account, when accepted, tends to weaken the role of morality in society. The theistic account tends to strengthen it. It is my assumption that we may learn something about the nature of reality, including God, from the theistic traditions.

All of this account is based on the assumption that sense experience is not our only source of knowledge of the world. The awareness cultivated in Eastern disciplines does not exclude sense experience, but it is not exhausted by it. The Jews have known from the beginning that their knowledge of God does not come from vision or touch. It is often expressed in terms of audition, but for the most part this should not be understood in terms of physical events in the ear. The biblical authors are speaking of the apprehension of meanings that are directly imparted. They find themselves called to act in particular ways, often in ways they would not have chosen.

Some thoughtful Westerners have rejected the idea that belief in God must be based either on direct sense experience or rational inference from that experience. They have appealed to "intuition" or "mystical" experience or special "spiritual" senses. Whitehead provides a much better way to approach these matters. He shows that our fundamental relationships to the external world are prehensive, that what is primarily prehended is a world of events, each of which is both physical and mental, and that the objectifying of some of these events in vision and touch is a high-level process that is quite abstract in comparison with the basic experience.

This view turns matters around. Experience of our own past and of other persons need not be mediated by sense experience. The same is true of our experience of God. The affirmation that we directly experience God does not require a special "religious sense," since it can fit into the most basic form of all experience. That our moral experience is partly informed by this experience of God is a meaningful hypothesis supported by widespread experience. The direct experience of our personal past, of the psyches of other persons, and of God rarely comes to clear consciousness. Such consciousness is largely reserved for the sense experience that has been so central to our intellectual history. But what is most clearly conscious may not be what is most fundamental to knowledge. Indeed, the fact that, practically speaking, we all know we live in a real world and that we cannot explain that knowledge through clearly conscious sense experience should warn us that there is a great difference.

If the religious beliefs in view are just those of traditional Christianity, then overcoming the bias against nonsensory perception will not reinstate credibility. The problem of evil, which I listed last in my account of reasons for skepticism, may be the most important reason for not accepting Christian teaching. It does not disappear with a changed epistemology. But if we are attentive to what moral and historical experience may actually teach us about God, we will not be drawn back into this quagmire. Nor will we end up with supernaturalist and absolutist doctrines. To believe that religious experience East and West tells us something about reality does not support dogmatic reaffirmations of all traditional teachings. These teachings have many sources other than such experience, and they are in urgent need of reformulation in our scientific and pluralistic context.

4. Believers from diverse traditions can communicate with one another.

That there can be communication among people who belong to different religious communities may seem too evident to note, but it has been seriously challenged. The challenge typically assumes the nonreferential character of language or, at least, of religious language. If indeed religious language has no reference in a shared world, the argument that there can be no communication among people of differing traditions is convincing.

I have rejected the idea that religious language is not referential. I believe that different traditions have selected, from the vastly complex world in which we all live, different aspects for attention. This has led to the cultivation of different types of experience. Even if this more moderate view is adopted, the problem of communication is acute.

The basis on which we normally translate from one language to another is the reference of words in different languages to similar features of a common world. Many languages have a word referring to trees. Even if the exact designation of the words in different languages differs—for example, changing or ignoring the boundary between "trees" and "shrubs"—the overlap is sufficient so that the translation is relatively successful. Perfection is not required. Even in a single language, there are diverse uses of the same term. The hearer may not understand exactly what the speaker intends. But there is still effective communication.

I am assuming, however, that among the religious communities, some have cultivated very different experiences and have ordered their worlds in quite distinct ways. If this is the case, is communication still possible? It certainly complicates the situation. It means, for example, that Abrahamic theists cannot assume that in other religious traditions there is a word for what they mean by "God." Sometimes there is, sometimes not. The effort to communicate on the assumption that equivalent terms must exist often leads to confusion rather than to mutual understanding.

Nevertheless, communication is not impossible. Suppose, for example, that *pratitya samutpada* is a Buddhist concept that is absent in Christian thinking. One cannot point to it and ask how Christians have named that. How then can communication across the barrier be possible?

Let us recognize that it is far from easy. Christians who underestimate the differences among religious traditions often suppose that they can find some idea or teaching in their own tradition that is similar to the Buddhist doctrine. If they try to identify some established Christian concept with the Buddhist one, they are likely to end up with serious misunderstanding. If we treat our given cultural-linguistic world as complete, and understand what we meet in others only insofar as it fits into that world, then the effort to communicate is often hopeless.

In fact, however, matters do not end there. The usual translation of *pratitya samutpada* is "dependent origination," which in turn is taken to be "emptiness" or "emptying." Here we have English words, but if we examine their meaning in English without constant recourse to the way that *pratitya samutpada* is used in its Buddhist context, it is unlikely that we will learn much from the Buddhists. Yet Buddhists can explain the meaning of these terms to Christians by pointing to features of experienced reality to which few Christians have previously attended. This leads progressively to understanding. Then either the Sanskrit words or the English translation may become useful and meaningful to Christians in expounding their new understanding of Buddhism. Having noticed previously unidentified features of experienced reality also expands the Christian's understanding of reality as a whole.

Thus, in dialogue, communication, imperfect but real, occurs. We do not live in fixed cultural-linguistic worlds. These worlds are constantly changing. One source of change is the encounter with words or ideas that do not fit well into our existing system. This encounter constitutes a challenge. We can misleadingly translate the strange words into familiar terms. We can simply reject them. Or we can live with them, seek to understand them through conversation and new experience, and then incorporate them into our own worlds, thereby expanding those worlds. Features of the indefinitely complex world in which we live that we have previously neglected can become important to us.

This statement presupposes that the words, in part, refer to nonlinguistic reality. If their meaning were exhausted by their references to other words, then they could not be abstracted from the entire cultural-linguistic system in which they reside. If, on the other hand, the word refers to some often neglected feature of the totality to which others also can attend, then the abstraction is possible. Certainly there will be some change in connotation and role for the word in its new context, but there will be real communication nevertheless.

CONCLUSIONS

I have not succeeded in separating assumptions clearly from the conclusions to which they have led me. For that I do not apologize. Even assumptions change, or should change, as one works with and from them. Also, these assumptions have assumptions, some of which I have partly expressed. In some ways, I have simply restated my ideas about how Christians can view other religious traditions.

However, I hope that what I have done here does supplement what I have written elsewhere. I usually write for fellow Christians in ways that do not make my commitment to Whitehead's philosophy fully explicit. I can do so, because most Christians share many of these assumptions, even if they do not have at hand a philosophical system that supports and clarifies them.

In this book, I can share my belief that there is a value in showing how Whitehead's philosophy, especially his doctrine of physical feelings or prehensions, makes possible views of the relations among religious traditions that are largely excluded from the academy because of its lack of this concept. For me, this not only helps us in dealing well with an urgent contemporary issue but also demonstrates once more the fruitfulness of Whitehead's conceptuality.

References

Abe, Masao. "Kenyotic God and Dynamic Sunyata." In John B. Cobb Jr. and Christopher Ives, eds., *The Empyting God: A Buddhist-Jewish-Christian Conversation*, 3–65. Maryknoll, NY: Orbis Books, 1990.

Ali, Abdullah Yusur. *The Meaning of the Holy Qur'an*. 11th ed. Beltsville, MD: Amana Publications.

Allen, E. L. *Christianity Among the Religions*. London: Allen & Unwin, 1960.

Angel, Marc D. "Pluralism and Jewish Unity." ROVE (Responsible Orthodox Viewpoints and Editorials), The Orthodox Caucus (www.yerushalayim.net/organizations/oc/projects/rove/angel3/htm).

Armstrong, Karen. *In the Beginning: A New Interpretation of Genesis*. New York: Alfred A. Knopf, 1996.

Arya, Ravi Prakash, ed. *Rigveda Samhita: Sanskrit Text, English Translation and Notes*. Delhi: Parimal Publications, 1997.

Aslan, Adnan. *Religious Pluralism in Christian and Islamic Philosophy*. Richmond, England: Curzon Press, 1988.

Aydin, Mehmet S. "Iqbal 'in Felsefesinde Allah-Alem Iliskisi" [The God-World Relation in Iqbal's Philosophy]. In *Islam Felsefesi Yazilari* [Writings on Islamic Philosophy]. Istanbul: Ufuk Kitaplari, 2000.

———. "Islam 'in Evrenselligi" [Universality of Islam]. In *Islam 'in Evrenselligi* [Universality of Islam]. Istanbul: Ufuk Kitaplari, 2001.

———. *Alemden Allah'a* [From Cosmos to God]. Istanbul: Ufuk Kitaplari, 2001.

Brihadaranyaka Upanishad. In *Upanishads*. Trans. Patrick Olivelle. Oxford: Oxford University Press, 1996.

Buber, Martin. *Israel and the World: Essays in a Time of Crisis*. 2nd ed. New York: Schocken Books, 1963.

Bulac, Ali. *Islam ve Demokrasi* [Islam and Democracy]. Istanbul: Iz Yayincilik, 1995.

Burch, George Bosworth. *Alternative Goals in Religion*. Montreal: McGill-Queen's University Press, 1972.

———. "Whitehead's Harvard Lectures, 1926–27." Ed. Dwight C. Stewart. *Process Studies* 4/3 (Fall 1974): 199–206.

Cheng, Chung-ying. "Philosophical Significances of *Guan* (Contemplative Observation): On *Guan* as Onto-Hermeneutical Unity of Methodology and Ontology." *Guoji Yixue Yanjiu* [International Journal in Yi Studies] 1/1 (1995): 59–79.

————. "Confucian Onto-Hermeneutics: Morality and Ontology." In *Journal of Chinese Philosophy* 17/1 (2000): 33–67.

————, ed. *Benti Yu Quanshi* [Ontology and Interpretation]. Beijing: Sanlian Publishing, 2000.

————, ed. *Benti Quanshi Xue* [Onto-Hermeneutics]. Beijing: Peking University Press, 2002.

Cobb, John B., Jr. *Living Options in Protestant Theology: A Survey of Methods*. Philadelphia: Westminster, 1962.

————. *A Christian Natural Theology: Based on the Thought of Alfred North Whitehead*. Philadelphia: Westminster, 1965.

————. *The Structure of Christian Existence*. Philadelphia: Westminster, 1967.

————. "A Whiteheadian Christology." In Delwin Brown, Ralph E. James Jr., and Gene Reeves, eds., *Process Philosophy and Christian Thought*, 382–98. Indianapolis: Bobbs-Merrill, 1971.

————. *God and the World*. Philadelphia: Westminster Press, 1969; Eugene, OR: Wipf and Stock, 1998 (reprint).

————. *Christ in a Pluralistic Age*. Philadelphia: Westminster, 1975.

————. *Beyond Dialogue: Toward a Mutual Transformation of Christianity and Buddhism*. Philadelphia: Fortress, 1982.

————. "Metaphysical Pluralism." In Joseph Prabhu, ed., *The Intercultural Challenge of Raimon Panikkar*. Maryknoll, NY: Orbis Books, 1996.

————. "Toward a Christocentric Catholic Theology." Originally in Leonard Swidler, ed., *Toward a Universal Theology of Religion* (1987). Reprinted in Cobb, *Transforming Christianity and the World* (1999), 76–91 (this latter pagination followed).

————. "Being Itself and the Existence of God." In John R. Jacobson and Robert Lloyd Mitchell, eds., *The Existence of God*, 5–19. Lewiston, NY: Edwin Mellen, 1988.

————. "Beyond 'Pluralism.'" Originally in D'Costa, ed., *Christian Uniqueness Reconsidered* (1990). Reprinted in Cobb, *Transforming Christianity and the World* (1999), 61–75 (this latter pagination followed).

————. "Being a Transformationist in a Pluralistic World." *Christian Century* 111/23 (August 10–17, 1994): 748–51.

————. *Transforming Christianity and the World: A Way beyond Absolutism and Relativism*. Ed. Paul F. Knitter. Maryknoll, NY: Orbis Books, 1999.

————, and David Ray Griffin. *Process Theology: An Introductory Exposition*. Philadelphia: Westminster, 1976.

————, and Christopher Ives, eds. *The Emptying God: A Buddhist-Jewish-Christian Conversation*. Maryknoll, NY: Orbis Books, 1990.

Cook, Francis. "This Is It: A Buddhist View of Ultimate Reality." *Buddhist-Christian Studies* 9 (1989): 127–42.

Coward, Harold. *Pluralism in the World Religions*. Oxford: Oneworld Publications, 2000.

Cupitt, Don. *Taking Leave of God*. New York: Crossroad, 1981.

Davis, Caroline Franks. *The Evidential Force of Religious Experience*. Oxford: Clarendon Press, 1989.

D'Costa, Gavin, ed. *Christian Uniqueness Reconsidered: The Myth of a Pluralistic Theology of Religions*. Maryknoll, NY: Orbis Books, 1990.

Devenish, Philip E., and George L. Goodwin. "Christian Faith and the First Commandment: The Theology of Schubert Ogden." In Devenish and Goodwin, eds., *Witness and Existence: Essays in Honor of Schubert M. Ogden*, 1–39. Chicago: University of Chicago Press, 1989.

DiNoia, Joseph A. "Varieties of Religious Aims: Beyond Exclusivism, Inclusivism, and Pluralism." In Bruce Marshall, ed., *Theology and Dialogue*. Notre Dame, IN: University of Notre Dame Press, 1989.

————. *The Diversity of Religions: A Christian Perspective.* Washington, DC: Catholic University Press, 1992.

Dobbins, James C. *Jodo Shinshu: Shin Buddhism in Medieval Japan.* Honolulu: University of Hawaii Press, 2002.

Dongyan, Dai. "Mengzi Ziyi Suzheng" [Commentaries on Words in Mencius]. In *The Complete Works of Dai Dongyuan.* Beijing: Qinghua University Press, 1911.

————. *Yuan Shan* [Inquiries into Goodness]. Trans. Chung-ying Cheng. Honolulu, HI: East-West Center Press, 1970.

Dorff, Elliot N., and Louis E. Newman, eds. *Contemporary Jewish Theology: A Reader.* Oxford: Oxford University Press, 1999.

Driver, Tom F. "The Case for Pluralism." In Hick and Knitter, eds., *The Myth of Christian Uniqueness* (1987), 203–18.

Eckel, Malcolm David. *To See the Buddha.* Princeton, NJ: Princeton University Press, 1992.

Farley, Edward, and Peter C. Hodgson. "Scripture and Tradition." In Peter C. Hodgson and Robert H. King, eds., *Christian Theology: An Introduction to Its Traditions and Tasks,* 2nd ed., 61–87. Philadelphia: Fortress, 1985.

Eugene J. Fisher, ed. *Visions of the Other: Jewish and Christian Theologians Assess the Dialogue.* New York: Paulist Press, 1994.

Fisher, Mary Pat. *Living Religions.* 4th ed. Upper Saddle River, NJ: Prentice Hall, 2002.

Frederiks, James. "Jodo Shinshu's Mission to History: A Christian Challenge to Shin Buddhist Social Ethics." In Kenneth K. Tanaka and Eisho Nasu, eds., *Engaged Pure Land Buddhism.* Berkeley, CA: Wisdom Ocean Publications, 1998.

Frymer-Kensky, Tikva, David Novak, Peter Ochs, David Fox Sandmel, and Michael A. Signer, eds. *Christianity in Jewish Terms.* Boulder, CO: Westview Press, 2000.

Gamwell, Franklin I. *The Divine Good: Modern Moral Theory and the Necessity of God.* San Francisco: Harper Collins, 1990.

Gandhi, Mohandas K. *Young India: 1919–1931.* Vol. VIII. Ahmedabad: Navajivan Publishing House, 1981.

Gethin, Rupert. *The Foundations of Buddhism.* New York: Oxford University Press, 1998.

Ghose, Aurobindo. *Essays on the Gita.* Pondicherry: Sri Aurobindo Ashram, 1983.

Gilkey, Langdon. "Plurality and Its Theological Implications." In Hick and Knitter, eds., *The Myth of Christian Uniqueness* (1987), 37–50.

Green, Arthur. "New Directions in Jewish Theology in America." In Dorff and Newman, eds., *Contemporary Jewish Theology* (1999), 486–93.

Greenberg, Irving. "Cloud of Smoke, Pillar of Fire: Judaism, Christianity, and Modernity after the Holocaust." In Dorff and Newman, eds., *Contemporary Jewish Theology* (1999), 396–416.

————. "The Ethics of Jewish Power." In Rosemary Radford Ruether and Marc Ellis, eds., *Beyond Occupation: American Jewish, Christian, and Palestinian Voices for Peace,* 22–74. Boston: Beacon Press, 1990.

————. "Judaism and Christianity: Covenants of Redemption." In Frymer-Kensky et al., *Christianity in Jewish Terms* (2000), 141–58.

————. "Judaism, Christianity, and the Partnership after the Twentieth Century." In Frymer-Kensky et al., *Christianity in Jewish Terms* (2000), 25–36.

————. "Judaism and Christianity: Their Respective Roles in the Strategy of Redemption." In Fisher, *Visions of the Other* (1994), 7–27.

————. "Yizhak Rabin and the Ethic of Jewish Power" (28-page pamphlet). New York: National Jewish Center for Learning and Leadership, 1995.

Griffin, David Ray. "Can Christians Learn from Other Religions?" (unpublished paper, 1976; available at the Center for Process Studies, 1325 N. College, Claremont, CA 91711).

——. "Parapsychology and Philosophy: A Whiteheadian Postmodern Perspective." *Journal of the American Society for Psychical Research* 87/3 (July 1993): 217–88.

——. *Parapsychology, Philosophy, and Spirituality: A Postmodern Exploration.* Albany: State University of New York Press, 1997.

——. *Unsnarling the World-Knot: Consciousness, Freedom, and the Mind-Body Problem.* Berkeley and Los Angeles: University of California Press, 1998.

——. "Introduction to SUNY Series in Constructive Postmodern Thought." In Nicholas F. Gier, *Spiritual Titanism: Indian, Chinese, and Western Perspectives,* xxi–xxvi. Albany: State University of New York Press, 2000.

——. *Religion and Scientific Naturalism: Overcoming the Conflicts.* Albany: State University of New York Press, 2000.

——. *Reenchantment without Supernaturalism: A Process Philosophy of Religion.* Ithaca: Cornell University Press, 2001.

——. "Creation out of Nothing, Creation Out of Chaos, and the Problem of Evil." In Stephen T. Davis, ed., *Encountering Evil: Live Options in Theodicy,* 2nd ed., 108–205. Louisville, KY: Westminster John Knox, 2001.

——. "Panentheism: A Postmodern Revelation." In Philip Clayton and Arthur Peacocke, eds., *In Whom We Live and Move and Have Our Being: Reflections on Panentheism for a Scientific Age,* 36–47. Grand Rapids: Eerdmans, 2004.

——. "Panentheism and Religious Pluralism" (unpublished paper).

——, and Huston Smith. *Postmodern Theology and Primordial Truth.* Albany: State University of New York Press, 1989.

Griffiths, Paul J. *An Apology for Apologetics: A Study in the Logic of Interreligious Dialogue.* Maryknoll, NY: Orbis Books, 1991.

——. "Beyond Pluralism" (review of S. Mark Heim, *Salvations*). *First Things,* January 1996: 50–52.

Halbfass, Wilhelm. *Tradition and Reflection.* Albany: State University of New York Press, 1991.

Hall, David, and Roger Ames. *Thinking from the Han.* Albany: State University of New York Press, 1998.

Hartman, David. *Conflicting Visions: Spiritual Possibilities of Modern Israel.* New York: Schocken Books, 1990.

——. "Judaism Encounters Christianity Anew." In Fisher, *Visions of the Other* (1994), 67–80.

——. "The Third Jewish Commonwealth." In Dorff and Newman, eds., *Contemporary Jewish Theology* (1999), 432–40.

——. *A Living Covenant: The Innovative Spirit in Traditional Judaism.* Woodstock, VT: Jewish Lights, 1997.

——. *A Heart of Many Rooms: Celebrating the Many Voices within Judaism.* Woodstock, VT: Jewish Lights, 1999.

——. "Auschwitz or Sinai?" (2001) (www.hartmaninstitute.com/davidhartman/teachings/archive/sinai.html).

——. "Religious Diversity and the Millenium" (2001) (www.hartmaninstitute.com/davidhartman/teachings/archive/diversity.html)

Harvey, Peter. *An Introduction to Buddhism: Teachings, History, and Practices.* New York: Cambridge University Press, 1994.

Hays, Richard B. *Echoes of Scripture in the Letters of Paul.* New Haven, CT: Yale University Press, 1989.

Heim, S. Mark. *Salvations: Truth and Difference in Religion.* Maryknoll, NY: Orbis Books, 1995.

——. *The Depth of the Riches: A Trinitarian Theology of Religious Ends.* Grand Rapids: Eerdmans, 2001.

Heschel, Abraham Joshua. *The Prophets,* vol. 2. New York: Harper & Row, 1962.

————. *Moral Grandeur and Spiritual Audacity*, ed. Susannah Heschel. New York: Farrar, Straus and Giroux, 1996.

Hick, John. *God and the Universe of Faiths*. London: Macmillan; New York: St. Martin's, 1973.

————. "Towards a Philosophy of Religious Pluralism." *Neue Zeitschrift für systematische Theologie und Religionsphilosophie* 22/2 (1980): 131–49.

————. *God Has Many Names*. Philadelphia: Westminster, 1982.

————. *Philosophy of Religion*. 3rd ed. Englewood Cliffs, NJ: Prentice-Hall, 1983.

————. *Problems of Religious Pluralism*. New York: St. Martin's, 1985.

————. *An Interpretation of Religion: Human Responses to the Transcendent*. London: Macmillan; New Haven, CT: Yale University Press, 1989.

————. "The Non-Absoluteness of Christianity." In Hick and Knitter, eds., *The Myth of Christian Uniqueness* (1987), 16–36.

————. *A Christian Theology of Religions: The Rainbow of Faiths*. Louisville, KY: Westminster John Knox, 1995.

————. "Religious Pluralism and Salvation." In Quinn and Meeker, eds., *The Philosophical Challenge of Religious Diversity* (2000), 54–66.

Hick, John, and Paul F. Knitter, eds. *The Myth of Christian Uniqueness: Toward a Pluralistic Theology of Religions*. Maryknoll, NY: Orbis Books, 1987.

Hirota, Dennis, ed. *Toward a Contemporary Understanding of Pure Land Buddhism: Creating a Shin Buddhist Theology in a Religiously Plural World*. Albany: State University of New York Press, 2000.

Hocking, William Ernest. *Living Religions and a World Faith*. New York: Macmillan, 1940.

————. *The Coming World Civilization*. New York: Harper & Brothers, 1956.

Hutchison, John A. *Paths of Faith*. New York: McGraw Hill, 1969.

Hakugen, Ichikawa. *Ichikawa Hakugen Chosakushu*, vol. 2. Kyoto: Hookan, 1993.

Huxley, Aldous. *The Perennial Philosophy*. New York: Harper & Row, 1944.

Inagaki, Hisao. *The Three Pure Land Sutras*. Kyoto: Nagata Bunshado, 1995.

————. *A Glossary of Shin Buddhist Terms*. Kyoto: Ryukoku University Research Center, 1995.

Inden, Ronald. *Imagining India*. Cambridge and Oxford: Blackwell, 1990.

Ingram, Paul O. *The Modern Buddhist-Christian Dialogue: Two Universalistic Religions in Transformation*. Lewiston, NY: Edwin Mellen, 1988.

Iqbal, Sir Mohammad. *The Reconstruction of Religious Thought in Islam*. Lahore: The Kapur Art Printing Works, 1930.

Ives, Christopher. "Ethical Pitfalls in Imperial Zen and Nishida Philosophy: Ichikawa Hakugen's Critique." In James W. Heisig and John C. Maraldo, eds., *Rude Awakenings: Zen, the Kyoto School, and the Question of Nationalism*, 16–39. Honolulu: University of Hawaii Press, 1995.

————. "The Mobilization of Doctrine: Buddhist Contributions to Imperial Ideology in Modern Japan." *Japanese Journal of Religious Studies* 26:1–2 (Spring 1999): 83–106.

Kalupahana, David. *The Buddha and the Concept of Peace*. Sri Lanka: Vishva Lekha Publishers, 1999.

Kamenetz, Rodger. *Stalking Elijah: Adventures with Today's Jewish Mystical Masters*. San Francisco: Harper, 1997.

Kanamatsu, Kenryo. *Naturalness: A Classic of Shin Buddhism*. Bloomington, IN: World Wisdom, 2002.

Katz, Stephen. "Language, Epistemology, and Mysticism." In Stephen Katz, ed., *Mysticism and Philosophical Analysis*, 22–74. New York: Oxford University Press, 1978.

Kaufman, Gordon K. "Religious Diversity, Historical Consciousness, and Christian Theology." In Hick and Knitter, eds., *The Myth of Christian Uniqueness* (1987), 3–15.

Keller, Catherine. *Face of the Deep: A Theology of Becoming*. New York and London: Routledge, 2002.

Kitagawa, Joseph. *Religion in Japanese History.* New York: Columbia University Press, 1966.

Klostermaier, Klaus K. *A Short Introduction to Hinduism.* Oxford: Oneworld Publications, 1998.

Knitter, Paul F. *No Other Name? A Critical Survey of Christian Attitudes toward the World Religions.* Maryknoll, NY: Orbis Books, 1986.

———. "Interreligious Dialogue: What? Why? How?" In Swidler et al., *Death or Dialogue?* (1990), 19–44.

———. "Preface." In Hick and Knitter, eds., *The Myth of Christian Uniqueness* (1987), vii-xii.

———. *Jesus and the Other Names: Christian Mission and Global Responsibility.* Maryknoll, NY: Orbis Books, 1996.

———, ed. John B. Cobb Jr., *Transforming Christianity and the World: A Way beyond Absolutism and Relativism.* Maryknoll, NY: Orbis Books, 1999. (Knitter wrote an introduction to the volume [1–11] and also an introduction to each of Cobb's essays.)

Kogan, Barry S. "Eternity and Origination: Averroes' Discourse on the Manner of the World's Existence." In Michael E. Marnura, ed., *Islamic Theology and Philosophy: Studies in Honor of George F. Hourani.* Albany: State University of New York Press, 1984.

Lerner, Michael. "A Jewish Renewal (Kabbalistic-Mystical-NeoHasidic) Approach to God" (www.tikkun.org/renewal/index.cfm/action/god.html).

Lessing, G. E. *Nathan the Wise* (1779). Trans. B. Q. Morgan. New York: Ungar, 1955.

Levenson, Jon D. *Creation and the Persistence of Evil: The Jewish Drama of Divine Omnipotence.* San Francisco: Harper & Row, 1988.

Long, Jeffery D. "Plurality and Relativity: Whitehead, Jainism, and the Reconstruction of Religious Pluralism." Ph.D. dissertation, University of Chicago, 2000.

———. "Multiple Aspects and Ultimate Notions." Unpublished paper, 2001.

Lubarsky, Sandra B. *Tolerance and Transformation: Jewish Approaches to Religious Pluralism.* Cincinnati: Hebrew Union College Press, 1990.

Marcaurelle, Roger. *Freedom Through Inner Renunciation: Śaṅkara's Philosophy in a New Light.* Albany: State University of New York Press, 2000.

May, Gerhard. *Creatio ex Nihilo: The Doctrine of "Creation Out of Nothing" in Early Christian Thought.* Trans. A. S. Worrall. Edinburgh: T. & T. Clark, 1994.

Meeker, Kevin, and Philip L. Quinn. "Introduction: The Philosophical Challenge of Religious Diversity." In Quinn and Meeker, eds., *The Philosophical Challenge of Religious Diversity* (2000), 1–28.

Milbank, John. *Theology and Social Theory.* Oxford: Blackwell, 1990.

Nasr, Seyyed Hossein. "To Live in a World with No Center—and Many." *Cross Currents* 46/3 (Fall 1996): 318–25.

Netton, Ian Richard. *Allah Transcendent: Studies in the Structure of Semiotics of Islamic Philosophy, Theology and Cosmology.* London and New York: Routledge, 1989.

Newman, Amy. "The Idea of Judaism in Feminism and Afrocentrism." In David Biale, Michael Galchinsky, and Susannah Heschel, eds., *Insider/Outsider: American Jews and Multiculturalism.* Berkeley: University of California Press, 1998.

Nikhilananda, Swami. *The Gospel of Sri Ramakrishna.* Abridged edition. New York: Ramakrishna-Vivekananda Center, 1958.

Nishida, Kitaro. *Last Writings: Nothingness and the Religious Worldview.* Trans. David Dilworth. Honolulu: University of Hawaii Press, 1987.

Nishitani, Keiji. "The Problem of Time in Shinran." *Eastern Buddhist,* New Series 11/1 (May 1978): 13–26.

Odin, Steve. *Process Metaphysics and Hua-Yen Buddhism.* Albany: State University of New York Press, 1982.

————. *The Social Self in Zen and American Pragmatism.* Albany: State University of New York Press, 1996.

————. *Artistic Detachment in Japan and the West.* Honolulu: University of Hawaii Press, 2001.

————. "'Leap of Faith' in Shinran and Kierkegaard." In *The Pure Land* Nos. 18–19 (December 2002): 50–65.

Ogden, Schubert M. *Christ without Myth: A Study Based on the Theology of Rudolf Bultmann.* New York: Harper & Brothers, 1961.

————. "Bultmann's Demythologizing and Hartshorne's Dipolar Theism." In William L. Reese and Eugene Freeman, eds., *Process and Divinity: The Hartshorne Festschrift,* 493–513. LaSalle, Ill.: Open Court, 1964.

————. *The Reality of God and Other Essays.* New York: Harper & Row, 1966.

————. *The Point of Christology.* San Francisco: Harper & Row, 1982.

————. "Problems in the Case for a Pluralistic Theology of Religions." *Journal of Religion* 68/4 (October 1988): 493–507.

————. *Is There Only One True Religion or Are There Many?* Dallas: Southern Methodist University Press, 1992.

Osman, Fathi. "Monotheists and the 'Other': An Islamic Perspective in an Era of Religious Pluralism." *The Muslim World* 88/3–4 (July-October, 1998): 353–63.

Padmarajiah, Y.J. *A Comparative Study of the Jain Theories of Reality and Knowledge.* Bombay: Jain Sahitya Vikas Mandal, 1963.

Pandit, Bansi. *The Hindu Mind: Fundamentals of Hindu Religion and Philosophy for All Ages.* Glen Ellyn, IL: B and V Enterprises, 1998.

Panikkar, Raimundo. *The Vedic Experience: Mantramañjari.* Delhi: Motilal Banarsidass, 1977.

————. "The Ongoing Dialogue." In Harold Coward, ed., *Hindu-Christian Dialogue: Perspectives and Encounters.* Maryknoll, NY: Orbis Books, 1989.

Pratt, James Bissett. *Naturalism.* New Haven, CT: Yale University Press, 1939.

Prabhavananda, Swami, and Christopher Isherwood. "Introduction to Shankara's Philosophy." In *Shankara's Crest-Jewel of Discrimination.* Translated and introduced by Swami Prabhavananda and Christopher Isherwood, 7–31. Hollywood, CA: Vedanta Press, 1978.

Reader, Ian. *Simple Guide to Shinto: The Religion of Japan.* Folkestone, England: Global Books, 1998.

Richards, Glyn, ed. *A Source-Book of Modern Hinduism.* Richmond, England: Curzon Press, 1985.

Quinn, Philip L. "Towards Thinner Theologies: Hick and Alston on Religious Diversity." In Quinn and Meeker, eds., *The Philosophical Challenge of Religious Diversity* (2000), 226–43.

Quinn, Philip L., and Kevin Meeker, eds. *The Philosophical Challenge of Religious Diversity.* New York and Oxford: Oxford University Press, 2000.

Race, Alan. *Christians and Religious Pluralism: Patterns in the Christian Theology of Religions.* London: SCM Press, 1983.

Rahman, Fazlur. *Islam.* Chicago and London: University of Chicago Press, 1979.

Ruether, Rosemary Radford. "Feminism and Jewish-Christian Dialogue: Particularism and Universalism in the Search for Religious Truth." In Hick and Knitter, eds., *The Myth of Christian Uniqueness* (1987), 137–48.

Sahn, Seung. *Only Don't Know: The Teaching Letters of Zen Master Seung Sahn.* San Francisco: Four Seasons, 1982.

Said, Edward W. *Orientalism.* New York: Vintage Books, 1978.

Schleiermacher, Friedrich. *The Christian Faith.* Trans. H. R. Mackintosh and J. S. Stewart. Edinburgh: T. & T. Clark, 1928.

Schuon, Fritjof. *The Transcendent Unity of Religions.* New York: Harper & Row, 1975.

Schwöbel, Christoph. "Particularity, Universality, and the Religions: Toward a Christian Theology of Religions." In D'Costa, ed., *Christian Uniqueness Reconsidered* (1990), 30–46.

Shinran, Shonin. *The Collected Works of Shinran.* Trans. Dennis Hirota, Hisao Inagaki, Michio Tokunaga, and Ryushin Uryuzu. Kyoto: Jodo Shinshu Hongwanji, 1997.

Simmons, Ernest Lee, Jr. "Process Pluralism and Integral Nondualism: A Comparative Study of the Nature of the Divine in the Thought of Alfred North Whitehead and Sri Aurobindo Ghose." Ph.D. dissertation, Claremont Graduate School, 1981.

———. "Mystical Consciousness in a Process Perspective." *Process Studies* 14/1 (Spring 1984): 1–10.

Smith, Huston. *Forgotten Truth: The Primordial Tradition.* New York: Harper & Row, 1977.

Smith, Wilfred Cantwell. *Towards a World Theology: Faith and the Comparative History of Religion.* Maryknoll, NY: Orbis Books, 1981.

———. "Idolatry in Comparative Perspective." In Hick and Knitter, eds., *The Myth of Christian Uniqueness* (1987), 53–68.

Soga Ryojin. "Dharmakaya Bodhisattva." In Frederick Franck, ed., *The Buddha Eye: An Anthology of the Kyoto School,* 221–31. New York: Crossroad, 1982.

Sölle, Dorothee. *Political Theology.* Trans. John Shelley. Philadelphia: Fortress, 1971.

Stcherbatsky, F. Th. *The Conception of Buddhist Nirvana.* Leningrad: Public Office of the Academy of Sciences of the USSR, 1927.

Strauss, David Friedrich. *The Life of Jesus Critically Examined.* Trans. George Eliot. Ed. Peter C. Hodgson. Philadelphia: Fortress, 1972.

Subramuniyaswami, Satguru Shivaya. *Dancing with Shiva: Hinduism's Contemporary Catechism.* Kapaa, HI: Himalayan Academy, 1997.

———. *Merging with Shiva: Hinduism's Contemporary Metaphysics.* Kapaa, HI: Himalayan Academy, 1999.

Suchocki, Marjorie Hewitt. "Theology and the World's Religious History." In Swidler, ed., *Toward a Universal Theology of Religions* (1987), 51–72.

———. "Coming Home: Wesley, Whitehead, and Women." *Drew Gateway* 57/3 (Fall 1987); reprinted in Bryan P. Stone and Thomas Jay Oord, eds., *Thy Nature and Thy Name Is Love: Wesleyan and Process Theologies in Dialogue,* 49–65. Nashville: Kingswood Books, 2001.

———. *God-Christ-Church: A Practical Guide to Process Theology.* New York: Crossroad, 1984; rev. ed., New York: Crossroad, 1989.

———. "In Search of Justice: Religious Pluralism from a Feminist Perspective." In Hick and Knitter, eds., *The Myth of Christian Uniqueness* (1987), 149–61.

———. *In God's Presence: Theological Reflections on Prayer.* St. Louis: Chalice Press, 1996.

———. "Pragmatic Pluralism." In Donald A. Crosby and Charley D. Hardwick, eds., *Religion in a Pluralistic Age: Proceedings of the Third International Conference on Philosophical Theology,* 49–67. New York: Peter Lang, 2001.

———. *Divinity and Diversity: A Christian Affirmation of Religious Pluralism.* Nashville: Abingdon, 2003.

Surin, Kenneth. "Towards a 'Materialist' Critique of 'Religious Pluralism': An Examination of the Discourse of John Hick and Wilfred Cantwell Smith." In Ian Hamnett, ed., *Religious Pluralism and Unbelief: Studies Critical and Comparative.* London: Routledge, 1990.

Swidler, Leonard, John B. Cobb Jr., Paul F. Knitter, and Monika K. Hellwig. *Death or Dialogue? From the Age of Monologue to the Age of Dialogue.* London: SCM Press; Philadelphia: Trinity Press, 1990.

Swidler, Leonard, ed. *Toward a Universal Theology of Religions*. Maryknoll, NY: Orbis Books, 1987.

Takeda, Ryusei. "Pure Land Buddhist View of Duhkha." *In Buddhist-Christian Studies* 5 (1985): 7–24.

Tanaka, Kenneth K. *Ocean: An Introduction to Jodo-Shinshu Buddhism in America*. Berkeley: Wisdom Ocean Publications, 1997.

Tapasyananda, Swami. *Sri Ramakrishna: Power and Glory*. Madras: Sri Ramakrishna Math, 1985.

Thelle, Notto R. *Buddhism and Christianity in Japan: From Conflict to Dialogue, 1854–1899*. Honolulu: University of Hawaii Press, 1987.

The Threefold Lotus Sutra. Trans. Bunno Kato. New York: Weatherhill, 1975.

Tillich, Paul. *Christianity and the Encounter of the World Religions*. New York: Columbia University Press, 1963.

Tindal, Matthew. *Christianity as Old as Creation*. London: Thomas Astley, 1730.

Tomoe, Moriya. *Yemyo Imamura: Pioneer American Buddhist*. Trans. Tsuneichi Takeshita. Ed. Eldred Bloom and Ruth Tabrah. Honolulu: Buddhist Study Center Press, 2000.

Toynbee, Arnold. "What Should be the Christian Approach to the Contemporary Non-Christian Faiths?" In Owen C. Thomas, ed., *Attitudes toward Other Religions: Some Christian Interpretations*, 153–71. New York: Harper & Row, 1969.

Tracy, David. *Plurality and Ambiguity: Hermeneutics, Religion, Hope*. University of Chicago Press, 1987.

———. *Dialogue with the Other: The Inter-Religious Dialogue*. Louvain: Peeters Press, 1990.

———. "Kenosis, Sunyata, and Trinity." In John B. Cobb Jr. and Christopher Ives, eds., *The Emptying God: A Buddhist-Jewish-Christian Conversation*, 135–54. Maryknoll, NY: Orbis Books, 1990.

Troeltsch, Ernst. "The Place of Christianity among the World Religions." In Owen C. Thomas, ed., *Attitudes toward Other Religions: Some Christian Interpretations*, 73–91. New York: Harper & Row, 1969.

Unno, Taitetsu. *River of Fire/River of Water: An Introduction to the Pure Land Tradition of Shin Buddhism*. New York: Doubleday, 1998.

———. *Shin Buddhism*. New York: Doubleday, 2002.

———. Review of *Toward a Contemporary Understanding of Pure Land Buddhism*, ed. Dennis Hirota. *Buddhist-Christian Studies* 22 (2002): 211–14.

The Upanishads. Trans. Eknath Easwaran. Petaluma, CA: Nilgiri Press, 1987.

Victoria, Brian. *Zen at War*. New York: Weatherhill, 2000.

Ward, Keith. "Truth and the Diversity of Religions." In Quinn and Meeker, eds., *The Philosophical Challenge of Religious Diversity* (2000), 109–25.

Waskow, Rabbi Arthur. "God and the Shoah" (www.shalomctr.org/html/comm36.html).

Wesley, John. *The Works of John Wesley*. Kansas City, MO: Nazarene Publishing House, 1958.

———. *Explanatory Notes Upon the New Testament*. Wimbledon: Epworth Press, 1976.

———. *A Plain Account of Christian Perfection*. Kansas City, MO: Beacon Hill Press, 1966.

Whitehead, Alfred North. (SMW) *Science and the Modern World* (1925). New York: Free Press, 1967.

———. (RM) *Religion in the Making*. New York: Macmillan, 1926; reprinted by Fordham University Press, 1996, with an introduction by Judith A. Jones and a glossary by Randall E. Auxier.

———. (S) *Symbolism: Its Meaning and Effect*. New York: Macmillan, 1927.

———. (PR) *Process and Reality: An Essay in Cosmology* (orig. ed. 1929). Corrected edition, ed. David Ray Griffin and Donald W. Sherburne. New York: Free Press, 1978.
———. (FR) *The Function of Reason* (1929). Boston: Beacon Press, 1958.
———. (AI) *Adventures of Ideas* (1933). New York: Free Press, 1967.
———. (MT) *Modes of Thought* (1938). New York: Free Press, 1968.
Whitson, Robley Edward. *The Coming Convergence of the World Religions.* New York: Paulist-Newman, 1971.
Williams, Paul. *Buddhist Thought: A Complete Introduction to the Indian Tradition.* New York: Routledge, 2000.
Yokota, John Shunji. "Sakyamuni within the Jodo Shinshu Tradition." *Pacific World* 2 (1986): 31–41. Published under the name John S. Ishihara.
———. "Rethinking the Doctrine of Satya-dvaya." *Journal of Chikushi Jogakuen College* 1 (January 1989): 63–86. Published under the name John S. Ishihara.
———. "Amida as the Christ: An Exercise Beyond Dialogue." *Journal of Chikushi Jogakuen College* 3 (January 1991): 121–48.
———. "A Call to Compassion: Process Thought and the Conceptualization of Amida Buddhism." *Process Studies* 23/2 (Summer 1994): 87–97.
———. "Understanding Amida Buddha and the Pure Land: A Process Approach." In Hirota, ed., *Toward a Contemporary Understanding of Pure Land Buddhism* (2000), 73–100.
———. "A Call to Compassion: A Response to Cobb and Kaufman." In Hirota, ed., *Toward a Contemporary Understanding of Pure Land Buddhism* (2000), 200–14.
———. "Nagarjuna, Shinran, and Whitehead." In Nagoya University Department of Indian Culture, ed., *Three Mountains and Seven Rivers: Essays in Tribute to Musashi Tachikawa on his 60th Birthday,* 247–270. New Delhi: Motilal Banarsidass, 2003.